BOY MEETS... GRAPH

BEST OF BISHONEN

はじめに

まず、本書の制作にご協力を頂いた多くの方々に、この場を借りて
心より御礼申し上げます。

本書は魅力的な少年・男性を描く漫画家・イラストレーター・キャ
ラクターデザイナー79名の作品と、プロフィール・コメントを掲載
しています。これまでに、刊行されているイラストレーターファイ
ル書籍は、どちらかといえば女性を描いた作品が多く掲載されてい
ました。
しかし、昨今、日本では漫画・ゲーム・アニメなどをはじめとする
様々な分野で、女性向けコンテンツが、かつてない盛り上がりを見
せているように感じます。女性向けコンテンツで必要とされるのは、
女性が"萌える""イケメン"です。「萌えるイケメン」と一言でいっ
ても、萌える要素は様々です。ツンデレだったり、ヤンデレだった
り、俺様だったり、ヘタレだったり、王子様だったり、アニキだっ
たり、リーマンだったり、軍服だったり、和服だったり、眼帯だっ
たり……。本当に様々です。

そのようなわけで、魅力的な少年・男性を描くことができるクリエ
イターの情報を求める声を広告業界・出版業界・ゲーム業界などか
ら受け、男性を描いたイラストに特化した、これまでにないクリエ
イターズファイルの制作に至りました。
本書が、"イケメンを描く名手"であるクリエイターの皆様と、読者
の皆様を様々な形でつなぐ1冊となれば幸いです。

編集部

First, we would like to extend words of gratitude to the many individuals who contributed to the realization of this book.

This volume introduces the works, profiles, and comments of 79 manga artists, illustrators, and character designers creating artistically irresistible youths and men. Past publications have introduced illustrators primarily drawing female characters.

In recent years, however, Japan has seen a considerable rise in female-oriented manga, games, anime, and the like. The prerequisite in female-oriented content is an *ikemen* (Japanese slang for "good-looking guy") with whom readers can be infatuated. Nevertheless, *ikemen* infatuation can be triggered in many ways. There is the hot/cold guy, the obsessed fellow, the pompous person, the weakling, the prince, the older gent, the businessman, the military figure, the male adorned in Japanese costume, and the character in the eyepatch. The variety is bountiful.

The advertising, publishing, and game industries have noted the public's wish for information on the individuals producing these irresistible youthful and mature male characters. This dedicated work highlights—for the first time— those very artists in their very own "creators' file."

We trust that this single tome will unite the *ikemen* master artists and their readers.

Editorial Department

掲載作家 Index

（あいうえお順）

Artist Index

BEST OF BISHONEN
Most Updated Boys Illustrations from Japanese Comics and Games

©2015 PIE International

All rights reserved. No part of this publication may be reproduced, stored in a retrieval system,
or transmitted in any form or by any means, graphic, electronic or mechanical, including photocopying and
recording, or otherwise, without prior permission in writing from the publisher.

PIE International Inc.

2-32-4 Minami-Otsuka, Toshima-ku, Tokyo 170-0005 JAPAN
sales@pie.co.jp

ISBN978-4-7562-4722-3 Printed in Japan

藤 未都也
FUJI MITSUYA

鈴木次郎
SUZUKI JIRO

尚 月地
NAO TSUKIJI

思春期
SHISHUNNKI

流れないテッシュ
NAGARENAI TESSYU

BOY MEETS SEASON

季節や季節から連想する
モチーフやイメージに少年・男性を絡め
5名のクリエイターにイラストを描いてもらいました。
素敵な競演をお楽しみください。

Five artists contributed dazzling
illustrations based on motifs and images related
to the seasons, adorned with boys and men.
Please enjoy their works created
exclusively for this project.

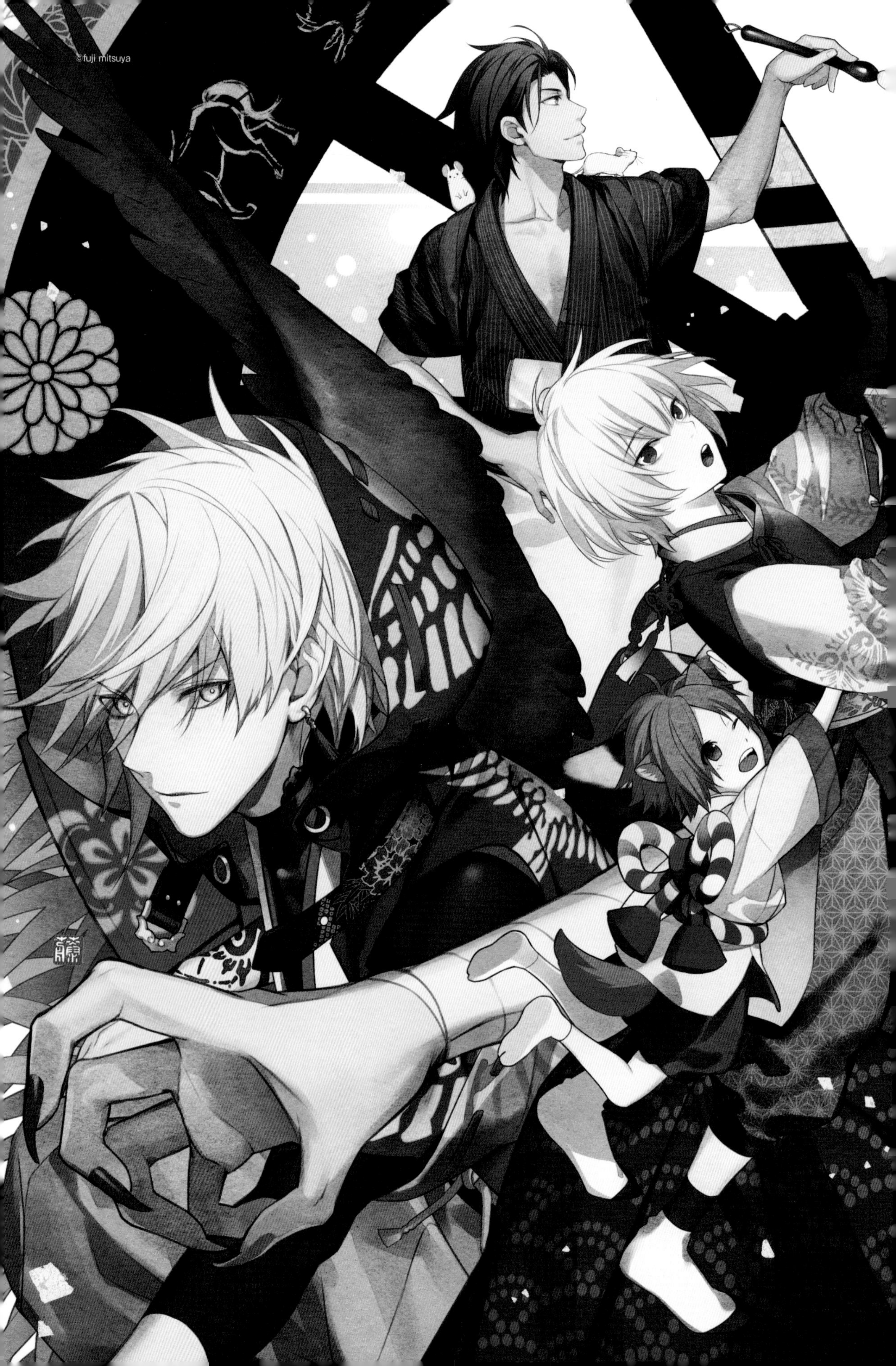
©fuji mitsuya

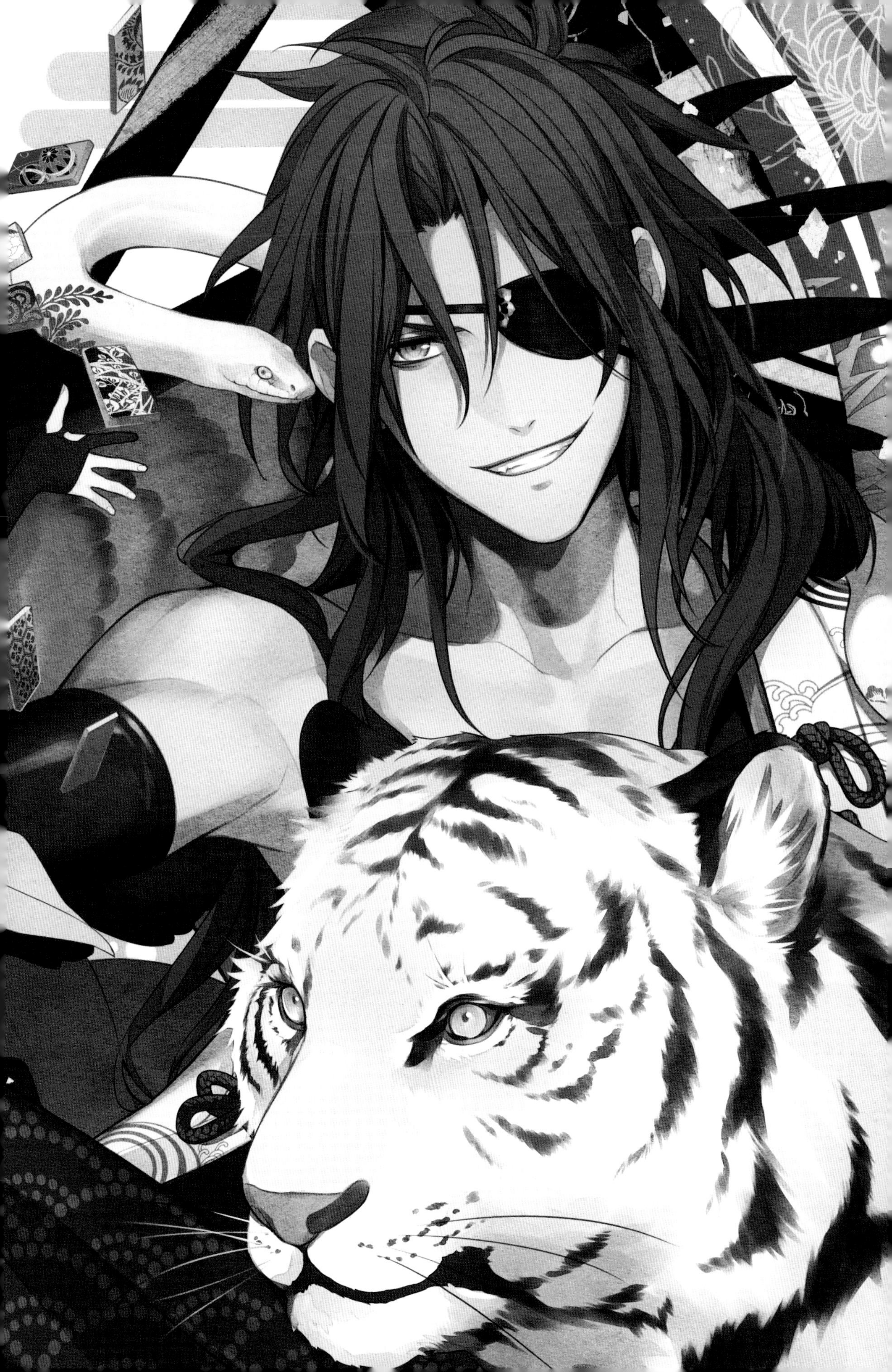

FUJI MI

新宴

今回はお話を頂いた時に「新年」というテーマから、安直に干支のキャラを使った構図にしました。
干支の順番を決めるために皆で集まってワイワイしてたら良いなというイメージです。
広がりや光源と言った魅せ方は今回の絵ではあえてなくして、一番描きたかった寅と辰（赤髪）を配置してから埋めていきました。
1色で複数の色が出せる効果が好きなので、ピンライトを被せながらの作業でしたが、
濃い色がなかなか出せなくて明暗を1キャラの中で整えるのに苦労しました。
（その他の作品・プロフィール掲載ページ→p.154-155）

TSUYA

Rough draft ©fuji mitsuya

藤 未都也

Shin-en (A New Spree)

When I received the story with "New Year" as the theme, I simply used the Chinese zodiac animals as characters for my composition. The image is the crazy fun of the animals clamoring around as they decided the sequential order they would represent. In this picture, I intentionally did not use expanse and light source for appeal, but initially placed the tiger and the dragon (redheaded) in the picture, as I wished to draw them first, and then filled in the rest. As I enjoy the effect of having one color produce various hues, I employed Photoshop's pinlight function to handle the work. Although it was difficult to produce darker shades that way, I labored and created light and darkness within each character.

Additional works and artist profile are found on pp. 154–155.

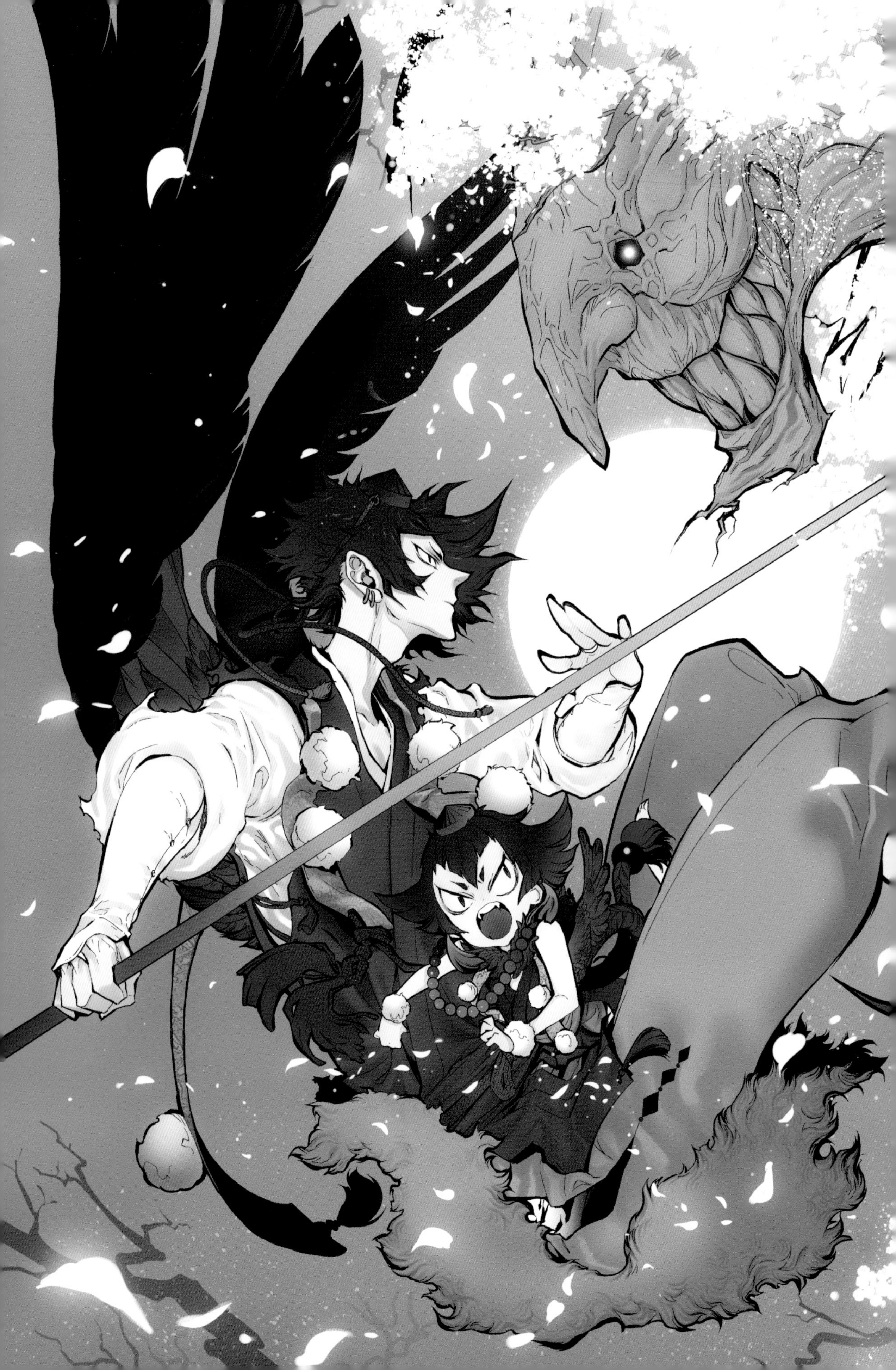

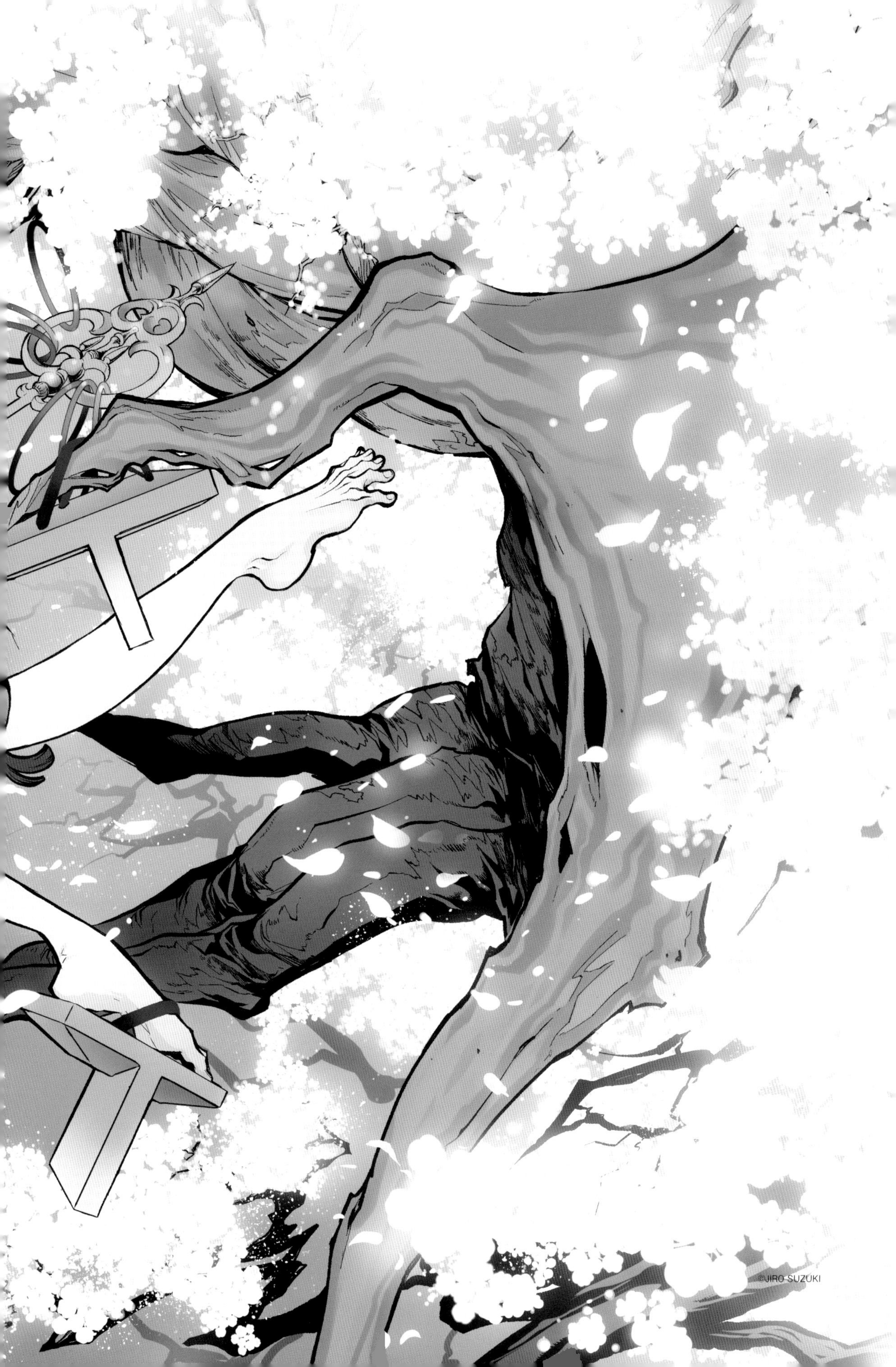

SUZUKI

春の幽惑

桜の妖老木が春のヨウキに浮かされ若い天狗にちょっかいを出している……というイメージです。
襲い掛かっているようにも、服従しようとしているようにも見えるといいなと思いながら描きました。
（その他の作品・プロフィール掲載ページ→p.102-103）

JIRO

Rough draft ©JIRO SUZUKI

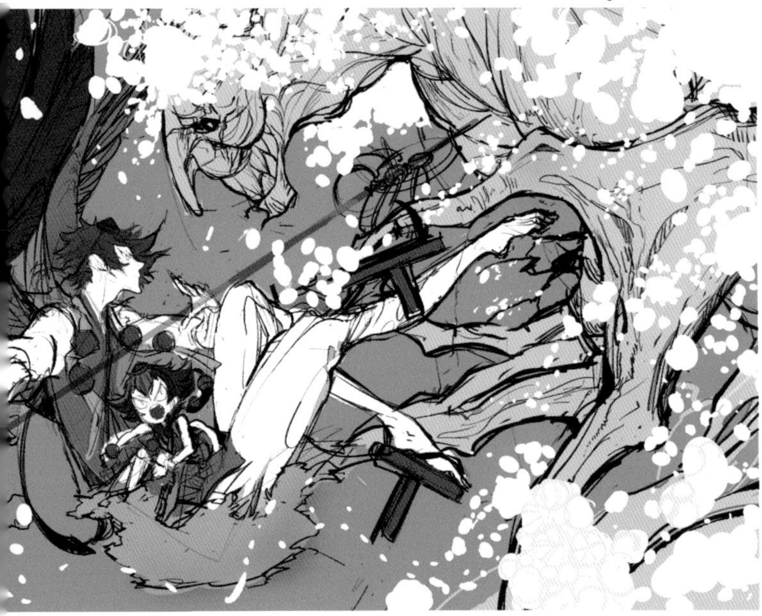

鈴木次郎

Haru no yuuwaku (Spring Decception)

The image is of a old sakura tree sprite getting carried away by the feeling of spring and meddling in a young forest devil's (known as a tengu) affairs. I would love to see it simultaneously appear as the tree swooping down on the young devil and yet being submissive to him.

Additional works and artist profile are found on pp. 102-103.

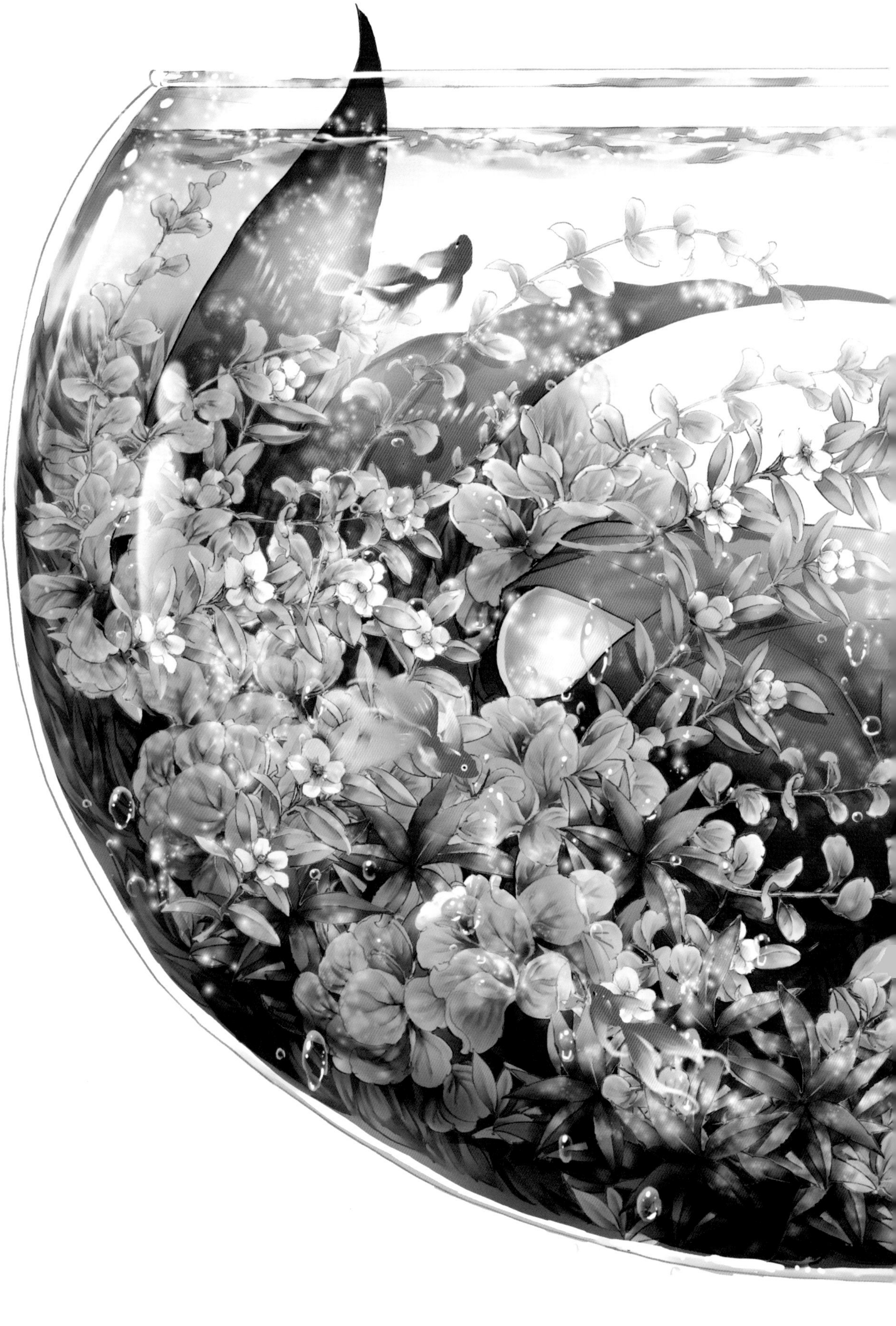

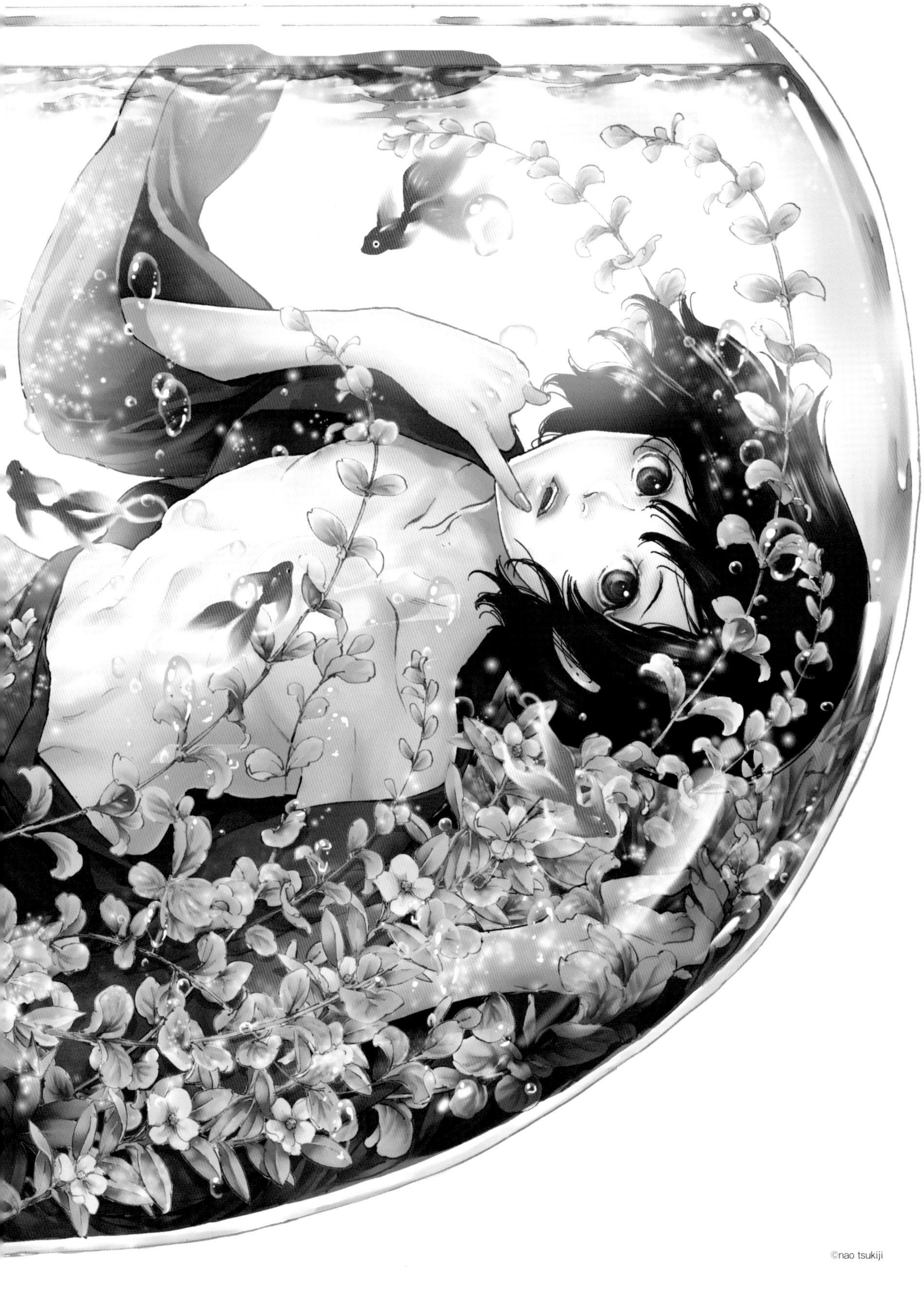

NAO TS

金魚

青少年の腹部やあばらの凹凸が好きなのでその辺りにこだわって描いています。
又、今回は、私が頂いたお題が「水」でしたので水のキラキラ感も楽しんで描きました。
(その他の作品・プロフィール掲載ページ→p.128-129)

UKIJI

Rough draft ©nao tsukiji

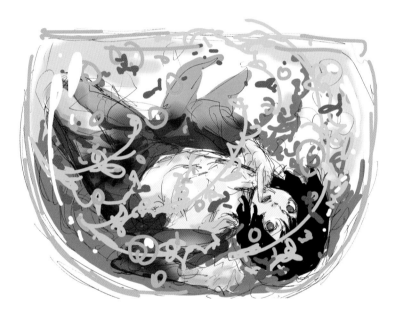

尚月地

Kingyo (Goldfish)

I really like the contours of young men's abs and ribs, and focus on them when I'm drawing. My most recent assignment centered on an aquatic theme, and I enjoyed drawing while enveloped in the sparkling sensation of water.

Additional works and artist profile are found on pp. 128-129.

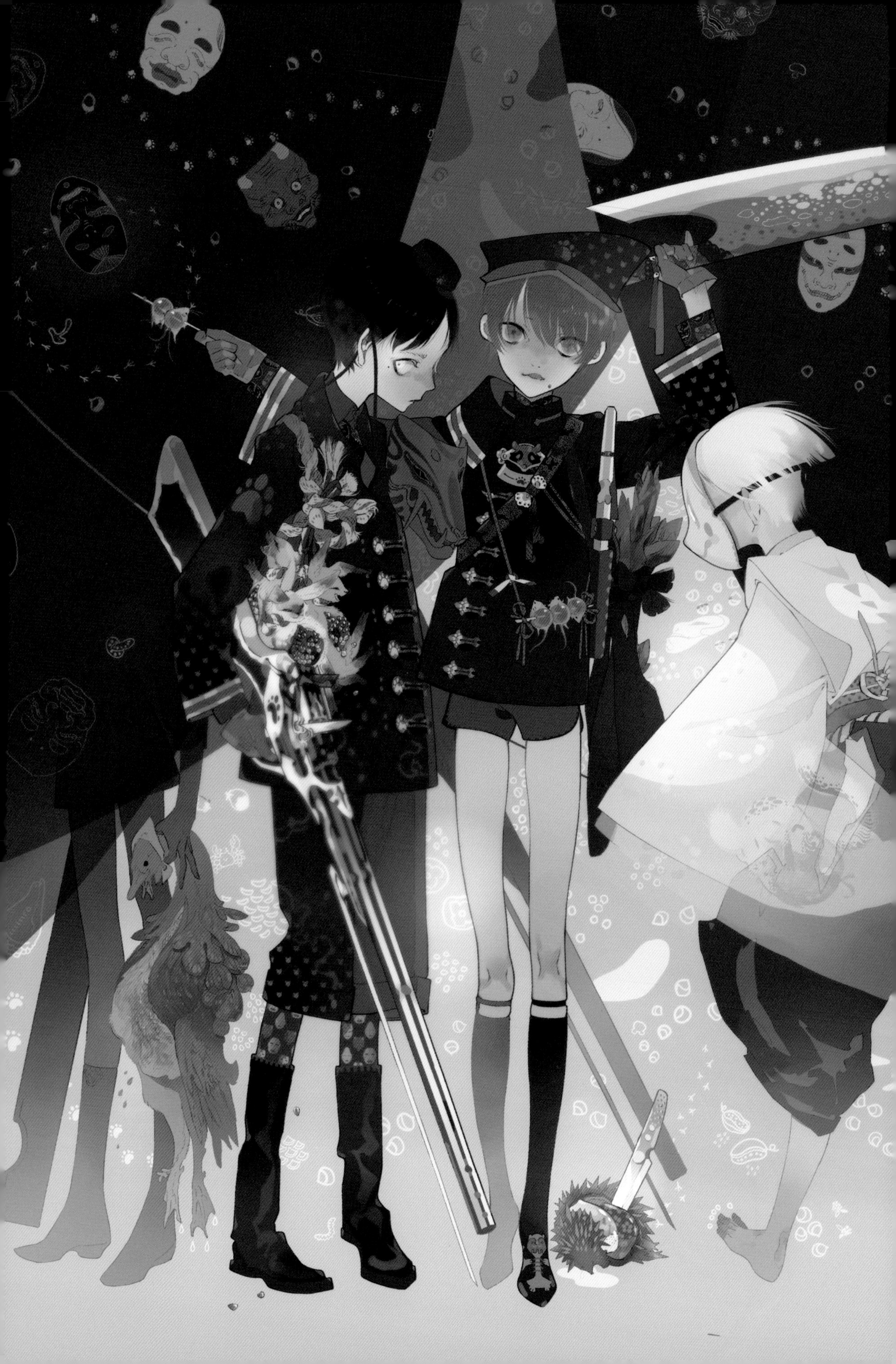

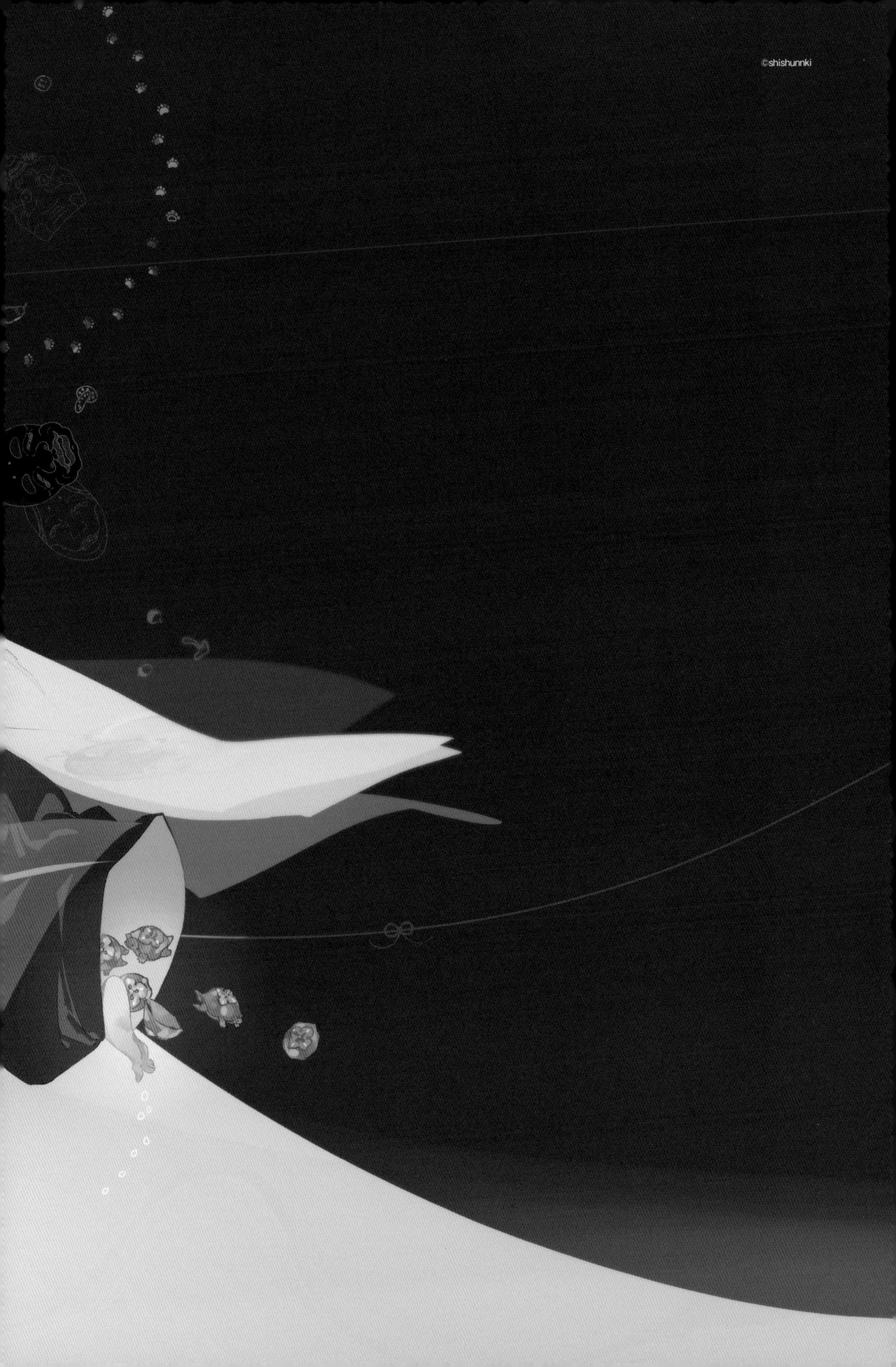
©shishunnki

SHISHU

待宵香

秋の味覚狩りをテーマに、実家の山で採れていた果物を思い出しながら描きました。
あの秋の恵み達に、逃げる手足があったらもっと愉しかったかも…。
大好きな冬の入り口でもある芳醇な季節、ちょっとでも味が伝わってくれれば幸いです。
（その他の作品・プロフィール掲載ページ→p.92-93）

NNKI

Rough draft ©shishunnki

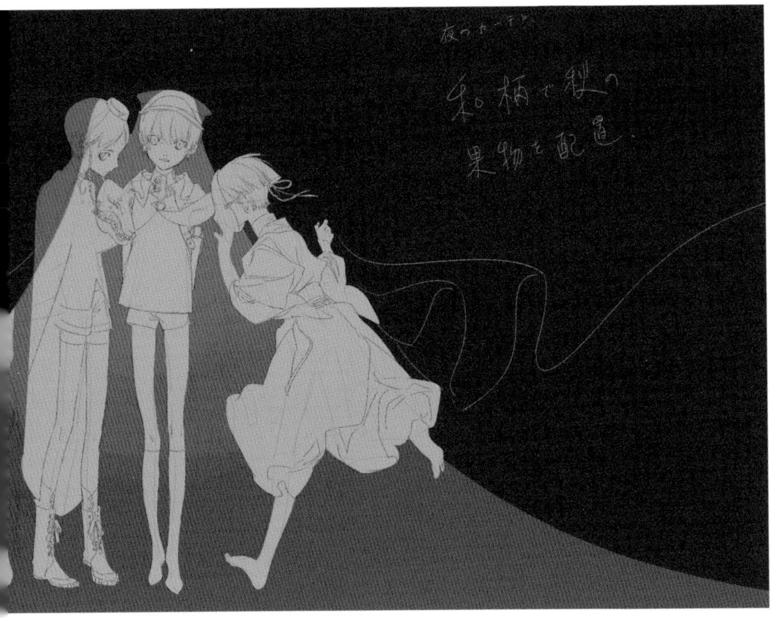
夜のカーテン
和柄で秋の
果物を配置.

思春期

Matsuyoi-koh (Heavenly Expectations)

I drew on memories of mountain fruit harvests near my childhood home to help me illustrate the theme of "pursuing the tastes of autumn." If all those fruits had only possessed limbs to escape, it might have been even more fun...
I would be delighted if my work conveyed even a little of what that rich season—the doorway to my winter—was like.
Additional works and artist profile are found on pp. 092-093.

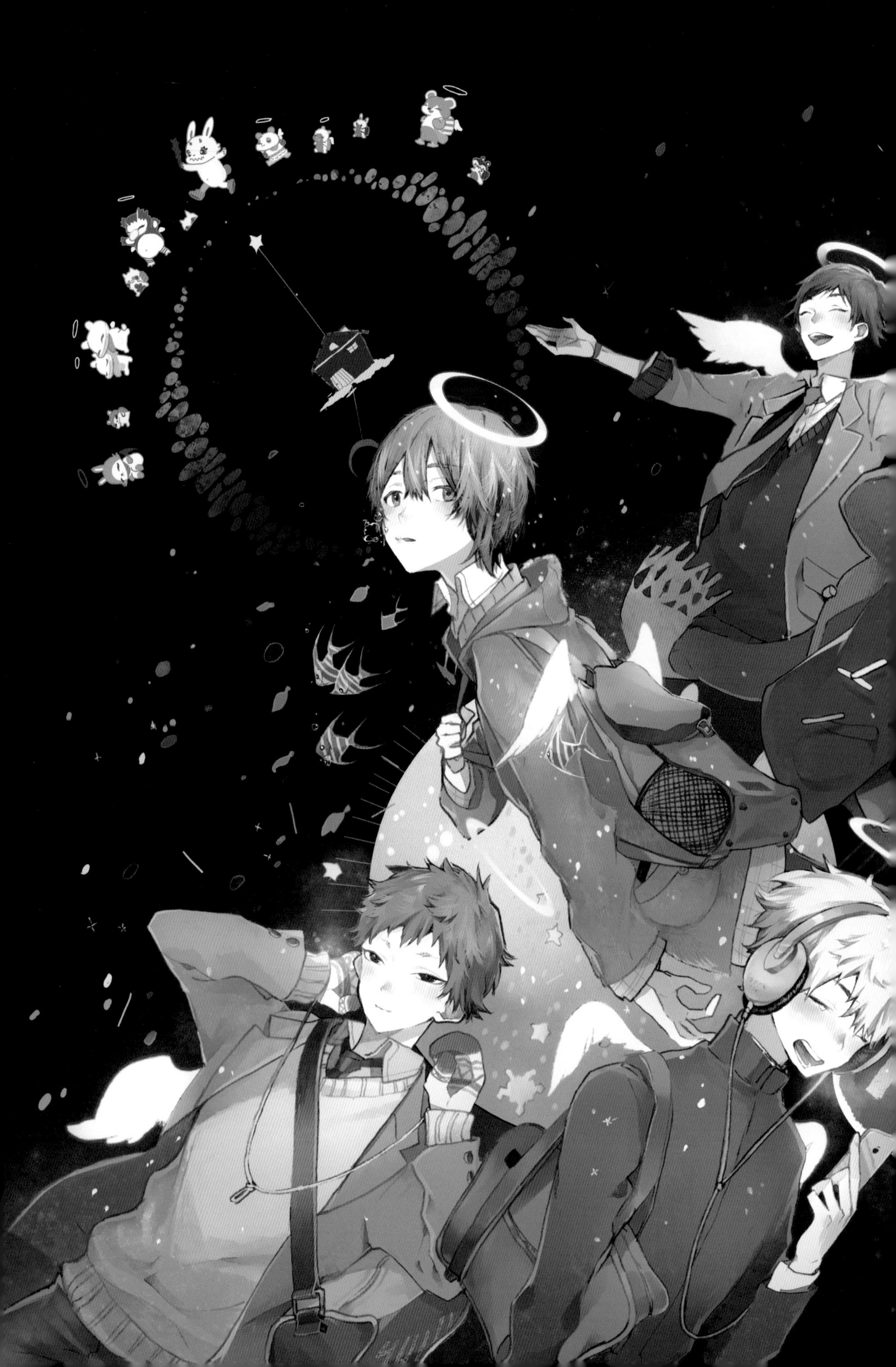

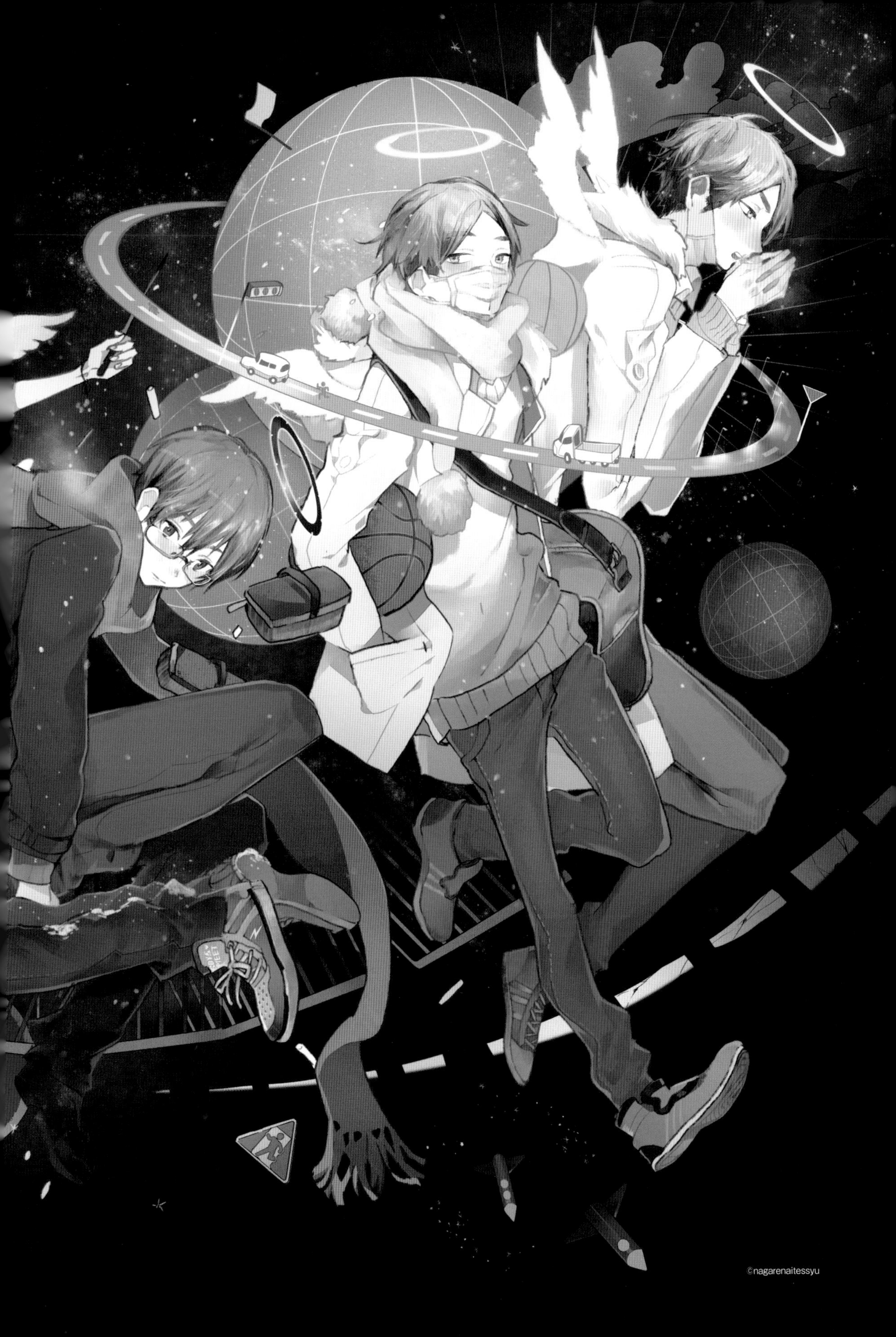

NAGARE TESSYU

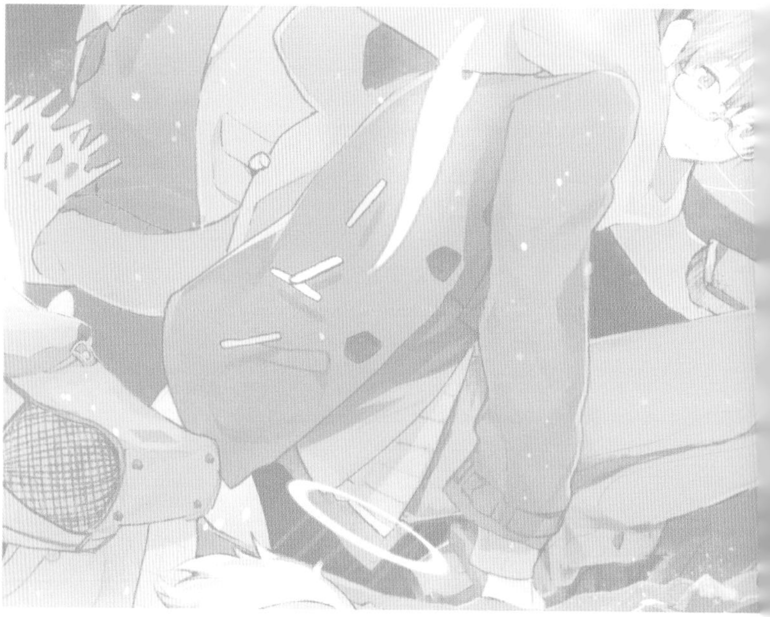

7:00

冬という大きなテーマをとても自由に描かせて頂きました。学生達の冬の通学路をイメージしています。
過酷だったり眠かったり毎日は同じ道のりだったりするのですが、冬場は日が昇るのが遅く普段と違う光景が味わえたり、
雪が降ってきて嬉しくなったりする、ちょっとだけ特別な気分になれるような通学路を詰め込みました。
(その他の作品・プロフィール掲載ページ→p.130-131)

NAI

Rough draft ©nagarenaitessyu

流れないテッシュ

7:00

I was given free rein to illustrate based on the expansive theme of winter. I imagined students beating the well-trodden path to school. Though harsh, sleepy, and invariable, the daily journey in winter creates a special feeling–with a later sunrise highlighting a different landscape and the joy of a snowfall–which I compacted into my work.

Additional works and artist profile are found on pp. 130–131.

本書の見方・留意事項
Notes on book layout

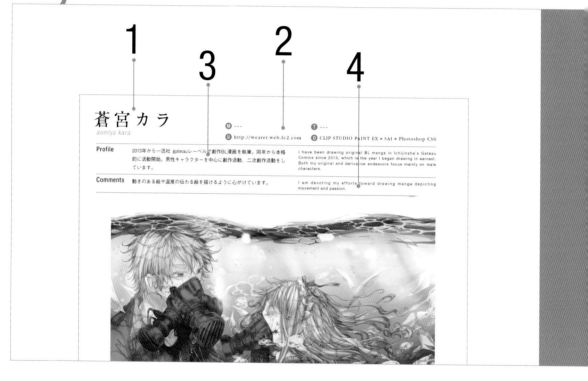

1
3
2
4

蒼宮カラ
aomiya kara

M ---
U http://wearer.web.fc2.com
T ---
D CLIP STUDIO PAINT EX ● SAI ● Photoshop CS6

Profile
2013年から一迅社 gateauレーベルで創作BL漫画を執筆。同年から本格的に活動開始。男性キャラクターを中心に創作活動、二次創作活動をしています。

I have been drawing original BL manga in Ichijinsha's Gateau Comics since 2013, which is the year I began drawing in earnest. Both my original and derivative endeavors focus mainly on male characters.

Comments
動きのある絵や温度の伝わる絵を描けるように心がけています。

I am devoting my efforts toward drawing manga depicting movement and passion.

1

作家名
作家名のローマ字表記は、名字・名前の順で記載しています。

Artists name
Artists' names are Romanized and listed alphabetically by surname, followed by given names.

2

- Ⓜ はメールアドレスです。
  an e-mail address.
- Ⓣ はツイッターIDです。
  a Twitter ID.
- Ⓤ はホームページアドレス(URL)です。
  a website (URL).
- Ⓓ は創作に使用するツール(Drawing tool)です。ハードウェアは記載していません。
  a drawing tool. (hardware is not specified).

3

作家のプロフィールです。
Artists profile

4

創作において心がけている点や、アピールしたい点などのコメントです。
Comments offered by the artist noting his or her creative aspirations and unique selling points.

※掲載作家の希望により、上記情報の一部を記載していない場合があります。
Some information has been omitted, per the artist's request.

※掲載情報は、2015年11月現在のものです。予告なく変更される場合があります。予めご了承ください。
The information noted above is current as of November 2015, and may change without prior notice.

※クレジットの企業名に付随する株式会社・有限会社等の法人格の表記は省略しております。
The official corporate names of companies acknowledged here have been omitted.

蒼宮カラ
aomiya kara

Ⓜ --- Ⓣ ---
Ⓤ http://wearer.web.fc2.com Ⓓ CLIP STUDIO PAINT EX ● SAI ● Photoshop CS6

Profile	2013年から一迅社 gateauレーベルで創作BL漫画を執筆。同年から本格的に活動開始。男性キャラクターを中心に創作活動、二次創作活動をしています。	I have been drawing original BL manga in Ichijinsha's Gateau Comics since 2013, which is the year I began drawing in earnest. Both my original and derivative endeavors focus mainly on male characters.
Comments	動きのある絵や温度の伝わる絵を描けるように心がけています。	I am devoting my efforts toward drawing manga depicting movement and passion.

Personal Work「水の中で」

「おこさまボックス」蒼宮カラ
gateau 2015年5月号 表紙イラスト / 一迅社

Personal Work「廃虚の街」

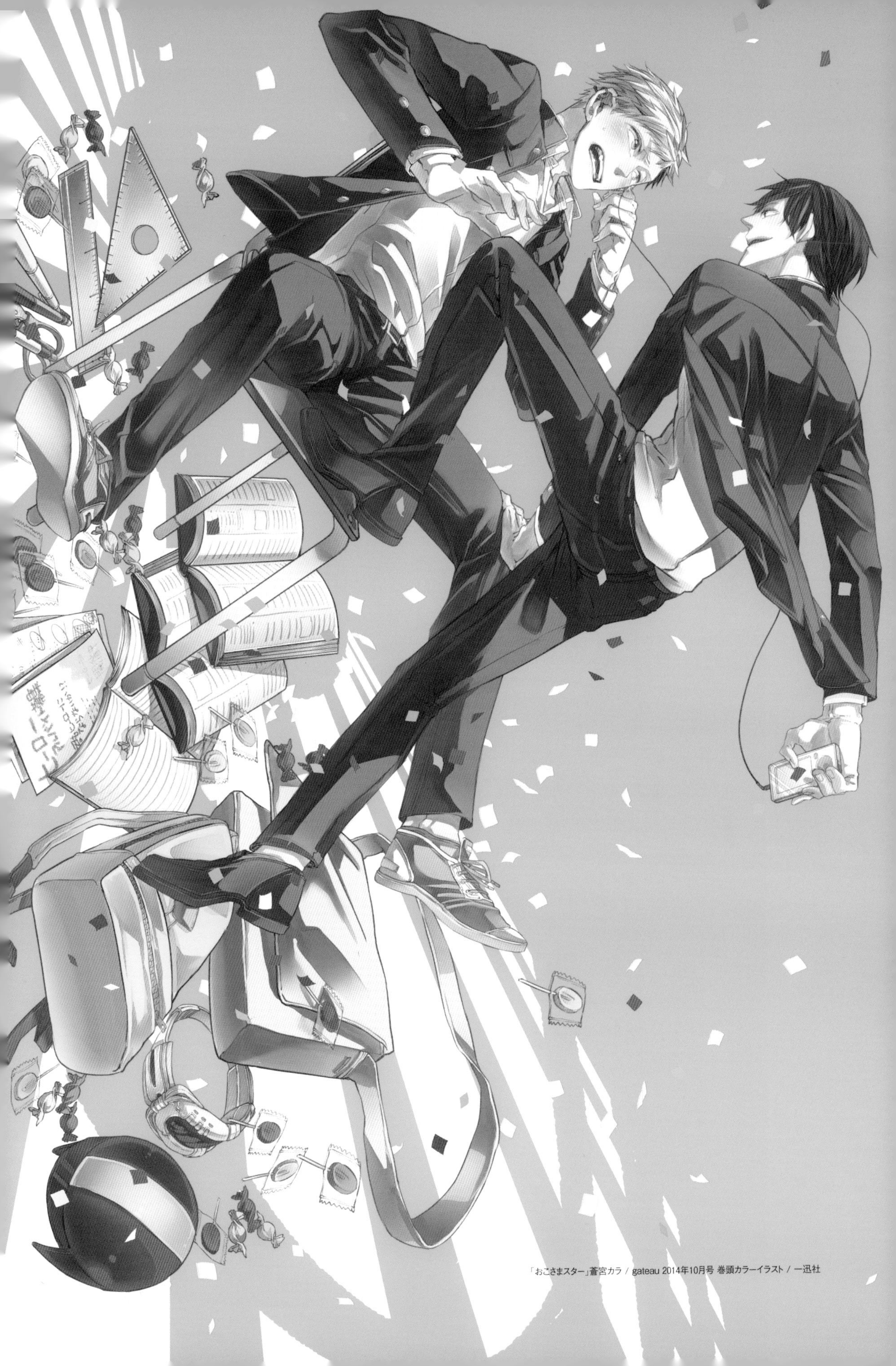

「おこさまスター」蒼宮カラ / gateau 2014年10月号 巻頭カラーイラスト / 一迅社

アキハルノビタ

AKIHARUNOBITA

M 5x2@zj.lomo.jp　**T** 52nbtn　**U** http://5x2.lomo.jp

D ComicStudio ● Painter ● SAI ● CLIP STUDIO PAINT

Profile	主にBL中心でまんがとイラストを描かせていただいております。
	I draw manga and illustrations mainly for BL.
Comments	基本的に楽んで描くようにしてます。あと、コンセプトに雰囲気に合わせつつも共通の個性が感じられるような作品を描ければと思っています。
	My basic stance is to enjoy myself as I draw. I also try to have my illustrations clarify shared characteristics, while ensuring they fit in with the concept and atmosphere.

「神様といっしょ。」アキハルノビタ / カバーイラスト　©アキハルノビタ / 大洋図書

「僕がゲイビ男優になった理由。」
アキハルノビタ / カバーイラスト
ダリアコミックス / フロンティアワークス
©アキハルノビタ / フロンティアワークス

Personal Work

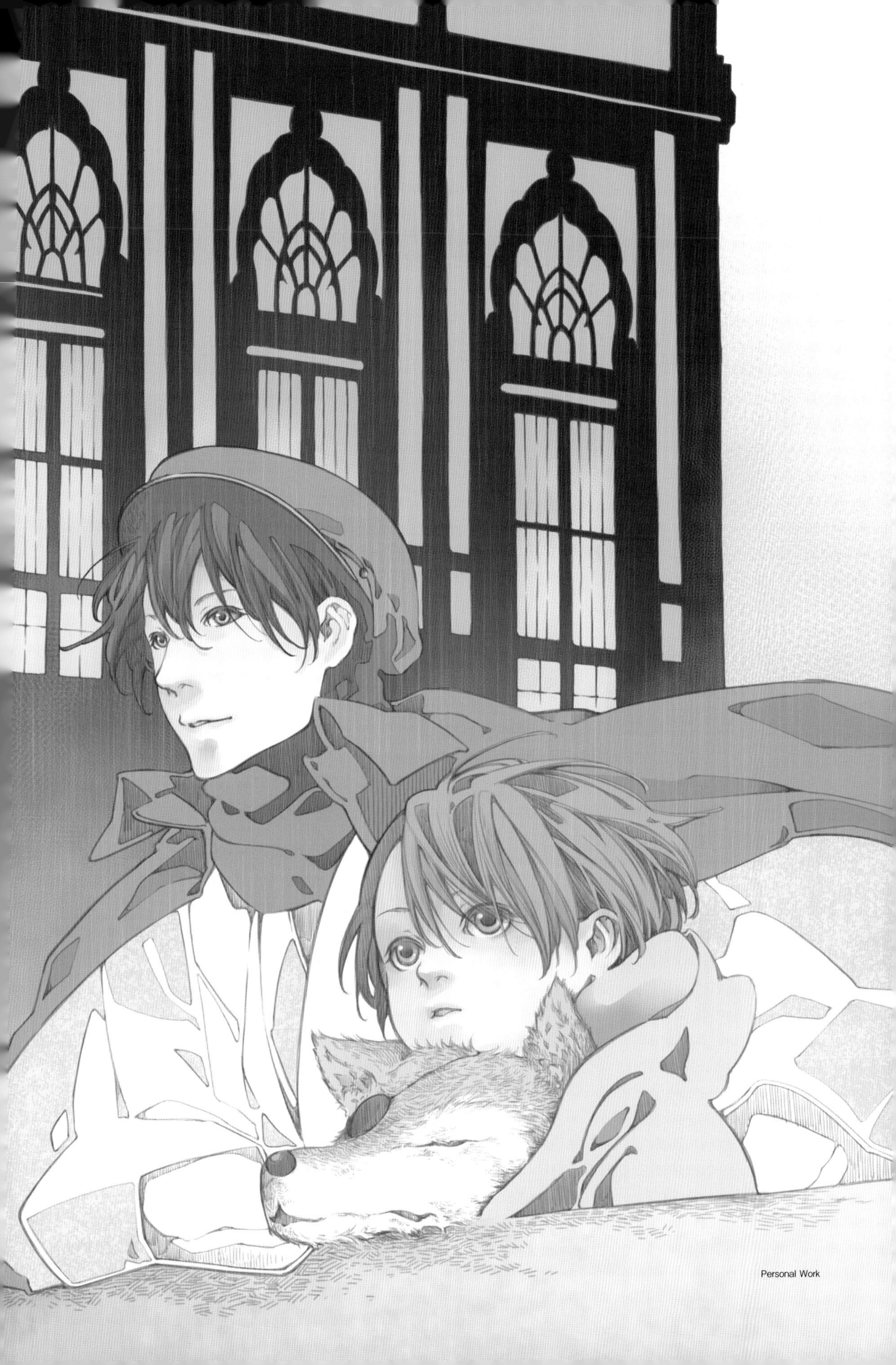

Personal Work

浅島ヨシユキ
Asajima Yoshiyuki

M ---
U http://www7b.biglobe.ne.jp/~plusl
T asjmysyk
D SAI • Photoshop

Profile	イラストレーター。シチュエーションCD、女性向けゲームアプリ、ソーシャルゲーム等のキャラクターデザイン、原画やイラストなど執筆。
	I am an illustrator. I create character designs for situation CDs (drama CD with only one voice actor), game applications for female consumers, and social games, for example, and do original stills and illustrations as well.
Comments	キャラクターの性格や個性など魅力を引き出せるよう意識して描いています。妖しさや透明感、色気のある男性キャラクターを描くのが好きです。
	When I draw, I try to ensure that my characters are fascinating by giving them personality, idiosyncrasies, and the like. I enjoy drawing male characters who are shady and transparent, and who have sex appeal.

「妖かし恋戯曲」/ メインビジュアル © XING INC. / OperaHouse Corporation

Personal Work「Knight」

Personal Work「昇華」

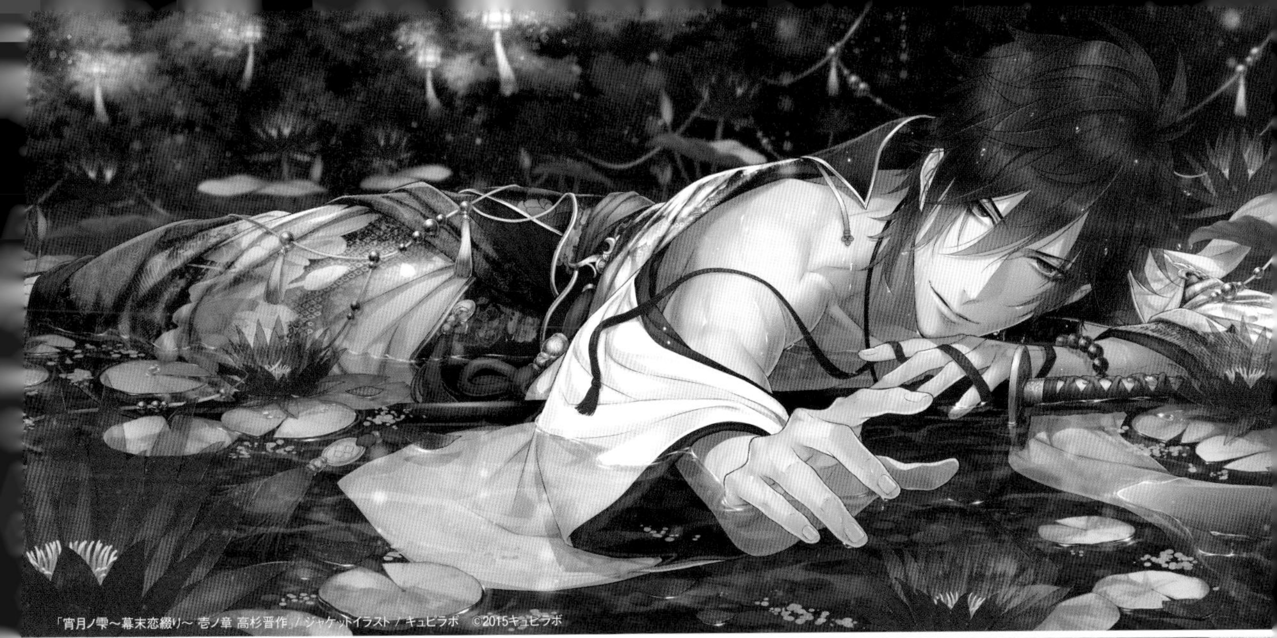
「宵月ノ雫～幕末恋綴り～ 壱ノ章 高杉晋作」/ ジャケットイラスト / キュピラボ ©2015キュピラボ

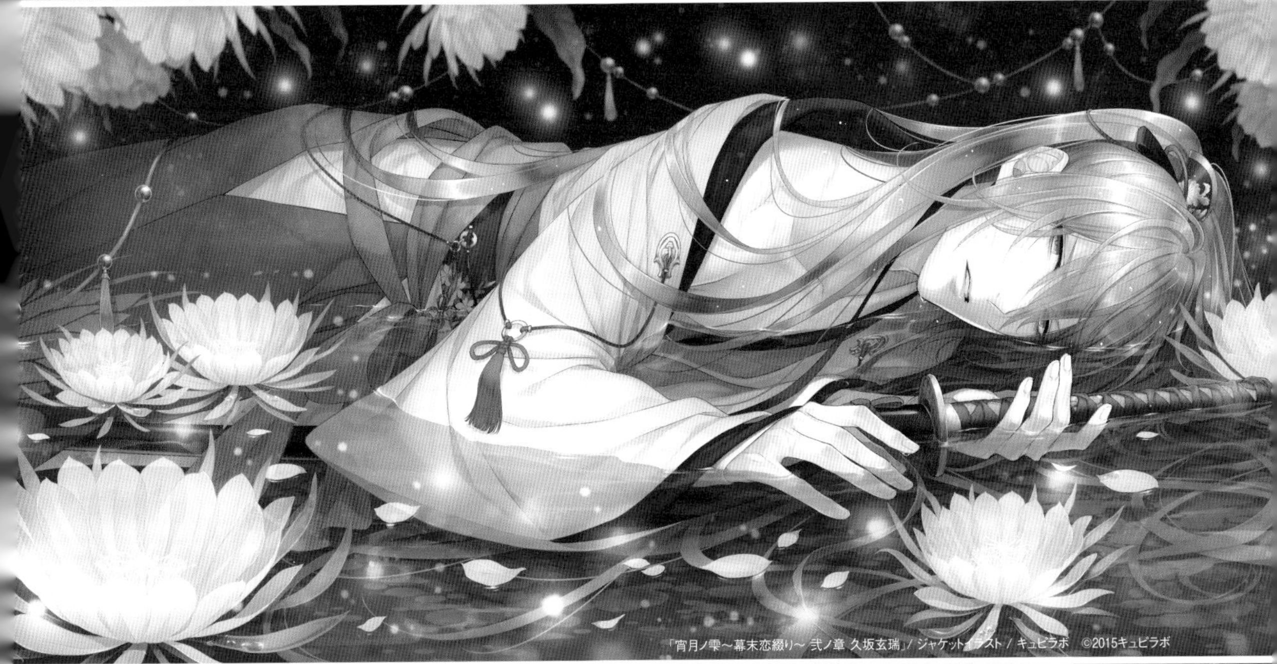
「宵月ノ雫～幕末恋綴り～ 弐ノ章 久坂玄瑞」/ ジャケットイラスト / キュピラボ ©2015キュピラボ

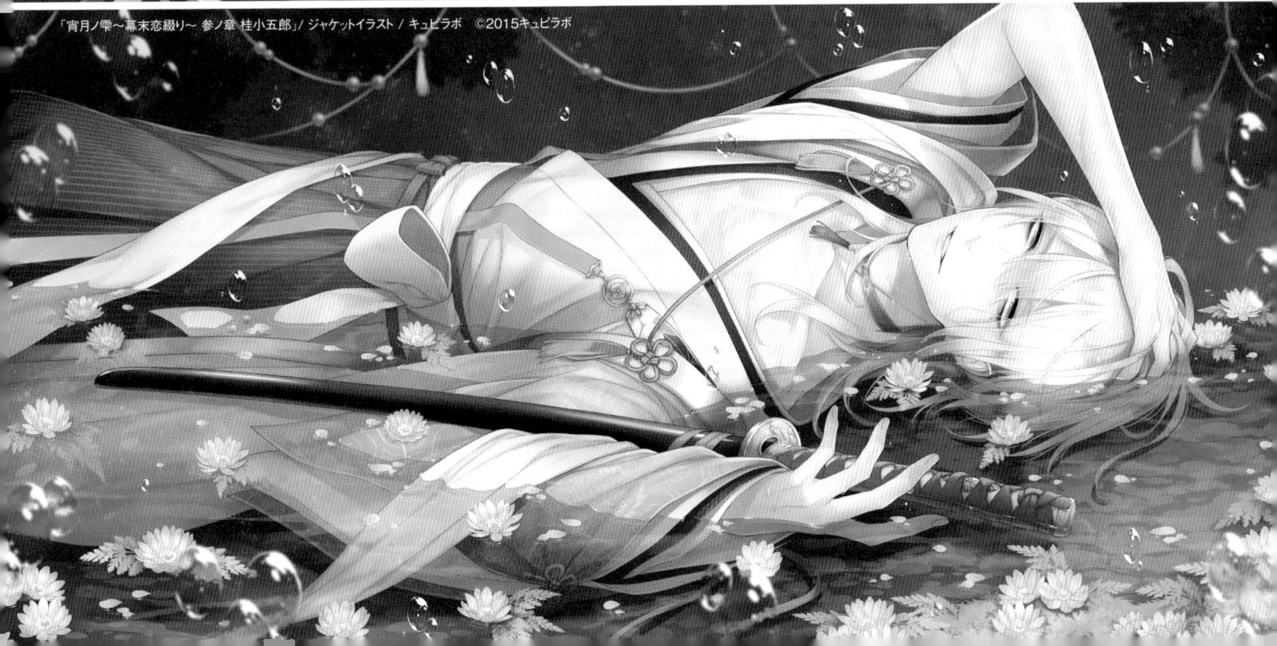
「宵月ノ雫～幕末恋綴り～ 参ノ章 桂小五郎」/ ジャケットイラスト / キュピラボ ©2015キュピラボ

ありいめめこ

ARII MEMECO

M ---　T memecocco　U http://memecocco.jugem.jp

D Maru pen • Photoshop Elements10 • Acrylic Paints • Crayons

Profile

漫画執筆をメインに活動しています。「ひとりじめマイヒーロー」（一迅社）、「かのこみち」（東京漫画社）を連載中。既刊に「ひとりじめボーイフレンド」（一迅社）、「闘う！ラブリーエプロン」（一迅社）、「嘘つきとスイーツ」（コアマガジン）　など。

I primarily draw manga. I'm now in the middle of creating serial comics for *Hitori-jime My Hero* (Ichijinsha) and *Kanokomichi* (Tokyo Mangasha). My earlier works include *Hitori-jime Boyfriend* and *Tatakau! Lovely Apron* (both from Ichijinsha), as well as *Usotsuki to Sweets* (Core Magazine).

Comments

小ネタをちょこちょこ入れて、よく見ると発見がある画面にしたいなと思っています。たまに見つけてもらえるととっても嬉しいので。自分で描いていて楽しいものを描きたいです。

By including bits of humor and offshoots here and there, I hope to create pictures offering discoveries to readers who look carefully. I'll be delighted if people notice these little additions once in awhile. I always like to draw what gives me pleasure.

「ひとりじめボーイフレンド」ありいめめこ
gateau 2014.10 / 一迅社　©ありいめめこ / 一迅社

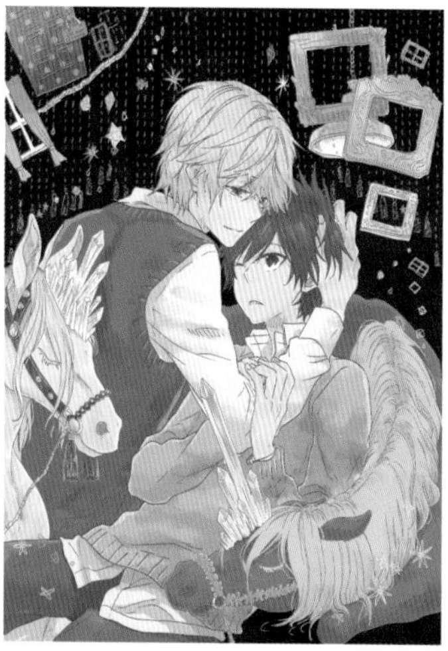

「ひとりじめマイヒーロー」ありいめめこ
gateau 2014.3 / 一迅社　©ありいめめこ / 一迅社

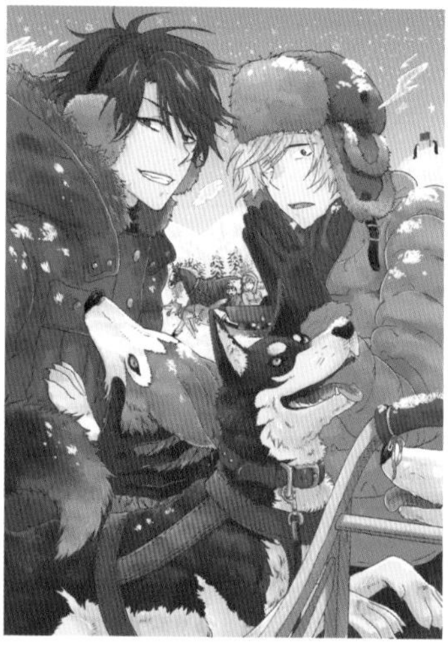

「かのこみち」ありいめめこ
Fig Vol.6 / 東京漫画社　©ありいめめこ / 東京漫画社

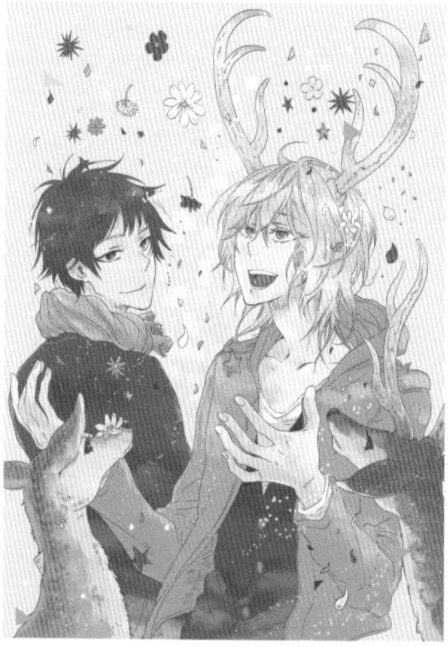

「ひとりじめマイヒーロー」ありいめめこ / gateau 2014.6 / 一迅社　©ありいめめこ / 一迅社

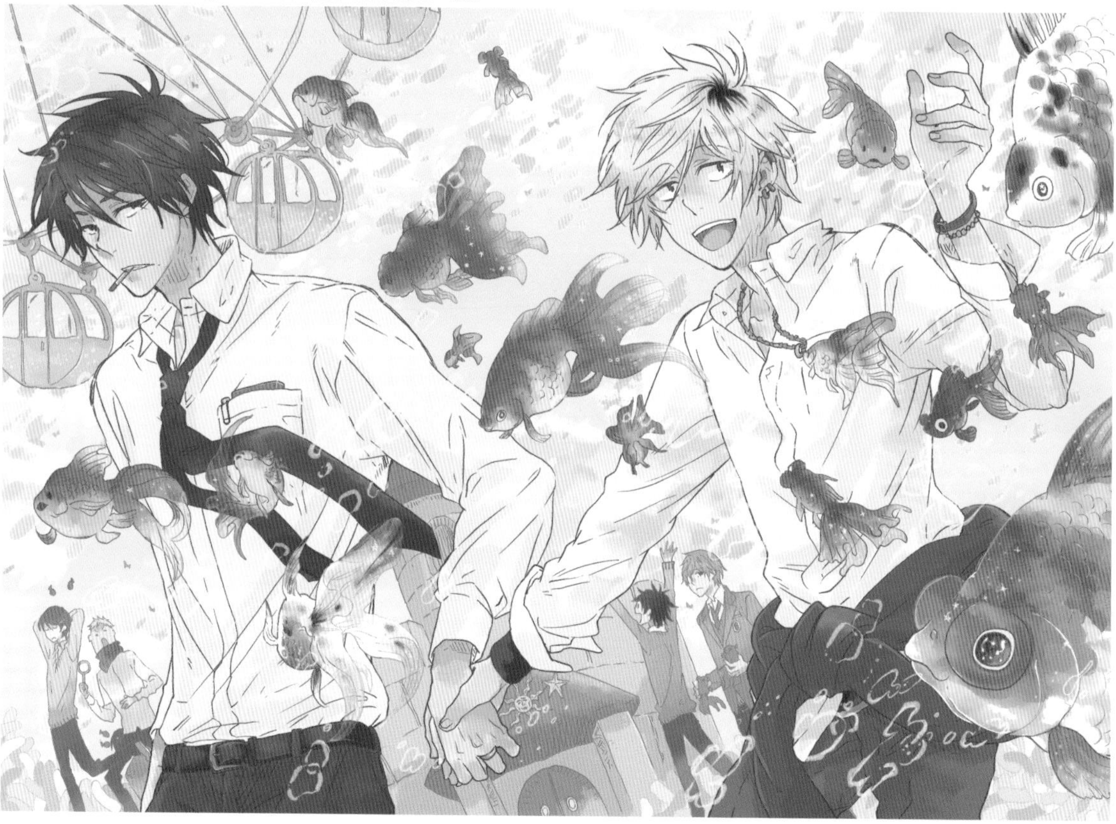

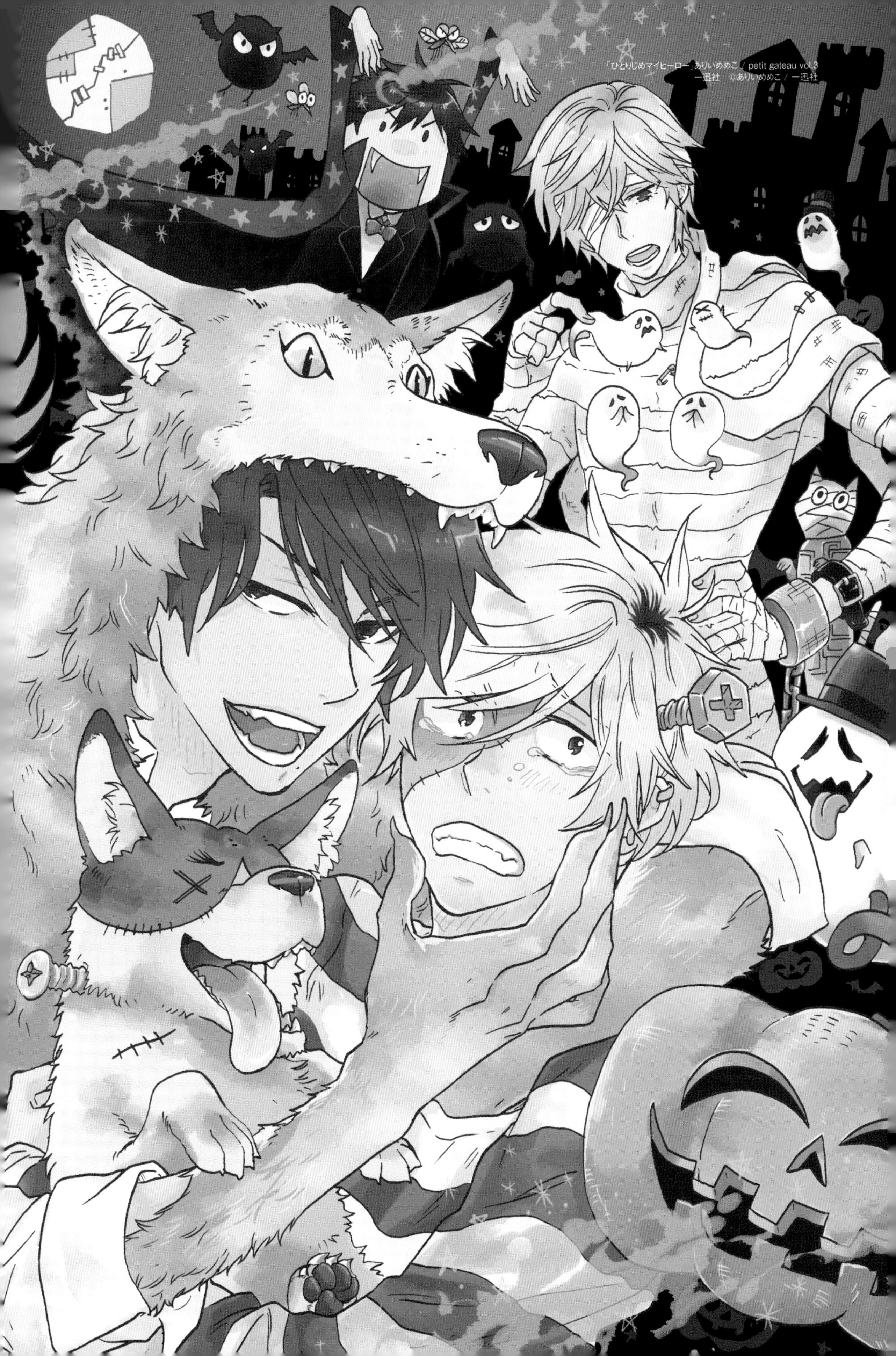
「ひとりじめマイヒーロー」ありいめめこ / petit gateau vol.3
一迅社　©ありいめめこ / 一迅社

ウダジョ
udajyo

M --- **T** udajyo
U --- **D** SAI • photoshop • CLIP STUDIO PAINT

Profile	「BROTHERS CONFLICT」「フォルティッシモ」等、女性向け企画のキャラクターデザイン、イラストを描かせていただいております。	I design and illustrate characters aimed at the female market, such as those in *BROTHERS CONFLICT* and *Fortissimo*.
Comments	キャラクターらしさを大切に、見た人が元気になるような絵を目指しています。	I value the identity of the characters, and try to energize the viewers with my rendering of them.

「BROTHERS CONFLICT」/ ポストカード / スクールカレンダー表紙イラスト / ©2015 ウダジョ / クロスワークス / KADOKAWA

ドラマCD「BROTHERS CONFLICT RARE TRACK」/ ジャケットイラスト
©2015 ウダジョ / クロスワークス / KADOKAWA

「BROTHERS CONFLICT」/ シルフ 2013年8月号 表紙イラスト
©2015 ウダジョ / クロスワークス / KADOKAWA

「フォルティッシモ」/ シルフ2014年9月号 表紙イラスト

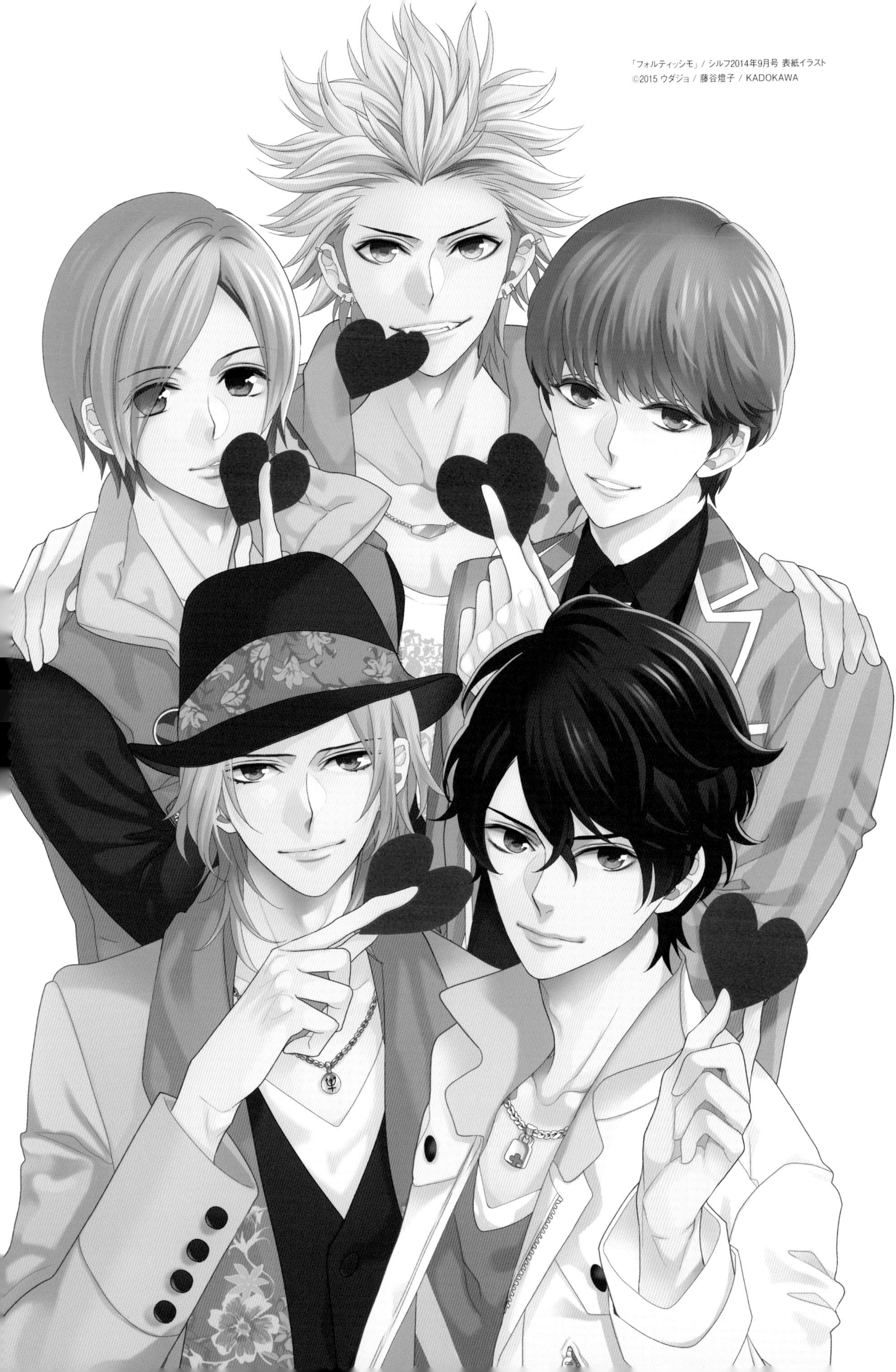

潤宮るか

Urumiya Ruka

M lovecom@bh.chu.jp

U http://lovecom.chu.jp/com

T ---

D SAI • Photoshop CS5

Profile

女性向けコンテンツのキャラクターデザイン、イラスト制作、監修等を中心に活動中です。

My work mainly involves work such as character design, illustrations, and editorial supervision for projects bearing female-oriented content.

Comments

キャラクターの内面に深く寄り添うようなデザインを心がけています。また、キャラクターとユーザー様の目線を合わせ、感情を共有できるようなイラスト制作ができたらと思います。

I attempt to create designs which allow profound access to the innermost hearts and minds of my characters. Another goal is to find common perspectives between my characters and the user so that they may share the same feelings.

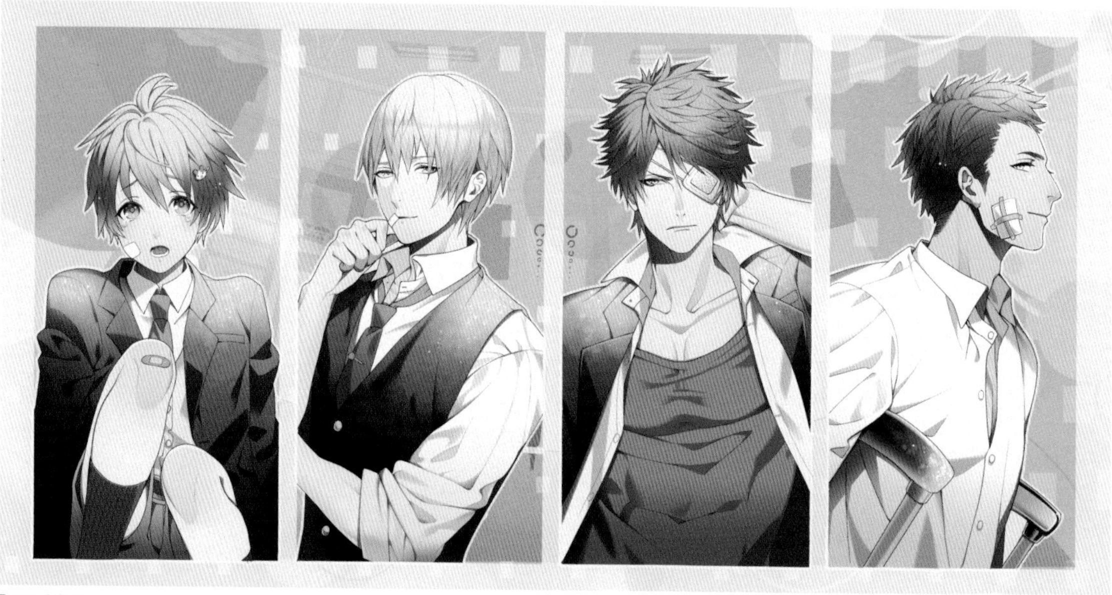

Personal Work

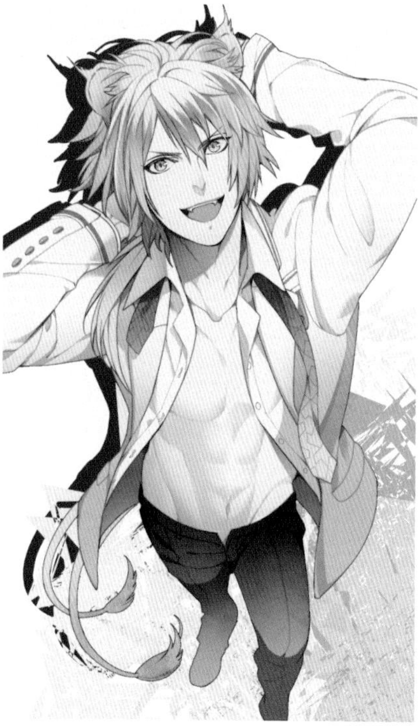

Personal Work

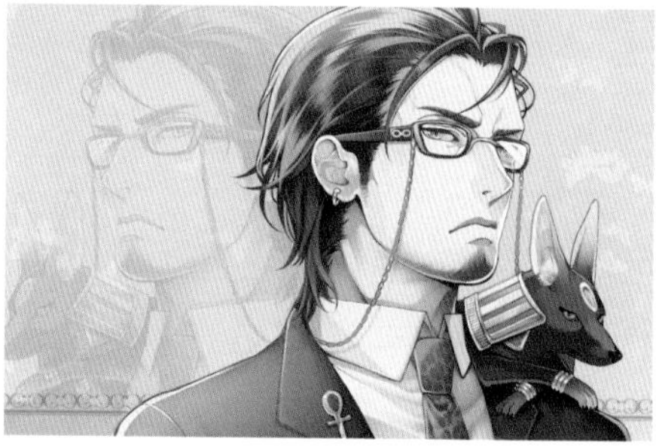

Personal Work

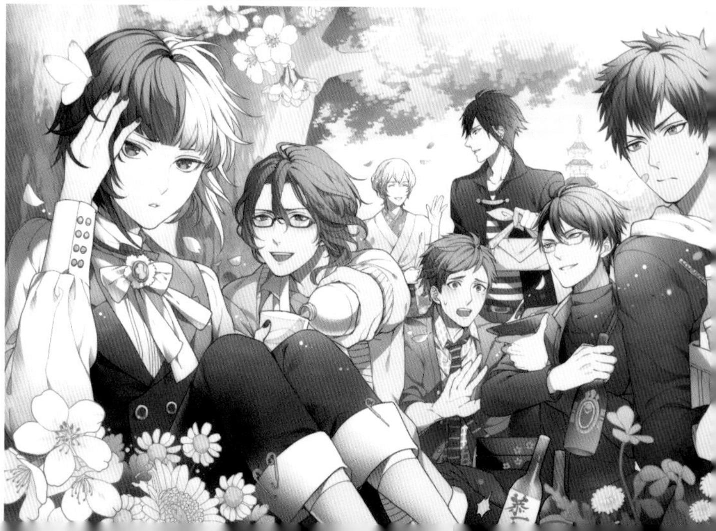

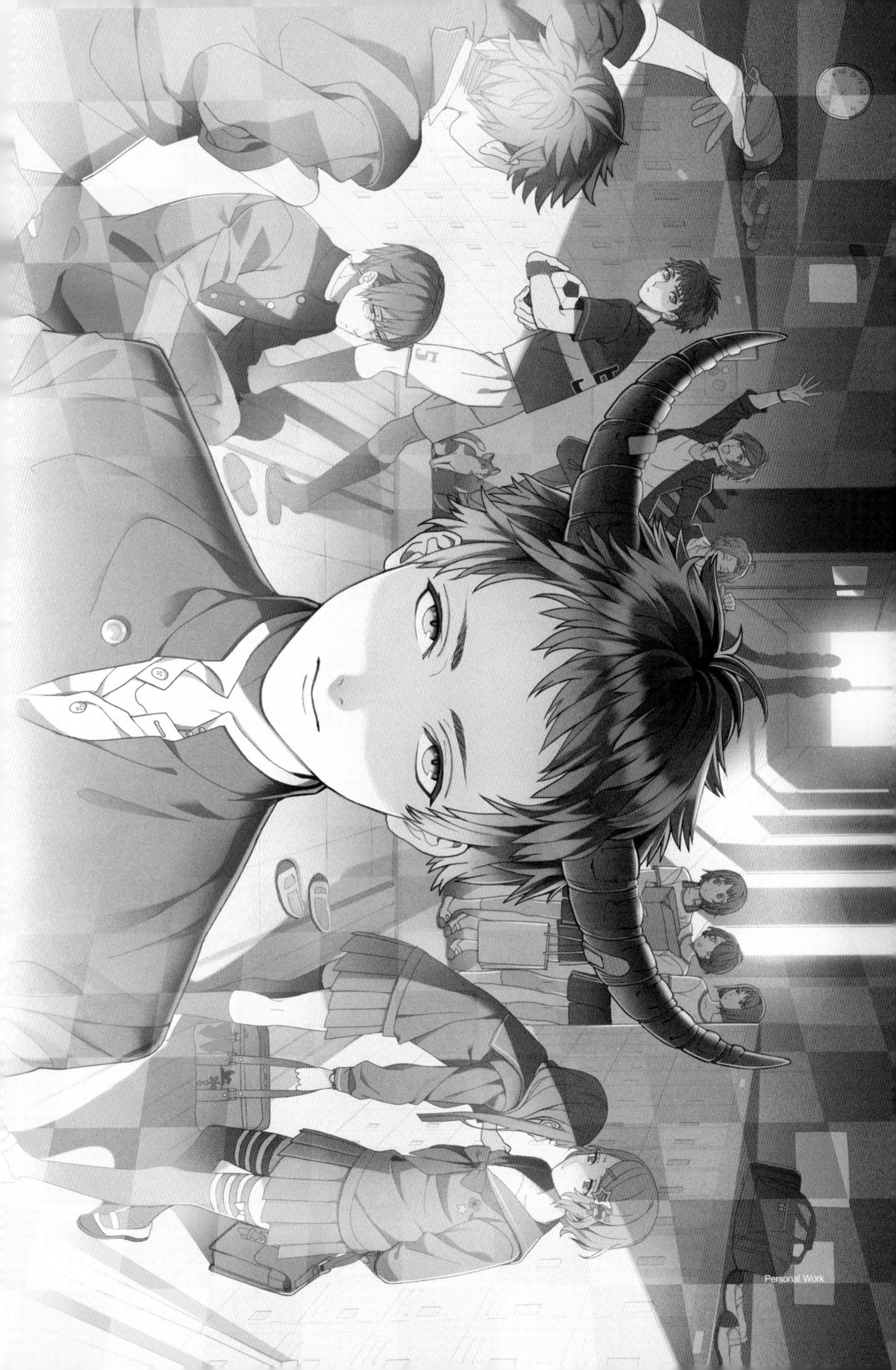

Personal Work

円陣闇丸

enjin yamimaru

M enjin_y@yahoo.co.jp
T enjin_y
U pixiv ID 6192128
D Color inks ● CLIP STUDIO PAINT EX

Profile

かれこれ15年以上BLメインに小説挿絵やイラスト、漫画を描いています。挿絵担当した小説100冊以上、コミックス8冊、イラスト集1冊など。スーツの似合う大人系の男性を描くことをご依頼頂くことが多いです。

For over 15 years, I have been illustrating novels and producing other illustrations and manga, primarily in the BL genre. I have illustrated over 100 novels and 8 comics, and other publications include one compilation of drawings. I'm often asked to draw pictures of adult males who look appealing in suits.

Comments

仕事で描く場合はまず、何を求められているか、期待されていることは何かを見極めることを念頭に、結果それ以上のものを出せたらベストと考えています。無茶ぶりも歓迎。と言いつつかっこいい男性を描くのが何より好きなのでそれだけを考えてやってきた部分もあります。趣味も仕事も男性ばかり描いてますが、男同士だけじゃなく女性を相手にした時の男性の色気の描写にもいくらか興味あり。しかしなかなか機会がなかったりします。

Whenever I accept a new assignment, I first determine what is being asked and expected of me. I keep that in mind and hope to exceed it in my results. I welcome even unreasonable assignments. That said, part of me has always preferred to draw good-looking males. Be it for work or a hobby, I only draw males, but my interest is not limited to male/male relationships; I do have some curiosity about males with sex appeal for females. However, I really don't have much chance to explore the latter in my work.

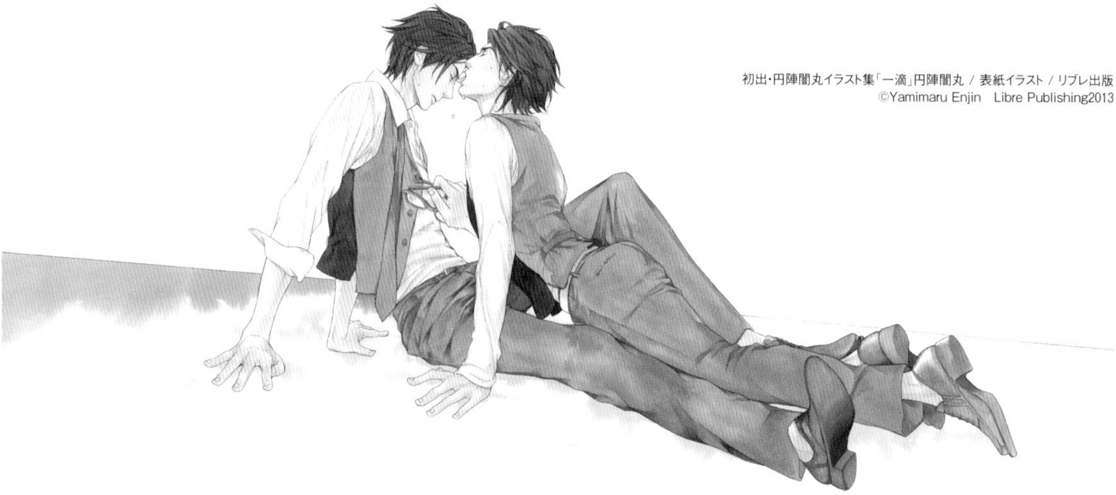

初出・円陣闇丸イラスト集「一滴」円陣闇丸 / 表紙イラスト / リブレ出版
©Yamimaru Enjin Libre Publishing2013

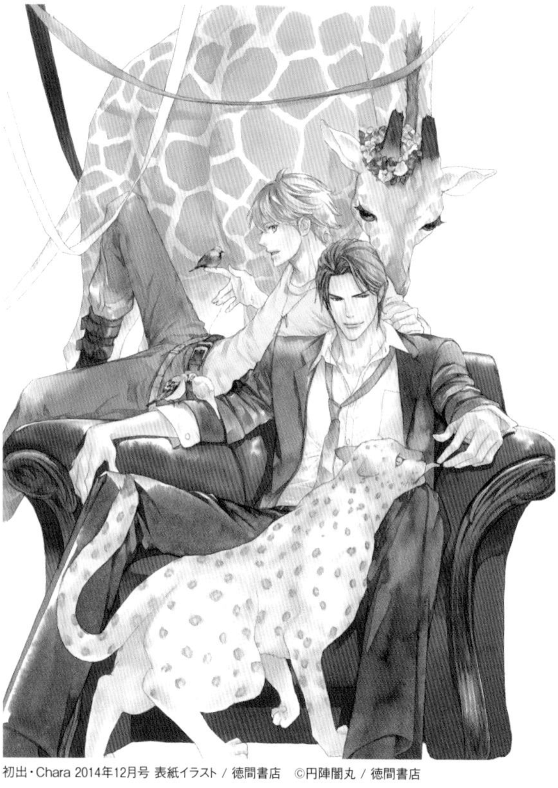

初出・Chara 2014年12月号 表紙イラスト / 徳間書店 ©円陣闇丸 / 徳間書店

「花嫁と誓いの薔薇：砂楼の花嫁2」遠野春日 / カバーイラスト
キャラ文庫 徳間書店 ©遠野春日・円陣闇丸 / 徳間書店

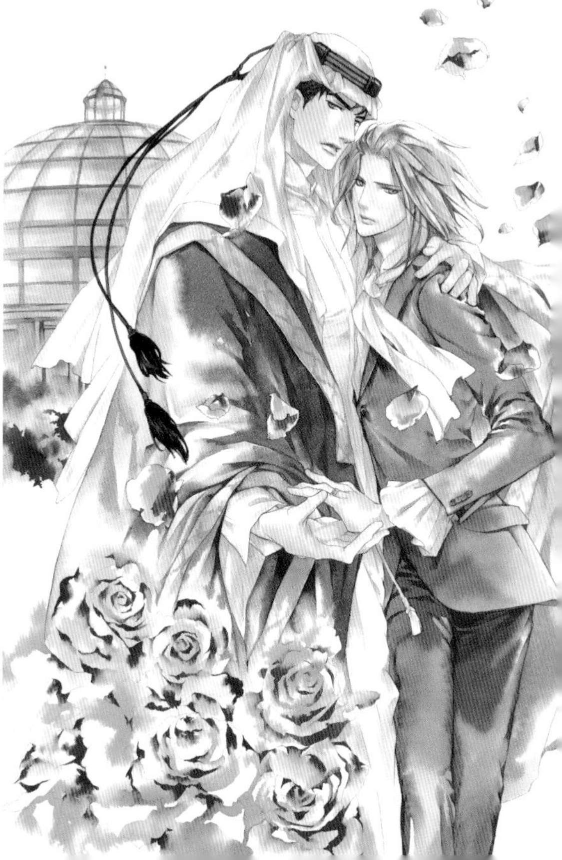

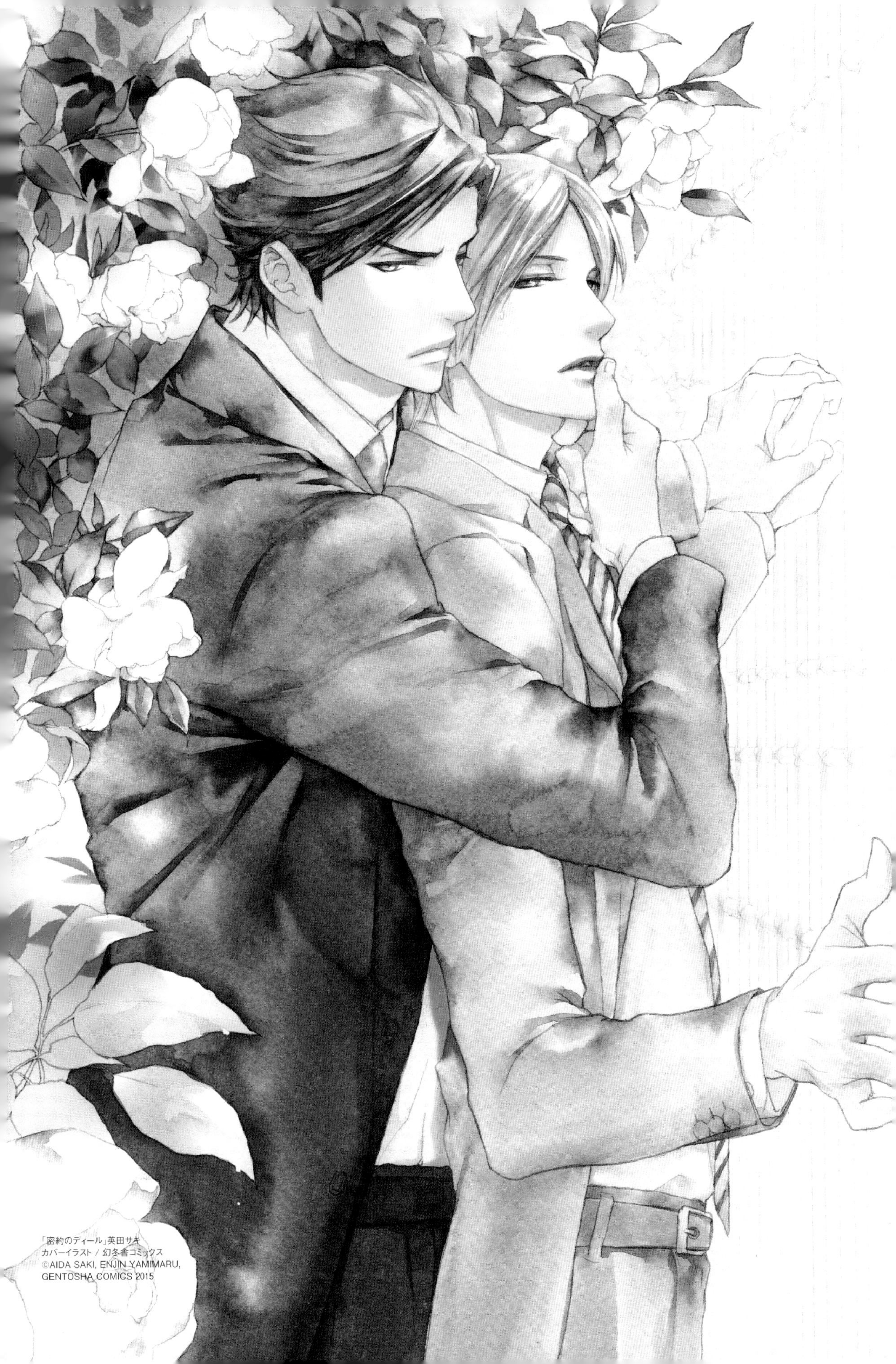
「密約のディール」英田サキ
カバーイラスト / 幻冬舎コミックス

遠田志帆

ENTA shiho

M techi@coo.plala.me
T techicoo
U www17.plala.or.jp/shiffon
D Photoshop CS4

Profile

秋田出身埼玉在住のイラストレーター。秋田大学教育文化学部卒業。主に小説の装画や挿絵を手掛けている。初画集『遠田志帆画集』が新書館より発売中。

I'm an illustrator—born in Akita Prefecture, but now living in Saitama Prefecture. I graduated from Akita University's Faculty of Education and Human Studies. I chiefly draw illustrations and book covers for novels. My first collection of drawings, *Enta Shiho Gashu*, is now available from Shinshokan publishers.

Comments

眼力、唇の立体感、髪の毛の表現に拘っています。最近は男性キャラを描くご依頼もいただくようになり、それらをうまく活かして男性ながらに艶っぽい魅力を出すのが楽しいです。本屋さんでお客さんが思わず目を留めてしまうような装画を目指すのはもちろん、読者の方が読後改めて表紙を見た時に納得してもらえるように心がけています。

I focus strongly on penetrating eyes, full lips, and presentation of hair. These days, I'm often asked to draw male characters, and I'm enjoying capitalizing on those characteristics to produce males with coquettish charm. Of course I'm trying to produce book covers which will unwittingly catch the eye of bookstore customers, but I'd also like to satisfy those customers as they revisit the covers after reading the books.

「真田十勇士 1 参上、猿飛佐助」小前亮 / 装画 / 小峰書店

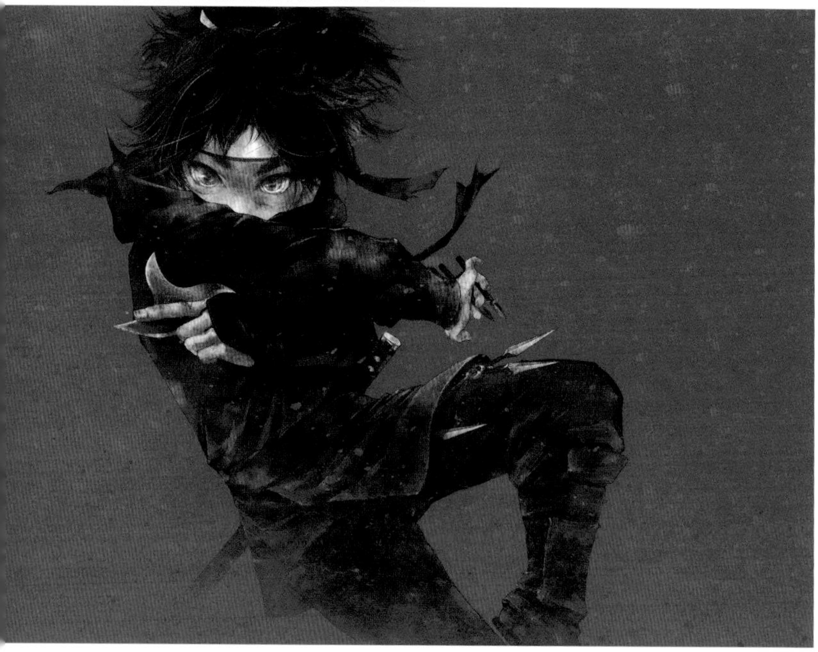

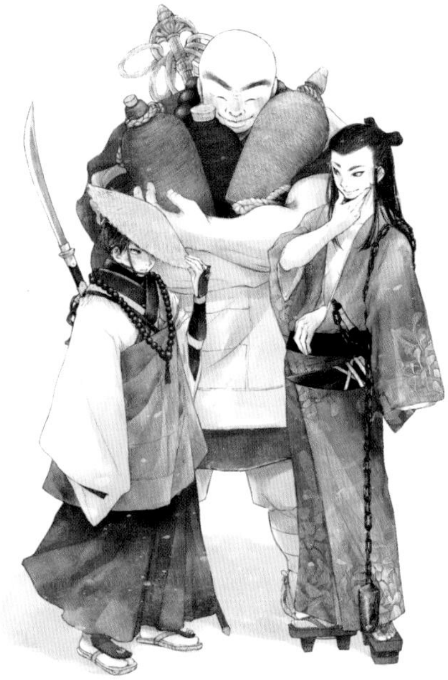

「真田十勇士 1 参上、猿飛佐助」小前亮 / 扉絵 / 小峰書店

「少年探偵」小路幸也 / 装画 / ポプラ社

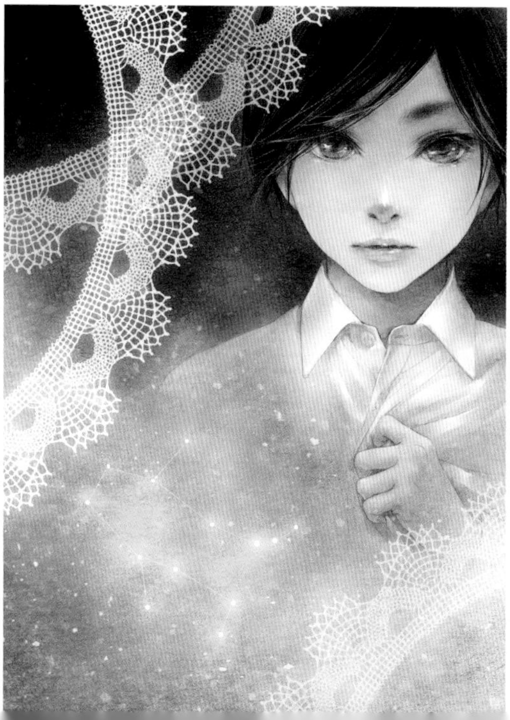

Personal Work「静燃」

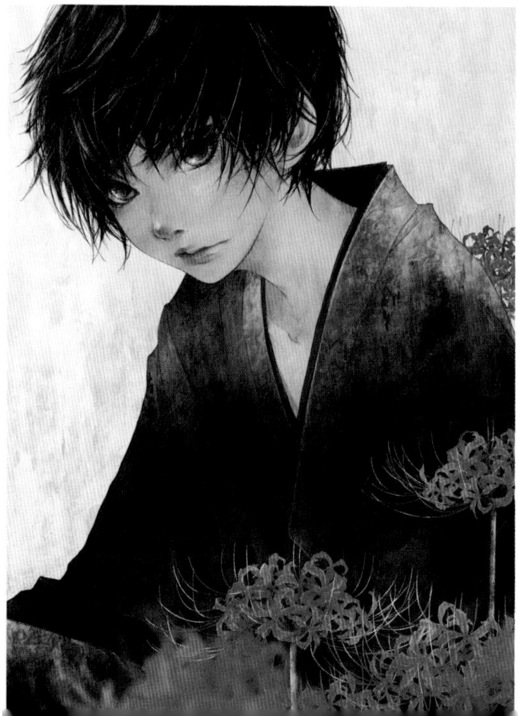

「薔薇十字叢書 天邪鬼の輩」著:愁堂れな　Founder:京極夏彦 / 装画 / KADOKAWA(富士見L文庫)

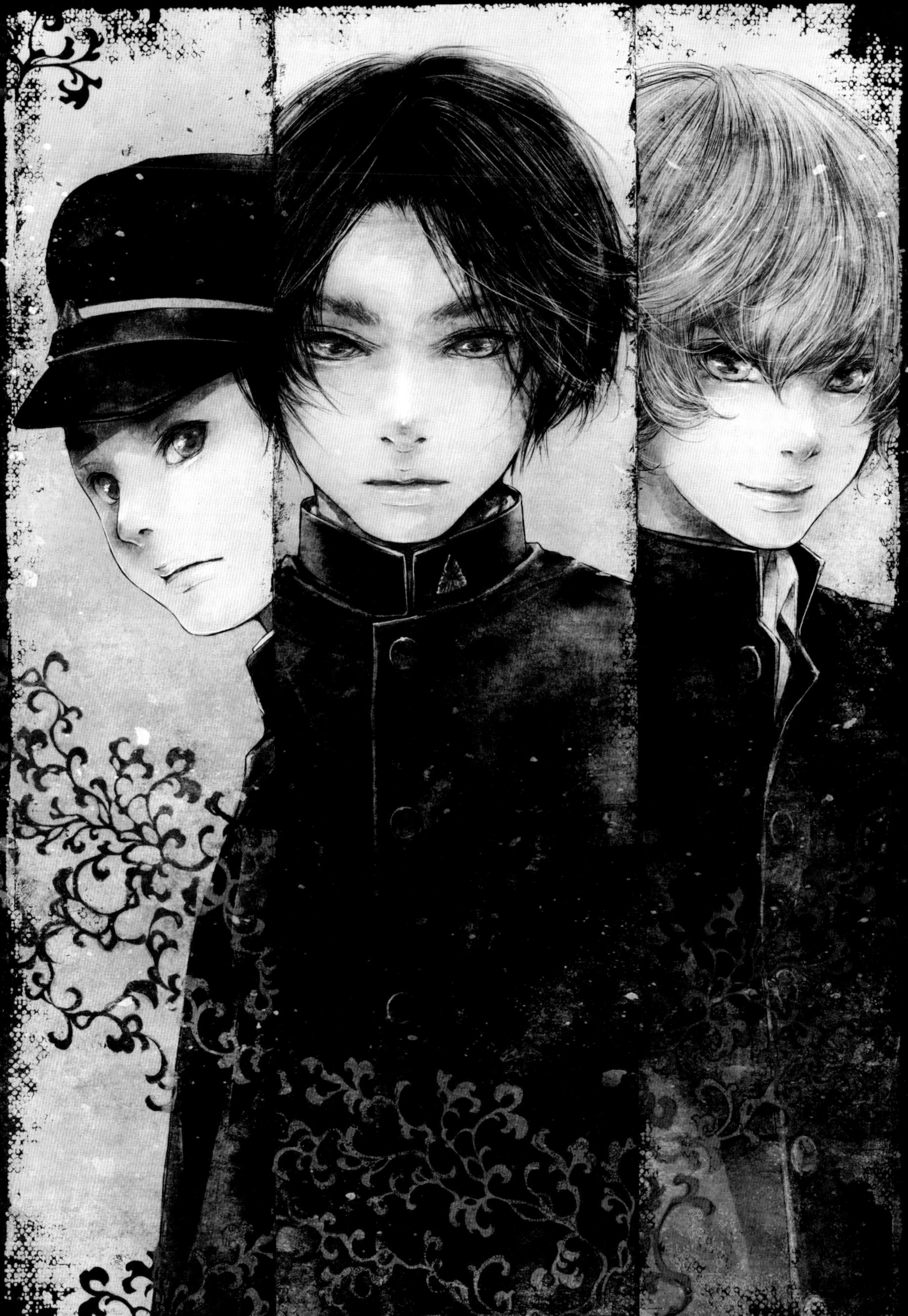

緒川千世
OGAWA CHISE

Ⓜ 135@sig-ma.sakura.ne.jp
Ⓤ ---
Ⓣ ---
Ⓓ SAI ● Photoshop CS5 ● ComicStudio EX

Profile

2011年デビュー。BL漫画家。シリアスからコメディまで様々な漫画を執筆している。他、イラスト・挿絵等も執筆。最新作：リブレ出版「カーストヘヴン1」海王社「終わらない不幸についての話」

I made my debut in 2011. I'm a BL manga artist. I draw all sorts of manga, from serious to humorous. I also illustrate books and other publications. Recent works: *Caste Heaven* 1 by Libre Publishing and *Owaranai Fukou ni Tsuite no Hanashi* by Kaiohsha.

Comments

読み易く、見易くがモットーです。イラストは作品の雰囲気に沿うように描いています。

My motto is: simple to read, simple to view. I render illustrations which are true to the feel of the content.

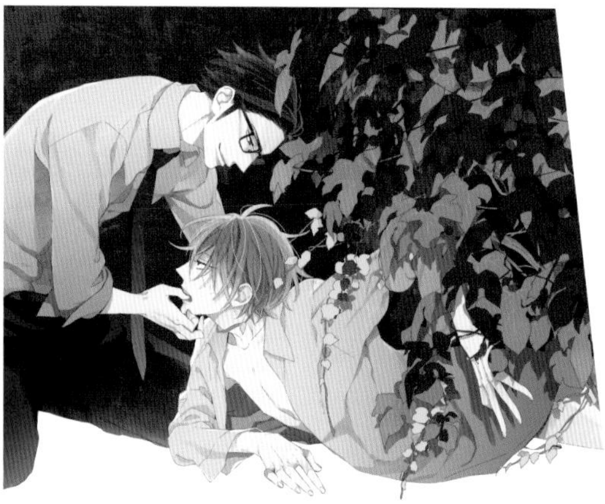

初出・MAGAZINE BE×BOY 2014年8月号「カーストヘヴン」扉イラスト / リブレ出版

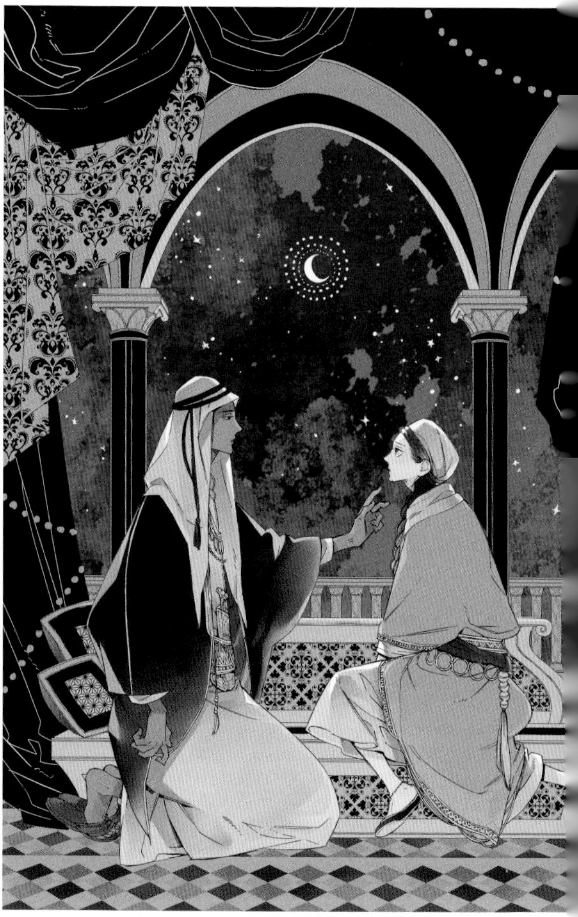

初出・BE・BOY GOLD 2013年12月号「ラクダ使いと王子の夜」扉イラスト / リブレ出版

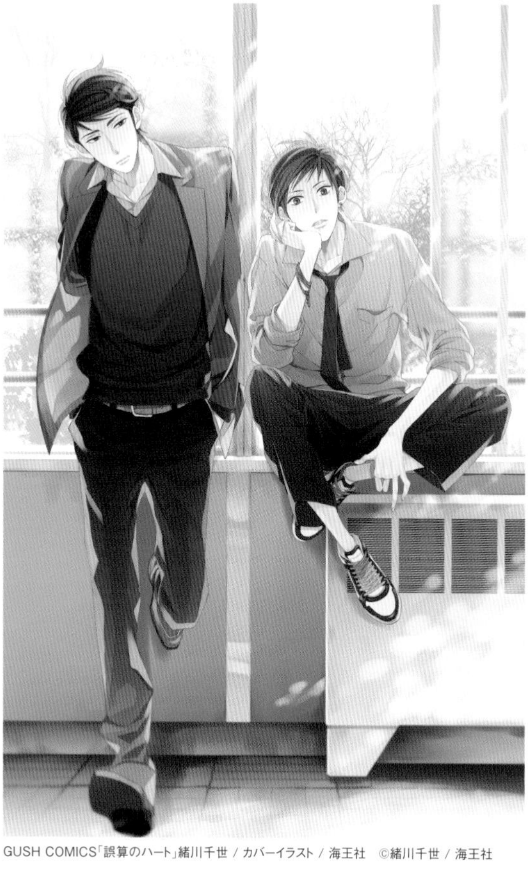

GUSH COMICS「誤算のハート」緒川千世 / カバーイラスト / 海王社

GUSH COMICS
「終わらない不幸についての話」緒川千世
カバーイラスト / 海王社

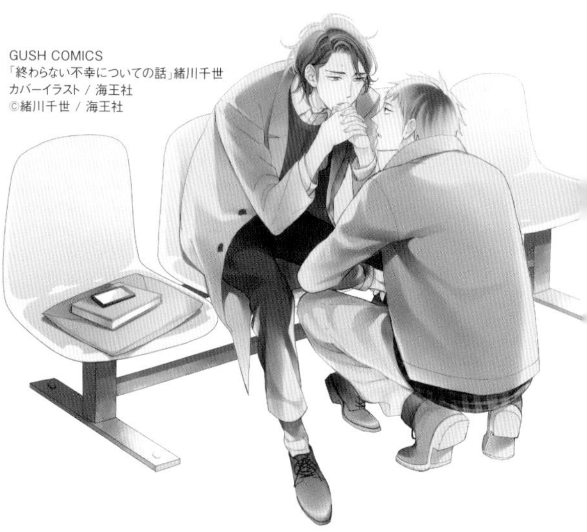

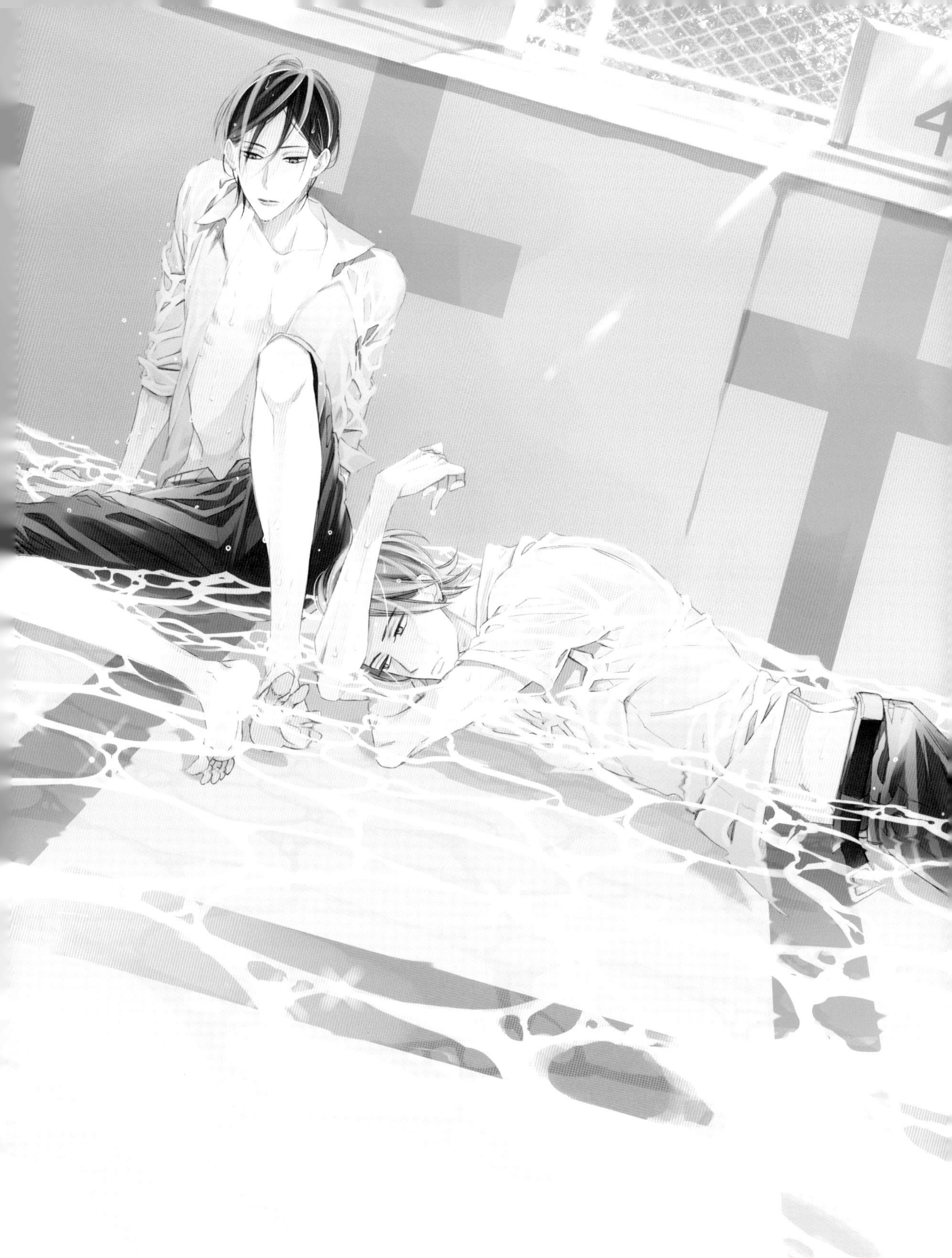

初出・MAGAZINE BE×BOY 2013年9月号「溺れる魚」扉イラスト / リブレ出版

緒田涼歌
ODA RYOKA

M hitsujisan1311@min.daa.jp **T** --- **U** http://min.sim.daa.jp

D Dr.ph.Martins Water Color Ink ● Copic sketch ● ComicStudio ● India ink ● Maru pen

Profile	奈良県民。時々 BL・TL小説の挿絵を描かせていただいております。	I live in Nara Prefecture. I sometimes illustrate works in the *Boys Love* as well as *Teens Love* genres.
Comments	とてもむずかしいけど…「ときめき」を心がけています。	It is really difficult, but the thrill of the work keeps me going.

「いつわりの花嫁」真船るのあ / カバーイラスト / コバルト文庫 / 集英社 2011

「花嫁御寮と銀の鬼」秋山みち花 / カバーイラスト
笠倉出版社 / ©Michika Akiyama ©KASAKURA PUBLISHING 2013

「暴君の初愛」中嶋ジロウ / カバーイラスト / 笠倉出版社 / ©Jiroh Nakashima ©KASAKURA PUBLISHING 2014

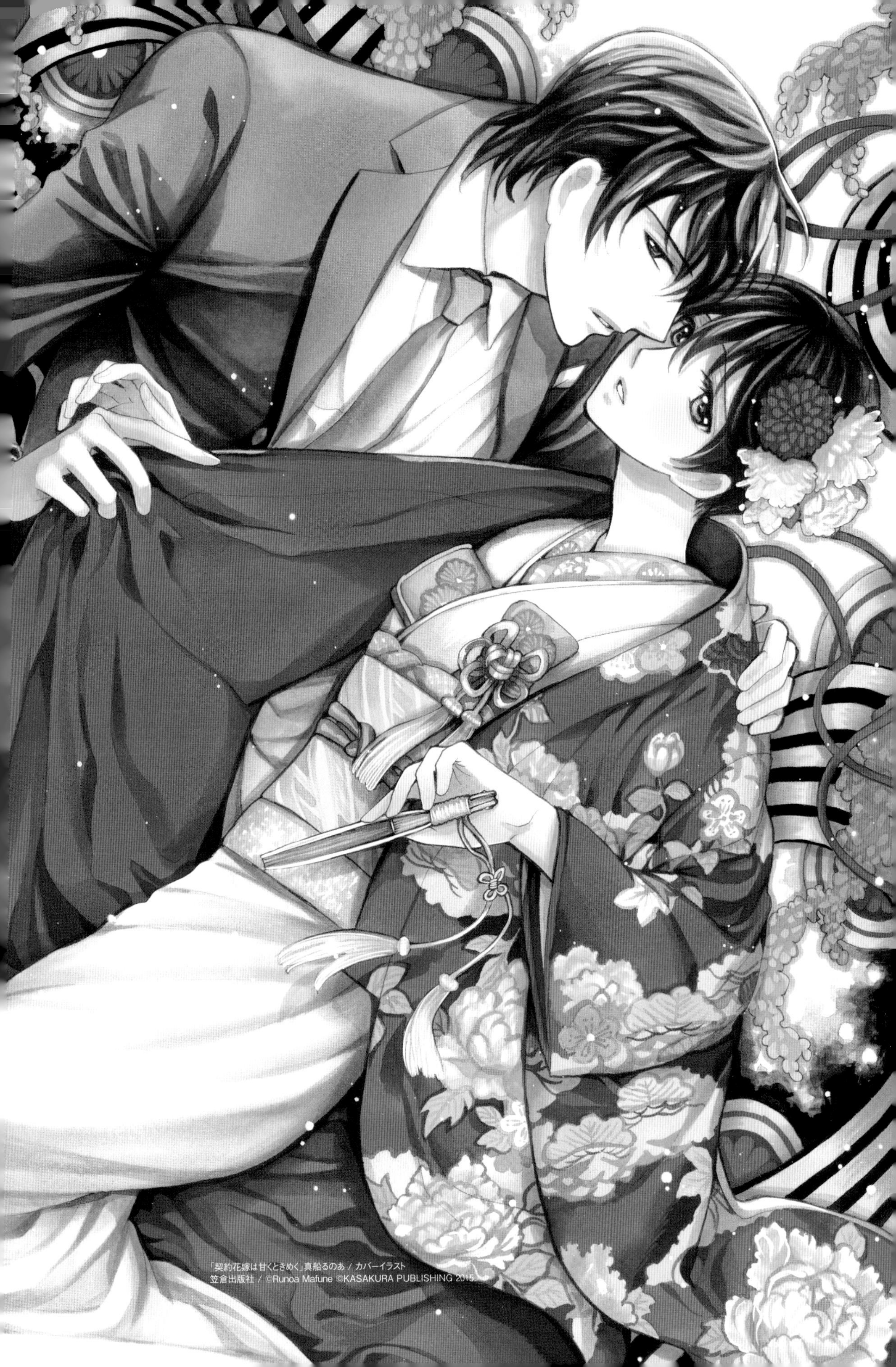

風李たゆ
kazaritayu

M kazaritayu@gmail.com
T kazari_tayu
U http://kazaritayu.tumblr.com
D SAI • Photoshop

Profile

主にゲームのキャラクターデザイン・イラストを手掛ける。最新の代表作はシチュエーションドラマCD「幽幻ロマンチカ」。着物と日本刀と猫をこよなく愛す。

I mainly work on character designs and illustrations for games. I recently completed a situation drama CD called *Yuugen Romantica*. I absolutely adore kimono, Japanese swords, and cats.

Comments

しっかりとした根底を元に着物や刀・ポージングを描けるよう現在勉強中です。背景はまだ苦手ですが、和モノ・ファンタジーの人物を描くのが得意です。

In addition to the fundamentals of illustration, I'm also studying how to properly draw characters posing in kimono or with Japanese swords. I'm not yet skilled at drawing backdrops, but I can portray Japanese things and fantasy characters well.

「天下統一クロニクル」/ キャラクターイラスト 【桜詩】源義家
サイバーエージェント © CyberAgent, Inc.

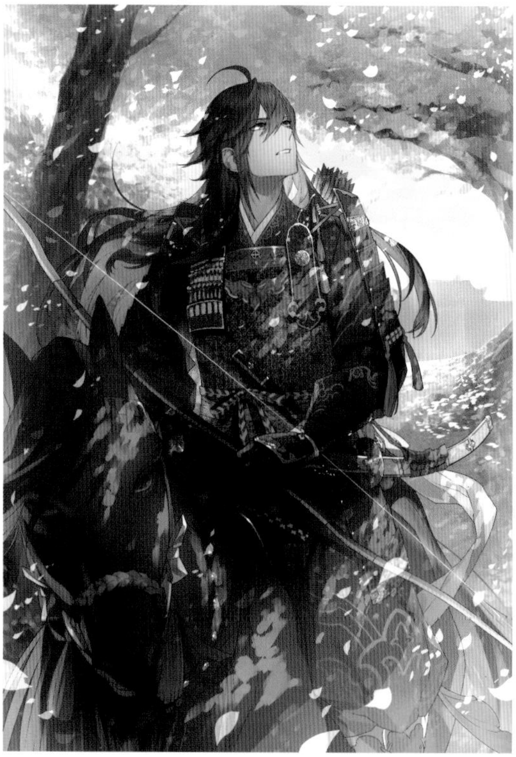

「天下統一クロニクル」/ キャラクターイラスト 藤林保武
サイバーエージェント © CyberAgent, Inc.

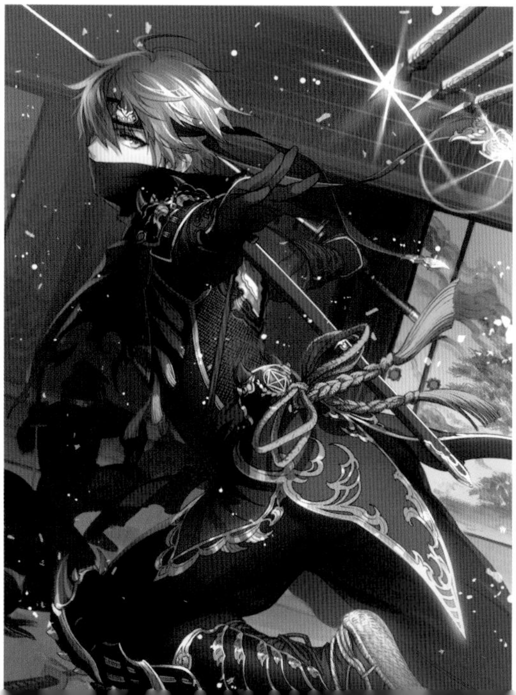

馬野馬追応援企画「第四回武者絵展」/ 出展イラスト
相馬野馬追「武者絵展」実行委員会 / 2015

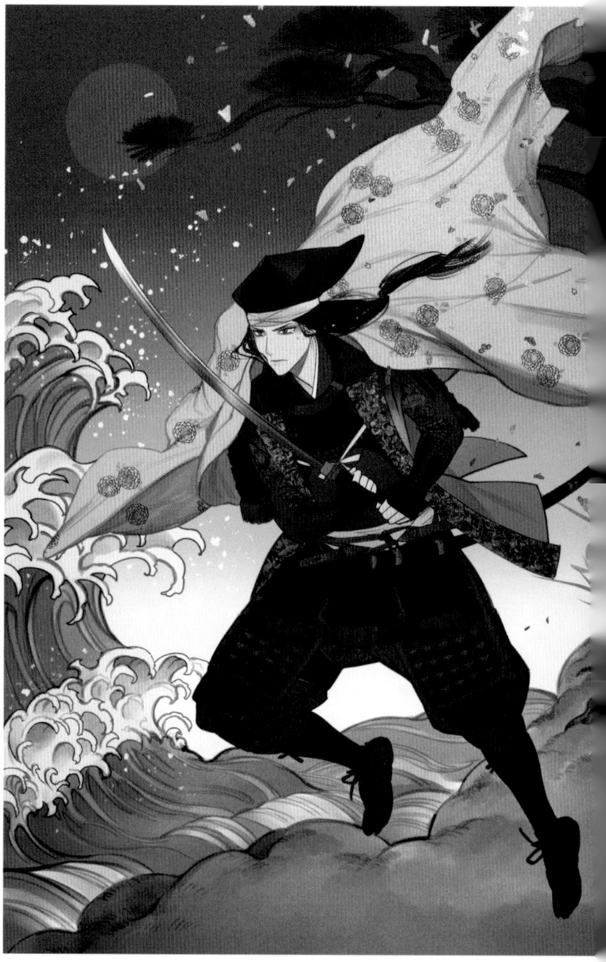

Personal Work

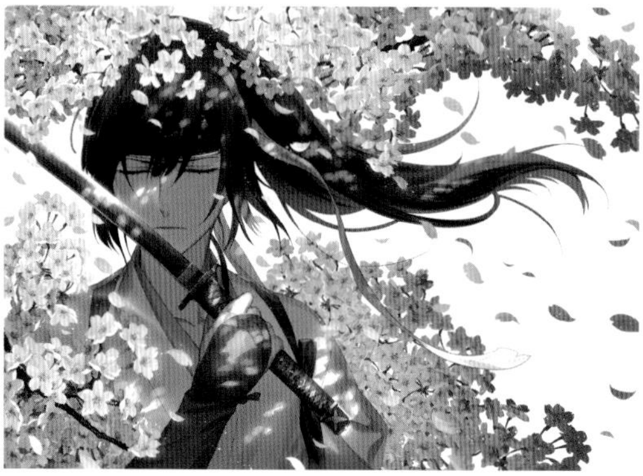

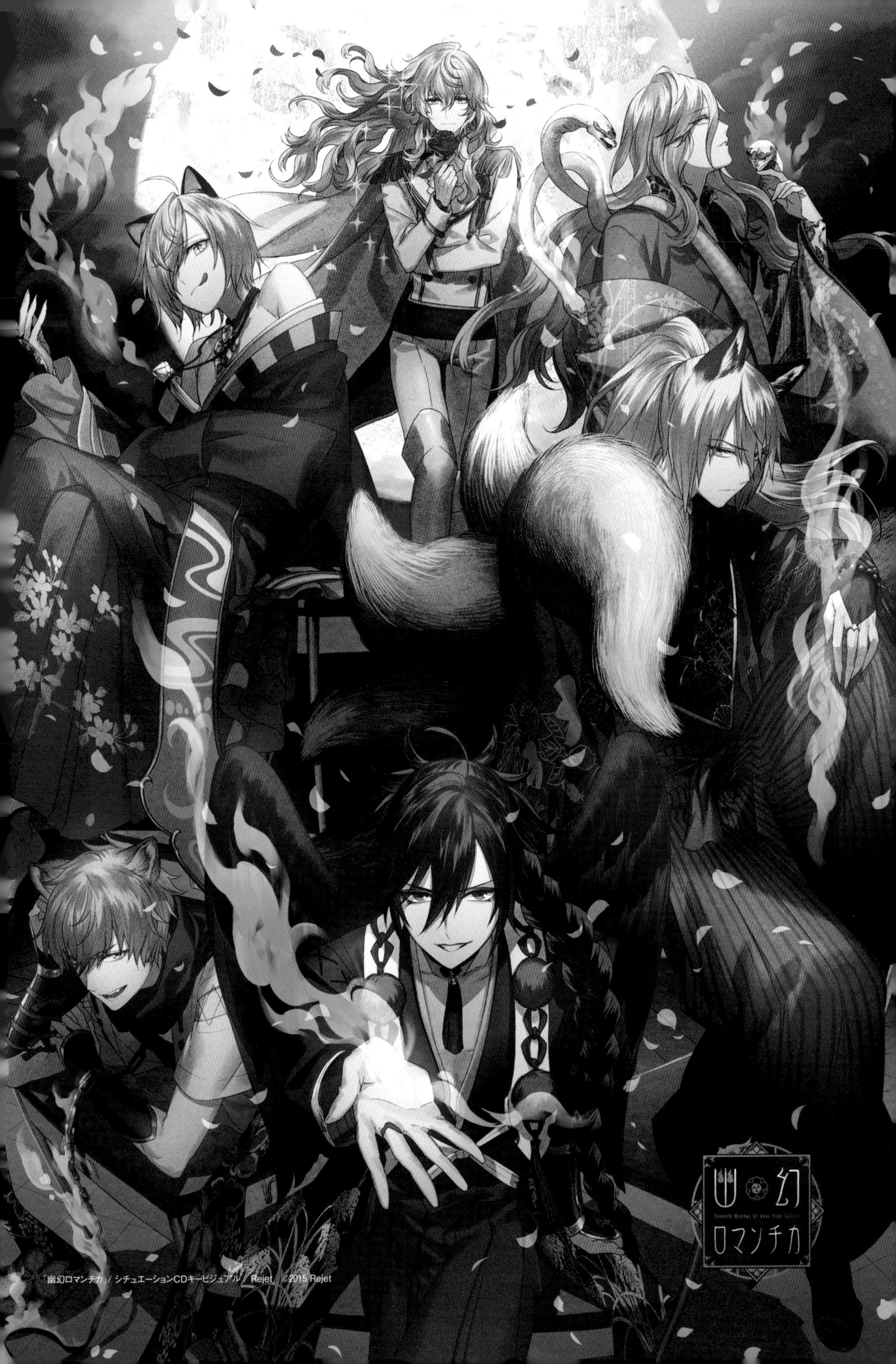
幽幻
ロマンチカ
「幽幻ロマンチカ」/ シチュエーションCDキービジュアル / Rejet ©2015 Rejet

冠城ちゆ
Kaburagi Chu

M merryxxchu@gmail.com   **T** merry_chu

U http://merryavantmerry.web.fc2.com   **D** Photoshop CC

Profile	カードイラスト、キャラクターデザイン、書籍のカバーイラスト・挿絵・漫画 etc. 全般のお仕事お受けしております。	I take on all kinds of work; I illustrate trading cards, create character designs, do book covers and illustrations, draw manga, etc.
Comments	色彩豊かに、表情豊かに、キャラクターが映えるような絵を心がけています。	I do all I can to make the characters in my drawings shine colorfully and expressively.

Personal Work「おとこのこ」

Personal Work「春」

Personal Work「シャンデリアカルーセル」

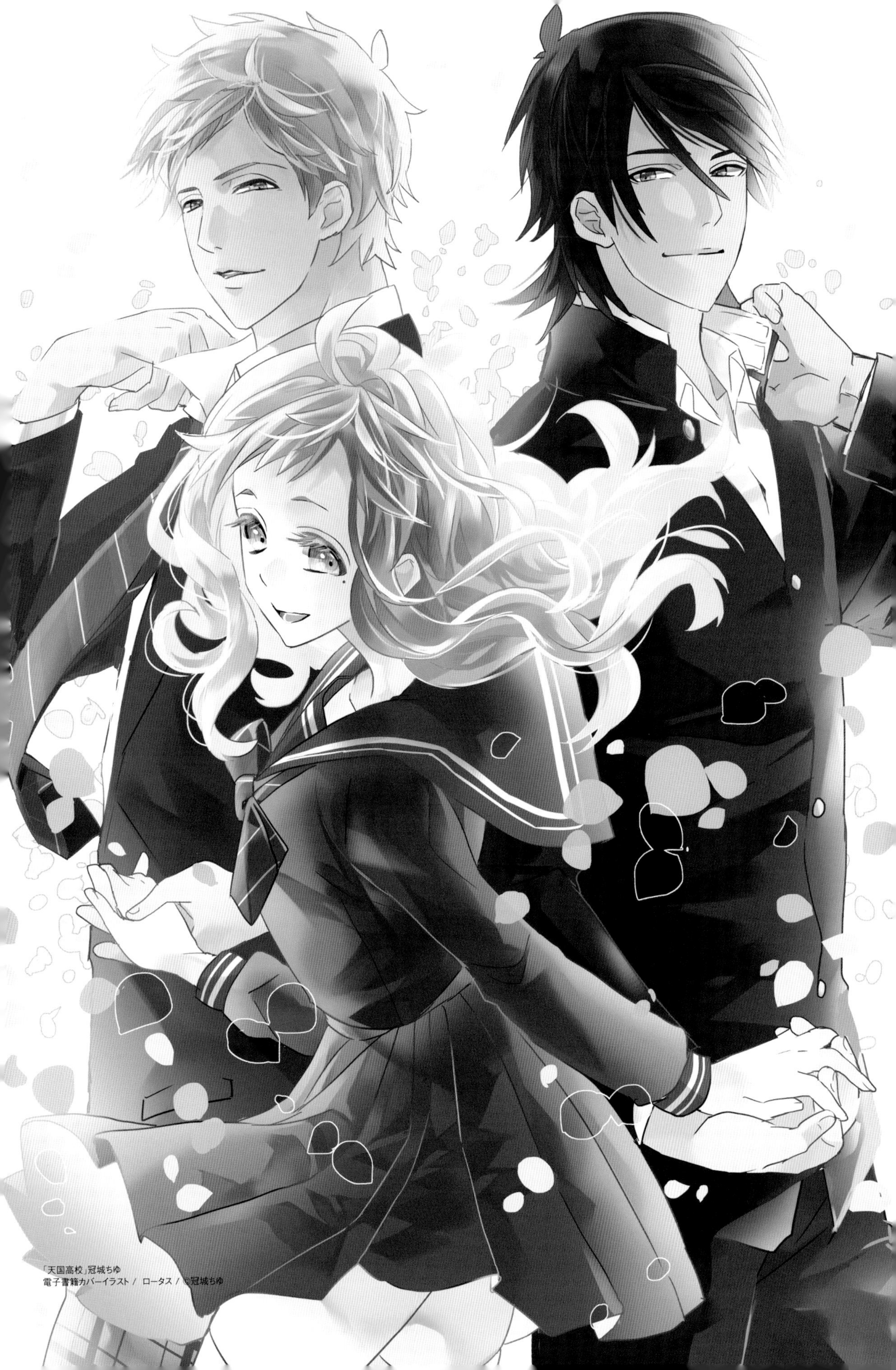

「天国高校」冠城ちゆ
電子書籍カバーイラスト / ロータス / ©冠城ちゆ

釜田みさと

KAMADA MISATO

M mi_kamada12@yahoo.co.jp
T mi_kamada
U http://mi-kamada.tumblr.com
D SAI • Photoshop CS4

Profile

漫画、イラストのお仕事をさせて頂いています。関西住まいです。略歴:「ジーンメタリカ - 機巧少女は傷つかない Re:Acta-」コミックジーン 2013年5月～2014年5月号連載 KADOKAWA MF刊　作画担当、他 ソーシャルゲームのイラスト作画等担当。

My work centers on manga and illustrations. I live in the Kansai region. My resume includes: illustrations for *Gene Metallica — Kiko Shojo wa Kizutsukanai Re: Acta*, serialized in Comic Gene from May 2013 to May 2014, published by KADOKAWA MF; illustrations for social games and other genre.

Comments

13～15歳の少年と現代に少しファンタジー感を足した絵を描くのが好きです。

I enjoy drawing boys aged 13-15 and contemporary settings with overtones of fantasy.

Personal Work

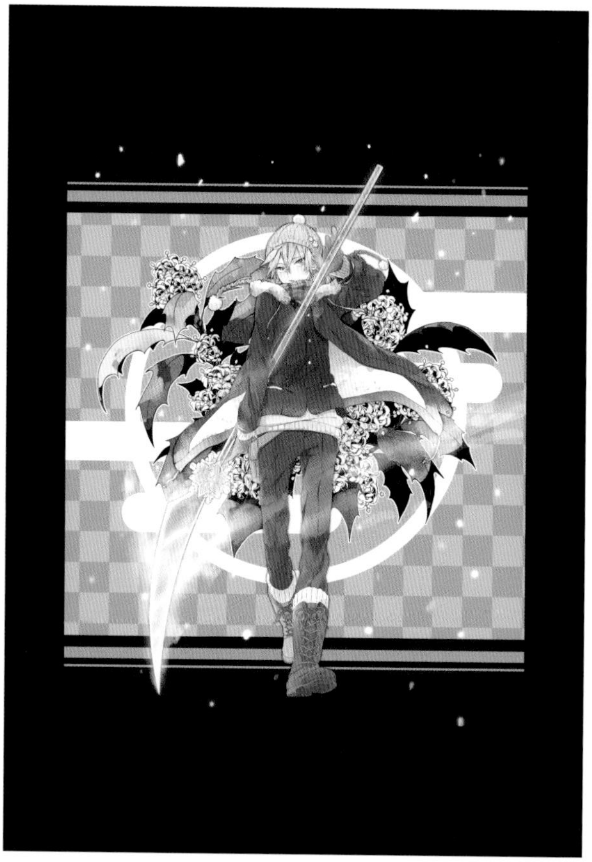

Personal Work

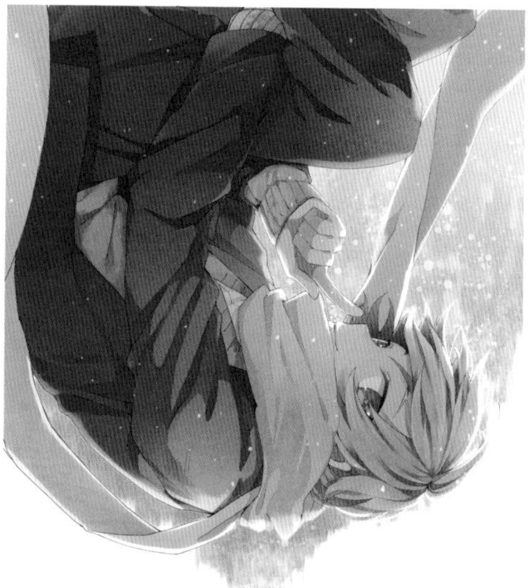

Personal Work

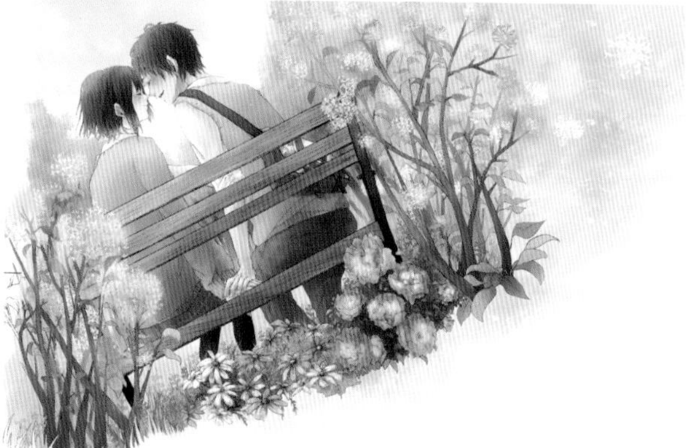

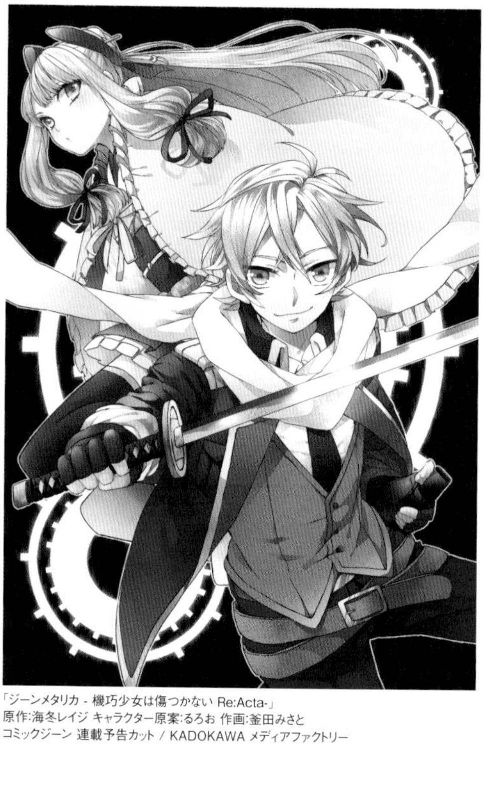

「ジーンメタリカ - 機巧少女は傷つかない Re:Acta-」
原作:海冬レイジ キャラクター原案:るろお 作画:釜田みさと
コミックジーン 連載予告カット / KADOKAWA メディアファクトリー

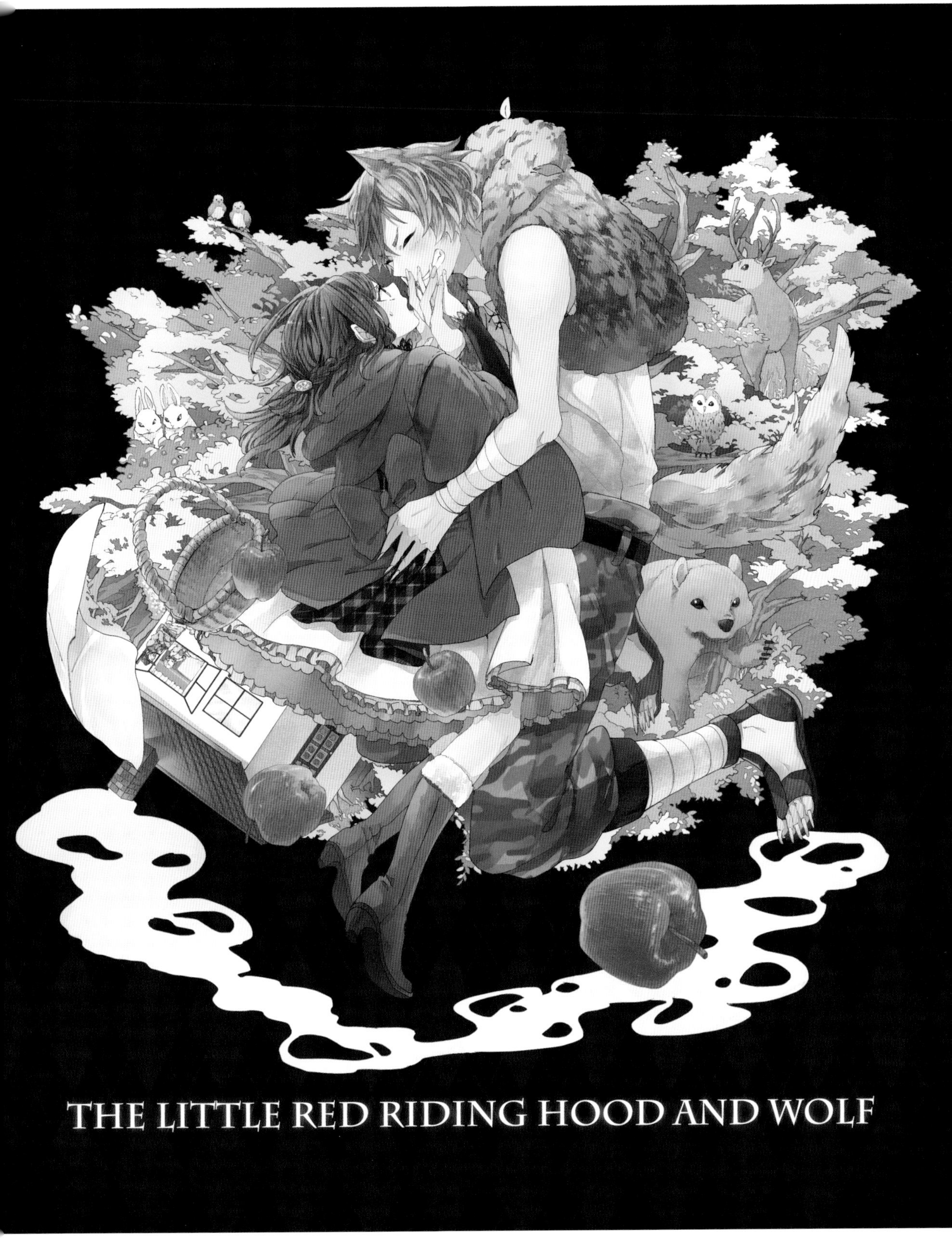
THE LITTLE RED RIDING HOOD AND WOLF

烏羽 雨
Karasuba Ame

M conronca.info@gmail.com
U http://conronca.flop.jp/
T conronca
D CLIP STUDIO PAINT ● Photoshop

Profile

イラストレーター。児童書や文芸の装画で活動中。関わった主な作品に「戦力外捜査官（河出書房新社）」など。講談社 月刊ヤングマガジンサードにて「ギルドレ」挿絵連載中。

I'm an illustrator. I create designs for the covers of children's books and other cultural publications. I have worked on *Senryokugai Sousakan* (Kawade Shobo Shinsha Publishers) and other projects. I am currently illustrating the serialized "Guildre" (Guilty Children) from Kodansha, Ltd.'s monthly *Young Magazine The 3rd*

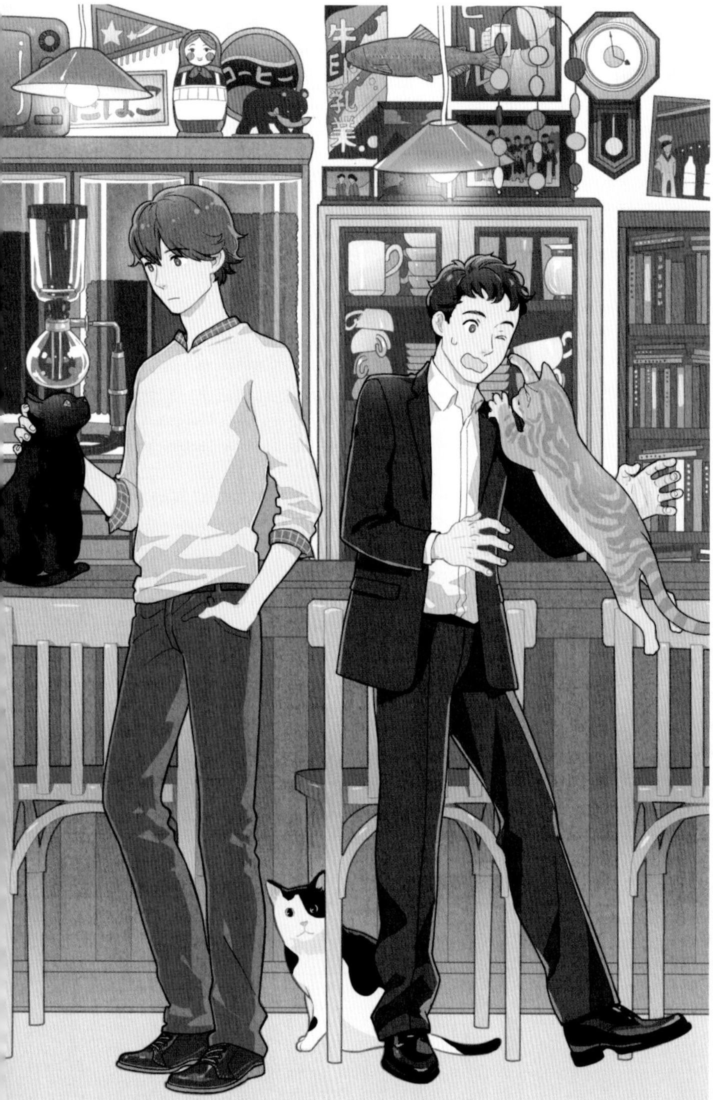

「名言探偵」著:北國浩二　装画:鳥羽雨 / カバーイラスト / PHP研究所

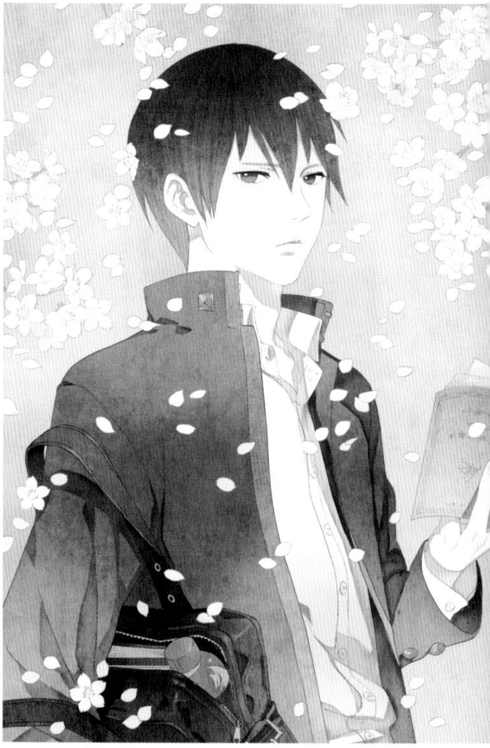

Personal Work「桜と少年」

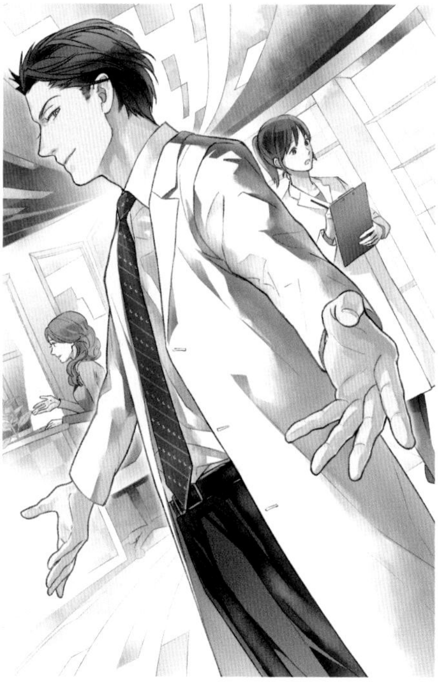

「改貌屋 天才美容外科医・柊貴之の事件カルテ」
知念実希人 / カバーイラスト / 幻冬舎文庫

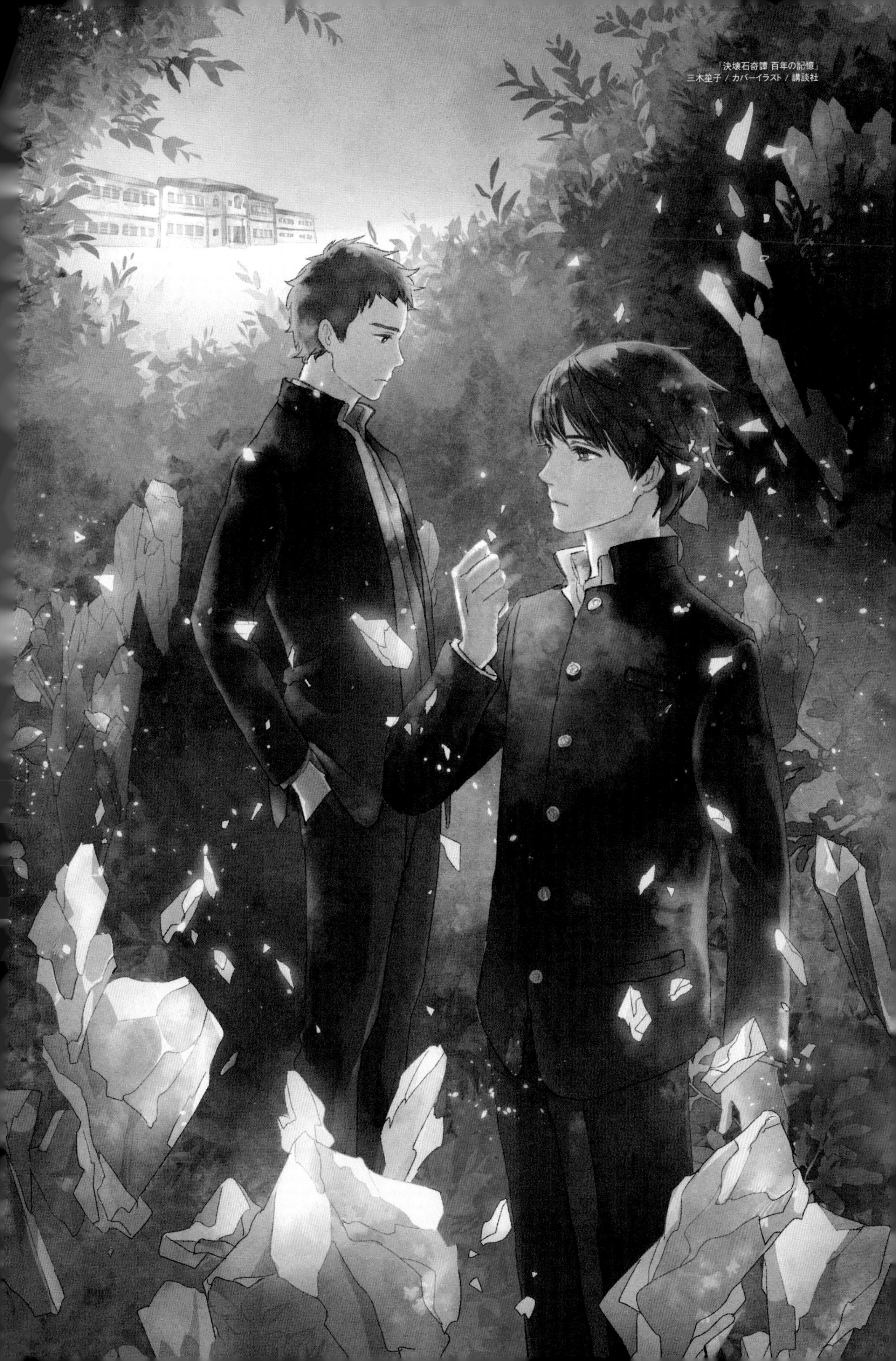
「決壊石奇譚 百年の記憶」
三木笙子 / カバーイラスト / 講談社

キナコ
KINAKO

M kamekichi6699@gmail.com   T kamabokoita
U http://marubotan.jimdo.com   D CLIP STUDIO PAINT PRO

Profile	キャラクターデザイン等イラストを描いています。	I do character designs and other illustrations.
Comments	自分にしか描けないようなものが描けていると嬉しいなと思いながら描いています。	I find happiness in creating unique works which other illustrators have yet to produce.

「栽培少年」/ キャラクターイラスト(ウシワカ)/ ネクシジョン

「栽培少年」/ キャラクターイラスト(キン)/ ネクシジョン

「フルボッコヒーローズX」/ キャラクターイラスト(寺田宗有)/ サイバーコネクトツー
©Drecom Co., Ltd. powered by CyberConnect2 Co., Ltd.

「フルボッコヒーローズX」/ キャラクターイラスト(バッハ)/ サイバーコネクトツー
©Drecom Co., Ltd. powered by CyberConnect2 Co., Ltd.

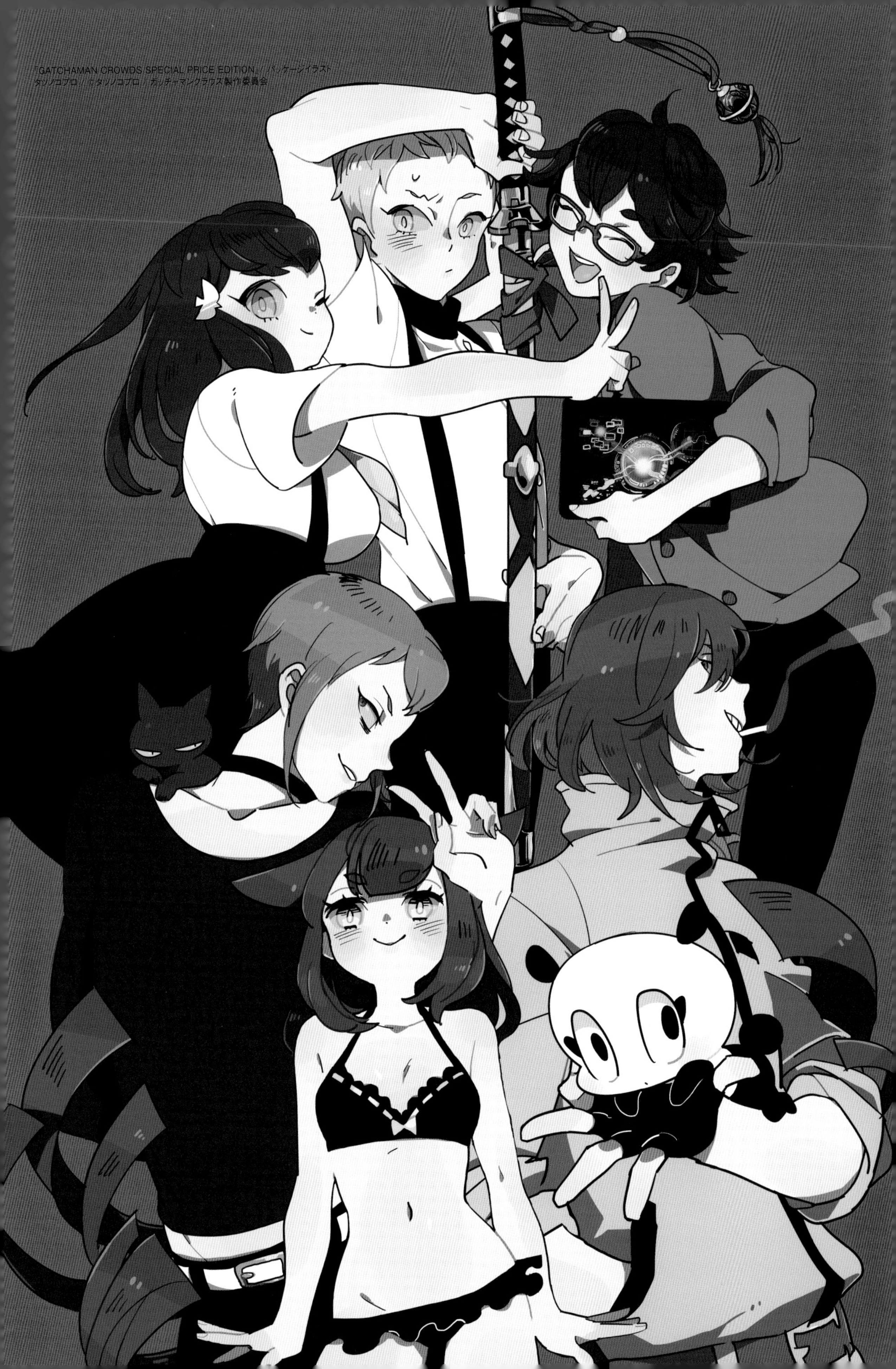

『GATCHAMAN CROWDS SPECIAL PRICE EDITION』/ パッケージイラスト
タツノコプロ / ©タツノコプロ / ガッチャマンクラウズ製作委員会

桐矢隆

Kiriya Takashi

M ibg6728@gmail.com
T ---
U http://ibg-00.wix.com/ibg0
D CLIP STUDIO PAINT EX

Profile

2008年頃からフリーランスで活動中。主に女性向け中心ですが依頼はジャンルを問わずお受けしています。

I've been freelancing since around 2008. Most of my job requests have centered on the female market, but I willingly draw for any genre.

Comments

個人的な趣味に拘り過ぎないように依頼には出来るだけ柔軟に対応するよう気をつけています。

I make an effort to remain flexible when new jobs come in, trying not to cling to my own comfort zone in terms of genre and taste.

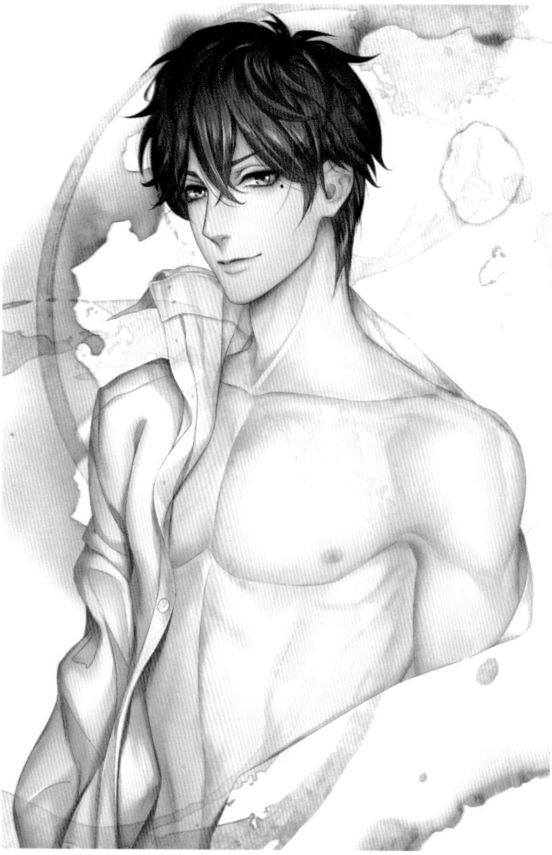

Personal Work ©桐矢隆

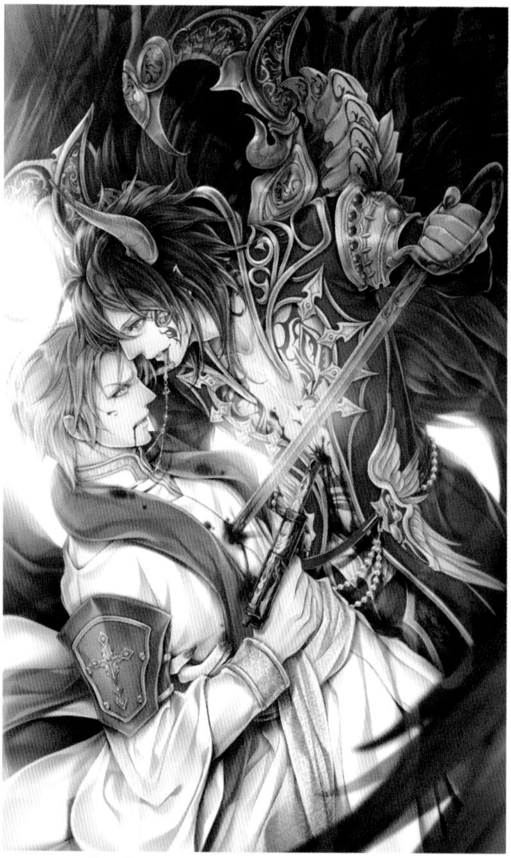

Personal Work「vs」©桐矢隆

Personal Work ©桐矢隆

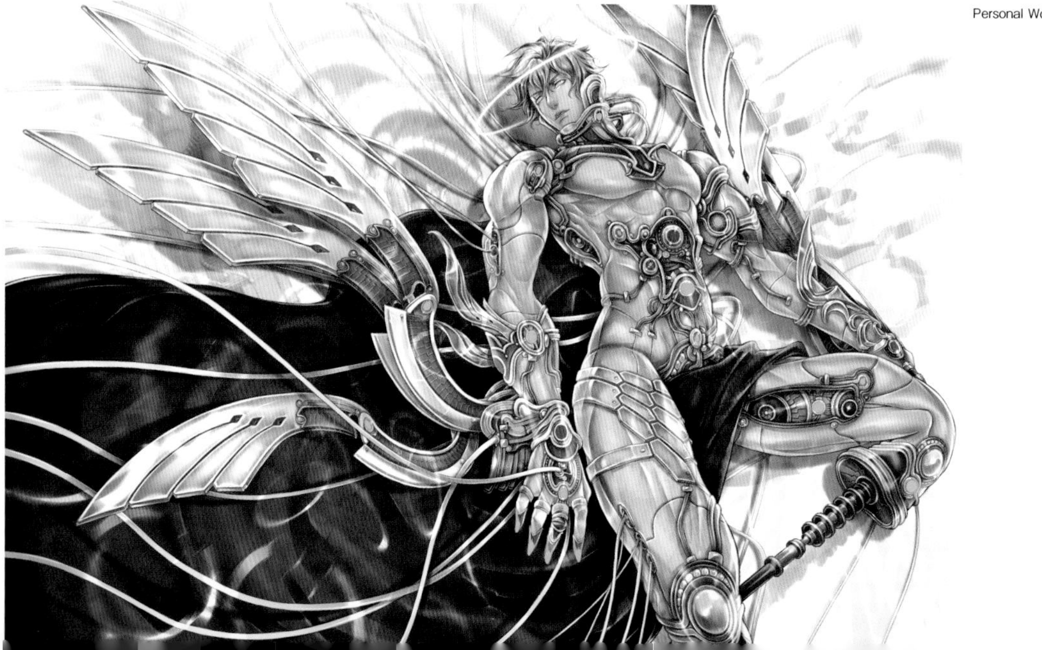

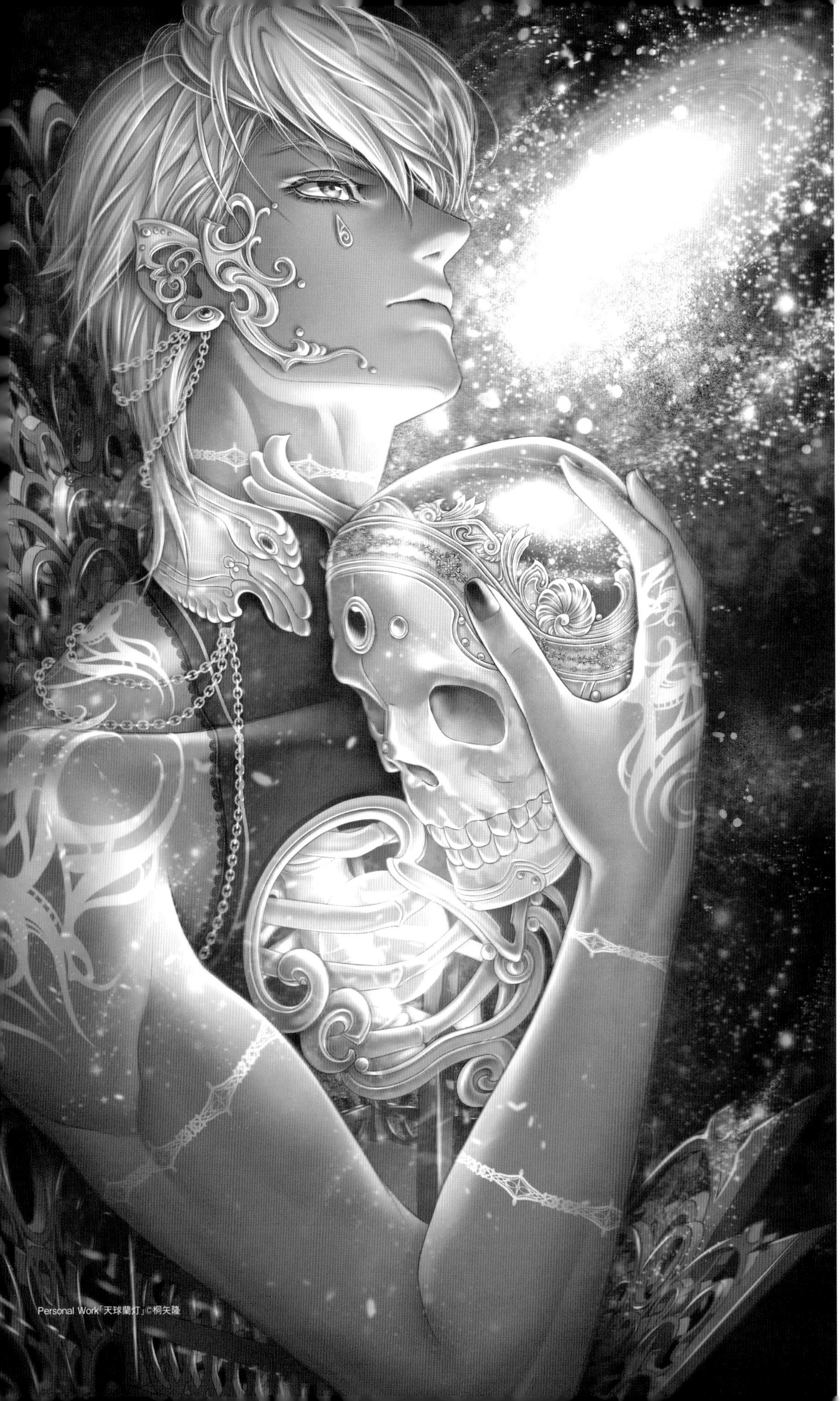

Personal Work「天球蘭灯」©桐矢隆

草間さかえ
kusama sakae

M mh-666@kcn.ne.jp

U ---

T penpen_kusa

D Painter11 ● Photoshop CS2

Profile	2003年頃から商業漫画と小説挿絵を描いてます。	I have been producing manga and story illustrations for commercial magazines since around 2003.
Comments	基本性別が男性でありさえすれば、幼～老年あまり年代関係なく好んで描きます。イラストであればなるべく依頼内容のイメージに沿うものにしたいと思っています。	As long as the basic gender is male, I enjoy drawing characters of any age from toddlers to seniors. I try to keep the content of my illustrations as faithful to the client's request as possible.

『OPERA』vol.23 -花- ©草間さかえ / 茜新社

萌え男子がたり2 / 「観葉植物男子」イラスト / ブックマン社

「天使の影」著:ジョシュ・ラニヨン 訳:冬斗亜紀 / カバーイラスト / 新書館
©Josh Lanyon・草間さかえ・新書館

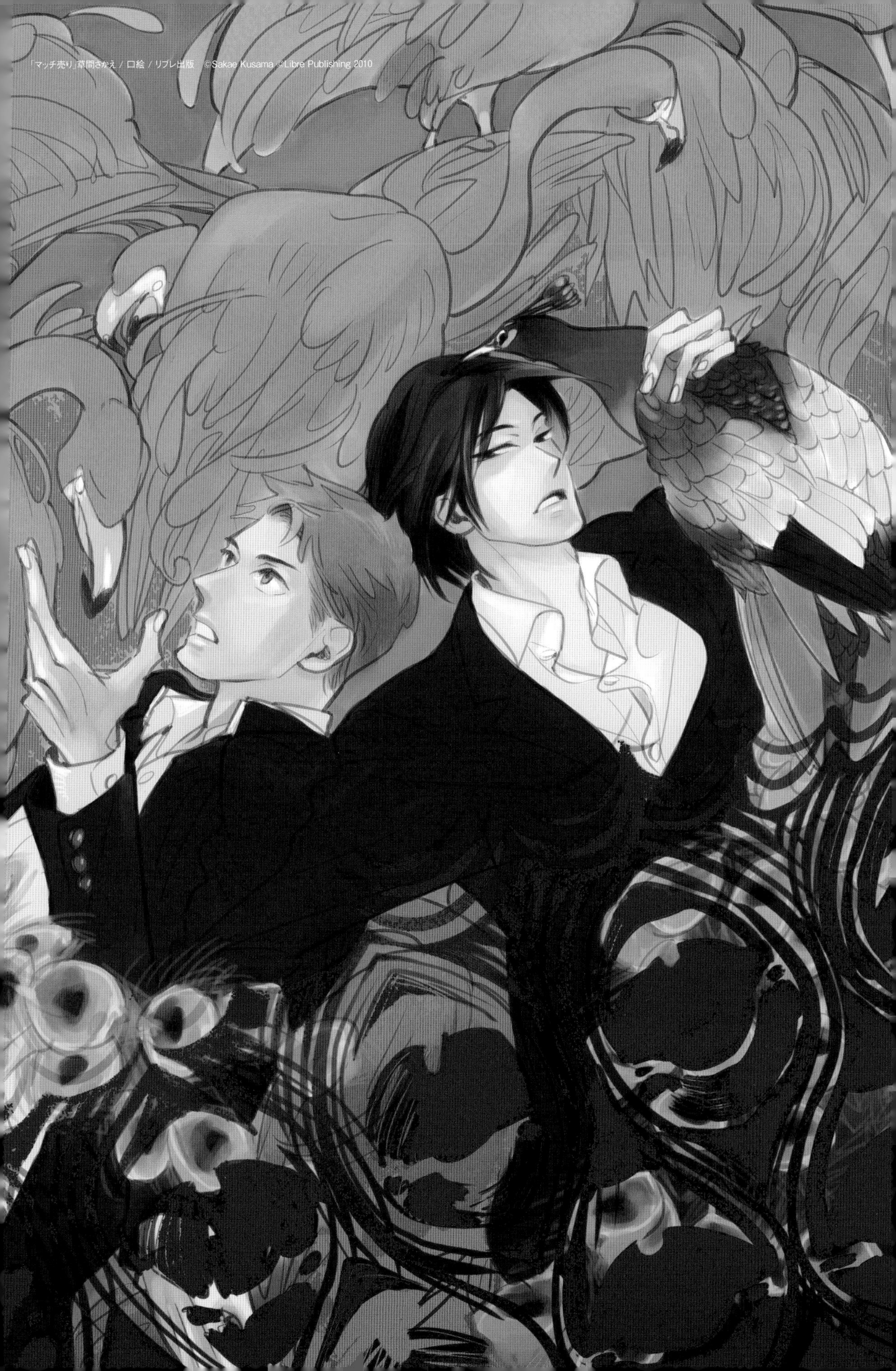

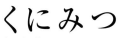

くにみつ
kunimitsu

M kunimitsu.nano@gmail.com　　T 9nimi2
U http://nove9nano.tumblr.com　　D Photoshop 7

Profile	千葉出身。ゲーム・書籍等でイラストを描いています。	I'm from Chiba Prefecture. I illustrate for games and books, among other items.
Comments	キャラクターイメージや世界観を出来るだけわかりやすく伝えることを心がけています。	I'm endeavoring to clarify the image and viewpoint of the characters through my illustrations.

PSPゲーム「宵夜森ノ姫」/ キービジュアル / éterire

「べろべろ男子」/ 雑誌掲載用イラスト / HuneX ©HuneX

Personal Work「白星探検隊」©くにみつ

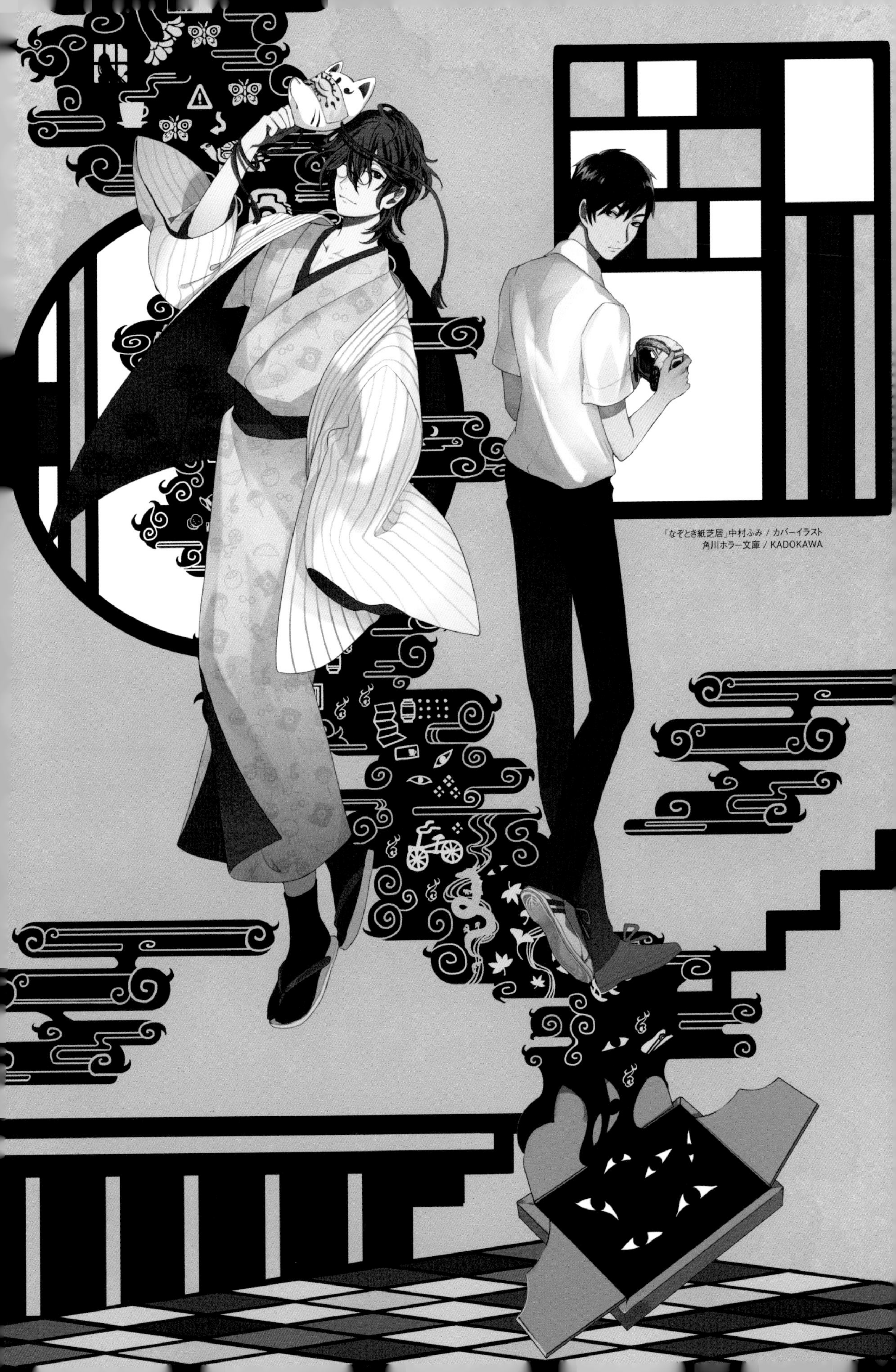
「なぞとき紙芝居」中村ふみ / カバーイラスト
角川ホラー文庫 / KADOKAWA

黒裄

kuroyuki

mail@nk-dk.skr.jp

http://nk-dk.skr.jp

krykkk

SAI

Profile

1990年1月16日生まれのO型。東京在住。2008年よりイラストレーターとして活動を開始。現在はゲームのキャラクターデザインと小説のカバーイラスト・挿絵を中心に活動中。

I was born on January 16, 1990, and have "O"-type blood. I currently live in Tokyo. I began working as an illustrator in 2008. At present, I mainly design game characters and illustrate book covers for novels.

Comments

ファンタジーな世界観と少年を描くのが好き。生き生きとした表情と、透明感のあるイラストを常に心がけています。

I enjoy drawing fantasy worlds and adolescent boys. I try to imbue my works with energy and transparency.

Personal Work

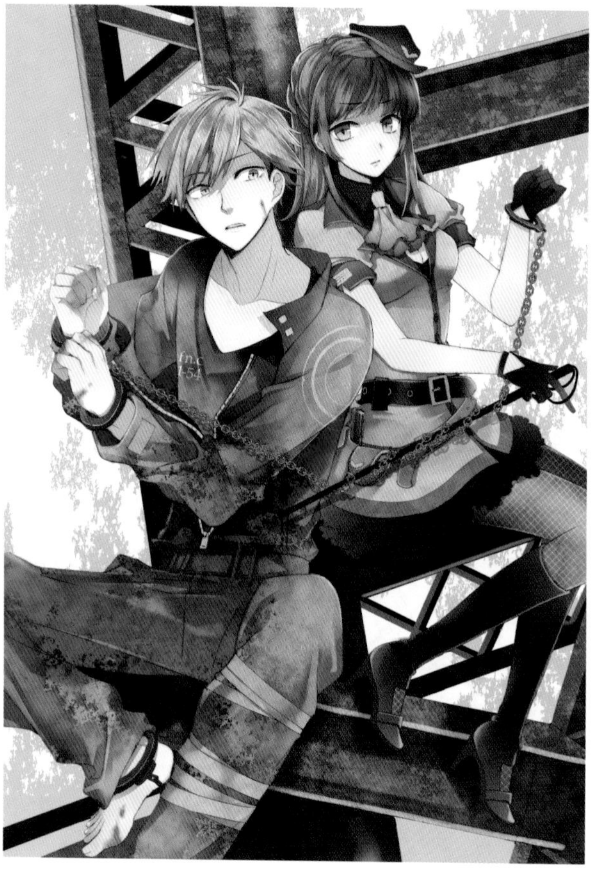

Personal Work

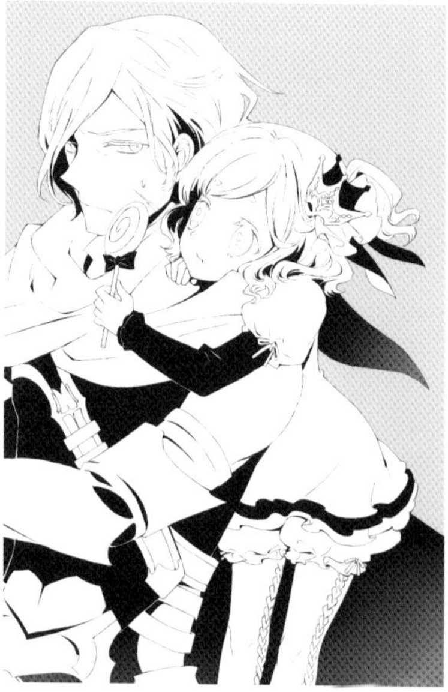

Personal Work

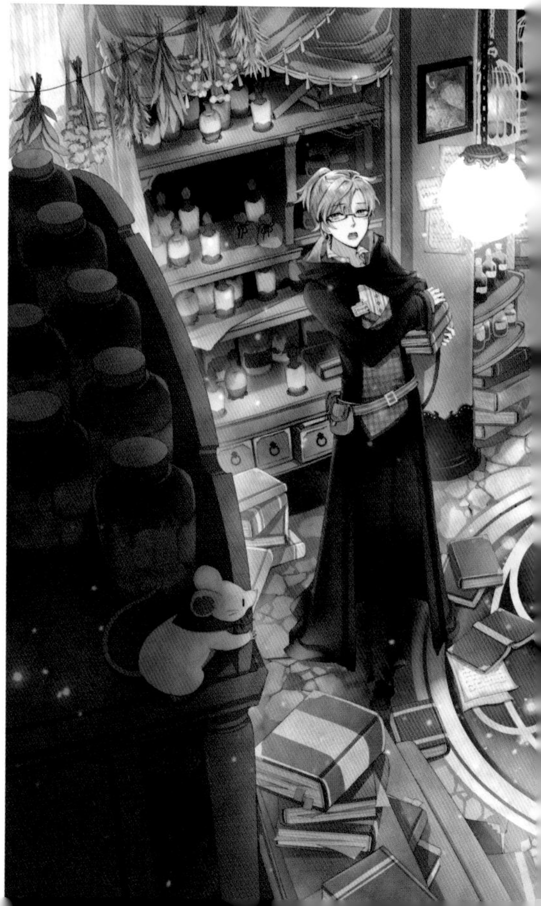

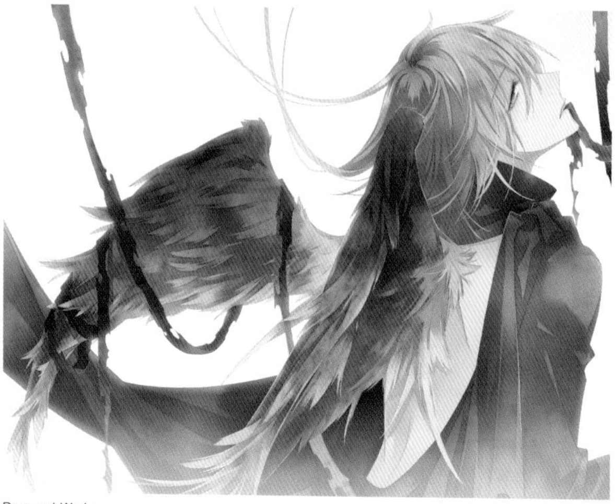

Personal Work

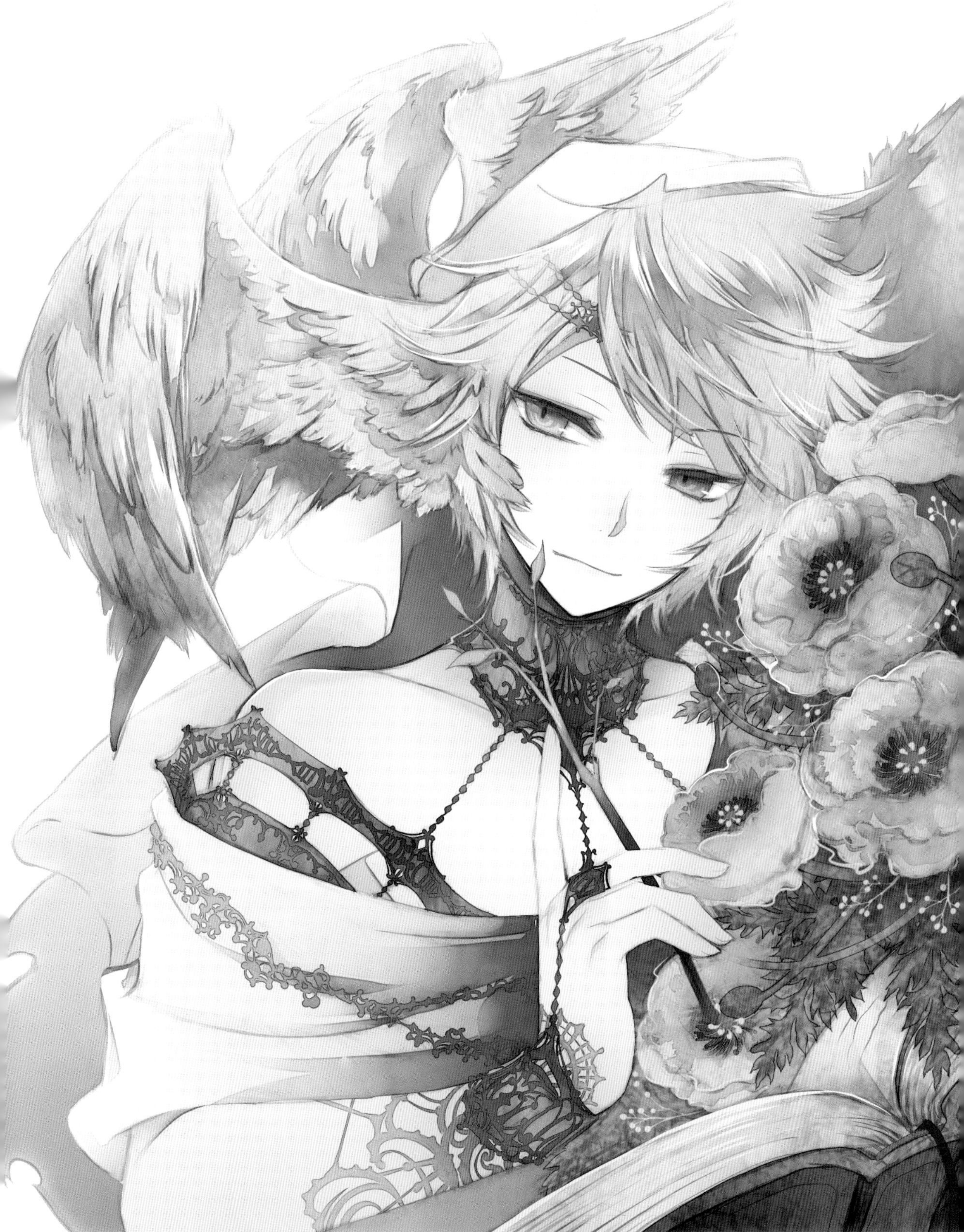

Personal Work

ここかなた

cocokanata

M cocokana.ovo@gmail.com
T ---
U http://cocokana.jugem.jp
D SAI ● Photoshop

Profile

和風から現代ものまで、キャラクターデザインを中心にお仕事させていただいております。女性にキュンとしていただけるテイストを心がけています。最近のお仕事では「ガム彼！」「au 三太郎二次元ver」「アイ★チュウ」など。

I primarily illustrate character designs, and I handle everything from traditional Japanese to contemporary. I work hard to create emotional characters that pull the heart strings of female readers. Recent efforts include *Gum Kare!*, and *au Santaro Nijigen ver, I★Chu*.

Comments

キャラクターデザインをさせていただくことが多いので、ぱっとみてわかりやすく、魅力的なキャラクターを産み出せるよう、頂いたキャラクター案から妄想を膨らましています。このキャラクターならこんなポーズや表情をとるかな、と考えている時が楽しいです。多種多様なジャンルでお手伝いさせて頂く機会があり、とても刺激になっています。いつか大好きなアニメーションのお仕事もさせていただけたらと日々精進しております。

As I'm often asked to create character designs, I take a plan and expand it into a obsession, which helps produce an appealing character that can be understood at first glance. I love thinking about the poses and expressions a given character might assume. I have been offered opportunities to work in a variety of genres, which I find greatly stimulating. I'm working toward the day when I will be asked to create animation, a great favorite of mine.

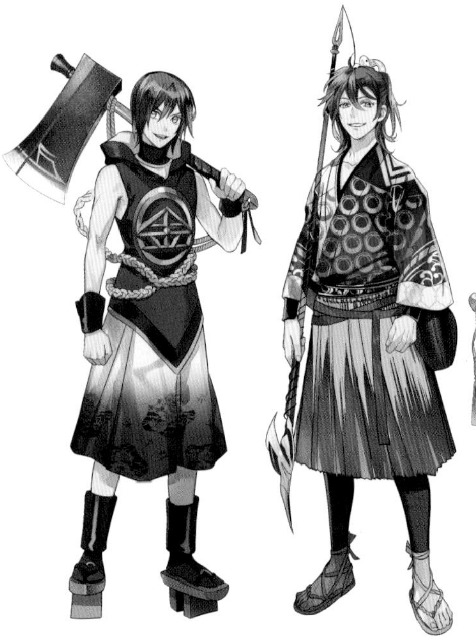

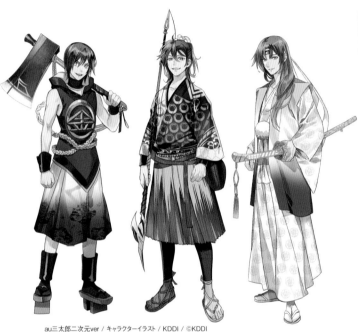

au三太郎二次元ver / キャラクターイラスト / KDDI / ©KDDI

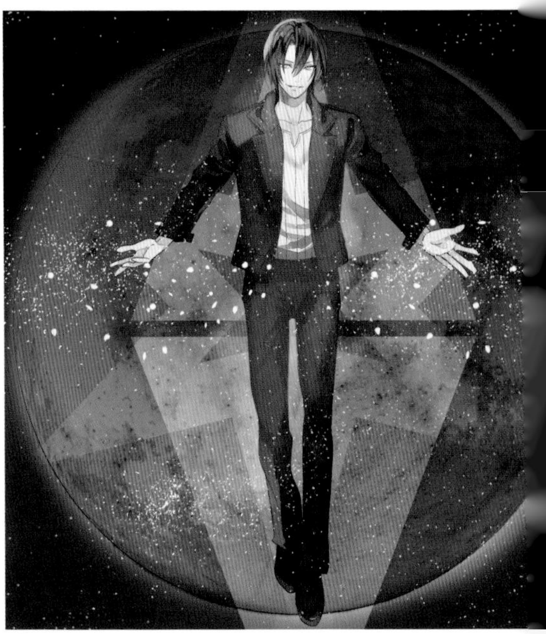

声優ユニットゆーたく / CDジャケットイラスト / ©ゆーたく

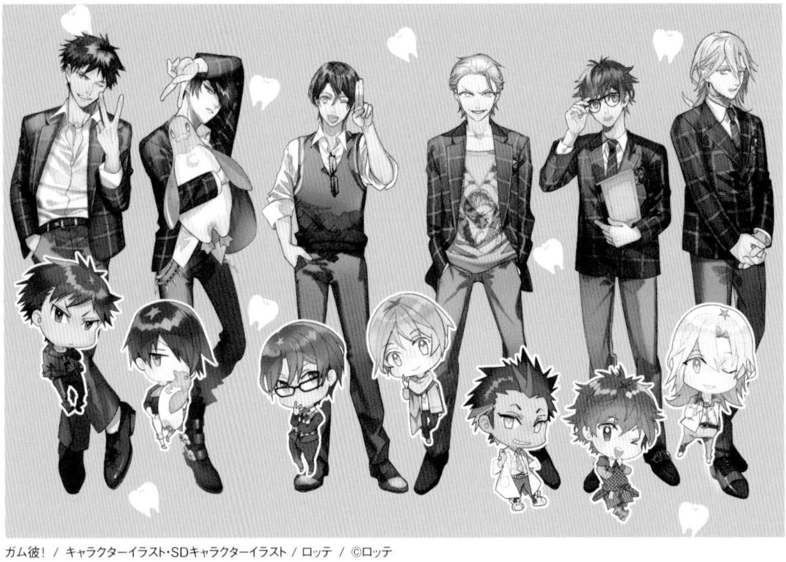

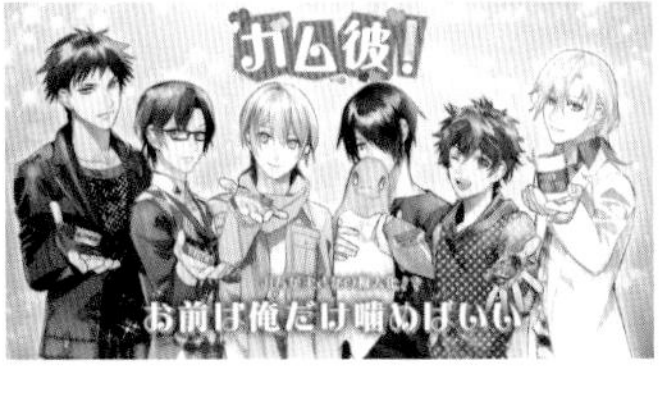
ガム彼!

ガム彼！ / キャラクターイラスト･SDキャラクターイラスト / ロッテ / ©ロッテ

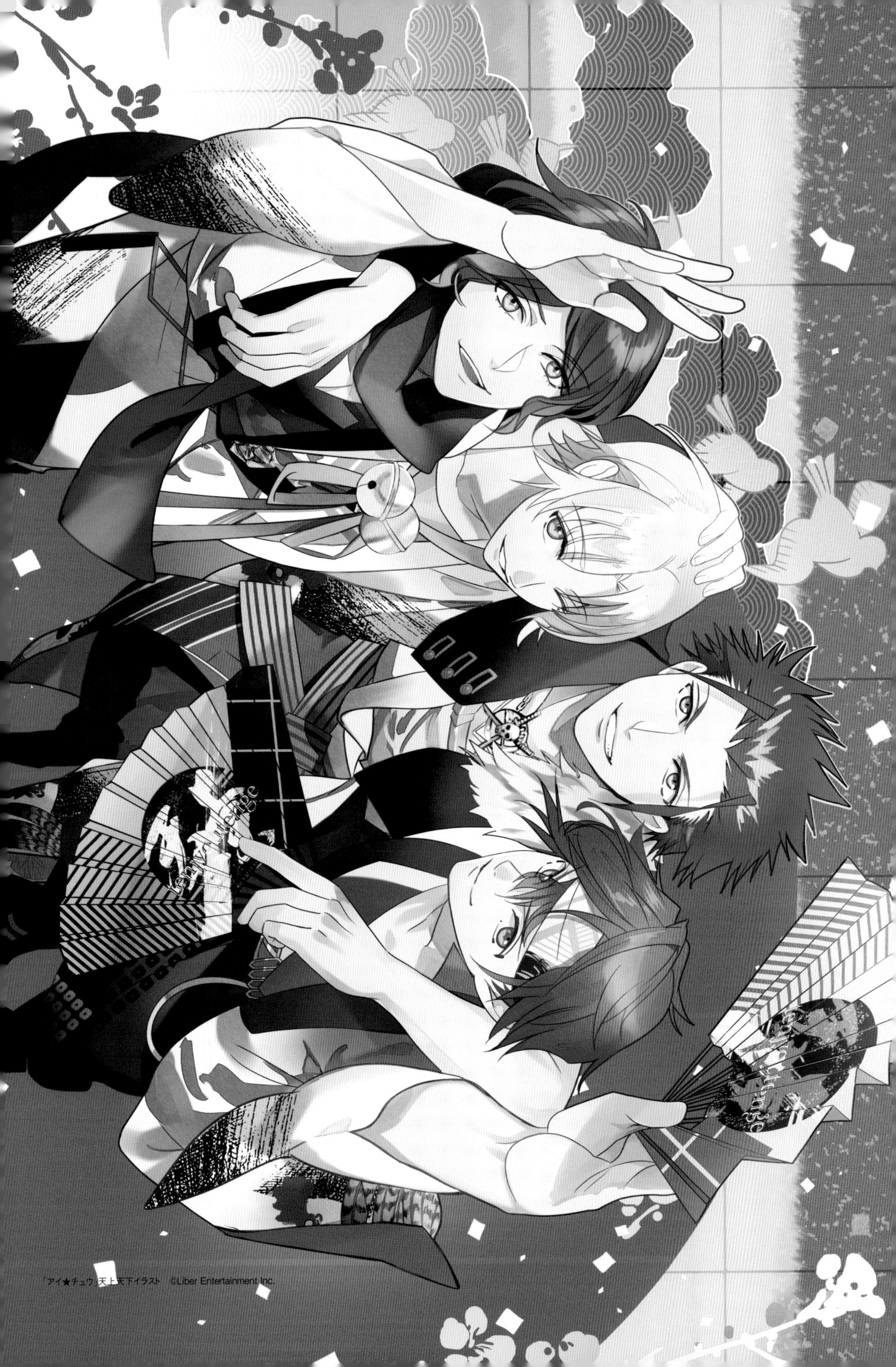

「アイ★チュウ」天上天下イラスト

湖住ふじこ

Kosumi Fujiko

M cobinrobin@yahoo.co.jp T KOSUMI225 U http://cobinrobin.com

D ComicStudio 4 ● CLIP STUDIO PAINT ● PhotoShop CS5 ● SAI

Profile

滋賀県長浜市出身・東京都在住。マンガ家。ゲーム・CD・ノベルのキャラクターデザイン、装画なども手掛ける。 代表作「サムライドライブ」「魔法使いと星降る庭」「うちの陛下が新米で。」「戦国ブラッド～薔薇の契約～(原作:広井王子)」など。

I'm from Nagahama City in Shiga Prefecture, but I now live in Tokyo. I'm a manga artist, designing characters for games, CDs, and novels, as well as book cover designs and other projects. My works include *Samurai Drive, Mahotsukai to Hoshi-furu Niwa, Uchi no Heika ga Shinmai de, and Sengoku Blood ~ Bara no Keiyaku* (original story: Ouji Hiroi).

Comments

少年少女の、特に動きのある絵を描くのが好きです。キャラクターの周りにそのキャラ独自の空気を感じるような作品が描ければと思っております。学生の制服姿が大好きです。

I enjoy drawing boys and girls, particularly illustrations with lots of action. I'm trying to capture the individual atmosphere surrounding each character in my illustrations. I like the image of students in their uniforms.

「汝、怪異を語るなかれ」宮沢龍生 / カバーイラスト / 中央公論新社

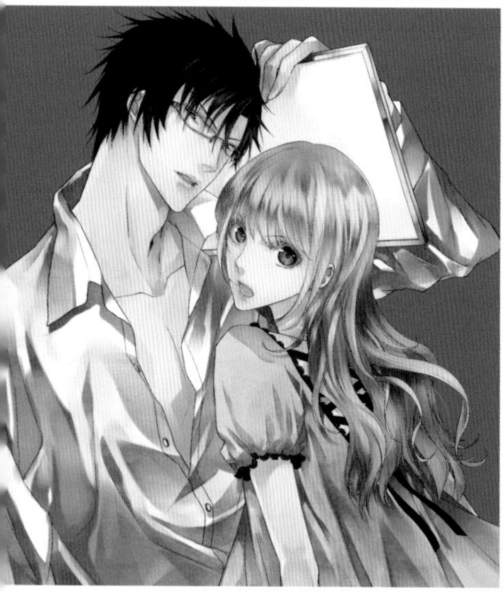

「魔法使いと星降る庭」湖住ふじこ / 扉イラスト
KADOKAWA ©湖住ふじこ / KADOKAWA

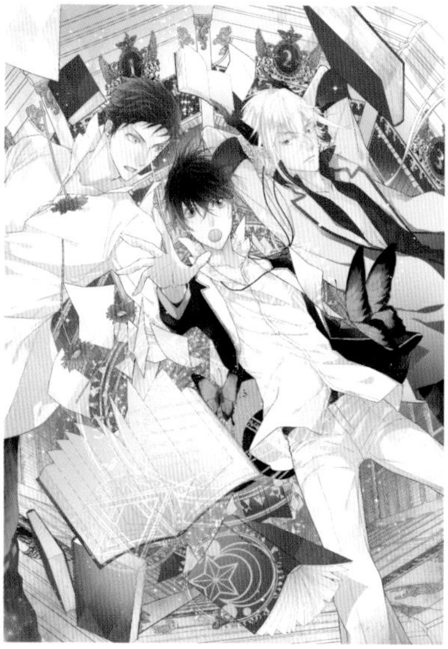

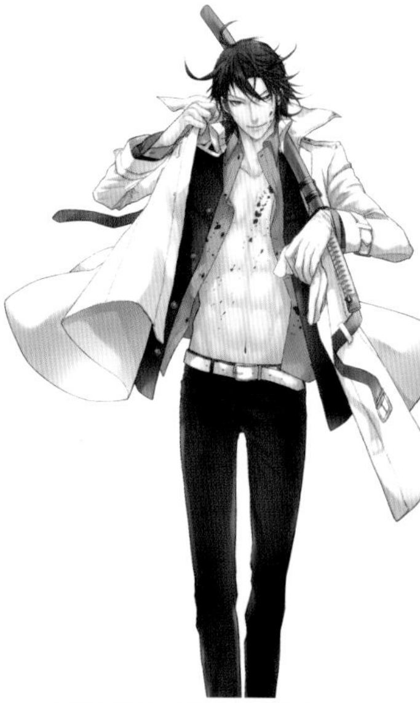

「サムライドライブ」湖住ふじこ / 3巻カバーイラスト
KADOKAWA ©湖住ふじこ / KADOKAWA

「愛してあげるワン! ー俺のペットー」/ CDジャケットイラスト / フロンティアワークス ©湖住ふじこ / フロンティアワークス

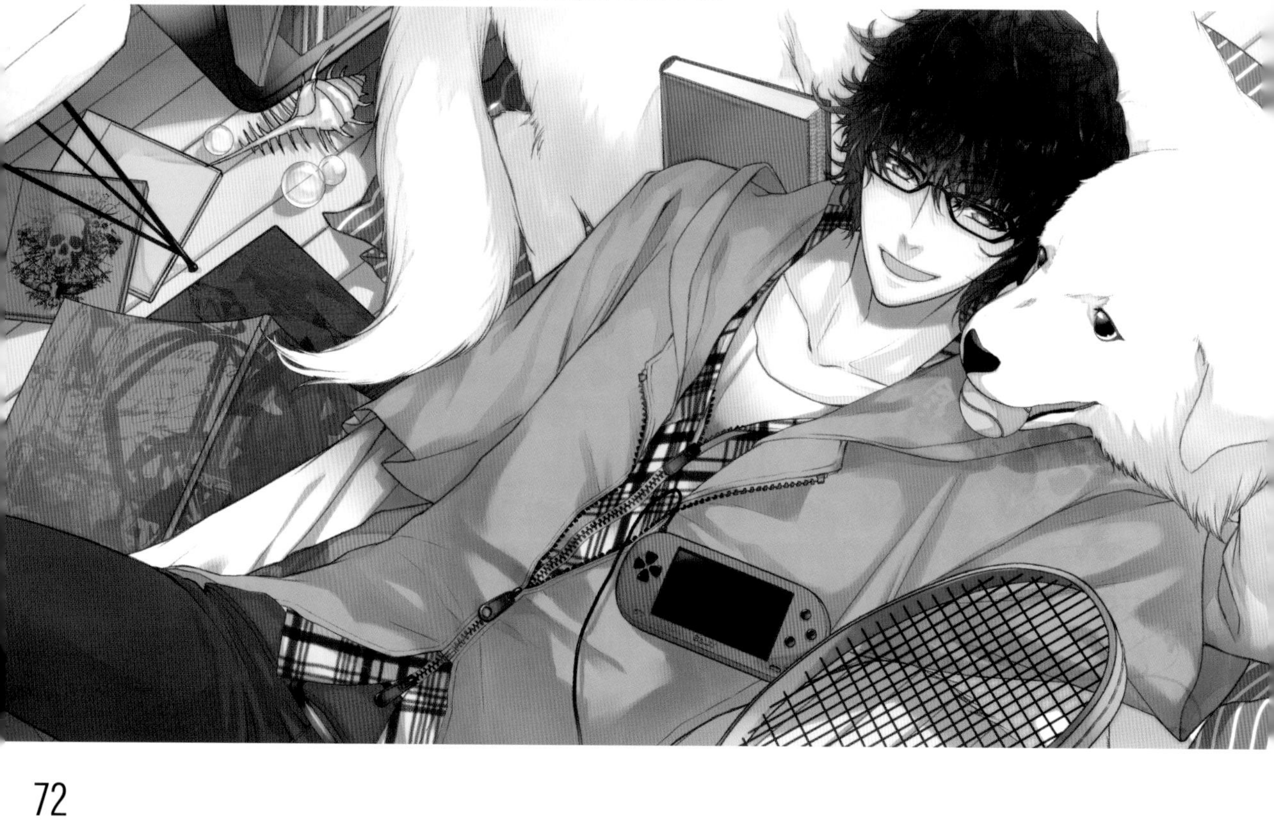

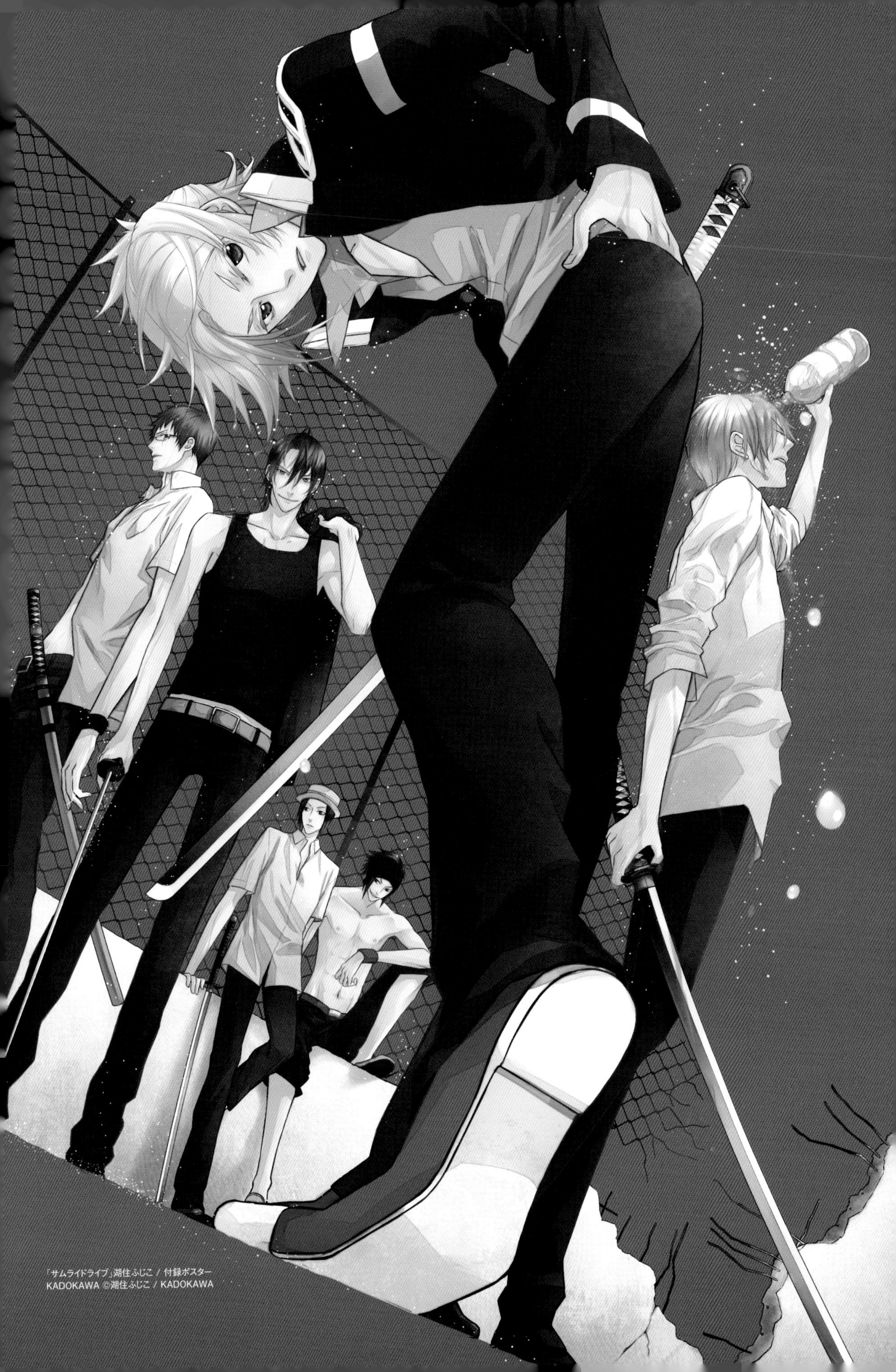

寿トロ

Kotobuki Toro

M zodiax@hotmail.co.jp
U http://taurus23.seesaa.net
T susizume
D ComicStudio ● Photoshop

Profile

ゲーム会社デザイナーを経て、現在、イラストレーター・漫画家をやっております。宜しくお願いします。

I used to work as a designer for a game company, but now I am an illustrator and manga artist.

Comments

技術に関してはまだ色々と模索中ではありますが、ポーズや表情、全体の雰囲気においてはキャラクターの「らしさ」を大事にしたいと思っています。

I'm still working on my artistic skills, but I hope to maintain the integrity of each character within their poses, expressions, and overall ambiance.

「簒奪皇帝1」漫画:寿トロ 原作:芝村裕吏
カバーイラスト / B's-LOG COMICS / KADOKAWA

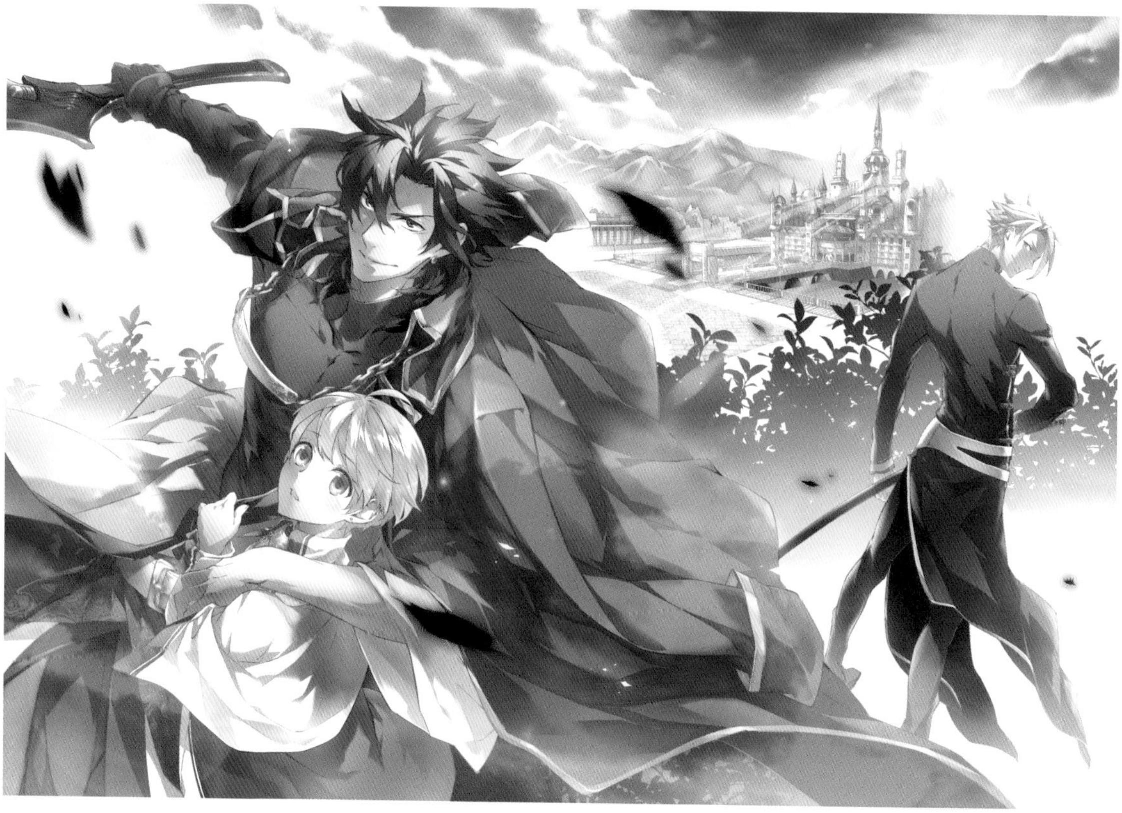

「簒奪皇帝1」漫画:寿トロ 原作:芝村裕吏
B's-LOG COMICS / KADOKAWA

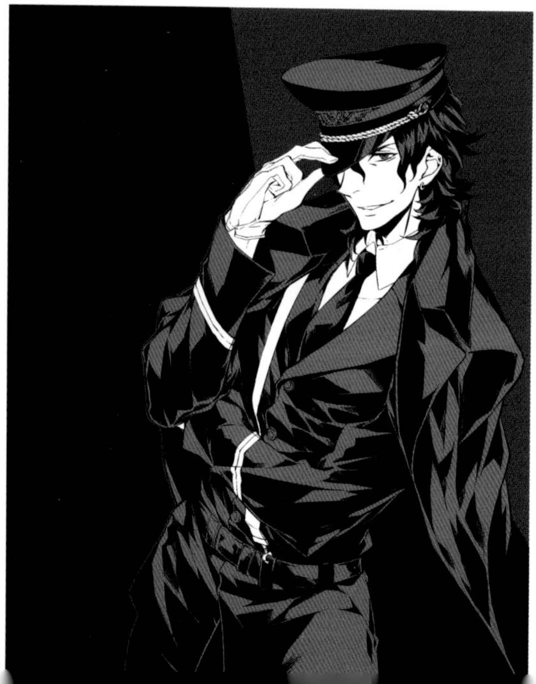

「はばたけ! 猛禽アパート」寿トロ / 告知用イラスト
B's-LOG COMICS / KADOKAWA

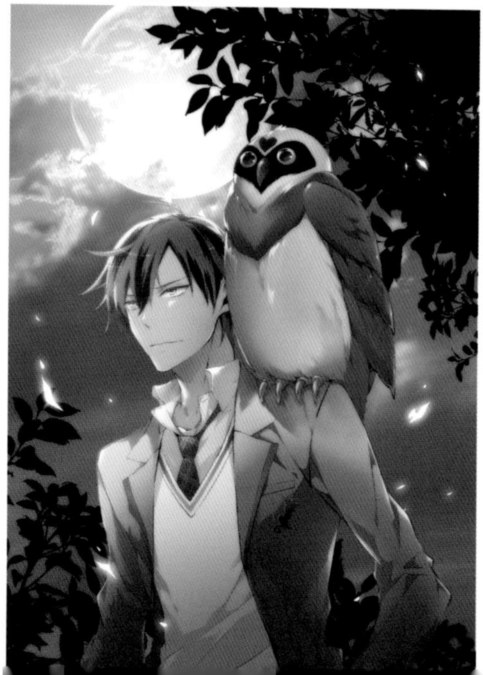

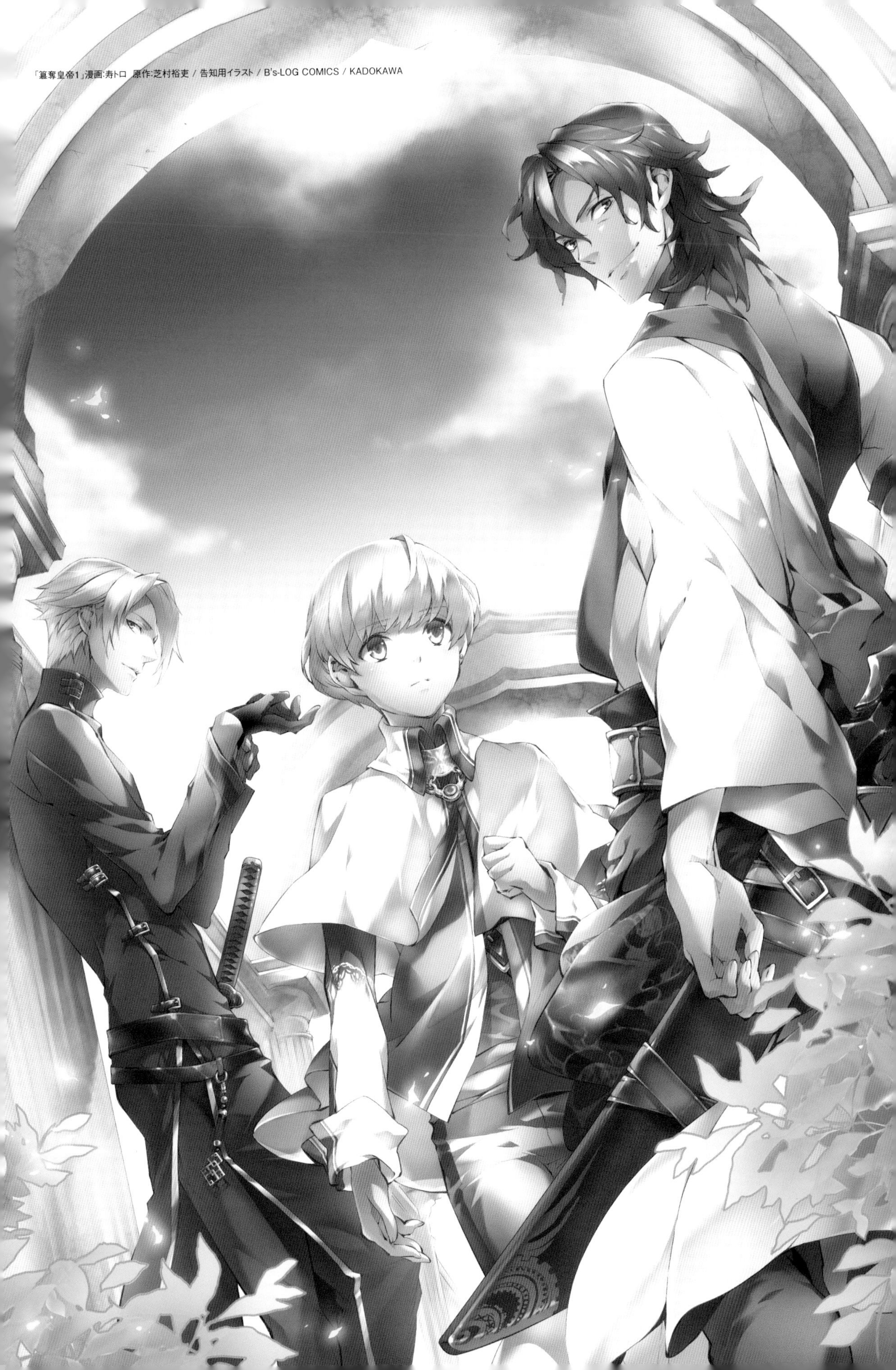
「簒奪皇帝1」漫画:寿トロ　原作:芝村裕吏 / 告知用イラスト / B's-LOG COMICS / KADOKAWA

榊 空也
Sakaki Kuya

M s9@theknights.xii.jp
U http://theknights.xii.jp
T higeing
D Photoshop CS4 ● SAI ● CLIP STUDIO

Profile

「お庭番望月蒼司朗参る！」シリーズなど、少女、BL、一般向け小説挿絵を中心に、ドラマCDイラスト、乙女ゲーム原画など、主に女性向けコンテンツで活動しています。

I primarily work on content aimed at female consumers, such as illustrations for the *Oniwaban Mochizuki Soshiro Mairu!* Series and other novels targeting young girls, BL, and general readership, as well as drama CD illustrations and *otome* game stills.

Comments

作品に合わせたものを描く時は、作品に求められている点を頭に置きながら、個性を殺さないようバランスを取る事を心がけています。空気感を大事に、表情のある生きたキャラクターを描いていきたいです。

When I'm drawing, I keep in mind the requirements imposed by the original work, and strive to maintain a balance which will not destroy my own creative style. Mood and atmosphere are important to me, and I also try to make my characters have expression and life.

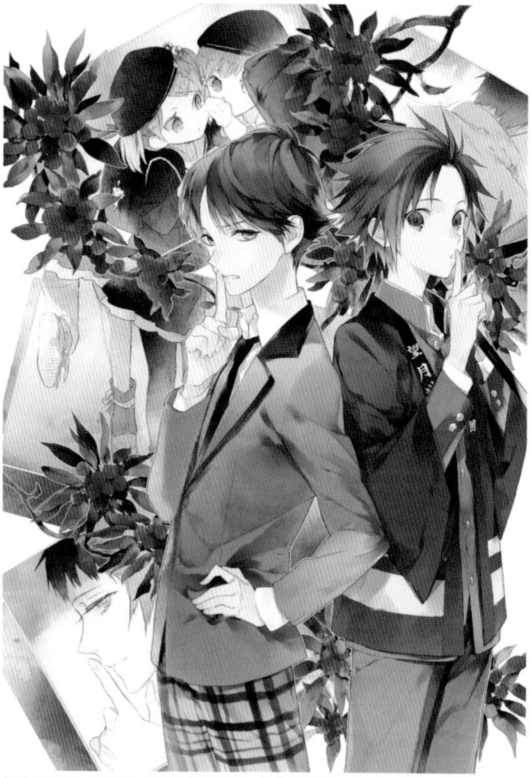

「お庭番望月蒼司朗参る! 内緒の蟲とお子さまの特権」流 星香
カバーイラスト / ビーズログ文庫(2014年4月) / KADOKAWA
©Seika NAGARE 2014

「しらつゆの怪」/ Otomate Maniax Vol.5 掲載イラスト
アイディアファクトリー ©IDEA FACTORY

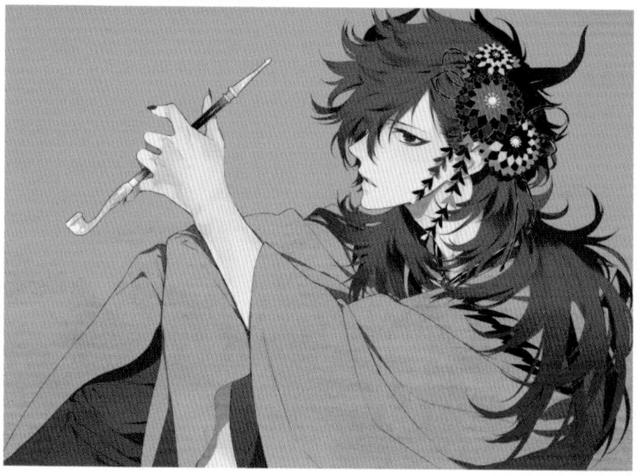

「その瞳が僕をダメにする」神奈木 智 / カバーイラスト / 幻冬舎コミックス
©KANNAGI SATORU, SAKAKI KUYA, GENTOSHA COMICS 2014

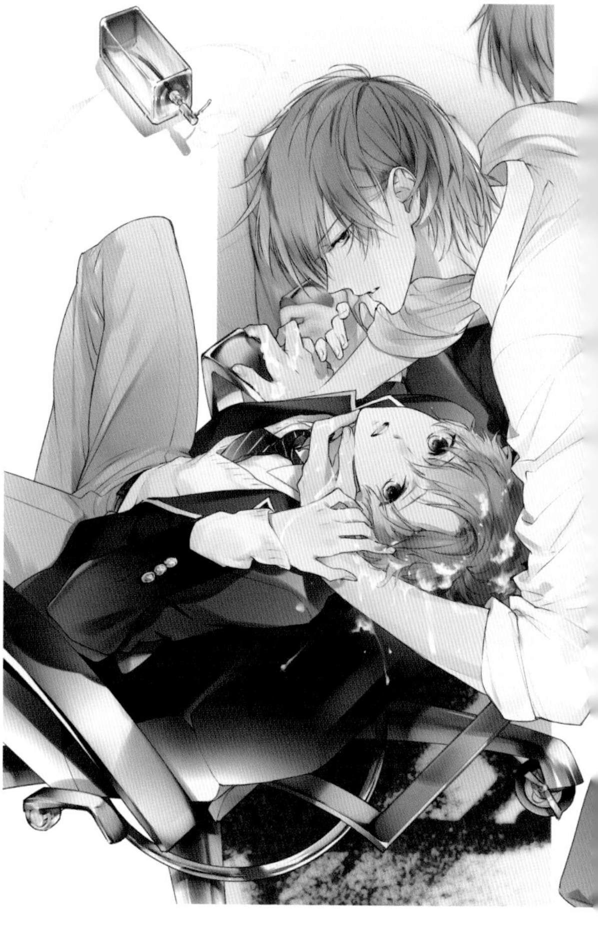

「異世界トリップ」榊 空也 / Chara 2015年10月号 ポスター / 徳間書店 ©徳間書店

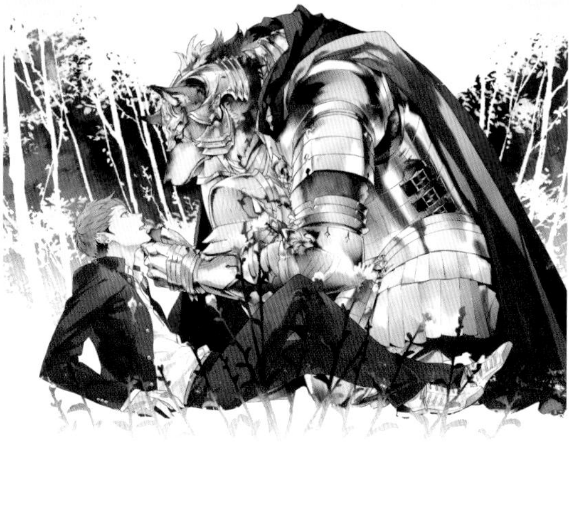

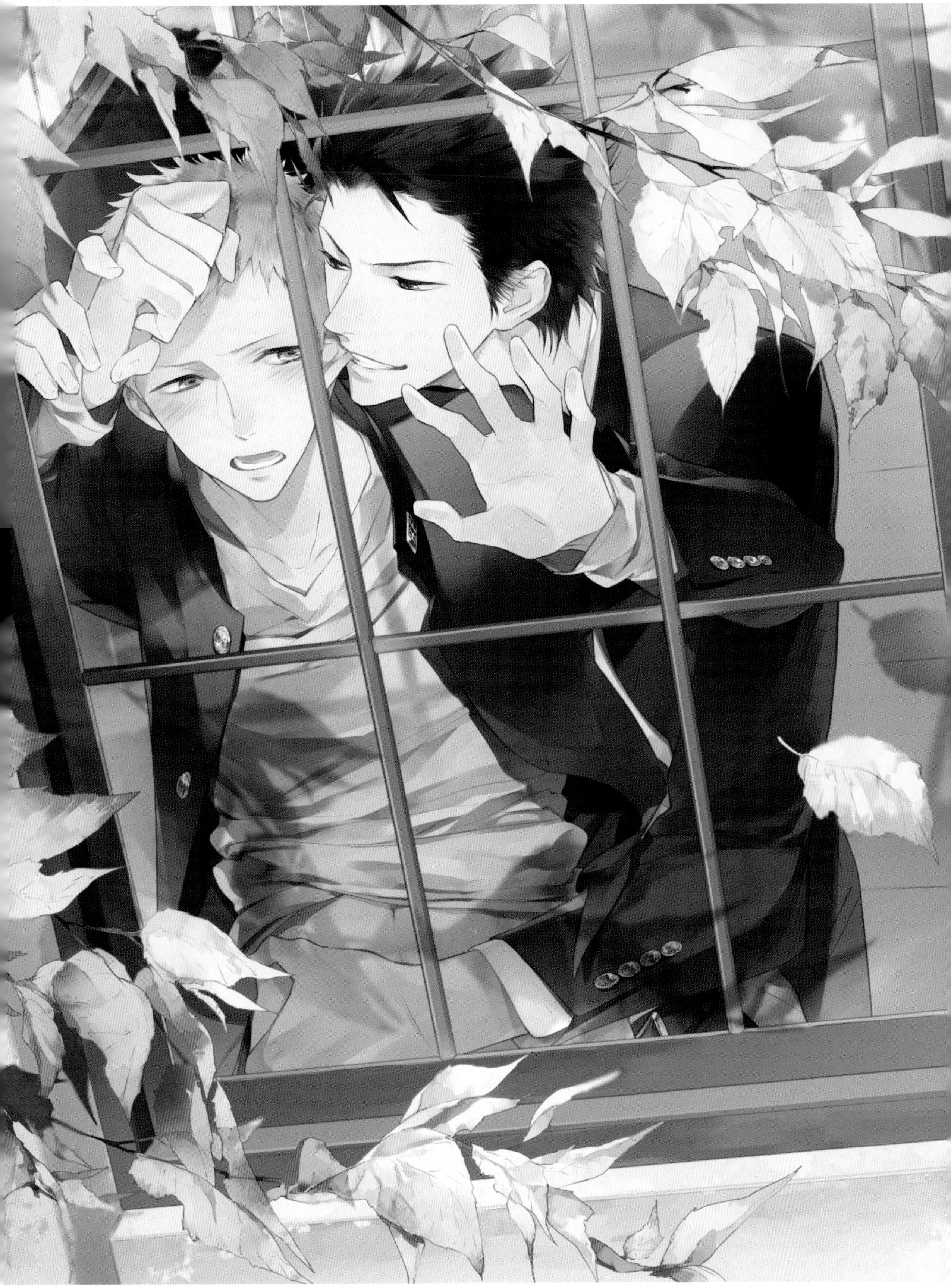

サガミワカ

Sagami Waka

M waka_t@nifty.com
T sagami_w
U http://sagami-waka.cocolog-nifty.com/blog
D Photoshop CS3 ● SAI

Profile

2008年「ドラマチック・マエストロ」(リブレ出版) でデビュー。主にBLジャンルでマンガを描いています。

I made my debut in 2008 with *Doramatic Maestro* (Libre Publishing). I am mostly illustrating manga in the BL genre.

Comments

イラストにはそのキャラらしい表情・色気が出るように心がけています。特にBLに関しては二人の関係性、距離感などが伝わるよう考えながら描いています。

I try to ensure that each character's unique expressions and sex appeal are reflected. In my BL work in particular, I keep the two characters' relationship and mutual distance in mind as I draw.

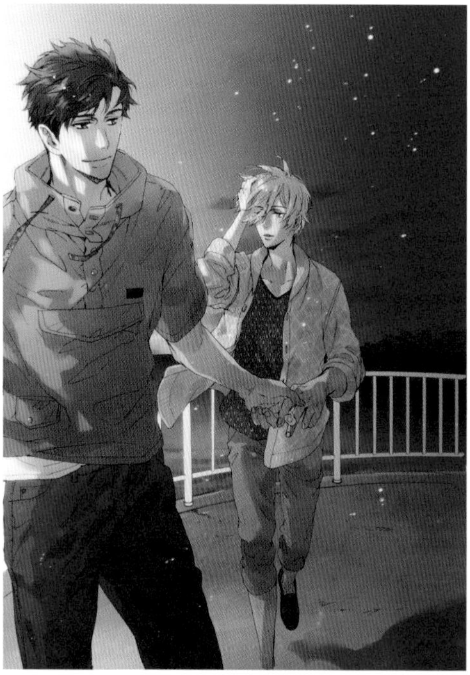

「うちの兄の恋愛事情」サガミワカ
初出・MAGAZINE BE×BOY 2015年6月号 作品扉イラスト / リブレ出版
©Waka Sagami ©Libre Publishing2015

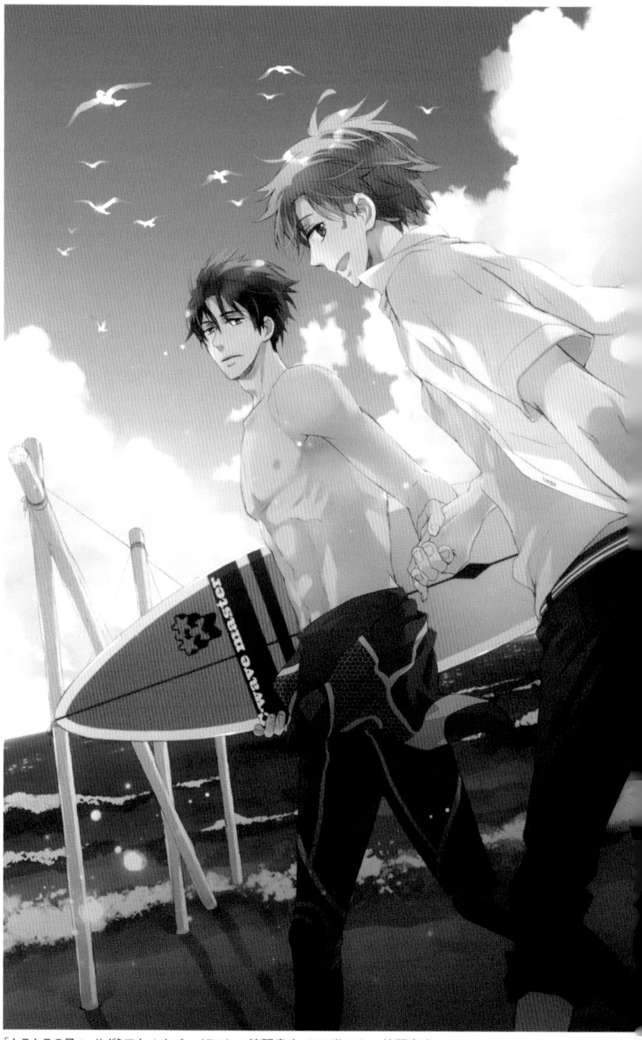

WAVE MASTER

「キラキラの日々」サガミワカ / カバーイラスト / 徳間書店 ©サガミワカ / 徳間書店

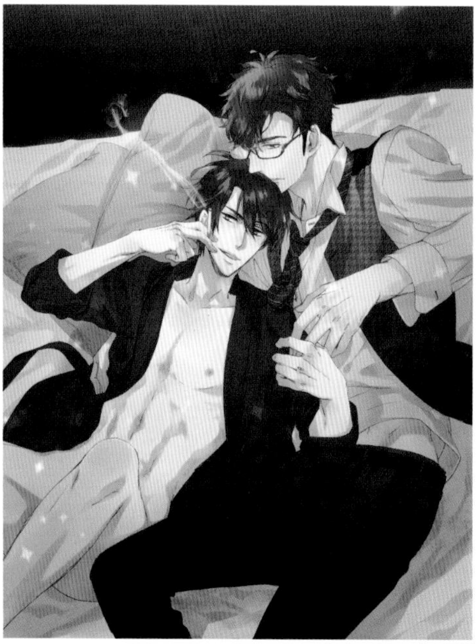

「くちづけは嘘の味」サガミワカ / GUSH2015年10月号 表紙イラスト / 海王社 ©サガミワカ / 海王社

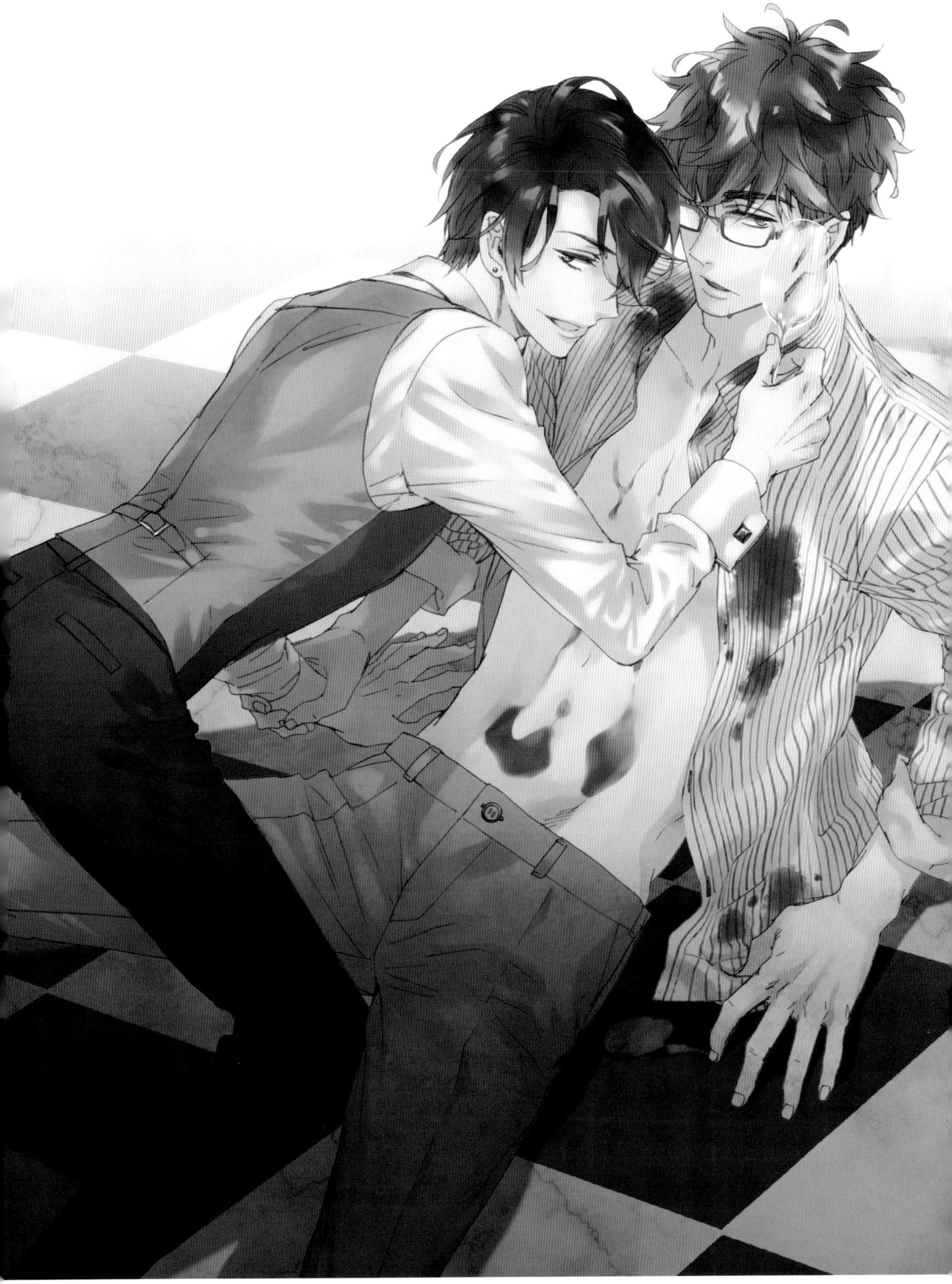

坂本あきら

SAKAMOTO AKIRA

M fwkt9855@mb.infoweb.ne.jp

U ---

T 48AKIRA69

D CLIP STUDIO PAINT EX

Profile

学生の頃に同人誌で二次創作を始め、そこから創作の道に。一般企業に入社し趣味で創作をしつつ出版社に持ち込み、スクウェア・エニックスのガンガンで漫画家デビュー。 少年誌、青年誌、乙女系、ゲームのキャラクターデザイン、などにて執筆中。

I began drawing for derivative works in self-publications (*doujinshi*) while I was a student, and continued along the creative path. I entered a regular company and continued drawing as a hobby, taking my work to publishers, ultimately debuting as a manga artist with the monthly *Shonen Gangan* by Square Enix. Now I draw for magazines aimed at lads and youths, respectively, as well as for the *otome-kei* romance stories for young women. I also design game characters.

Comments

顔だけではなく手の仕草などからもキャラクターの感情が伝わるようにと思っています。内側に秘められた攻撃性や仄暗い感情や覚悟、追い詰められた時のギリギリの選択…などの、ただ見た目の綺麗さより、泥臭く生臭く仄暗く激しく暴力的で反抗的でエロスとグロの境界線を彷徨うような絵が一番自分の得意ジャンルです。

I try to communicate characters' expressions not only through their faces, but also by hand gestures and other means. My forte in terms of genre is delineating that fine line between the rebellious and violent erotic and grotesque worlds in which the uncouth, depraved, and gloomy characters lurk; I prefer that concealed aggressive and gloomy feeling and the characters feeling trapped with choices left until the last moment, over drawings in which everything is simply pretty at first glance.

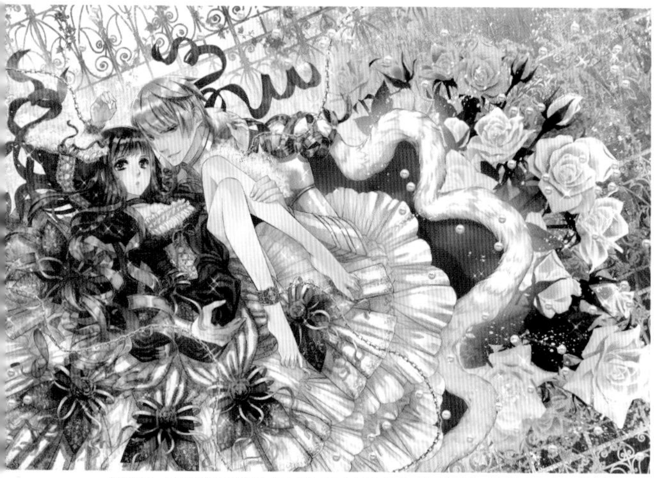

「愛の檻　騎士に淫らに触れられて」漫画:坂本あきら 原作:永谷圓さくら / カバーイラスト / 宙出版
©AKIRA SAKAMOTO / SAKURA NAGATANIEN / 宙出版 / プランタン出版

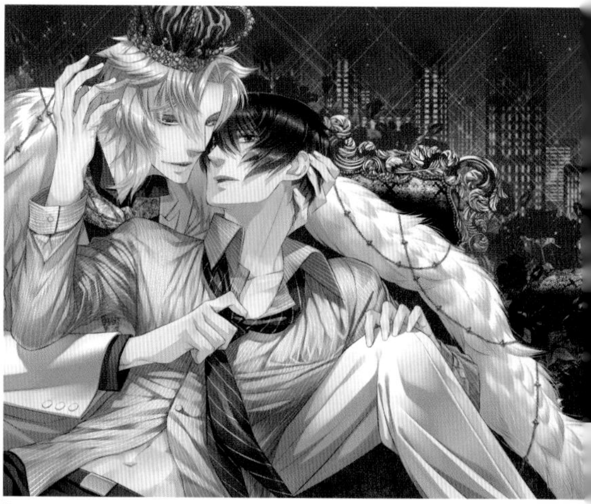

「王子様のオトコ。」坂本あきら / カバーイラスト / B's-LOVEY COMICS / KADOKAWA
©2014 Akira Sakamoto

「東京陰陽師」坂本あきら / 一周年 WEB用イラスト / TYRANT / ©TYRANT

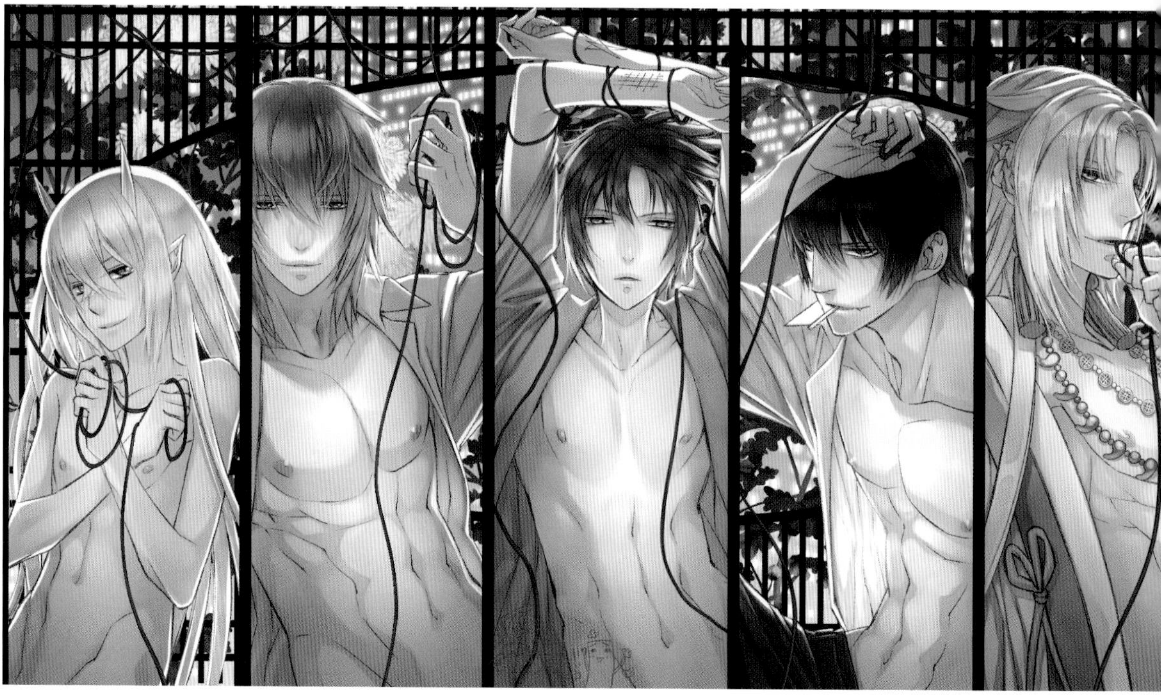

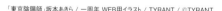

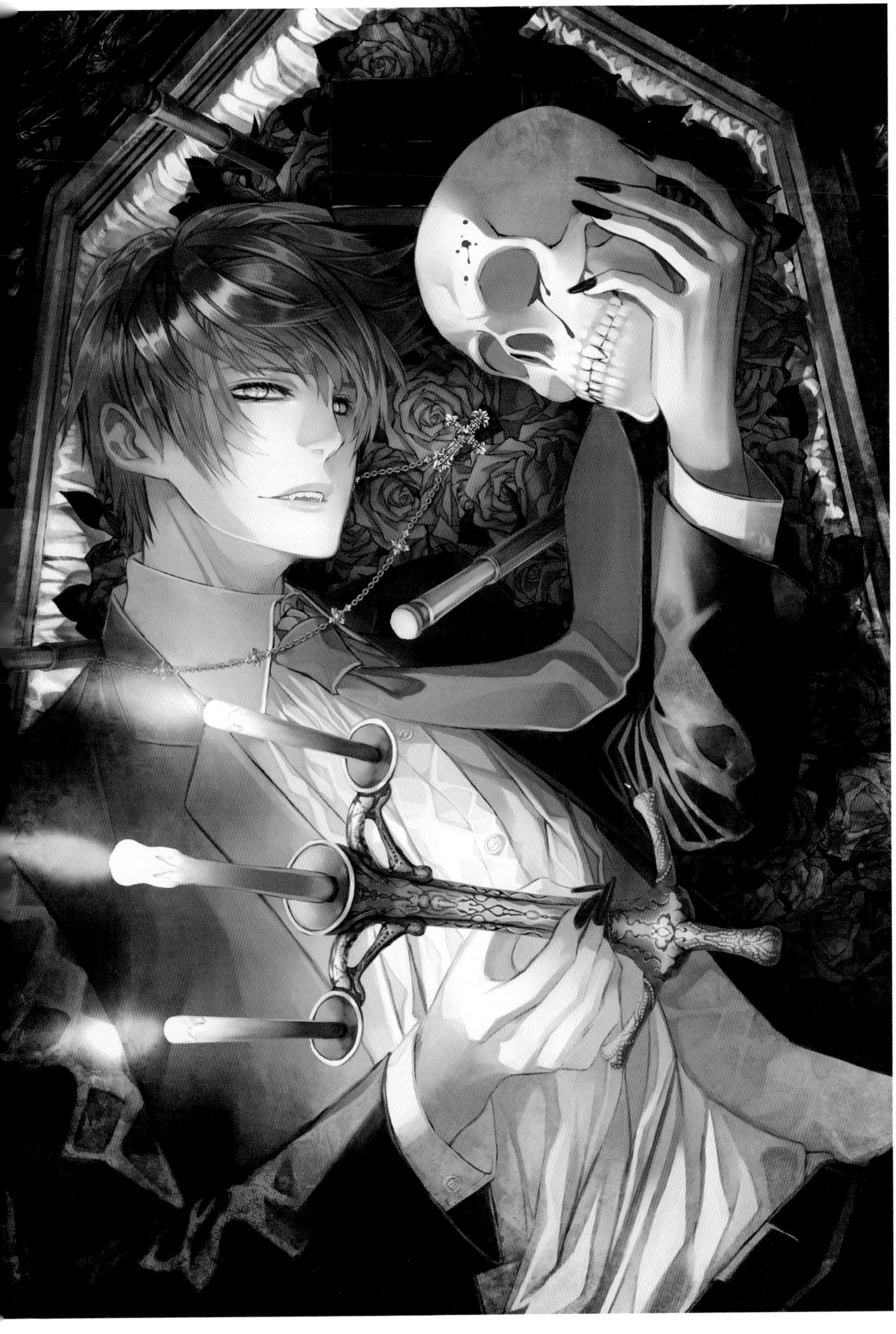

佐木郁
SAKI KAORU

M sakikaoru0808@gmail.com
U http://sakikaoru08.wix.com/saki-kaoru
T sakikaoru08
D SAI ● Photoshop

Profile

フリーのイラストレーターとして、男性イラスト、カップルイラストなどを多く描いています。書籍カバーやCDジャケットなどを主とし活動中。2015年秋、ワニブックス様より恋愛ショートコミックを題材とした初の書籍を発売いたしました。

As a freelance illustrator, I often draw males and couples. I mainly work on book covers and CD jackets. In the fall of 2015, Wani Books began marketing my first publication, a short comic book centered on romantic love.

Comments

中性的な男性を得意とするため、特に男性の表情においては「色気」を意識して描いています。イラスト、ショートコミックともに目線や表情からそのキャラクターの性格や心情が伝わるようなものを描きたい、と常に考えながら作業をしています。「誰の絵よりも、自分の描く男性がいちばん好み！」という自負をもちながら創作を続けています。

Since my forte is androgynous males, I concentrate on producing sexy expressions, particularly for my male characters. Whenever working on my illustrations or short comics, I want to ensure that when I draw, each character's gaze and expression will communicate his or her personality and emotions. As I create, I can't help feeling that I prefer my own drawings of male characters over those of anybody else.

「EXIT TUNES PRESENTS ACTORS3」/ 千本桜 PV用イラスト一部 / エグジットチューンズ ©EXIT TUNES Character Design:めか

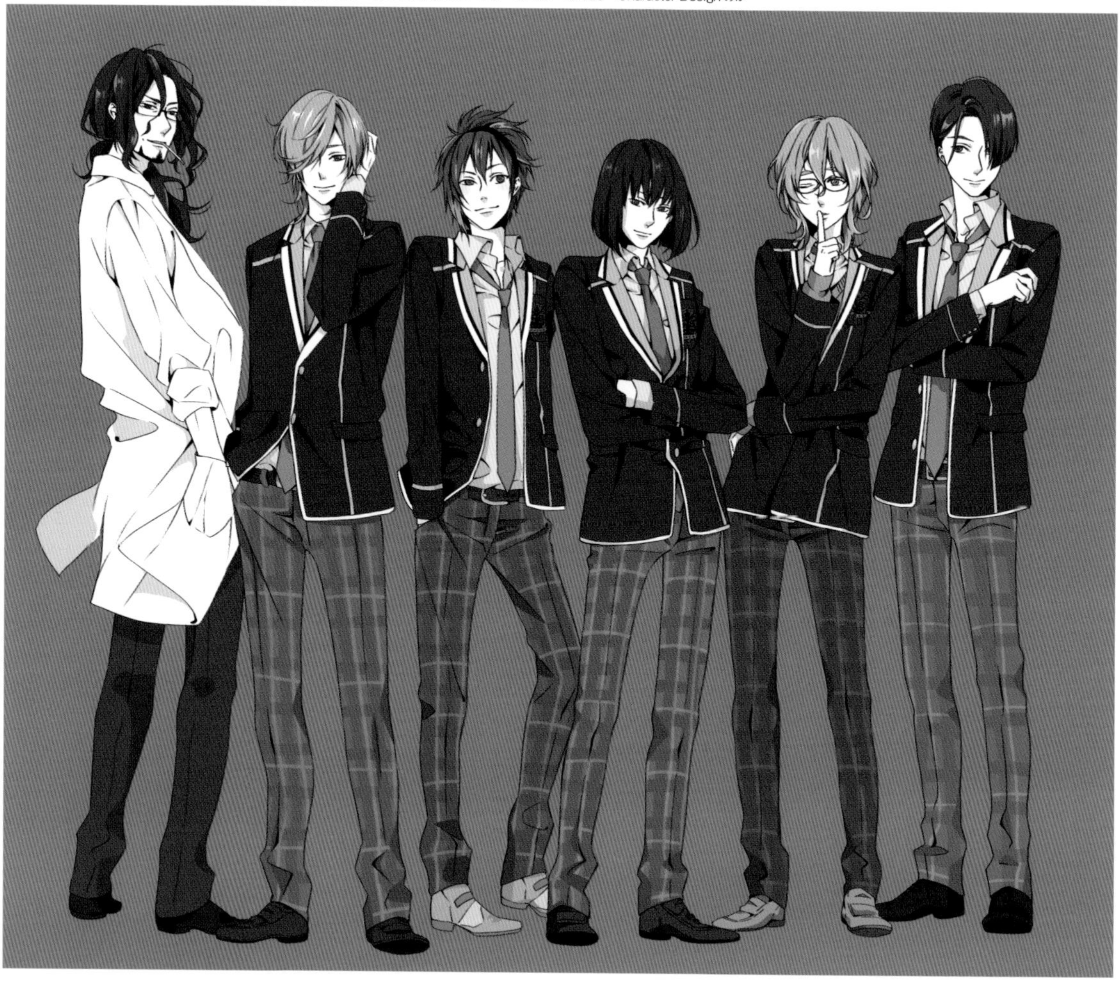

初出・「Voice Colors Series～Kiss～」(2014年6月25日発売)
ジャケットイラスト2 / マリン・エンタテインメント ©MARINE ENTERTAINMENT

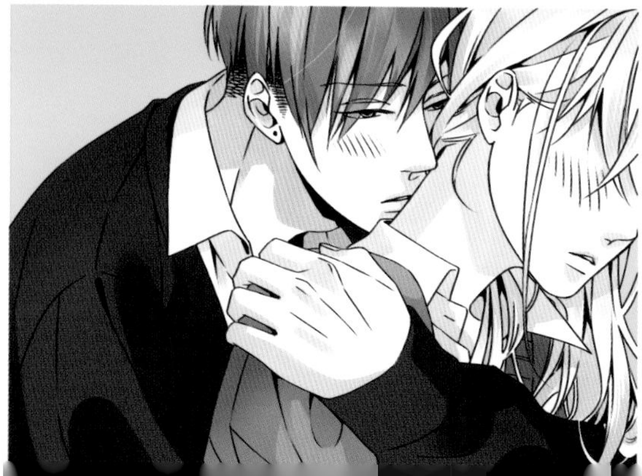

Personal Work「箱入りスーツ」

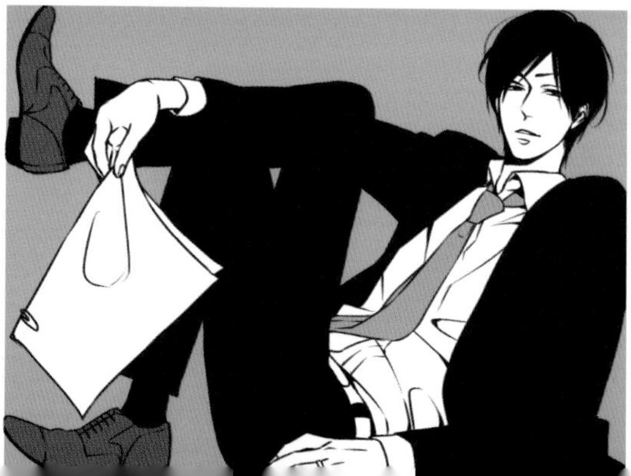

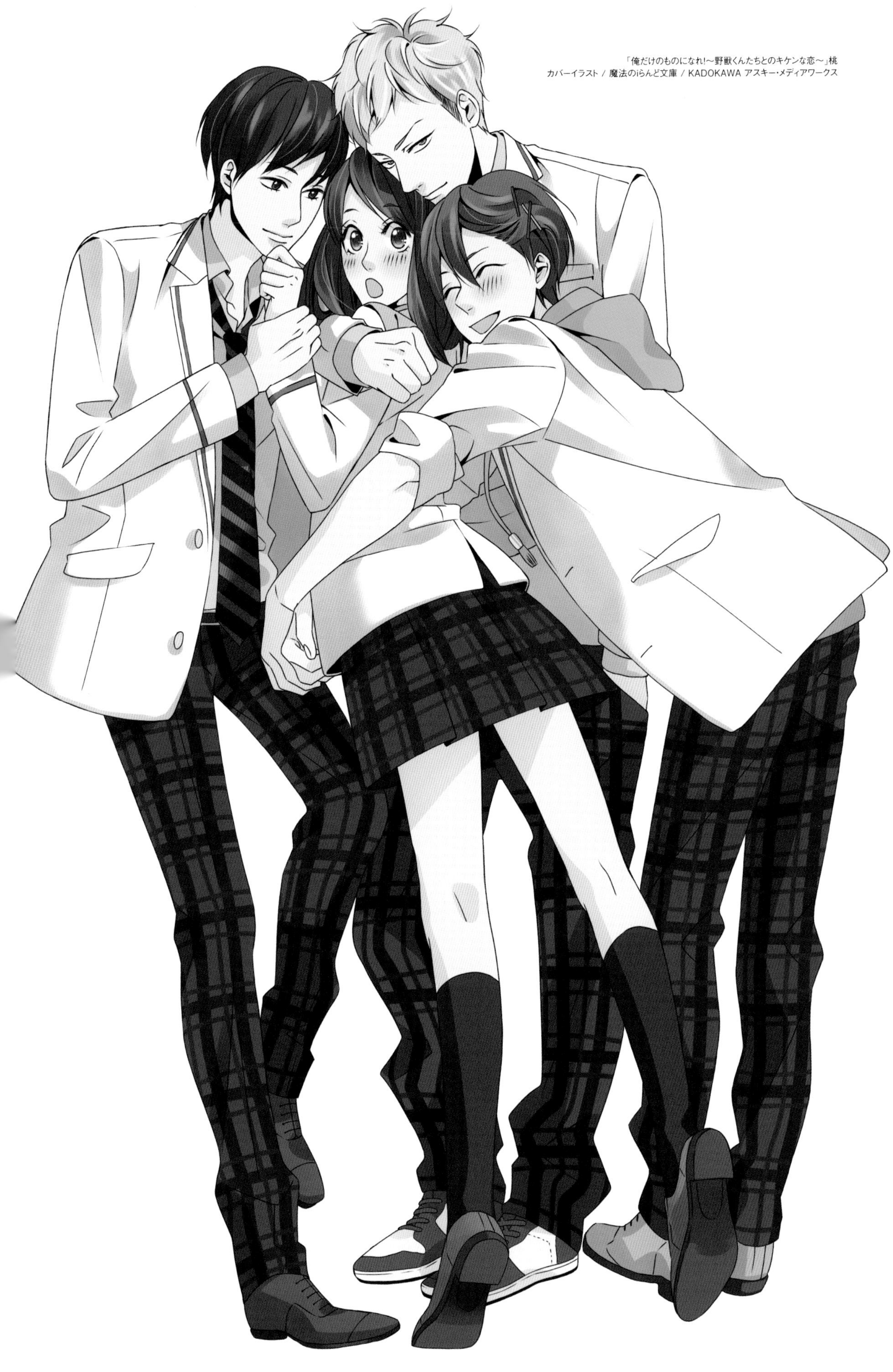

「俺だけのものになれ!～野獣くんたちとのキケンな恋～」桃
カバーイラスト / 魔法のiらんど文庫 / KADOKAWA アスキー・メディアワークス

漣一弥

Sazanami Ichiya

M info@3373hp.com
T 3373ichiya
U http://3373hp.com
D Photoshop ● CLIP STUDIO PAINT

Profile

漫画家兼イラストレーター。「第九のマギア」、「あやなしの君」、「革命機ヴァルヴレイヴ 裏切りの烙印」、「吟遊戯曲 BlackBard」など、オリジナルからコミカライズ作品まで、ジャンルを問わず描いています。

I wear two hats: those of manga artist and illustrator. I create original works, including *Magia The ninth*, *Ayanashi no Kimi*, *Kakumeiki Valvrave Uragiri no Rakuin*, and *Ginyugikyoku BlackBard*, as well as manga based on novels, films, and the like.

Comments

男性はかっこよく、女性はかわいく描くことを心がけています。黒とビビットな色の組み合わせが好きで、ファンタジー・ゴシック風の描写が一番得意です。

I do my best to draw cool male characters and cute female ones. I love combining black colors with vivid hues, and am best at portraying fantasy and goth.

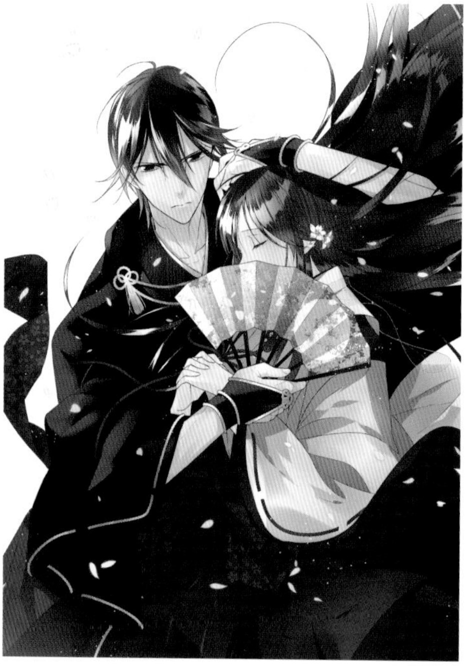

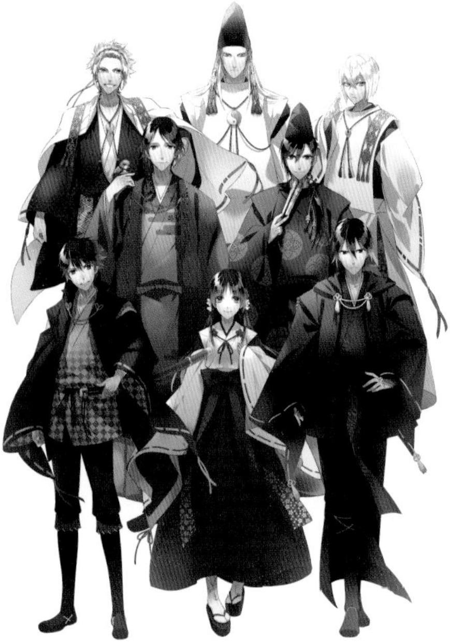

「あやなしの君 一」イラスト:漣一弥
シナリオ: 水野隆志
カバー・キャラクターイラスト
シルフコミックス / KADOKAWA
アスキー・メディアワークス
©2015 Sazanami ichiya / Mizuno Takashi

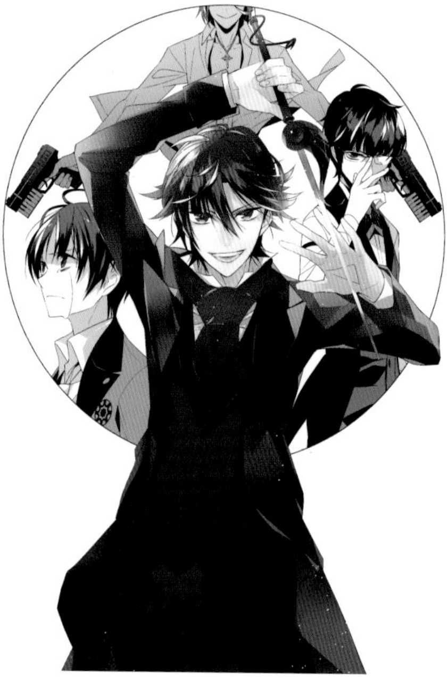

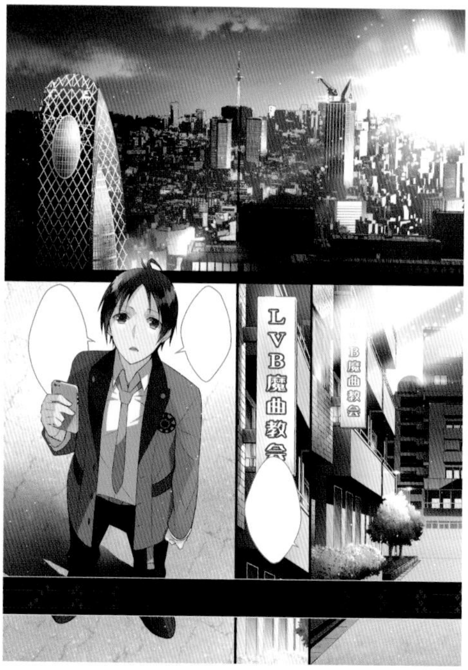
LVB魔曲教会

「第九のマギア」漣一弥
監修:堀江宏樹 / カバー・口絵
コミックジーン / KADOKAWA
メディアファクトリー
©2015 Sazanami ichiya / KADOKAWA

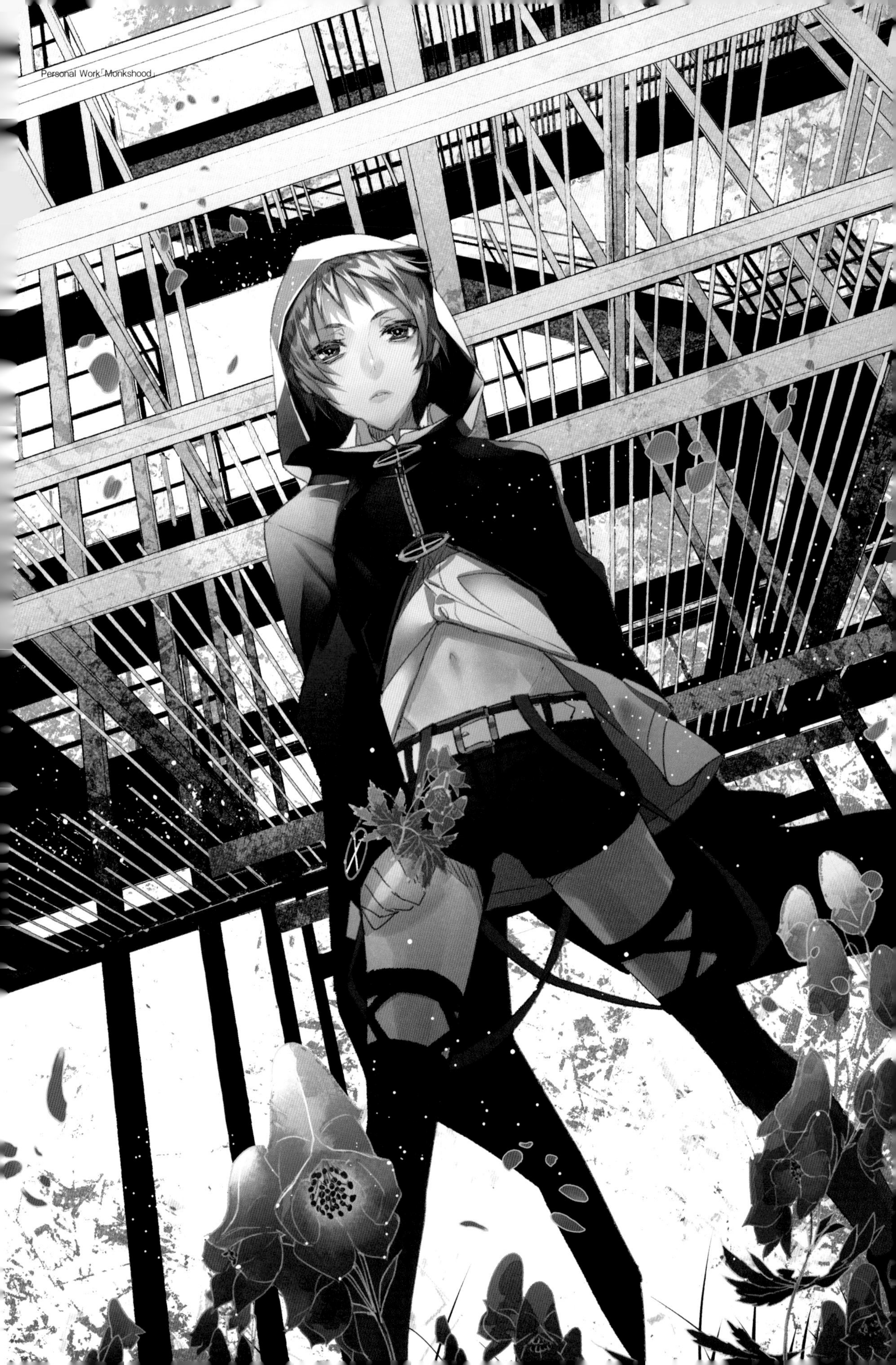

Personal Work「Monkshood」

ZAKK/石江 八

ZAKK / ISHIE HACHI

Ⓜ arxzakk@yahoo.co.jp(ZAKK) / ishiehachi@gmail.com(石江 八)

Ⓣ ZAKK_ccc(ZAKK) / ishiehachi(石江 八)　Ⓤ ---

Ⓓ Writing brush ● Milli Pen ● Photoshop CS5

Profile

ZAKK名義でBLを、それ以外は石江 八名義で活動しています。(ZAKK：茜新社『OPERA』にて「CANISシリーズ」連載中。石江 八：リブレ出版『クロフネZERO』にて「路地裏ブラザーズ」連載中。)

I do my BL work under the name ZAKK, with all my other work attributed to Ishie Hachi. As ZAKK, I'm currently working on the *CANIS* series for OPERA, published by Akaneshinsha. As Ishie Hachi, I'm now involved in the *Rojiura Brothers* for Kurofune ZERO, put out by Libre Publishing.

Comments

男性を描く時に心がけていることは、たとえ線の細い美形だろうが中性的な人であろうが、どこかしらに"無骨さ"を出すというところ。女性では表現できない色気があるように思います。

When I draw, sure, my males are androgynous and the lines are slender and beautiful, but somehow, I inject a boorishness into the character. My female characters have a sexiness which cannot fully be expressed.

「CANIS -Dear Hatter- #1」ZAKK
カバーイラスト / 茜新社
©ZAKK / akaneshinsha

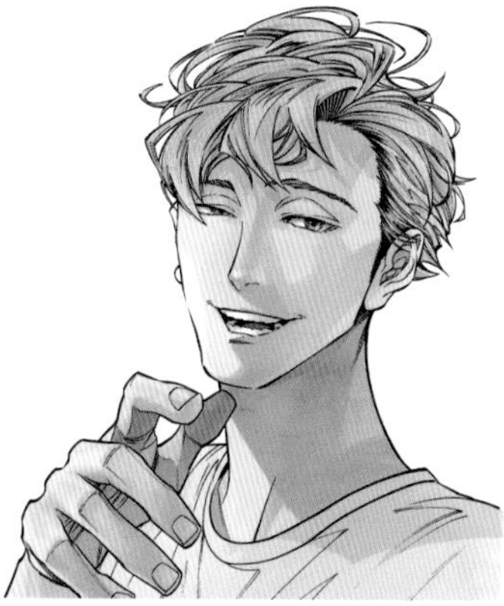

Personal Work ©Hachi Ishie

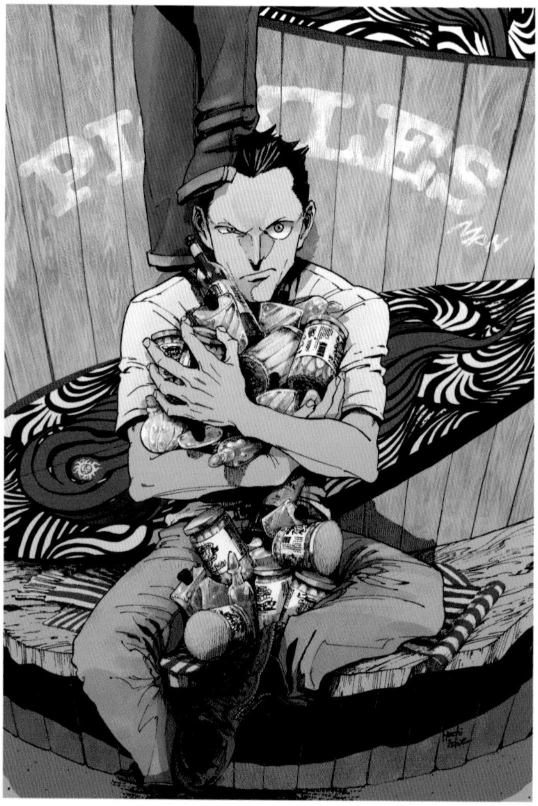

「路地裏ブラザーズ ①」石江八 / 口絵 / リブレ出版　©Hachi Ishie / Libre Publishing 2015

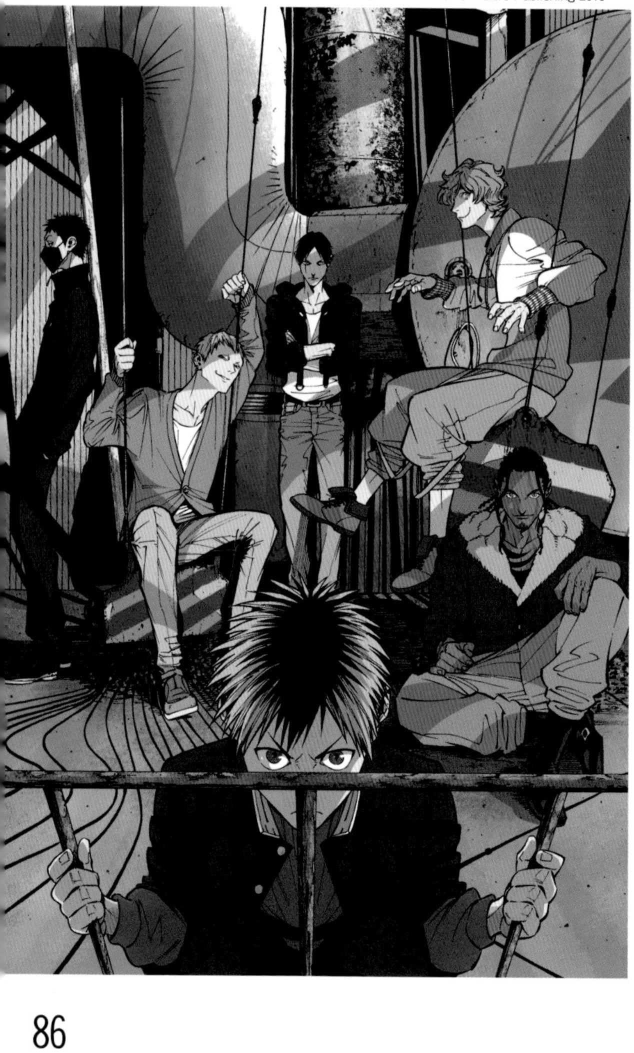

Personal Work ©Hachi Ishie

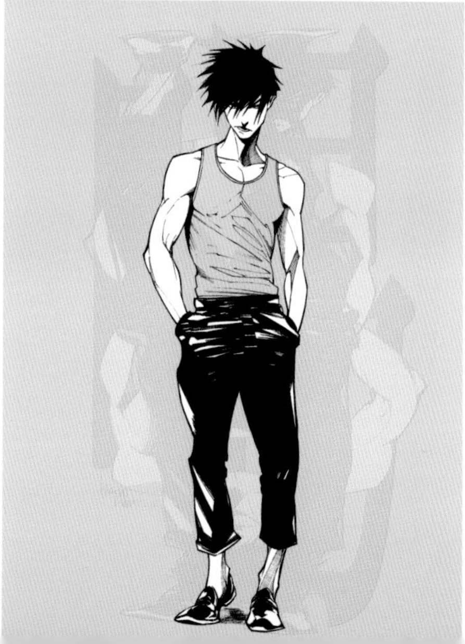

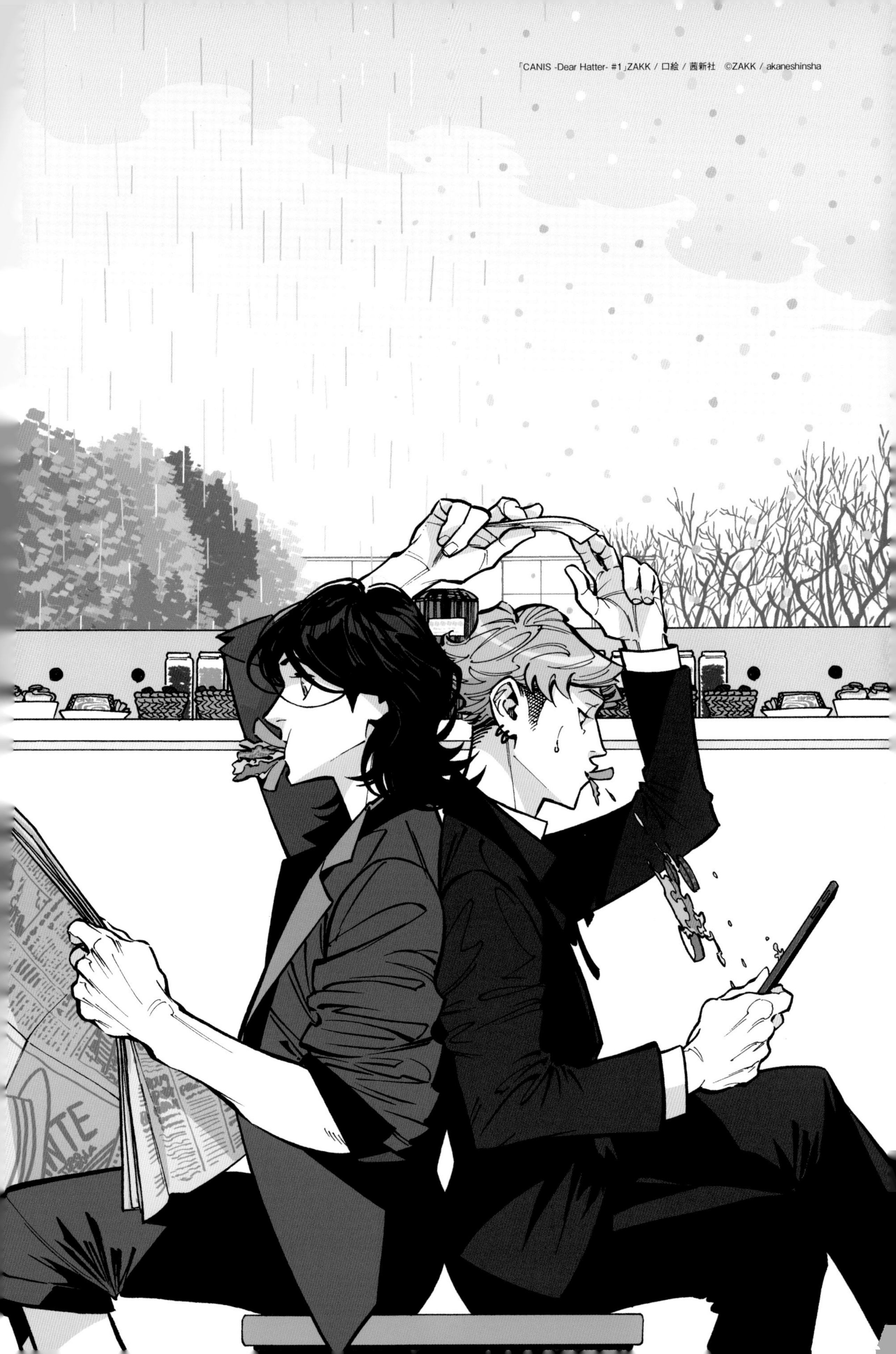

しきみ
Shikimi

M keeggy@yahoo.co.jp
U http://keeggy.com
T keeggy
D SAI • Photoshop 6

Profile

都内在住のイラストレーター。主に書籍の装画やゲームのキャラクターデザイン、カードイラストなどを描かせて頂いております。

I'm an illustrator living in Tokyo. I primarily work on book covers, character designs, and trading card illustrations.

Comments

テーマ性、物語性を常に意識しています。無機質な人物を描くのが好きです。

I keep theme and story line in mind when I work. I enjoy drawing emotionless, rather mechanical characters.

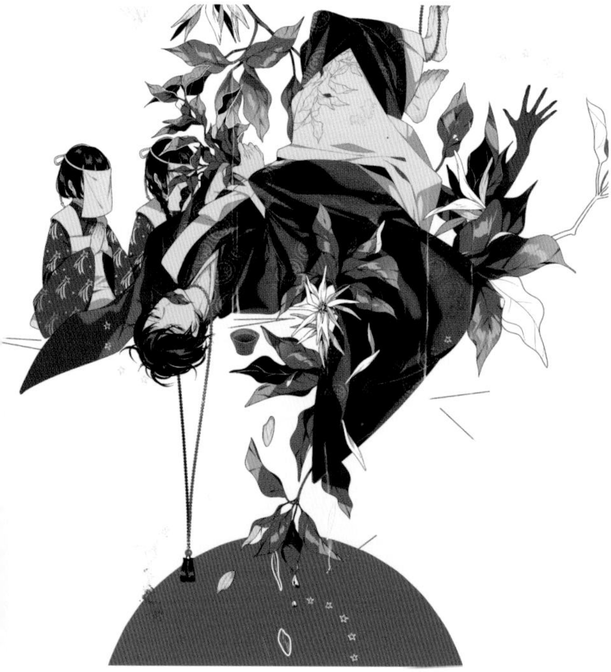

Personal Work「死に水」

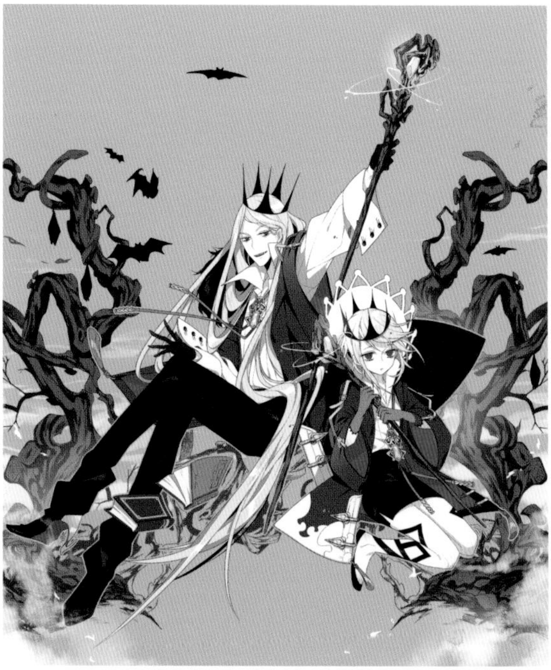

Personal Work「Spell and Epitaph」

Personal Work「昔日」

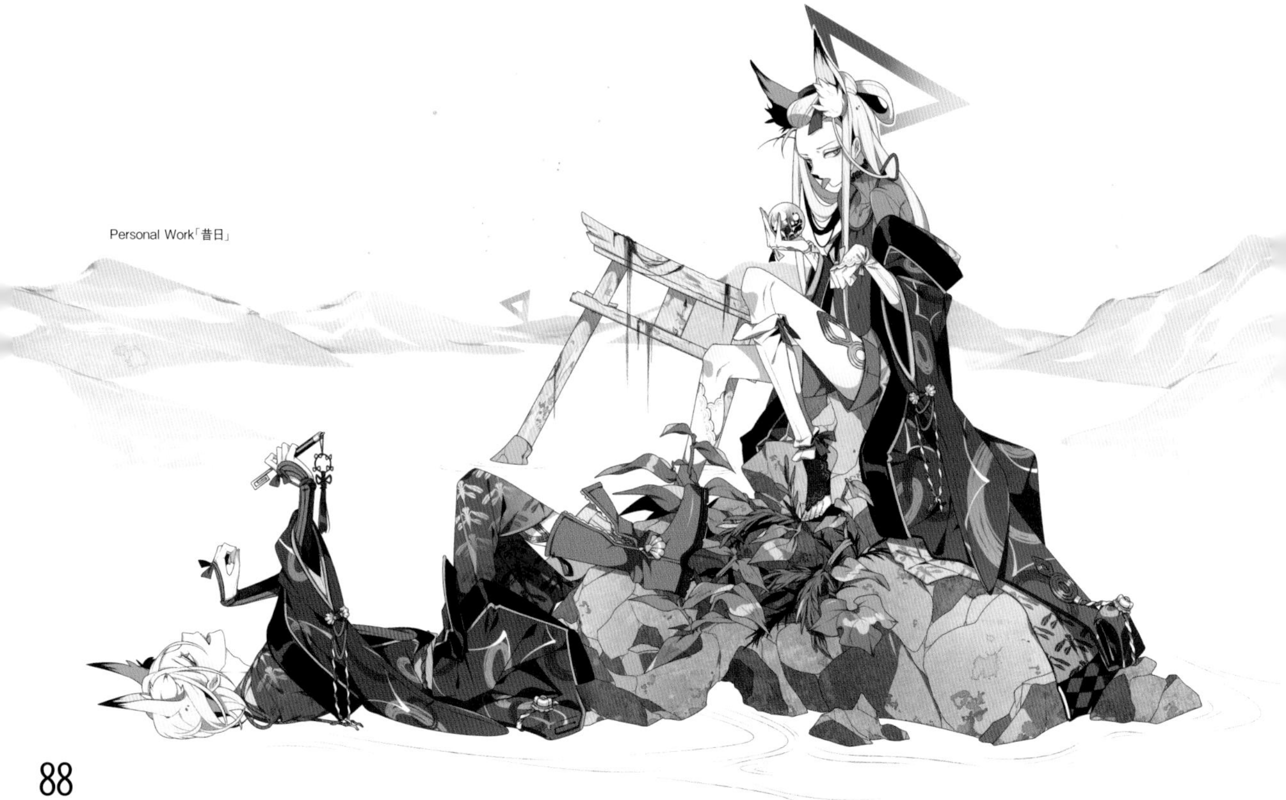

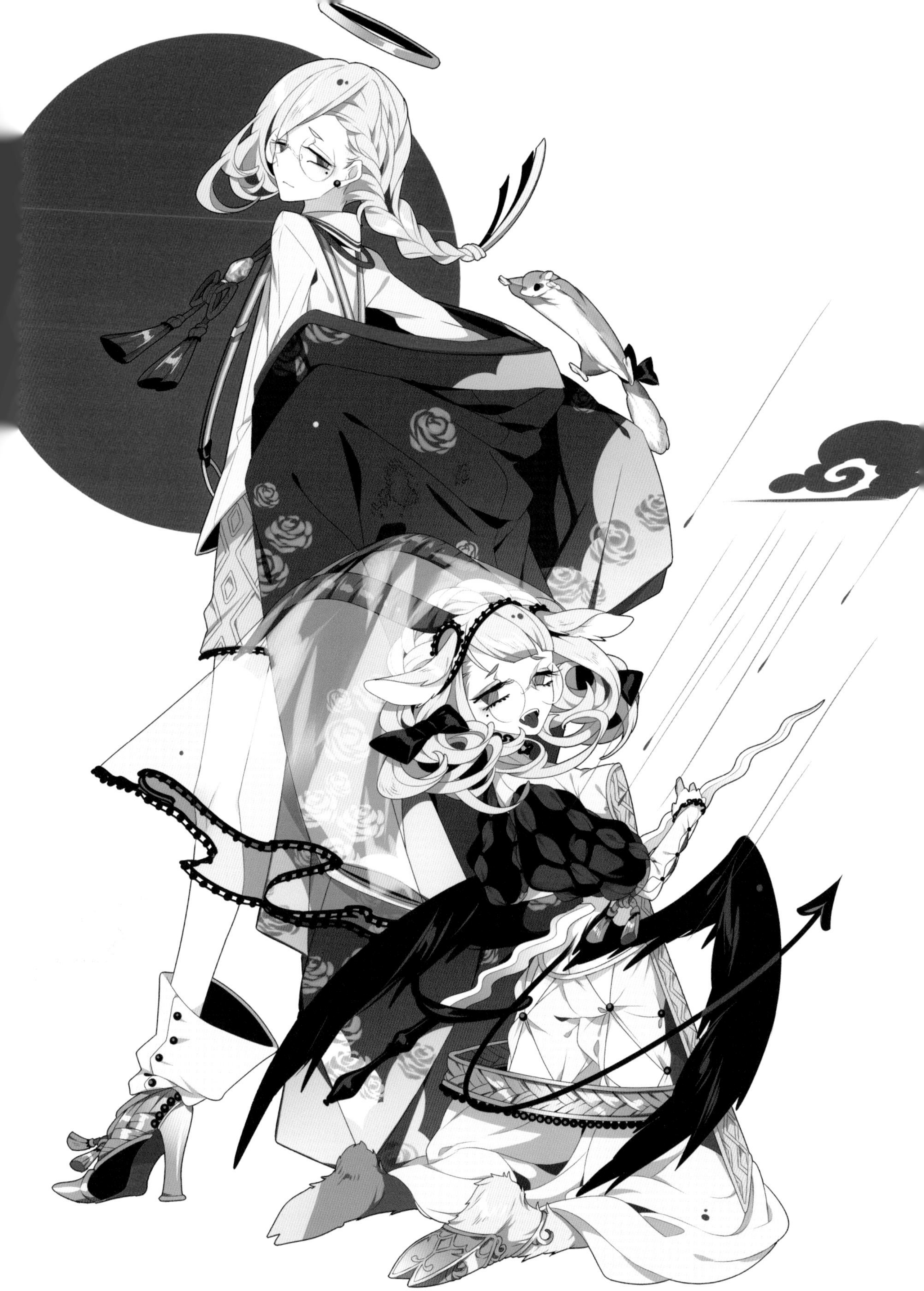

Personal Work「Liquid sunshine」

志島とひろ

Shijima Tohiro

M het_u23k_ri19p@yahoo.co.jp
T tohiro1
U http://th-cuddle.jimdo.com
D SAI ● Photoshop

Profile

主に、女性向けコンテンツのキャラクターデザインをさせて頂いております。雑誌内では声優ラジオのイラストを初回から担当、短編コミックのお仕事等も受けております。 現在はフリーで活動中で、10〜30代くらいの男性を描くご依頼を頂く機会が多いです。

I mainly design characters for female-oriented publications. My initial job was illustrating radio voice actors, but now I'm drawing short comic strips. I'm currently a freelancer, and mainly drawing males whose ages range from about ten through their thirties.

Comments

手や首筋といった細かい体のパーツを大事にして、女性目線でぐっとくる男性像を描けるように意識しています。直接的な表現がなくても、目線や体の流れで絵から深読みができたり、男性の色気を感じたり…という表現が好きなので、イラスト上で目をひくポイントができるように心がけています。

I concentrate on subtle, delicate parts of the body such as the hands and neck, and consciously try to turn out male characters which will garner a response in female readers. I like picking up on male sex appeal not necessarily through direct expression in an illustration, but rather by reading into the gaze or body flow. That's why I'm striving to produce illustrations with specific eye-catching features.

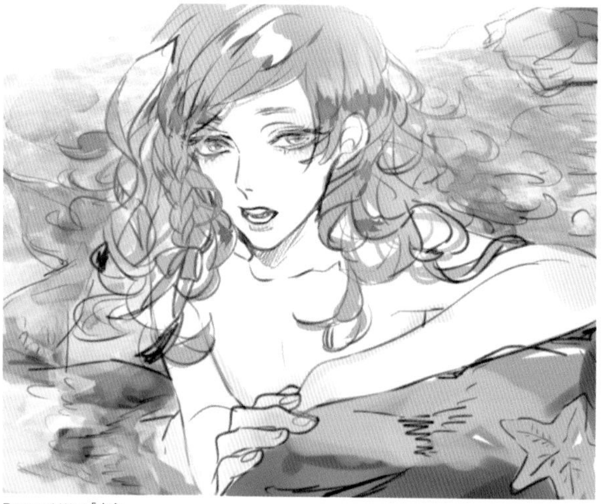

Personal Work「人魚」

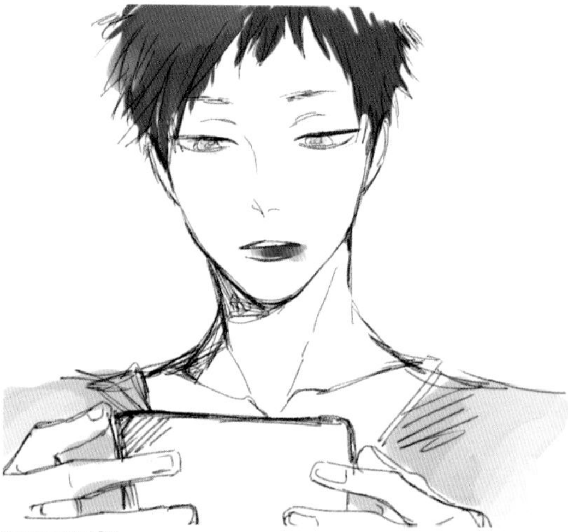

Personal Work「紅」

Personal Work

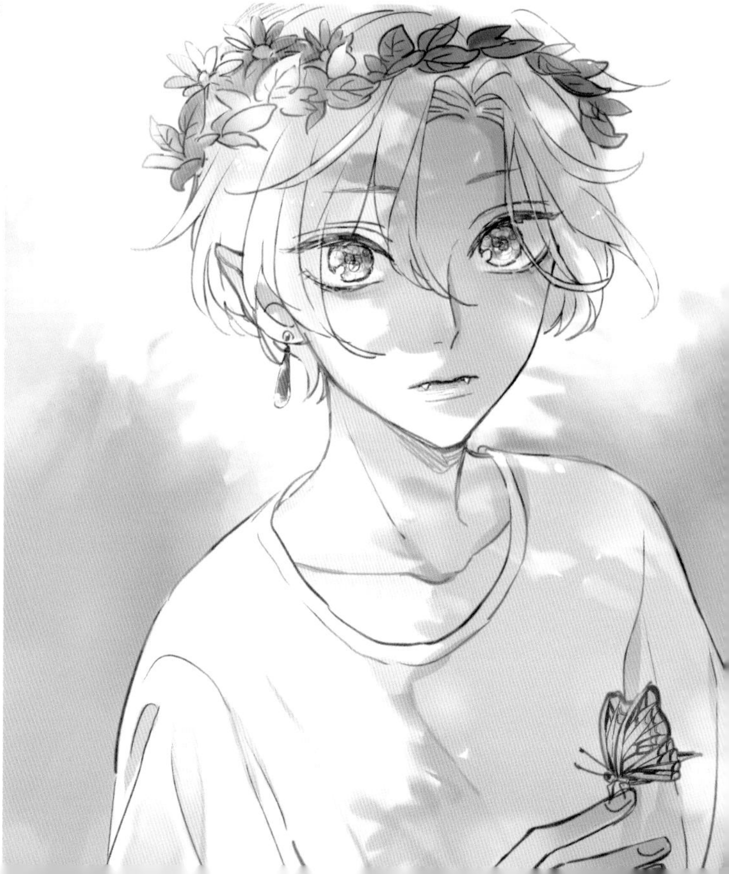

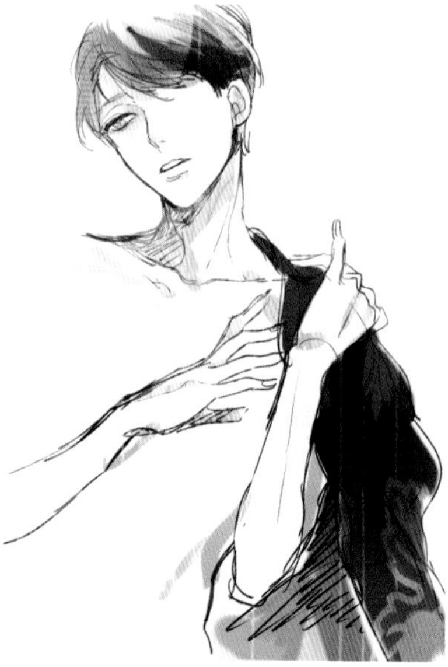

Personal Work

「ALIVE Side:G」/ ジャケットイラスト / ムービック ©TSUKIPRO

思春期
shishunnki

M poroporocinq@gmail.com   T siroimorino

U ---   D SAI • Photoshop • Illutrator • Pencil • Pen

Profile	たまにイラストのお仕事を頂きながら趣味で絵を描いています。肉の薄い少年と骨と、ダンディなおじさまが大好きです。	I continually draw as a hobby, with a few paid illustration jobs here and there. I like creating wispy adolescent boys, skeletal frameworks, and middle-aged dandies.
Comments	この身体にはきちんと骨や内臓が収まって、生きて動いてるんだな、と思って頂けるような人の表現ができるようになりたいです。	I hope that someday I'll be good enough so that people will comment favorably on my portrayal of how amazingly our frames and organs fit precisely within our bodies.

Personal Work

Personal Work「着き草頭」

Personal Work

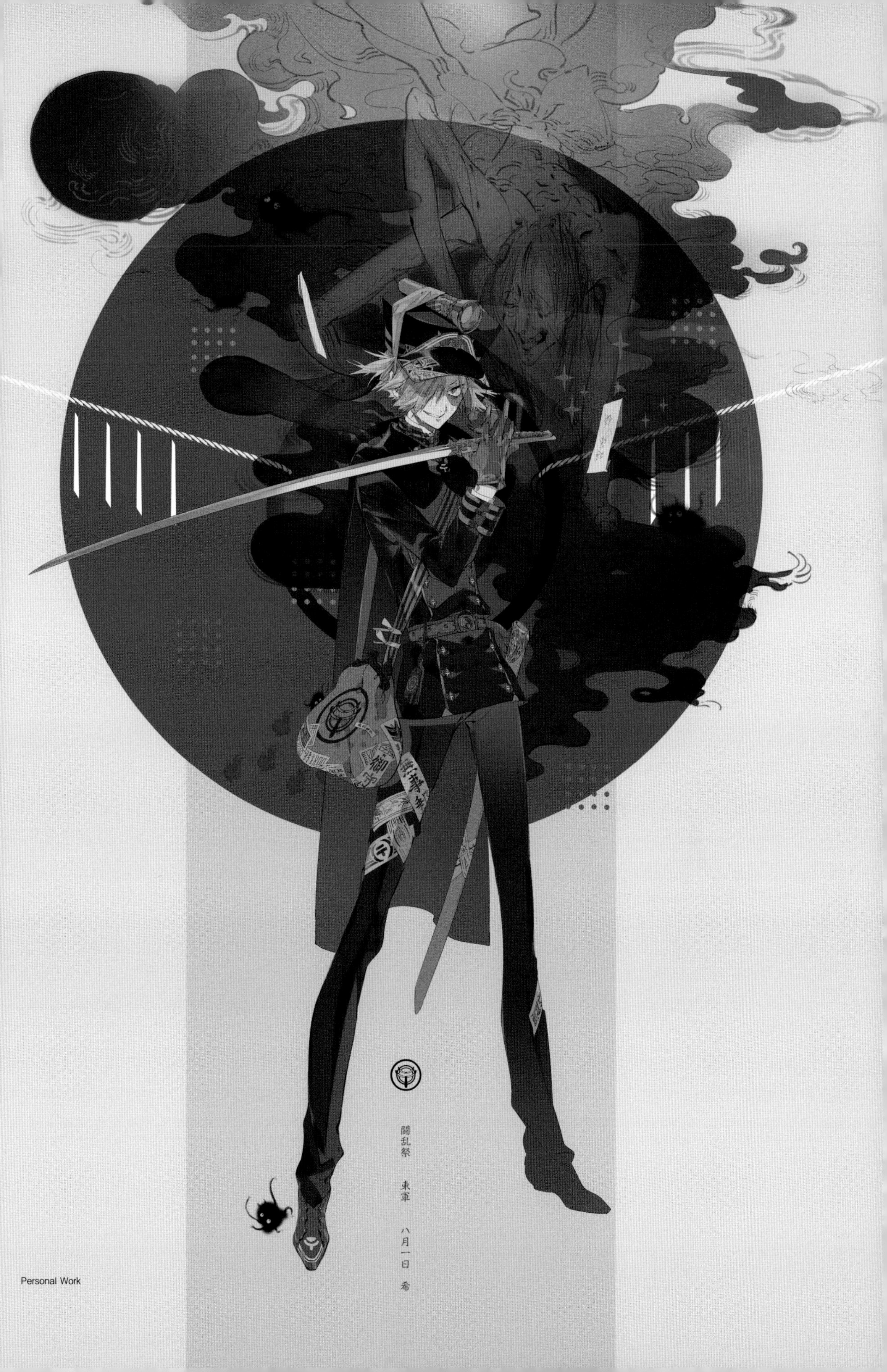
闘乱祭　東軍　八月一日　希

Personal Work

しまこ（花梨エンターテイメント）

Shimako (Karin entertainment)

M info@karin-e.jp

U ---

T ---

D SAI ● Photoshop 7, CS5

Profile

花梨エンターテイメント所属グラフィッカー。茨城県出身。「BLシチュエーションCD 黒薔薇の館」ではキャラクターデザイン・ジャケットイラストを担当。"ほんわかした絵柄"と言われることが多く、SDキャラクターを描くことも。甘いものと散歩が好き。

I'm a computer game artist associated with Karin entertainment. I'm from Ibaraki Prefecture. I do character designs and jacket illustrations for BL Situation CD *Kuro Bara no Yakata*. People often comment that my artwork has a warm and cozy feel. I also draw SD (super deformed) characters. I enjoy eating sweets and taking walks.

Comments

絵柄や彩色は１つの手法に制限するのではなく、世界観に合わせて柔軟に変化させるようにしています。等身の高いキャラやＳＤキャラ、水彩塗り、厚塗り、パス塗りなど様々な手法から1番効果的なものを選ぶようにしています。人物を描く際は、特に肌の塗りや服のシワの表情のつけ方などに、自分なりのこだわりをもって描いています。

I don't limit myself to a single approach to design and coloration; rather, I flexibly adapt to the perspective reflected in any given job. In rendering tall figures and SD characters, I choose whichever method is most successful, be it watercolor, thick paints, pastels, or something else. When I draw figures, I use my own unique discretion, particularly in how to render skin or expressive wrinkles in clothing.

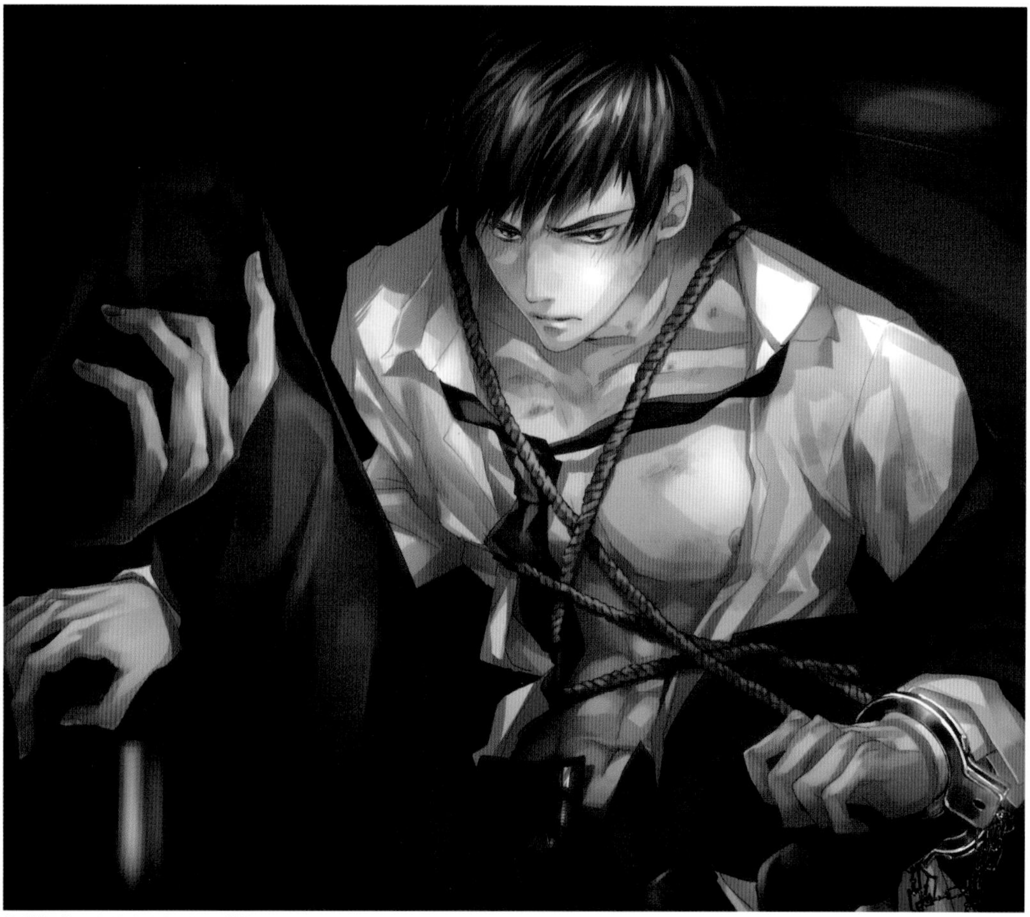

「黒薔薇の館」/ CDジャケットイラスト / ©花梨シャノアールΩ

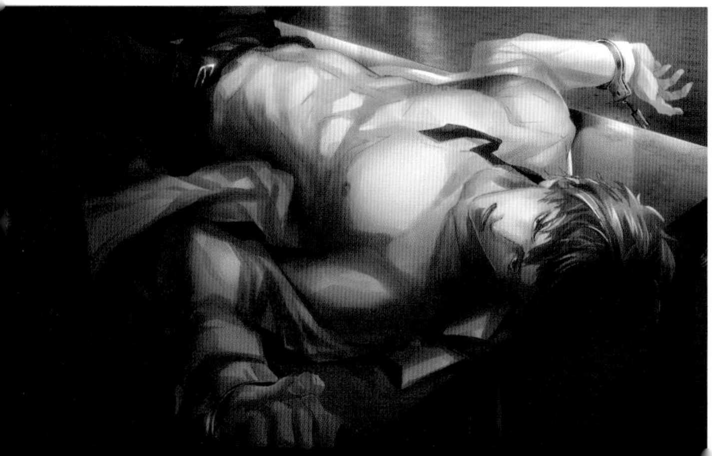

「黒薔薇の館」/ 雑誌描き下ろしイラスト / ©花梨シャノアールΩ

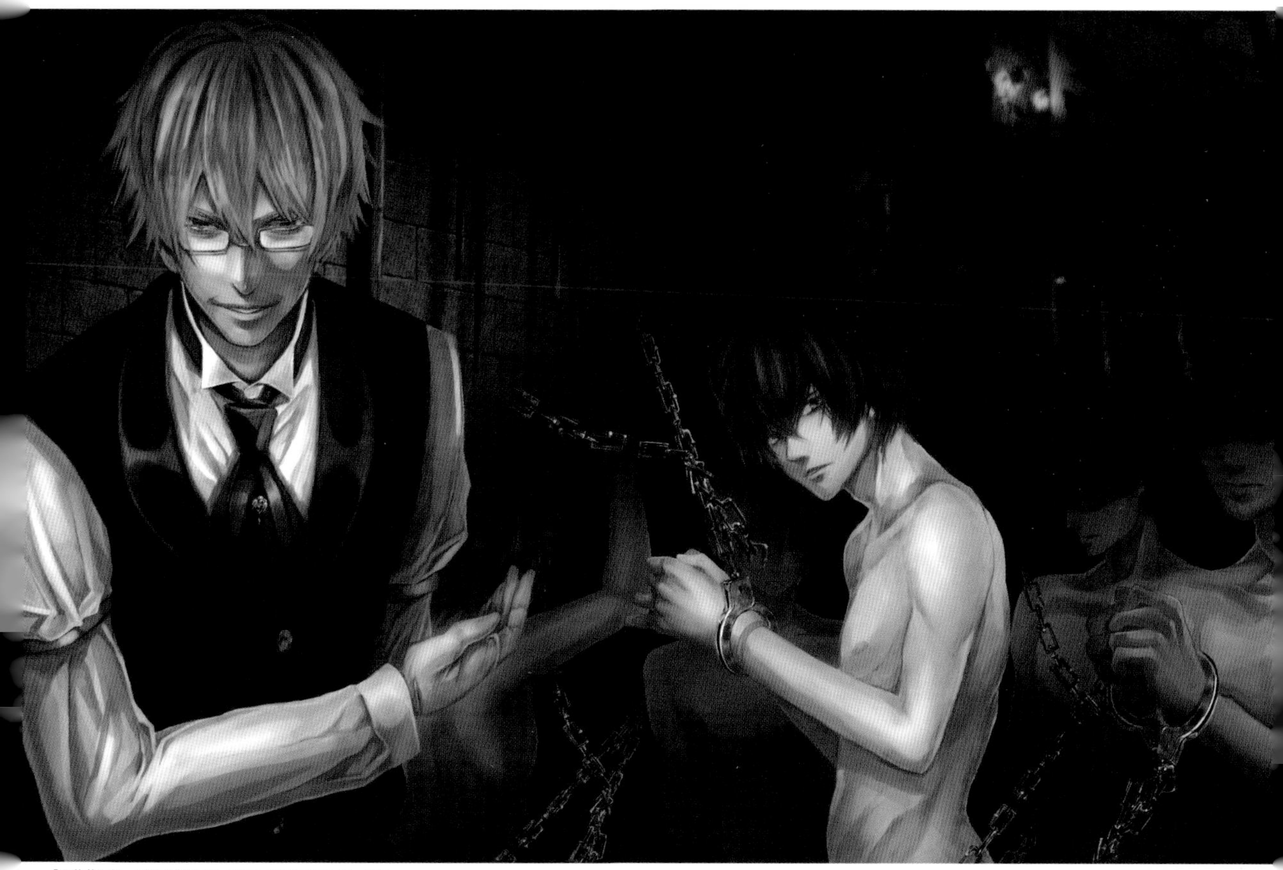

「黒薔薇の館」/ 雑誌描き下ろしイラスト / ©花梨シャノアールΩ

「黒薔薇の館」/ 雑誌描き下ろしイラスト / ©花梨シャノアールΩ

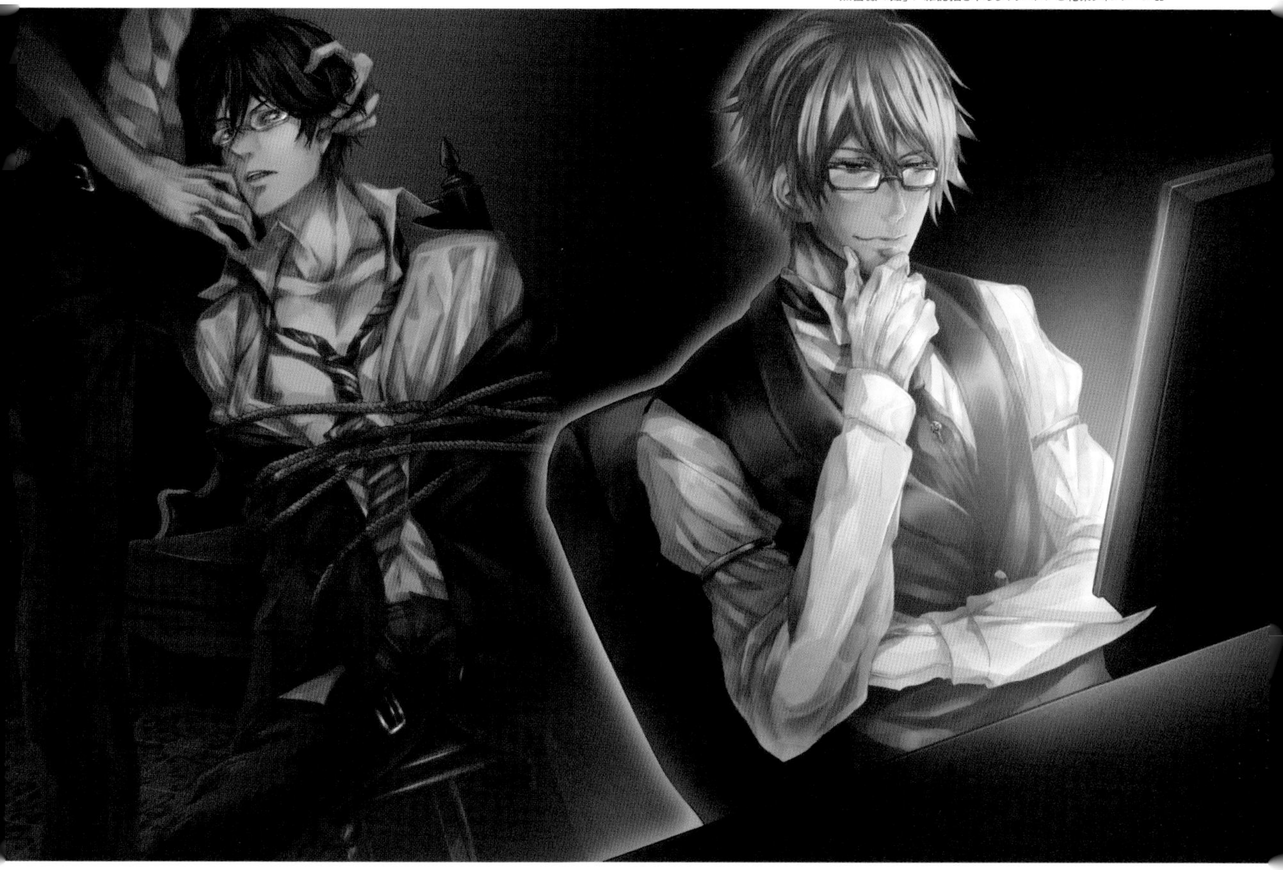

じゃのめ

jyanome

M jyanome4162@gmail.com
T jyanome29
U http://jyanome29.tumblr.com
D ComicStudio EX 4.0 ● Photoshop CC

Profile

2012年「笑い話のようだ」(ふゅーじょんぷろだくと刊)でデビュー。既刊に「キライの恋人」「カラフルな君とモノクロな僕」(幻冬舎コミックス刊)2015年現在は角川CIEL、幻冬舎コミックスリンクスなどで連載中。BL漫画を中心に色んな漫画を描きたいです。

I debuted in 2012 with *Warai-banashi no Yo Da* by Fusion Product publishers. My earlier work includes *Kirai no Koibito and Colorful na Kimi to Monokuro na Boku* by Gentosha Comics. In 2015, I began working on serial stories for, among others, CIEL (KADOKAWA publishers) and LYNX (by Gentosha Comics). I draw various types of manga, but primarily BL comics.

Comments

ちょっとだけ、かっこ悪くて変わってる男子を、描きたいと心がけています。カラーイラストは、物語を感じてもらえるように気をつけています。良かったら漫画も読んでもらえると嬉しいです。

I concentrate on drawing sort of strange and unattractive males. I'm trying to let readers sense a storyline from my color illustrations. I will be pleased if people decide to have a look at my manga.

「カラフルな君とモノクロな僕」じゃのめ / 初出・雑誌リンクス 2014年 5月号　巻頭カラーイラスト / 幻冬舎コミックス　©JYANOME, GENTOSHA COMICS 2014

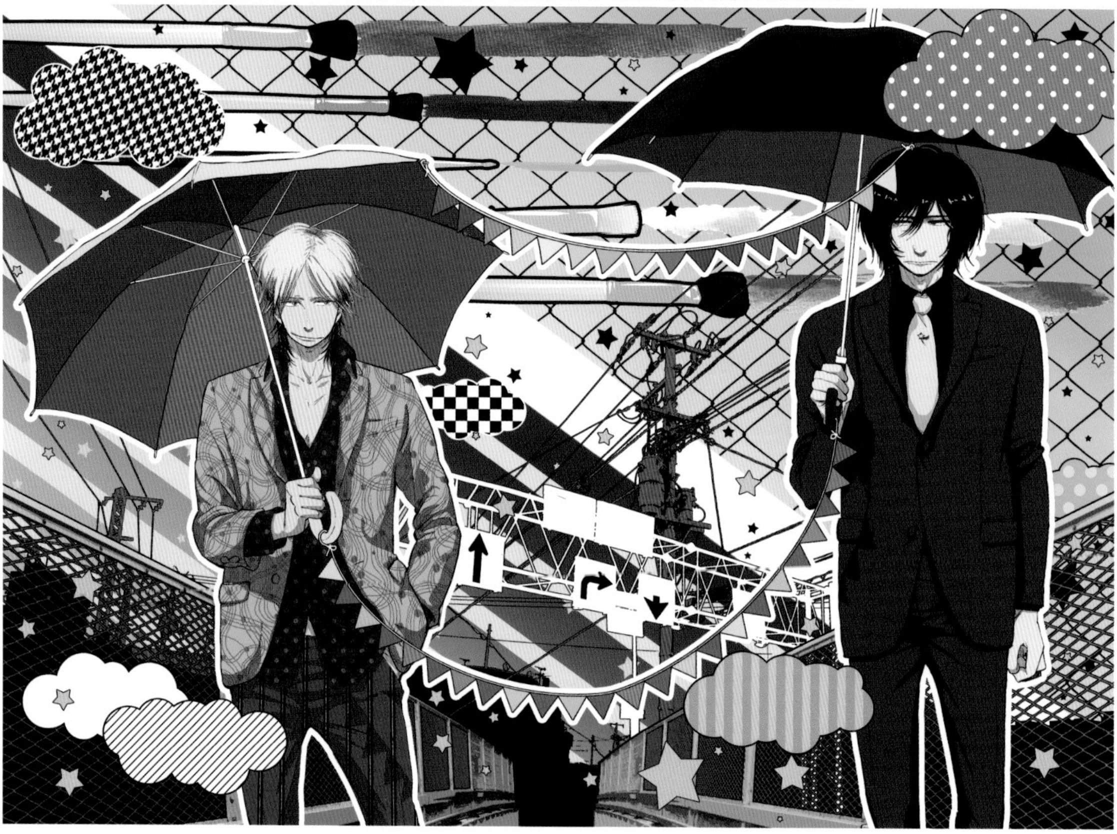

「カラフルな君とモノクロな僕」じゃのめ / カバーイラスト
幻冬舎コミックス　©JYANOME, GENTOSHA COMICS 2014

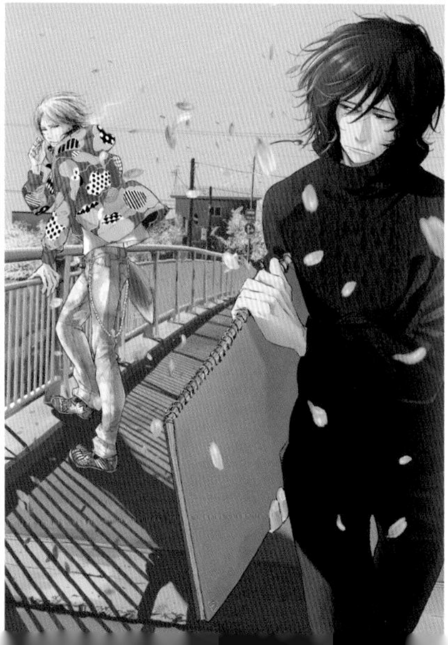

「無敵すぎるマイラバー」じゃのめ / 初出・JUNK!BOY 2015年はるやすみ号
作品扉イラスト / リブレ出版　©Jyanome ©Libre Publishing2015

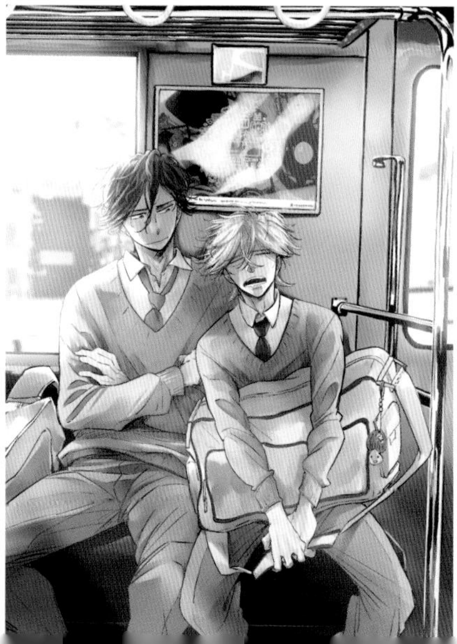

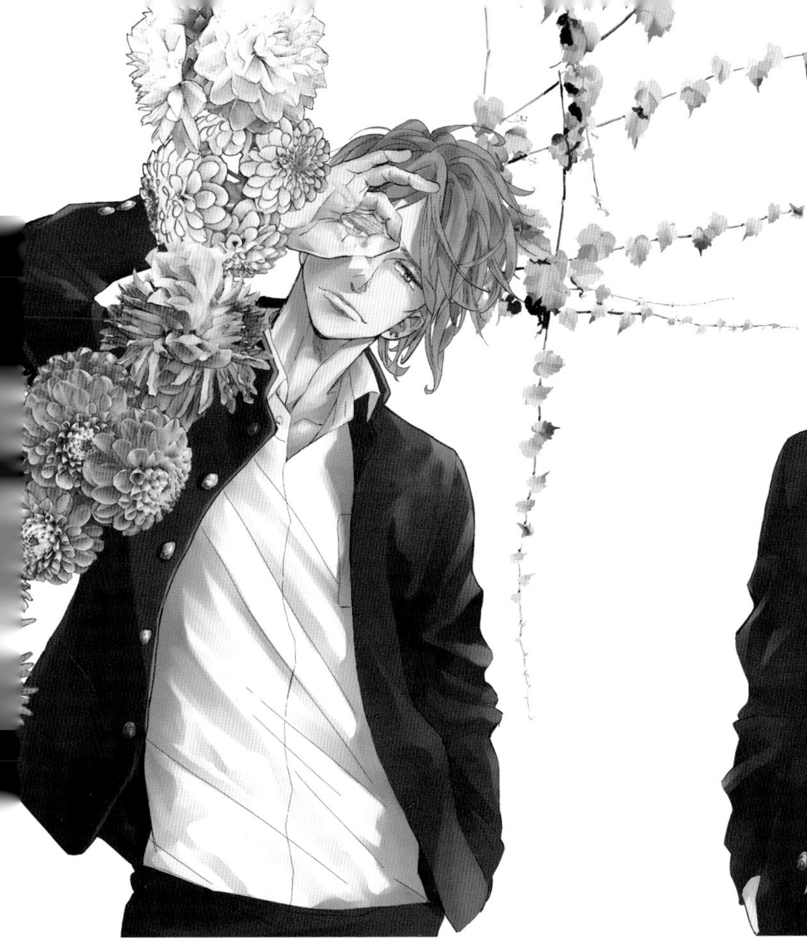

「曲がり角に、犬」じゃのめ / 初出・雑誌リンクス 2015年 7月号 巻頭カラーイラスト / 幻冬舎コミックス
©JYANOME, GENTOSHA COMICS 2015

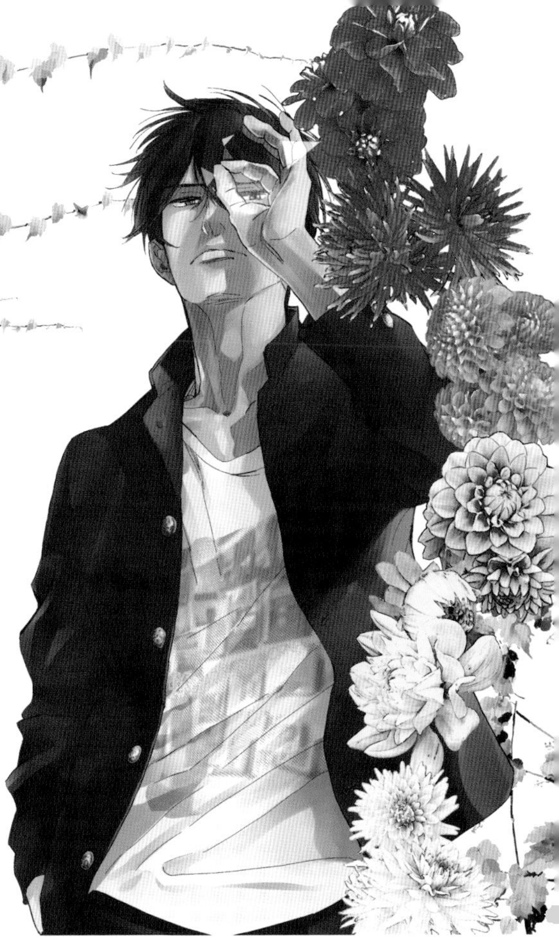

「キライの恋人」じゃのめ / カバーイラスト / 幻冬舎コミックス
©JYANOME, GENTOSHA COMICS 2013

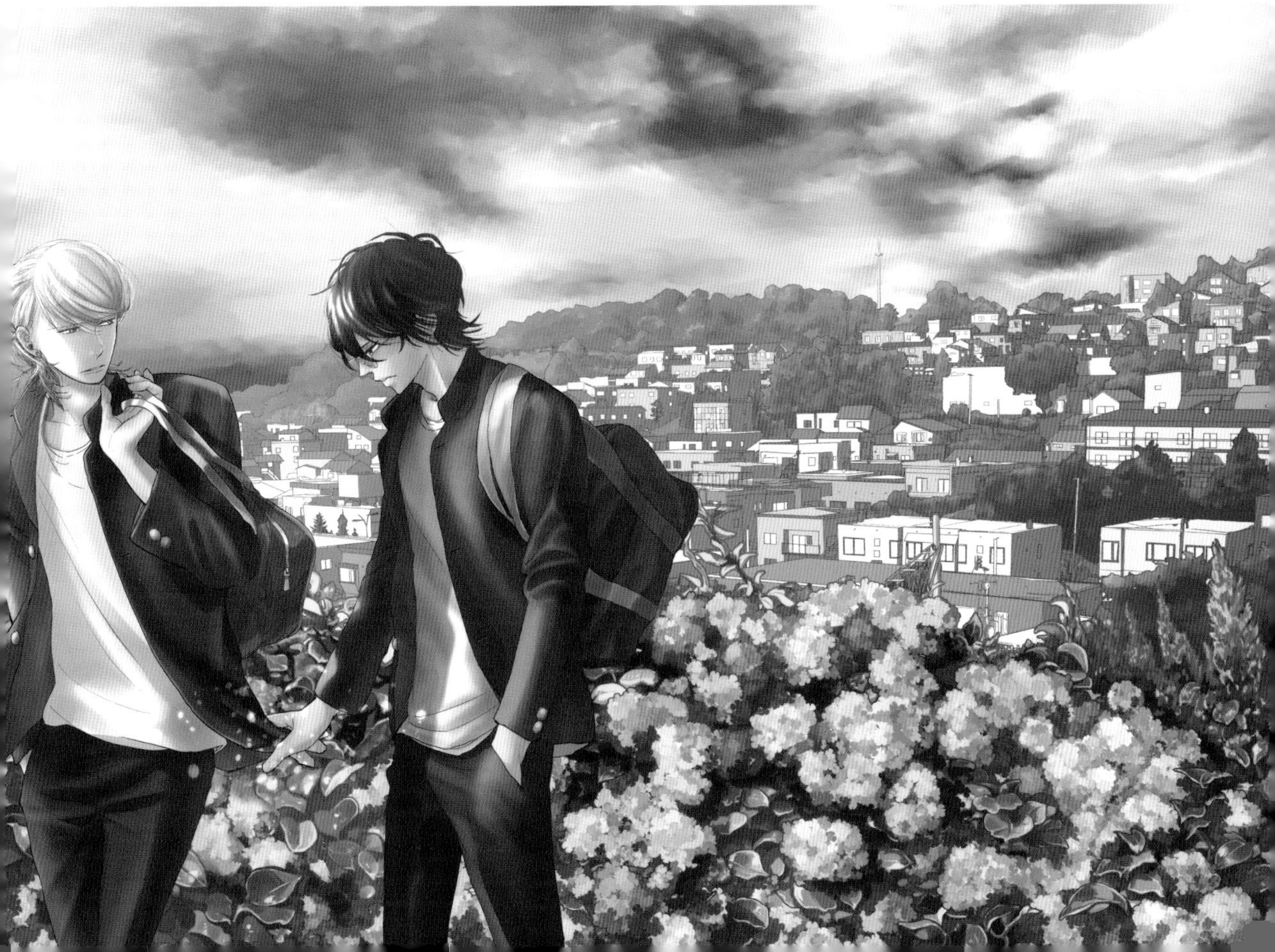

SHOOWA

M ---
T shoowa
U http://yaplog.jp/monimonika
D ComicStudio ● SAI ● Watercolors ● Mechanical pencil ● Dip pen ● Ballpointing pen

Profile

2005年芳文社よりデビュー。現在BL漫画家。

I debuted in 2005 with Hobunsha publishers. I am currently a BL manga artist.

Comments

商用イラストはきっちり塗ったデジタルカラーが多いですが、本来の描き方と塗り方は、デジタルアナログ共にラフな線画と水彩塗りです。ツイッターなどのぞいていただけると分かります。よろしくお願いします。

Commercial illustration usually requires neatly applied digital color, but my style of drawing and coloring involve both digital and analog methods, resulting in rather rough line drawings enhanced with watercolors. You can get an idea of my style by having a look at my Twitter posts.

Personal Work「cafe」©SHOOWA

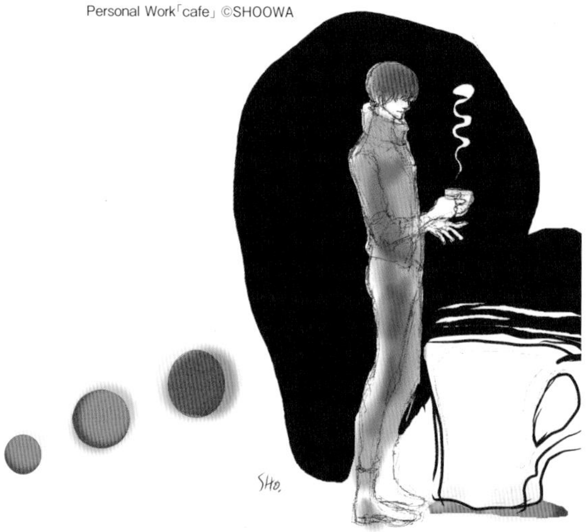
SHO.

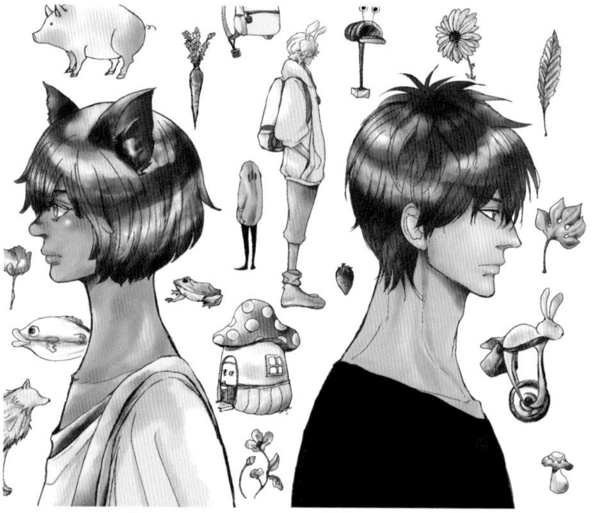

「ニィーニの森」SHOOWA / カバーイラスト ©SHOOWA / 祥伝社 onBLUE comics

「パパ'sアサシン。～ダニエルは飛んでゆく。～」SHOOWA / カバーイラスト ©SHOOWA / 大洋図書

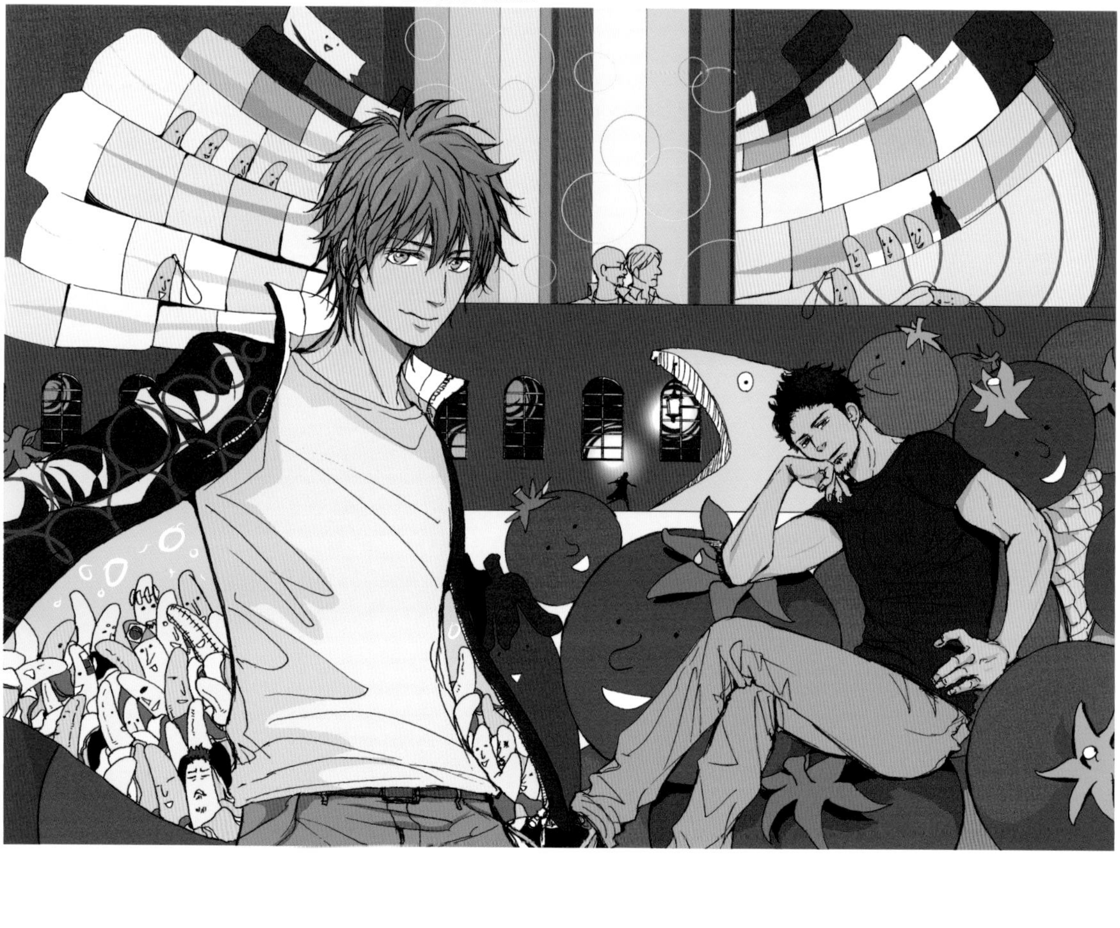

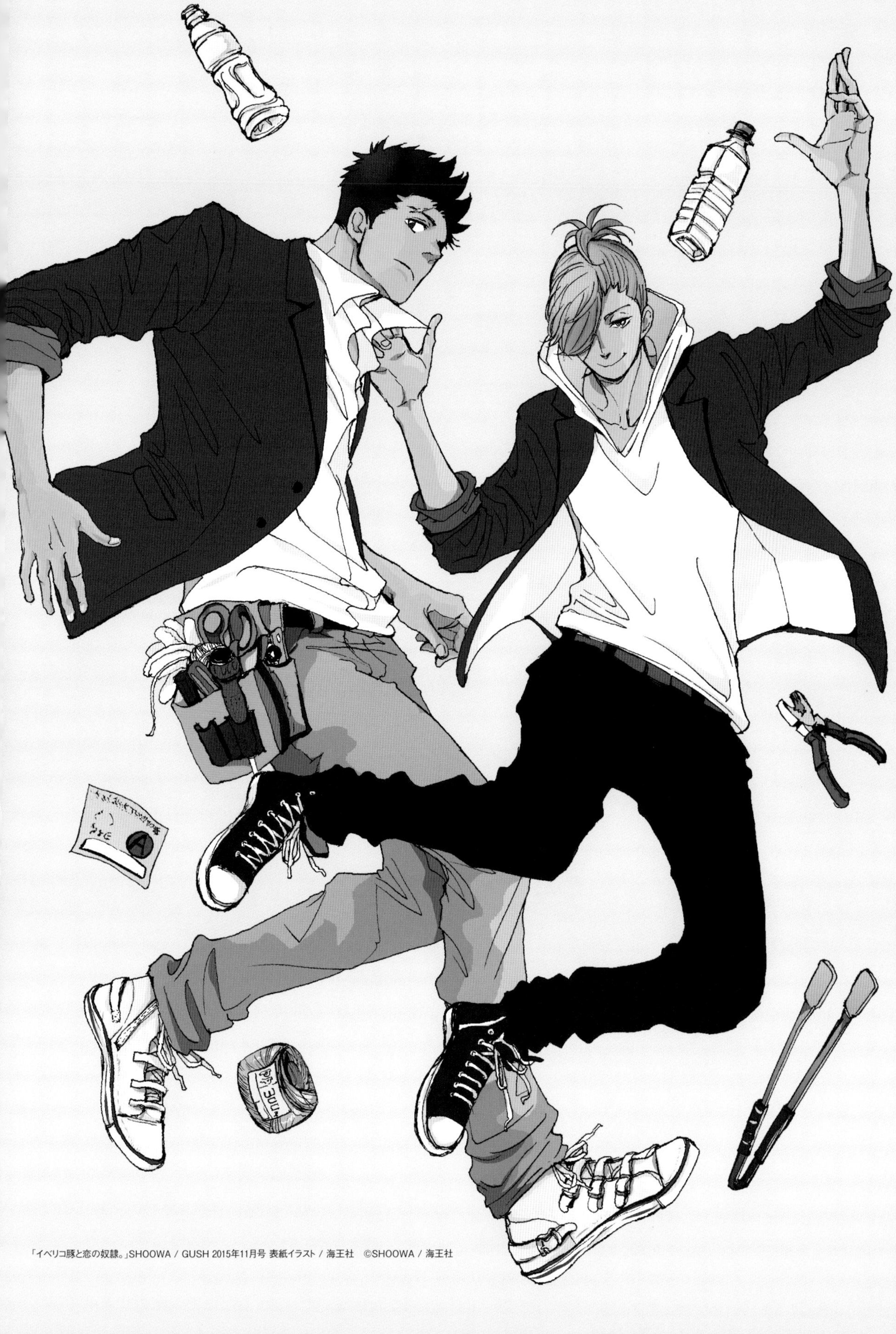

「イベリコ豚と恋の奴隷。」SHOOWA / GUSH 2015年11月号 表紙イラスト / 海王社

しろま(花梨エンターテイメント)

Shiroma (Karin entertainment)

M info@karin-e.jp
U http://460.boo.jp
T _460_
D SAI ● Photoshop 7, CS2

Profile

花梨エンターテイメント所属イラストレーター、グラフィッカー。書籍のイラストや乙女ゲームのキャラクターデザイン・原画を務める。しばしば"上品な絵柄"との評価を受ける、可愛い女の子と筋肉質な男性を描くのが好きな人。紅茶とアクションゲームが大好き。

I'm an illustrator and computer game artist associated with Karin entertainment. I work on book illustrations along with character designs and still pictures for games aimed at the female market. I enjoy drawing cute girls and muscular males, and am often praised for my elegant designs. I like to drink English tea and play action games.

Comments

男性は男性らしく、女性は女性らしくを心がけています。キャラクターデザイン時には個性が出るように、目の描き方や唇の厚さ、眉の形などに変化を付け、性格もそこから読み取れるように心がけています。アピールポイントは手。立体感を意識して、表情をつけながら描くのが好きです。その手も男性らしさ、女性らしさを意識しています。

I focus on making my male characters manly and my females feminine. In my character design work, I concentrate on variations in eyes, lip thickness, eyebrow shape, and the like as ways my readers can note individual character personalities. Hands are key. I enjoy keeping three-dimensionality in mind when drawing, along with adding expressiveness. I'm always keenly aware of whether I'm drawing masculine or feminine hands.

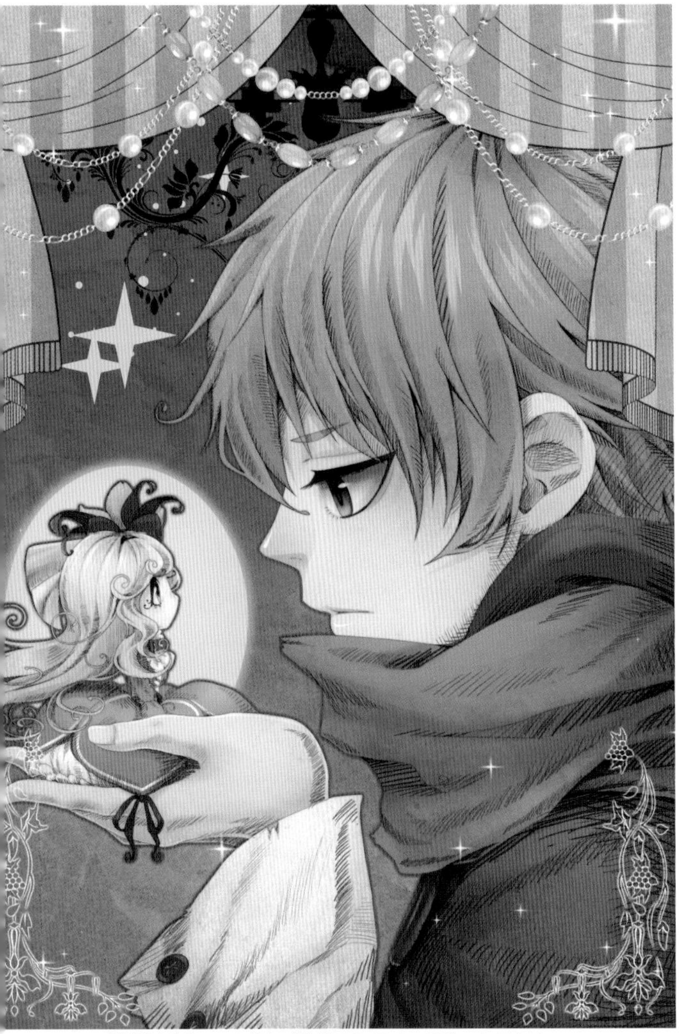

「絶対迷宮 秘密のおやゆび姫」/ 雑誌描き下ろしイラスト / ©花梨エンターテイメント

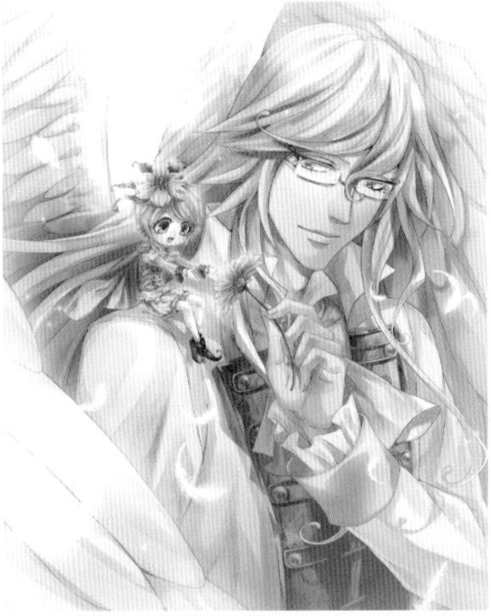

「絶対迷宮 秘密のおやゆび姫」/ 雑誌描き下ろしイラスト
©花梨エンターテイメント

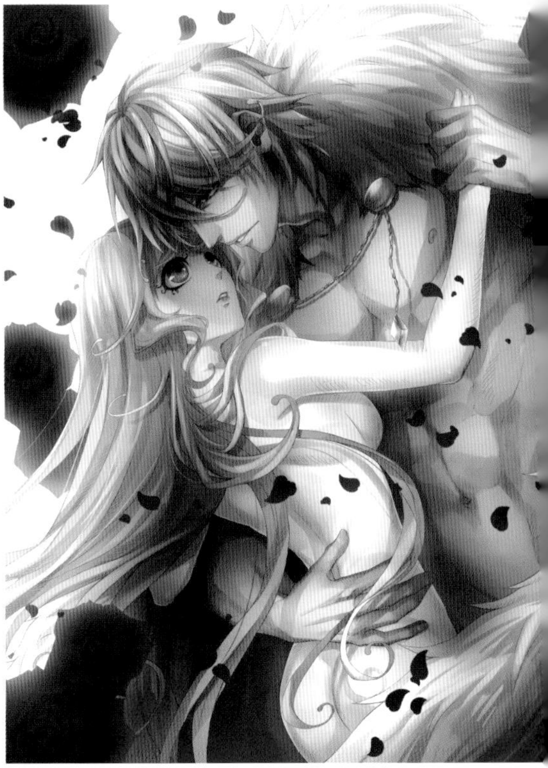

「絶対迷宮 秘密のおやゆび姫」/ 雑誌描き下ろしイラスト / ©花梨エンターテイメント

「絶対迷宮 秘密のおやゆび姫」/ 描き下ろし店舗特典イラスト / ©花梨エンターテイメント

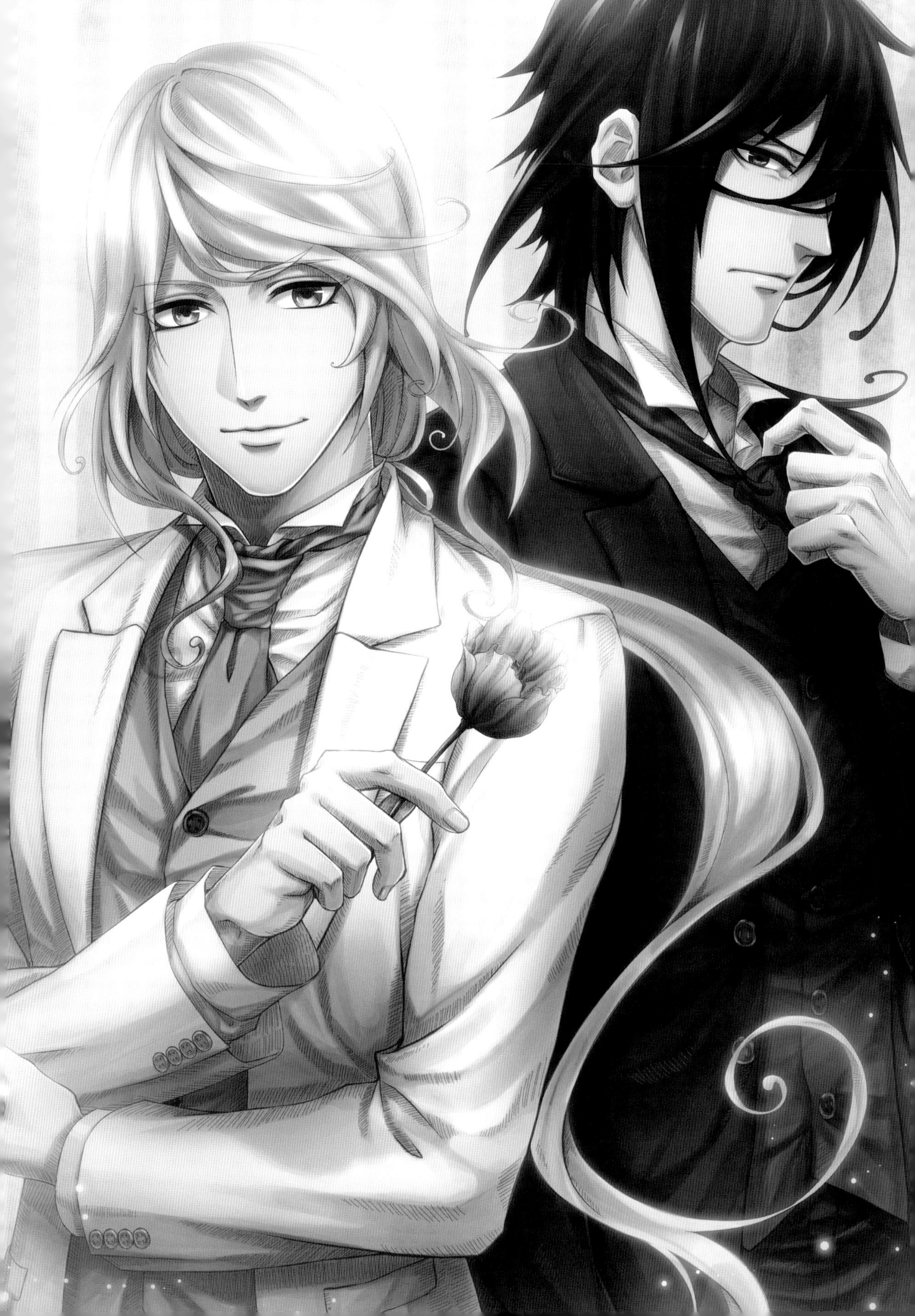

鈴木次郎
SUZUKI JIRO

M kokutoumami@gmail.com
U http://ameblo.jp/jirosuzuki
T jirosuzuki
D CLIP STUDIO PAINT ● Photoshop

Profile	東京都在住。主に漫画家ですが、イラストレーターとしてもお仕事を頂いています。最近の関連作品は月刊「Gファンタジー」にて「学園K」原作GoRA・GoHands(スクウェア・エニックス)、「刀剣乱舞-ONLINE-」(DMMゲームズ／ニトロプラス)等	I live in Tokyo. I'm fundamentally a manga artist, but I also work as an illustrator. My recent efforts include *Gakuen K* for the monthly *G Fantasy* (original work by GoRA / GoHands, Square Enix) and *Toukenranbu -ONLINE-* (DMM Games / Nitroplus).
Comments	なんとなく描く、という事をしないよう、自身が楽しみつつ、キャラクターの表情がいきいきするようにいつも心がけてます。	I try to draw with focus, enjoying what I do and keeping my characters' expressions buoyant.

「学園K」漫画:鈴木次郎 ストーリー原作:鈴木鈴(GoRA) 原作:GoRA・GoHands
月刊「Gファンタジー」2014年8号付録B3ポスター／スクウェア・エニックス
©GoRA・GoHands／k-project ©JIRO SUZUKI / SQUARE ENIX

「刀剣乱舞-ONLINE-」
キャラクターイラスト ©2015 DMMゲームズ/Nitroplus

「まじかる無双天使 突き刺せ!! 呂布子ちゃん」
鈴木次郎／8巻カバーイラスト／スクウェア・エニックス
©JIRO SUZUKI / SQUARE ENIX

「拡散性ミリオンアーサー」／カードイラスト／スクウェア・エニックス ©SQUARE ENIX

「マルタ・サギーは探偵ですか？Ⅰ ～レド・ビァ事件～」
野梨原花南 / カバーイラスト / KADOKAWA

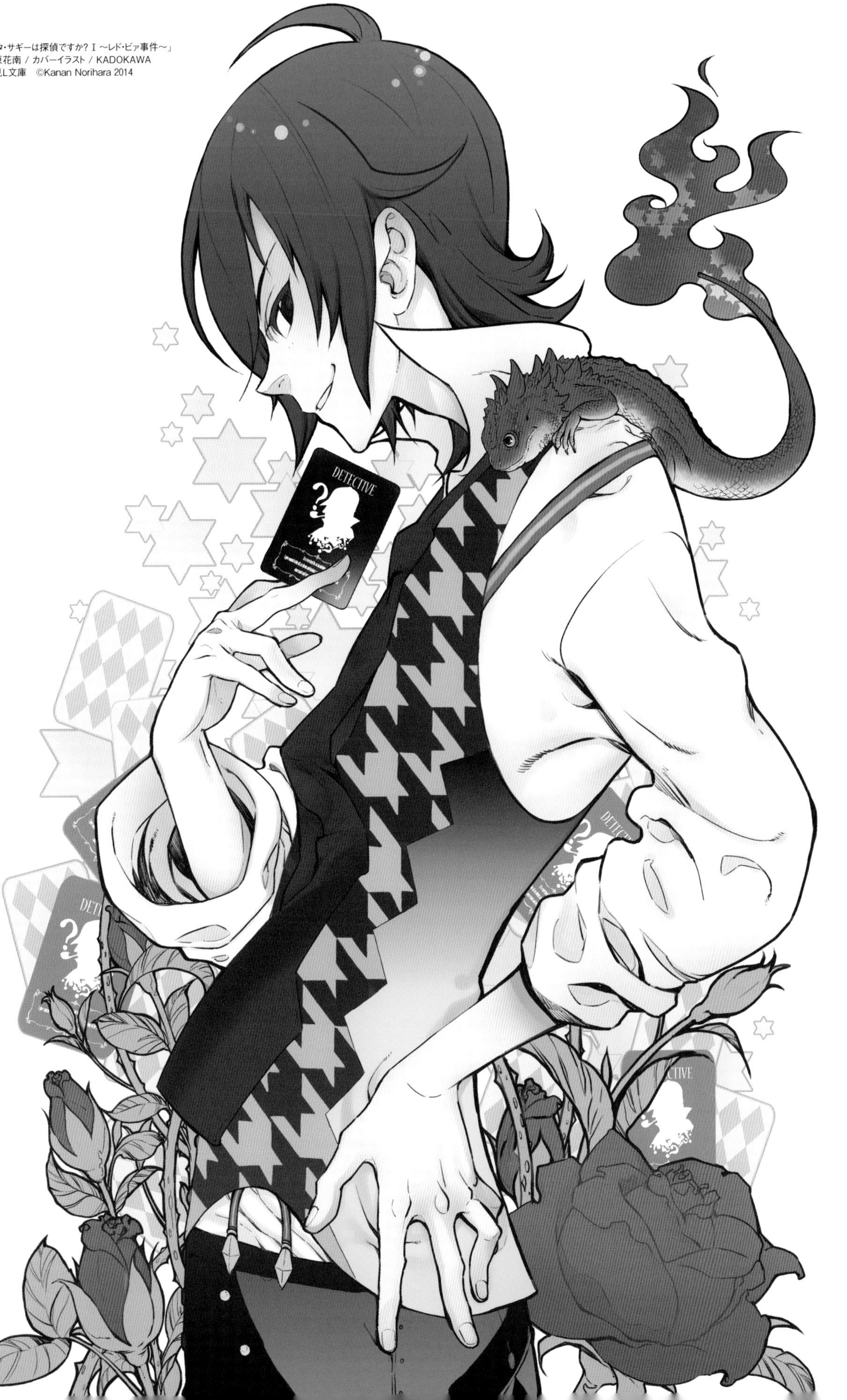
DETECTIVE
DETECTIVE
DETECTIVE
DETECTIVE

スズケン

SUZUKEN

M kaleido@zy.sub.jp
U http://kaleido.sub.jp
T ---
D Photoshop ● SAI

Profile

BL・乙女両方の原画作業をメインに、彩色業務・イラスト・マンガなど幅広く活動しております。代表作「俺の下であがけ」「三国恋戦記」「ヴァルプルガの詩」「モサモサ通信」B's-LOGにて掲載中です！

My chief work is still pictures of BL and *otome* girls, but my work covers a broad range including coloration, illustrations, and manga, among other things. My work can be seen on B's LOG, and includes: *Ore no Shita de Agake, Sangoku Rensen-ki, Walpurga no Uta*, and *Mosa-mosa Tsushin*.

Comments

できる限り表情豊かに、幅広いキャラクターをもたせられるよう心がけています。ギャップ萌えと意外性が大好きです！

I'm doing my best to create a wide range of characters and ensure that each character is very expressive. I love discrepancies and unpredictability in characters.

とらのあな 冬の大感謝祭 特典イラスト ©とらのあな

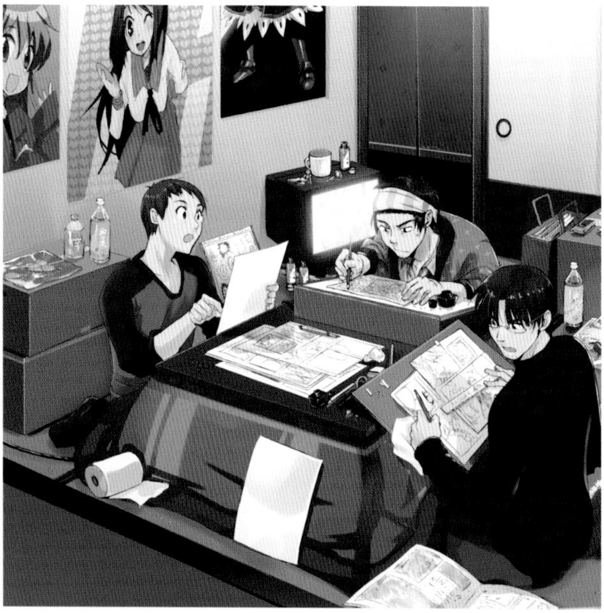

とらのあな C83カタログ 特典イラスト ©とらのあな

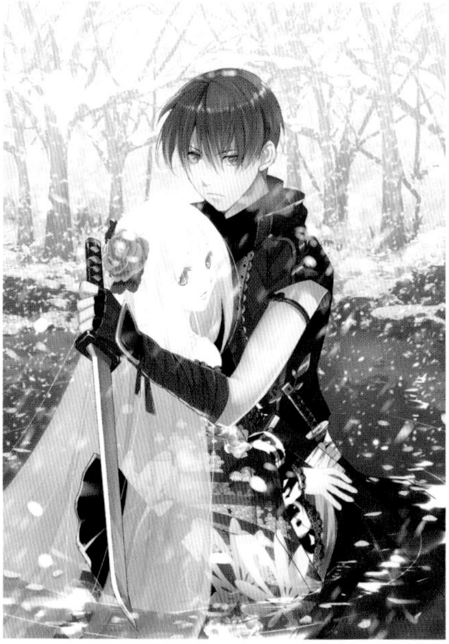

「ヴァルプルガの詩」/ 雑誌掲載イラスト / 3Daisy ©3Daisy

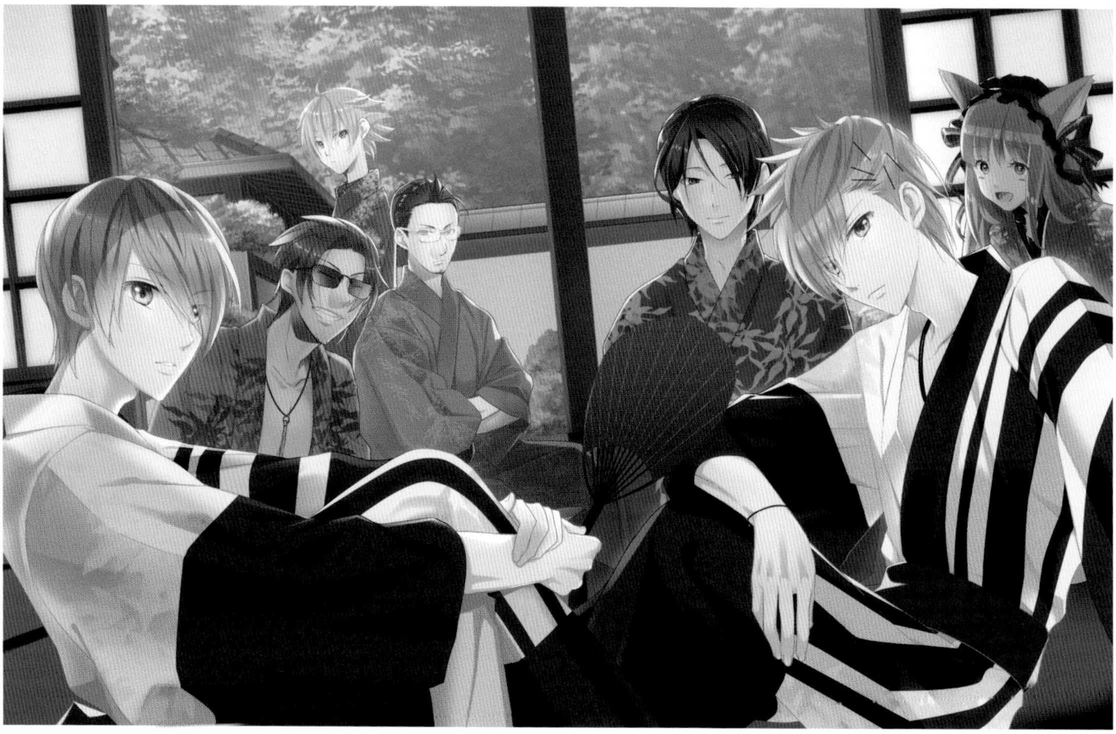

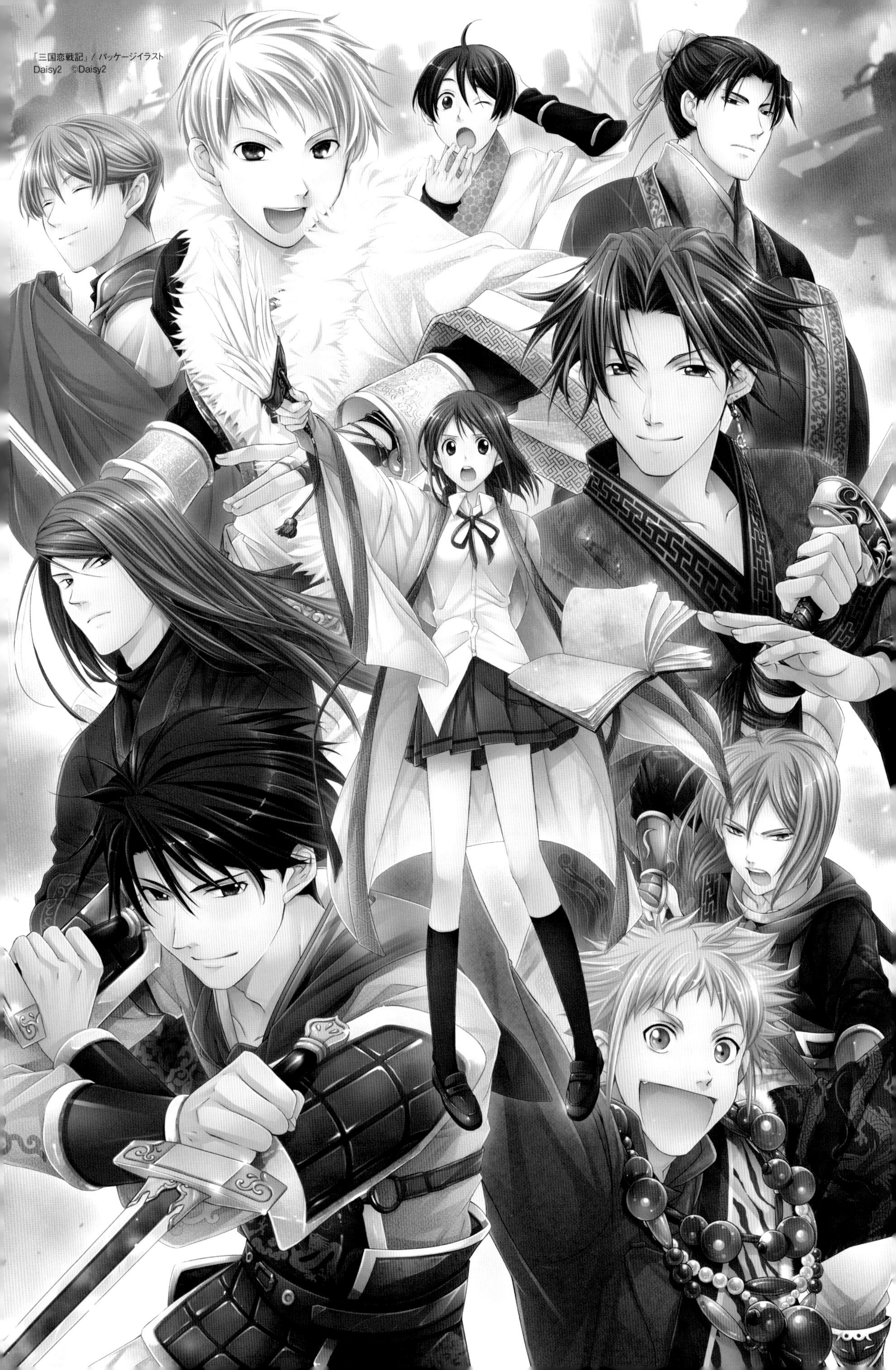
「三国恋戦記」/ パッケージイラスト
Daisy2　©Daisy2

セカイメグル

Sekai Meguru

M elevatedrailroad@gmail.com

U http://elevatedrailroad.tumblr.com

T sekamegu

D CLIP STUDIO PAINT EX ● Photoshop CS6

Profile	九州出身の田舎育ちです。小説の挿絵などを描いています。
	I was born in Kyushu and reared in a rural area. I do book illustrations and other similar work.
Comments	絵の中にある物語や雰囲気を感じ取っていただけるようにと心がけています。人物が何を思っているかなどの表情、周りの空気感などを大切にしています。 背景を描くことやキャラクターデザインなど、とても好きです。
	I try to let readers pick up on the atmosphere of the story from drawings. Among the things I find important are the expressions revealing characters' thoughts and the surrounding atmosphere. I love drawing backgrounds and designing characters.

Personal Work

Personal Work

Personal Work

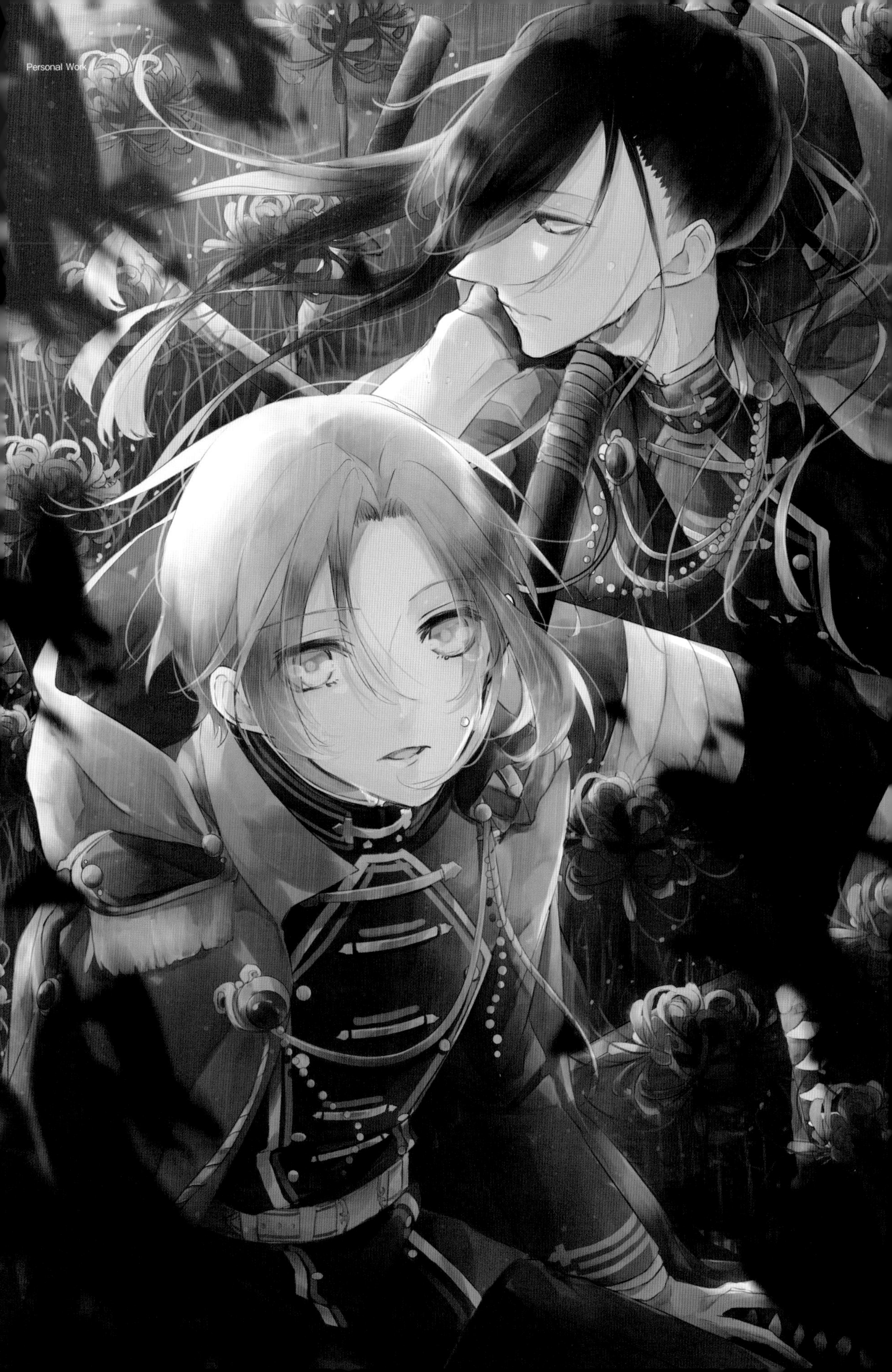

serori

Ⓜ tomato22000@yahoo.co.jp
Ⓤ http://sero2.tumblr.com
Ⓣ serori0000000
Ⓓ SAI ● Photoshop CS5 ● Illustrator CS5

Profile

2012年より書籍の表紙や挿画、ＣＤジャケット、キャラクターデザインを中心に活動しております。「ぼくらは虚空に夜を視る」上遠野浩平/ 星海社、「CeVIO Creative Studio タカハシ」、「ハーレクインキャストノベル朗読ＣＤ」など。

Since 2012, I have worked mainly on book covers and illustrations, CD jackets, and character design. My efforts have included *Bokura wa Kokuu ni Yoru wo Miru* by Kouhei Kadono for Seikaisha publishers, the *Takahashi character for CeVIO Creative Studio*, and *Harlequin Cast* audio books on CDs.

Comments

キャラクターの生き様や物語を感じるイラストを心がけています。描く前に、何を伝えたいのか、自分の中でハッキリするまで考えたり、担当さんと話し合いをすることが多いです。誠実に絵と向き合い、良いと思うものを世に表現していけたら、と思います。

I try to illustrate so that viewers can feel the character's lifestyle and personal story. Before embarking on the illustration, I often spend time thinking, trying to clarify what I wish to communicate, and I also consult with the client. My aim is faithful production of expressive work which I myself feel is good.

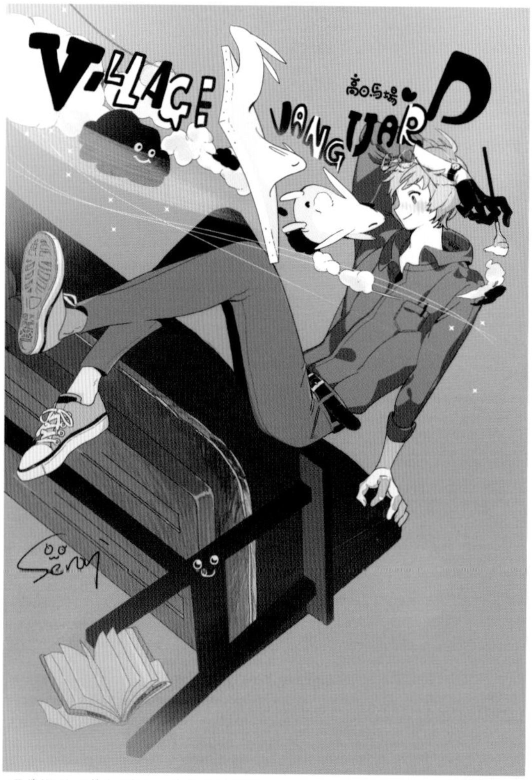
VANGUARD

コラボイラスト / ヴィレッジヴァンガード 高田馬場店

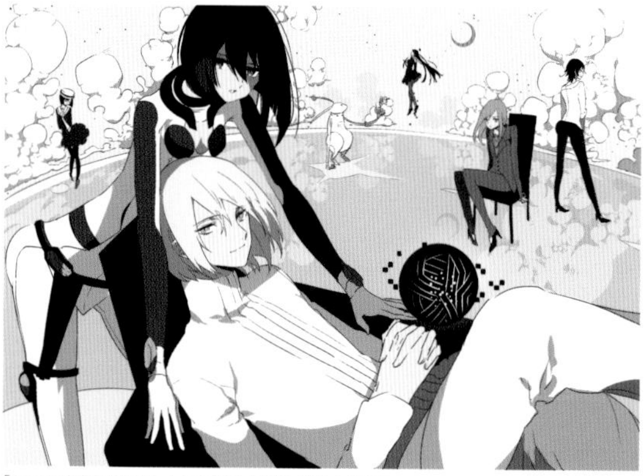

「わたしは虚夢に月を聴く」上遠野浩平 / 表紙・挿画 / 星海社

「あなたは虚人と星に舞う」上遠野浩平
表紙・挿画 / 星海社

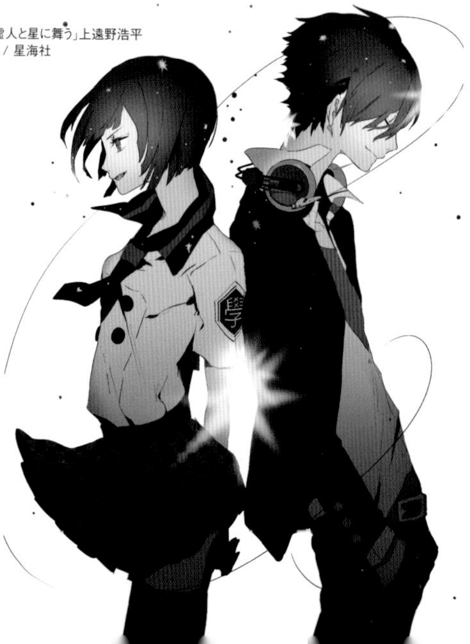

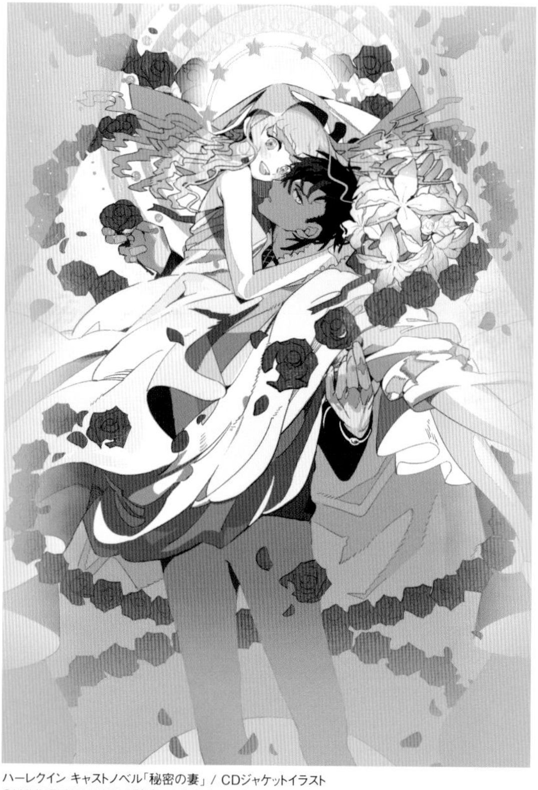

ハーレクイン キャストノベル「秘密の妻」/ CDジャケットイラスト
©LYNNE GRAHAM / 読広エンタテインメント

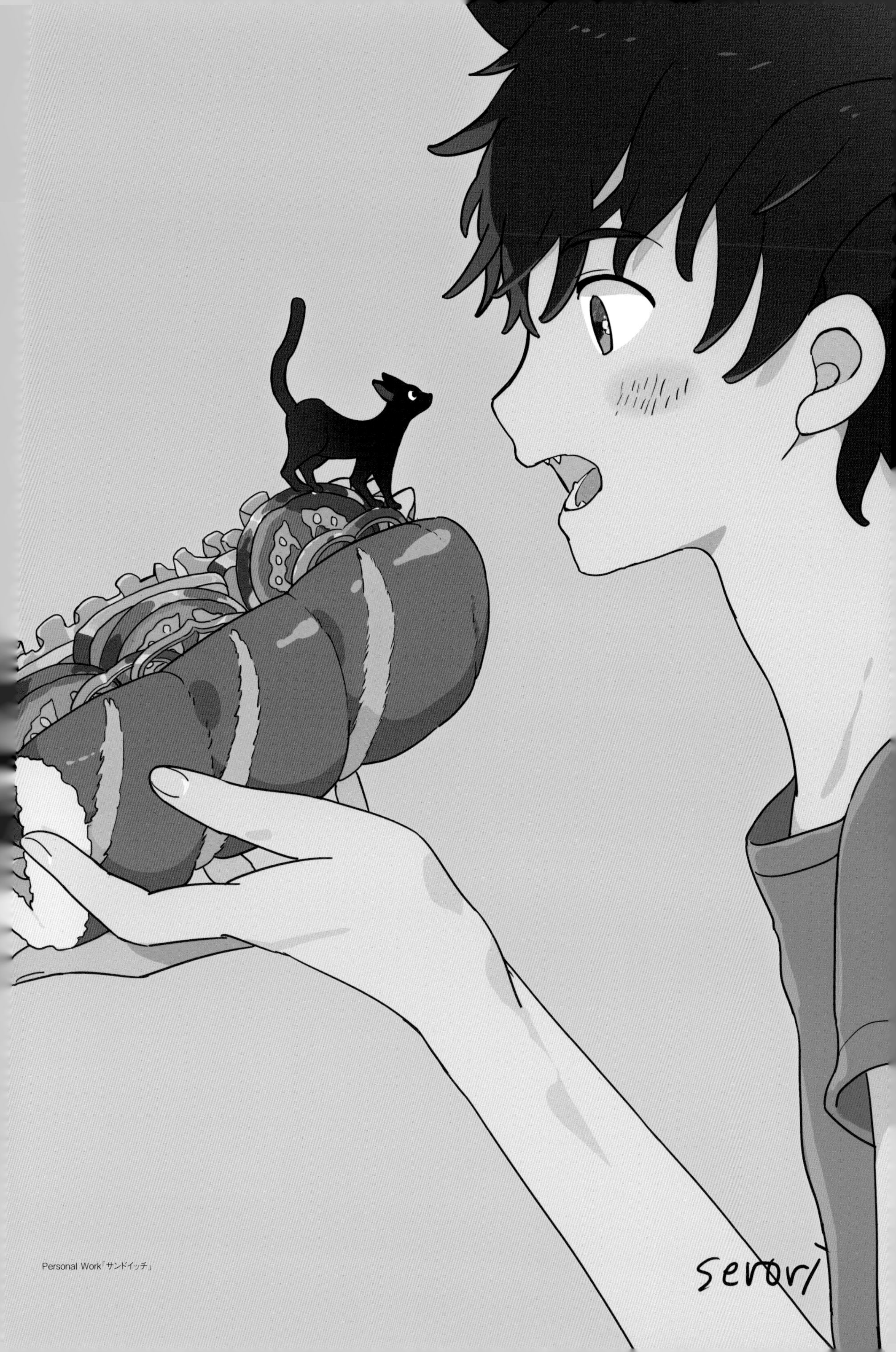
serori

Personal Work「サンドイッチ」

先崎真琴

Senzaki Makoto

Ⓜ http://senzakimakoto.com/contact
Ⓤ http://senzakimakoto.com
Ⓣ senzakimakoto
Ⓓ Photoshop ● SAI

Profile

ときめきメモリアルGirl'sSideシリーズに携わり『ときめきレストラン☆☆☆』でキャラクターデザイン・イラストを担当。2015年1月コナミを退社。フリーランスとなった現在は、同タイトルと『コンビニカレシ』を平行して担当中。

I worked on character designs for *Tokimeki Restaurant*☆☆☆, which was part of the Tokimeki Memorial Girl's Side series. I left Konami Digital Entertainment in January 2015. At present, I am a freelancer and am working simultaneously on *Tokimeki Restaurant and Konbini Kareshi*.

Comments

お客様のニーズに応えるデザインや絵作りを心がけ、リアリティある男性像を提供することを得意としています。恋愛物にこだわらず、ミステリーやファンタジー等幅広いジャンルを視野に入れ活動中です。

I keep client needs in mind when doing character designs and drawing pictures, and am skilled at offering male figures steeped in "reality." I don't limit myself to romance, but consider a wide spectrum of genre including, for example, mystery and fantasy.

「コンビニカレシ」/ キャラクター イラスト
©コンビニカレシプロジェクト

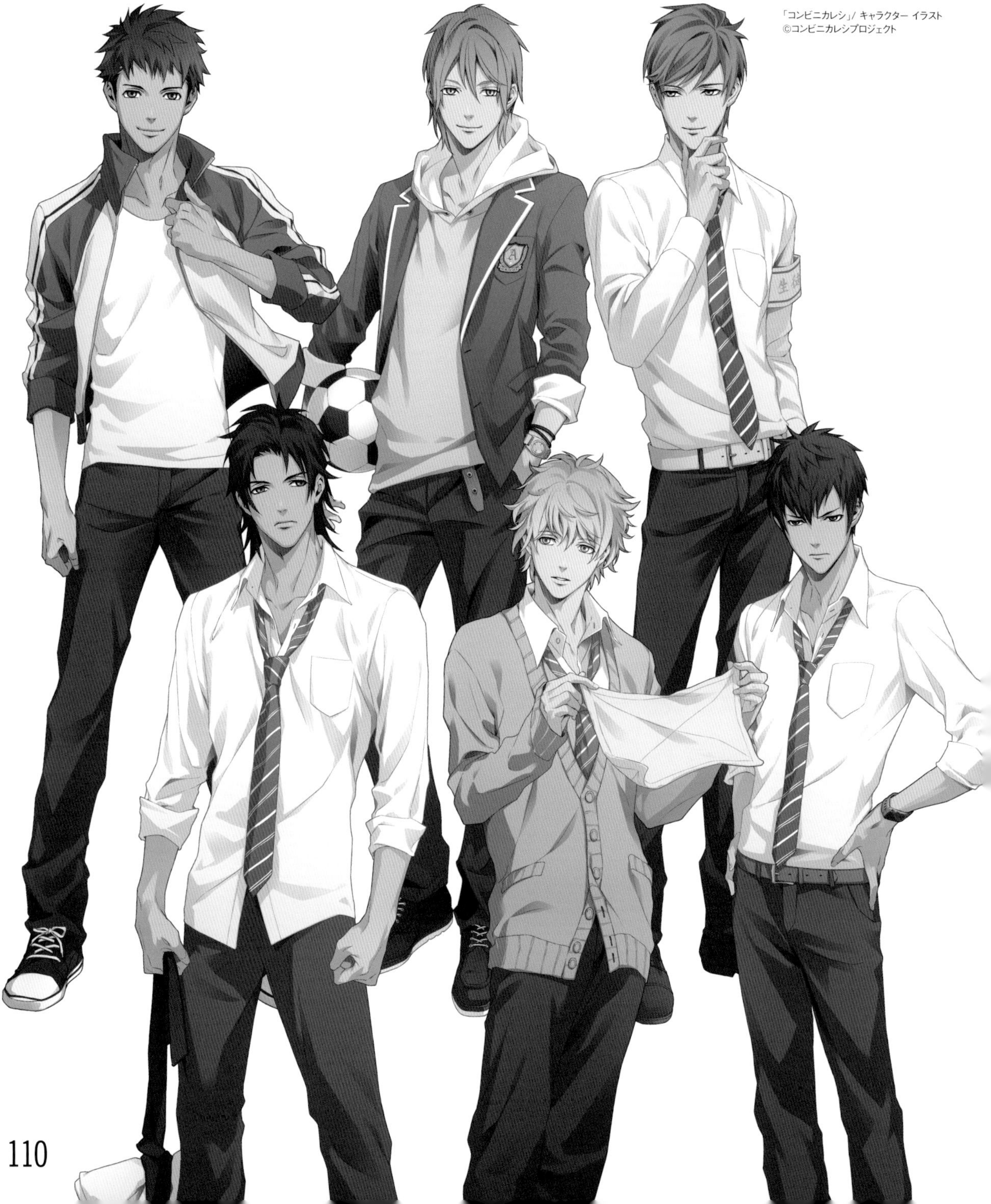

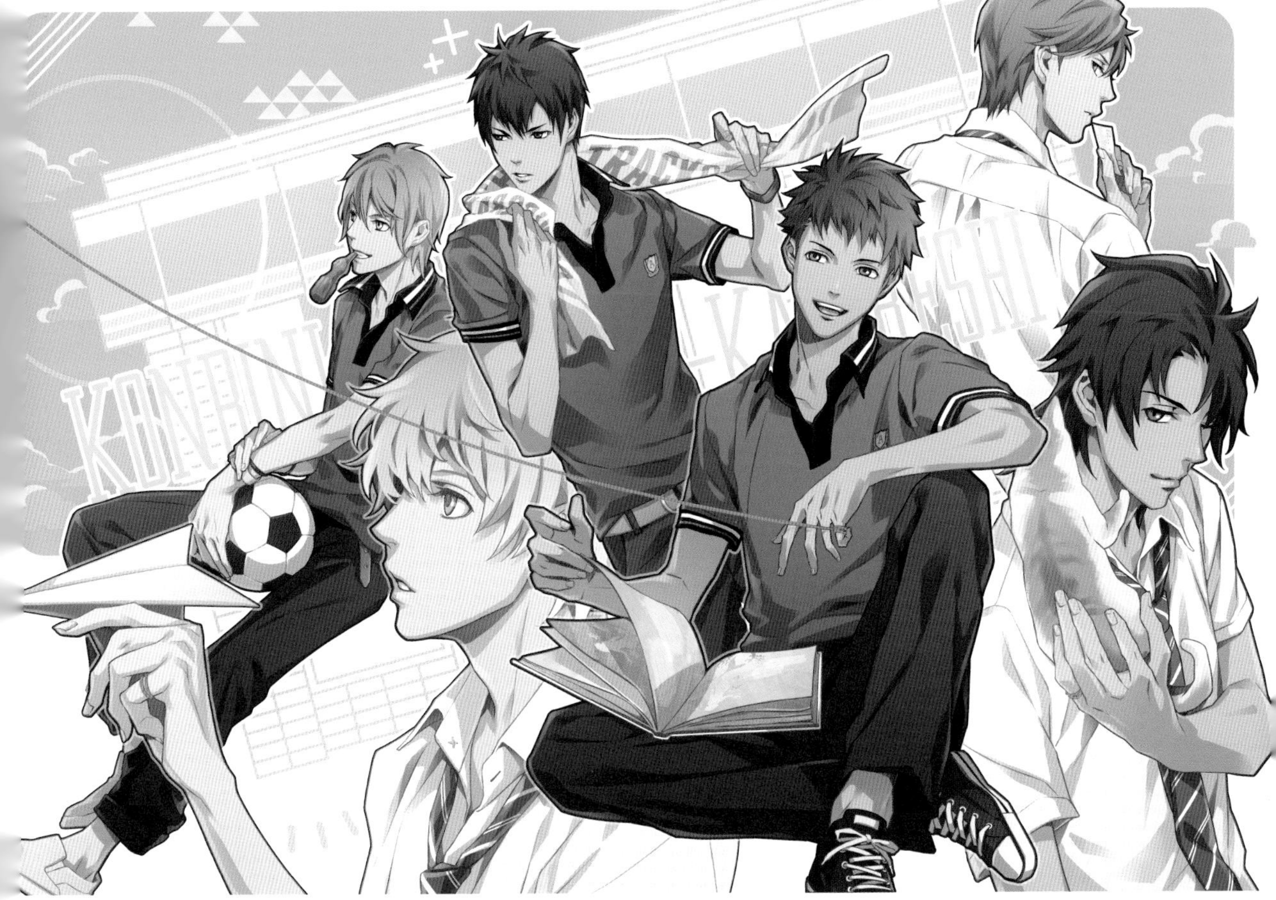

「コンビニカレシ」/ ノベル 表紙イラスト / KADOKAWA
エンターブレイン　©コンビニカレシプロジェクト

「コンビニカレシ」/ B's - LOG 2015年8月号 ピンナップ / KADOKAWA
エンターブレイン　©コンビニカレシプロジェクト

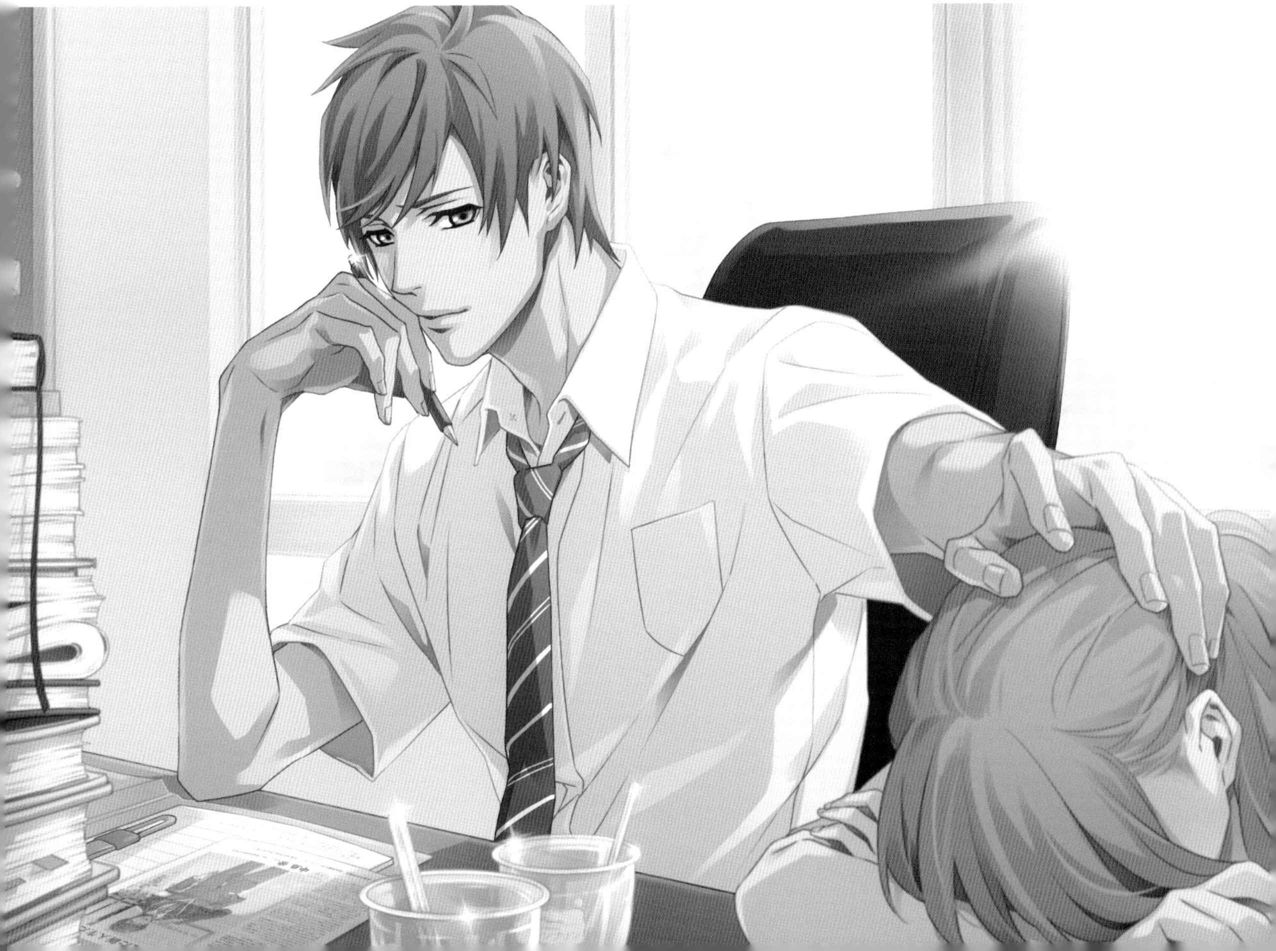

高階 佑

Takashina Yuh

M takashina.yuh@gmail.com
T kazusat
U ---
D ComicStudio 4.0 EX ● SAI

Profile

主にＢＬ小説の挿絵や漫画を描かせていただいています。英田サキ先生原作「DEADLOCK」コミカライズ連載中

I primarily illustrate BL novels and draw manga. I am currently drawing for a comic book serialization of Saki Aida's *DEADLOCK*.

Comments

男性を色っぽく描きたいと思っています。特にスーツの男性や銃を描くのが好きです。

My aim is to make my male characters sexy. I especially enjoy drawing be-suited males and guns.

小説Dear+ 2014年フユ号 カバーイラスト / 新書館 / ©Takashina Yuh ©shinshokan

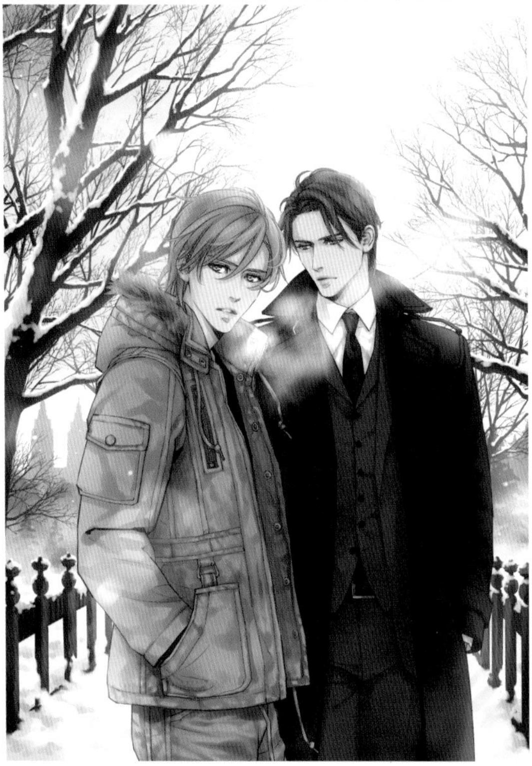

初出・小説b-Boy 2010年4月号表紙 / リブレ出版 ©Takashina Yuh Libre Publishing 2010

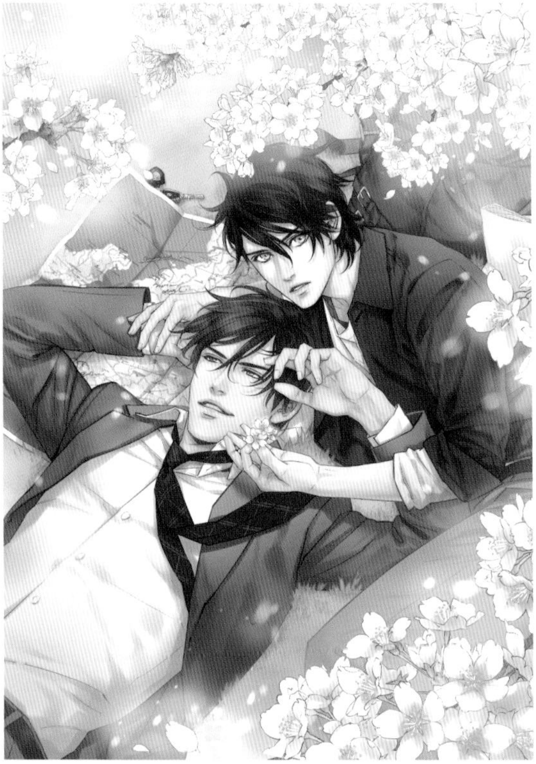

小説Dear+ 2014年ハル号 カバーイラスト / 新書館 / ©Takashina Yuh ©shinshokan

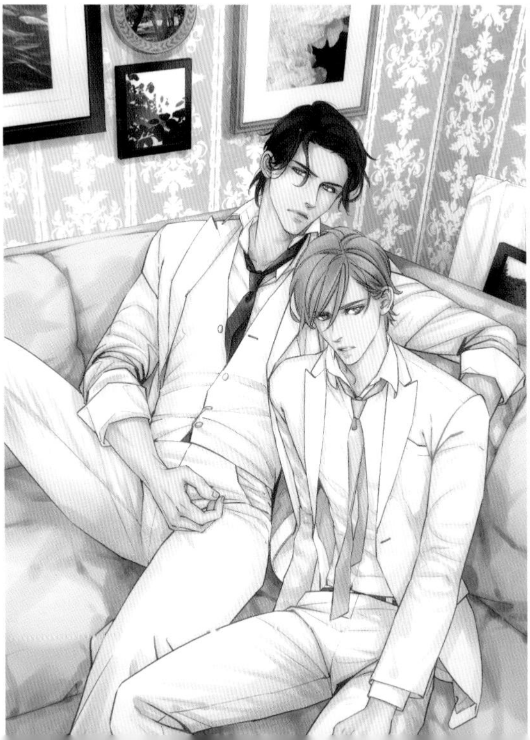

「Bule Rose」榎田尤利 / カバーイラスト / 大洋図書SHYノベルス
©Takashina Yuh ©Yuuri Eda ©Taiyo Tosho SHY Novels

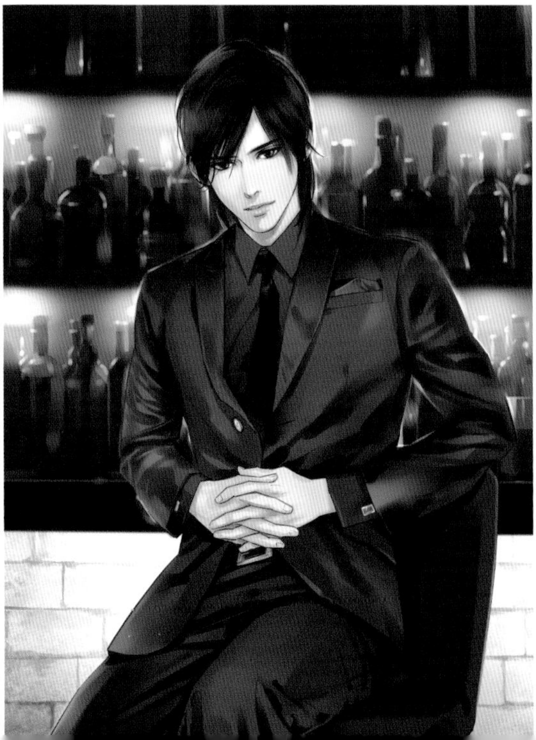

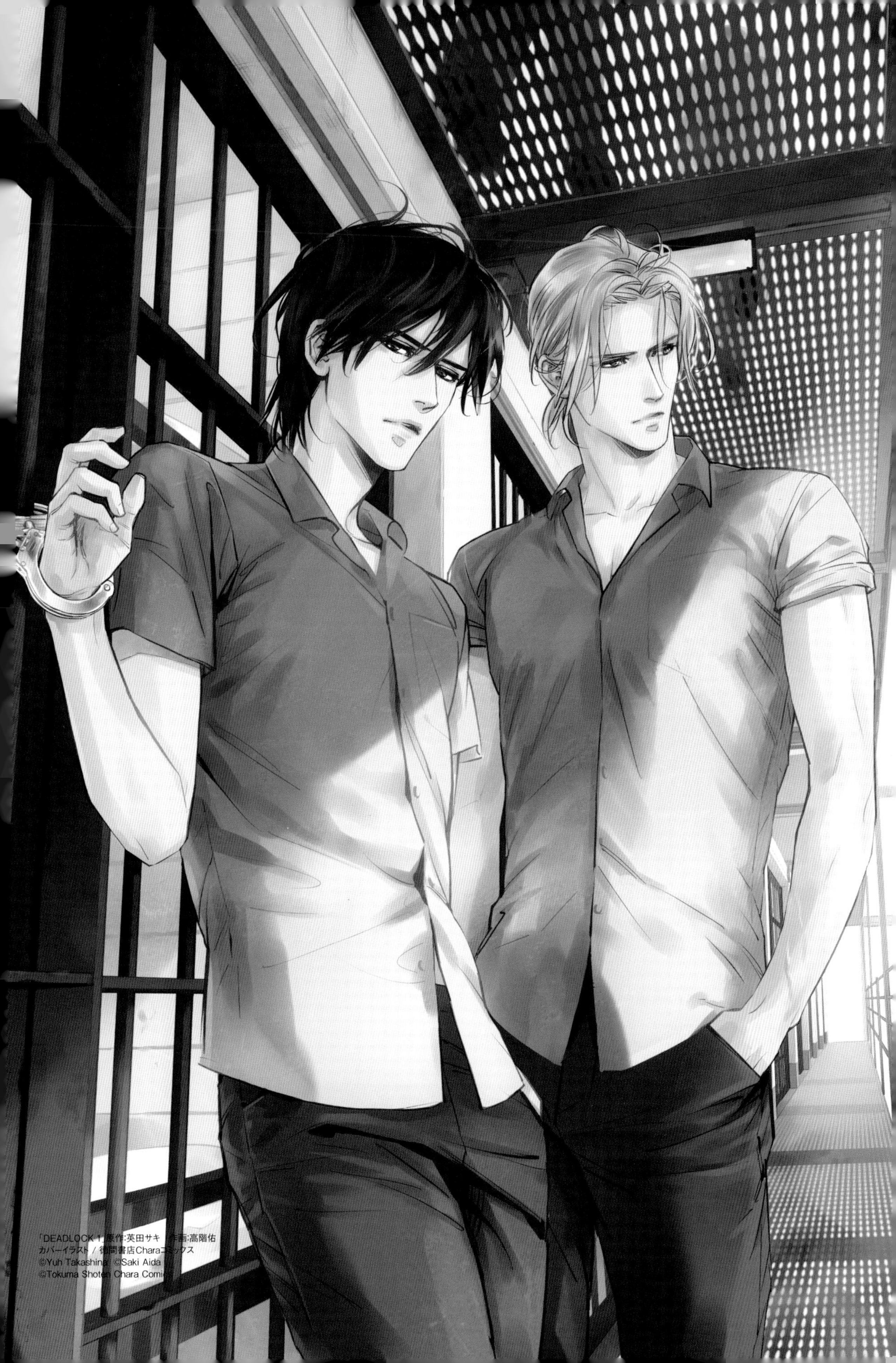
「DEADLOCK 1」原作:英田サキ 作画:高階佑
カバーイラスト / 徳間書店Charaコミックス
©Yuh Takashina ©Saki Aida
©Tokuma Shoten Chara Comics

高永ひなこ
Takanaga Hinako

Ⓜ anagura@anaguranz.com Ⓣ tkhina Ⓤ http://anaguranz.blog95.fc2.com
Ⓓ HOLBEIN DRAWING INK ● KAIMEI DRAWING SOL K ● Kabura Pen ● G Pen ● Maru Pen

Profile

1995年デビュー。主にBL漫画・BL小説の挿絵等を描いています。主な作品「恋する暴君」9巻以下続刊：連載中（海王社）、「不器用なサイレント」5巻以下続刊：連載中（リブレ出版）、「きみ恋シリーズ」全6巻「花と蝶（ひらり）」連載中（KADOKAWA）。

I began work in 1995. I mainly draw BL manga and illustrate BL novels. My main works include: *Koi Suru Bo-kun* (Volumes 1-9, serialized) by Kaiohsha publishers, *Bukiyo na Silent* (Volumes 1-5, serialized) by Libre Publishing, and *Kimi Koi* series (all 6 volumes) along with *Hana to Cho (Hirari)*, both serials published by KADOKAWA.

Comments

独りよがりにならないよう、解りやすく読みやすい漫画を心がけています。絵だけより自分は漫画込みの作風だと思っているので出来れば全体的に絵もお話もバランス良く、すべてが平均よりちょっと上、を狙いたい。

I try to remain vigilant in creating manga which are understandable and easy to read. I feel it's not only about the pictures, but also the manga's literary style, and therefore seek a balance between the two which hits just above expectations in terms of average quality.

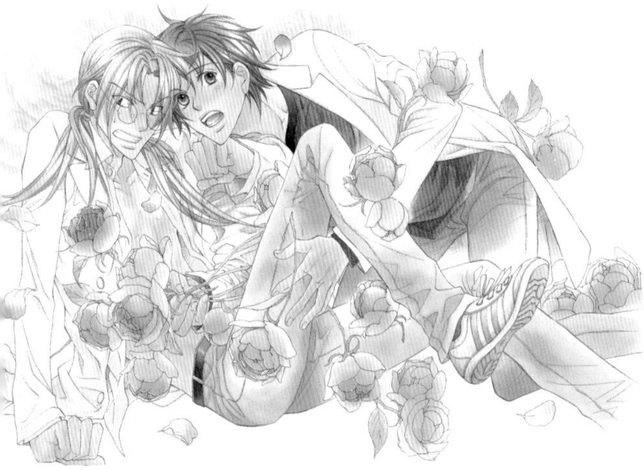

「高永ひなこイラスト集 恋する暴君」高永ひなこ / カバーイラスト / 海王社 ©高永ひなこ / 海王社

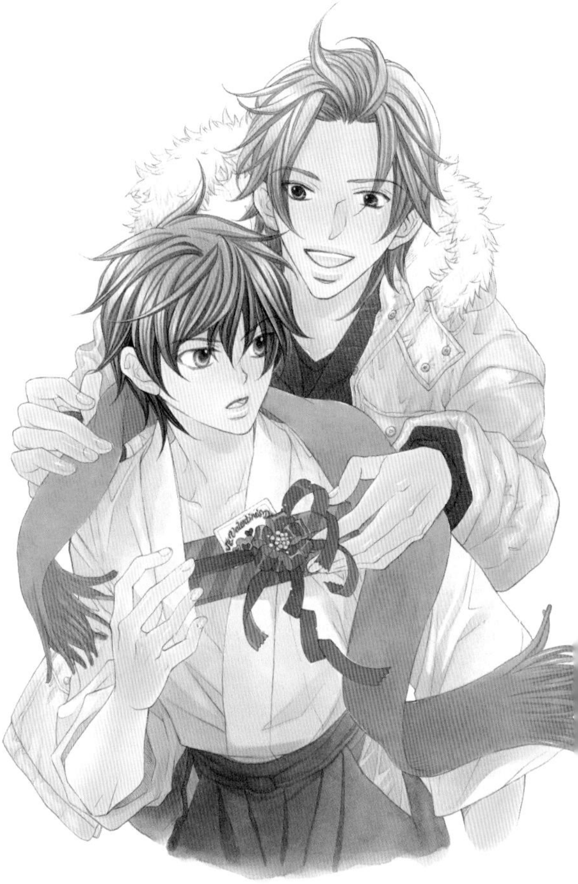

CIEL 2015年3月号 / 表紙イラスト / KADOKAWA ©KADOKAWA2015

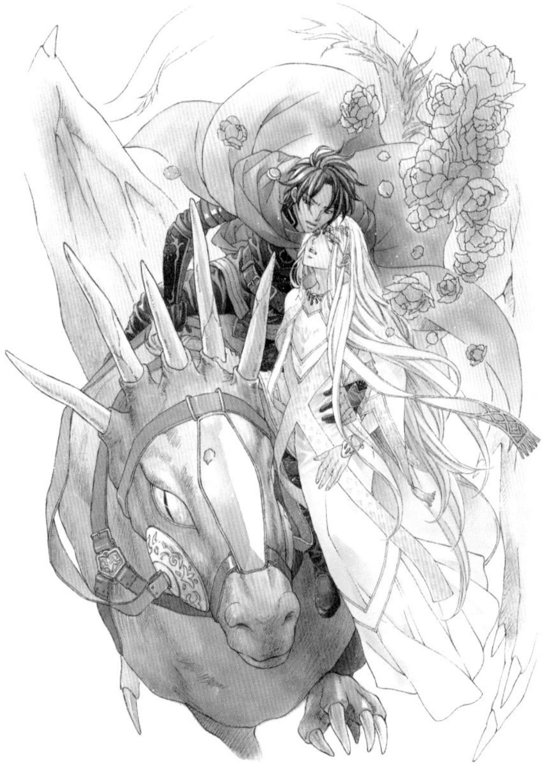

ガッシュ文庫「神官は王に操を捧ぐ」/ 吉田珠姫 / カバーイラスト
海王社 ©吉田珠姫 / 海王社

ドラマCD「有罪」/ 和泉桂 / 高永ひなこ / ジャケット / ダリアレーベル
フロンティアワークス ©フロンティアワークス

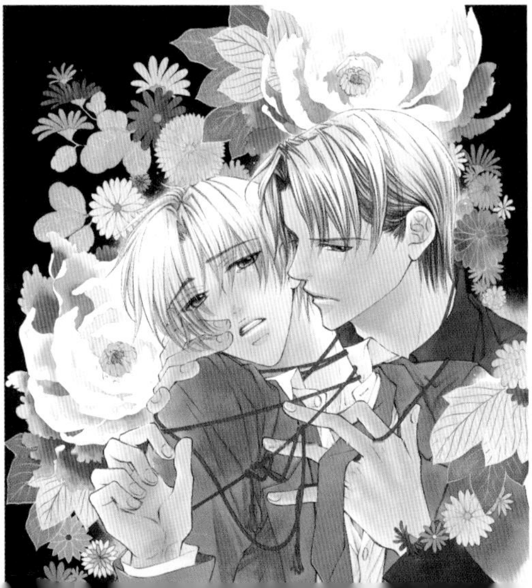

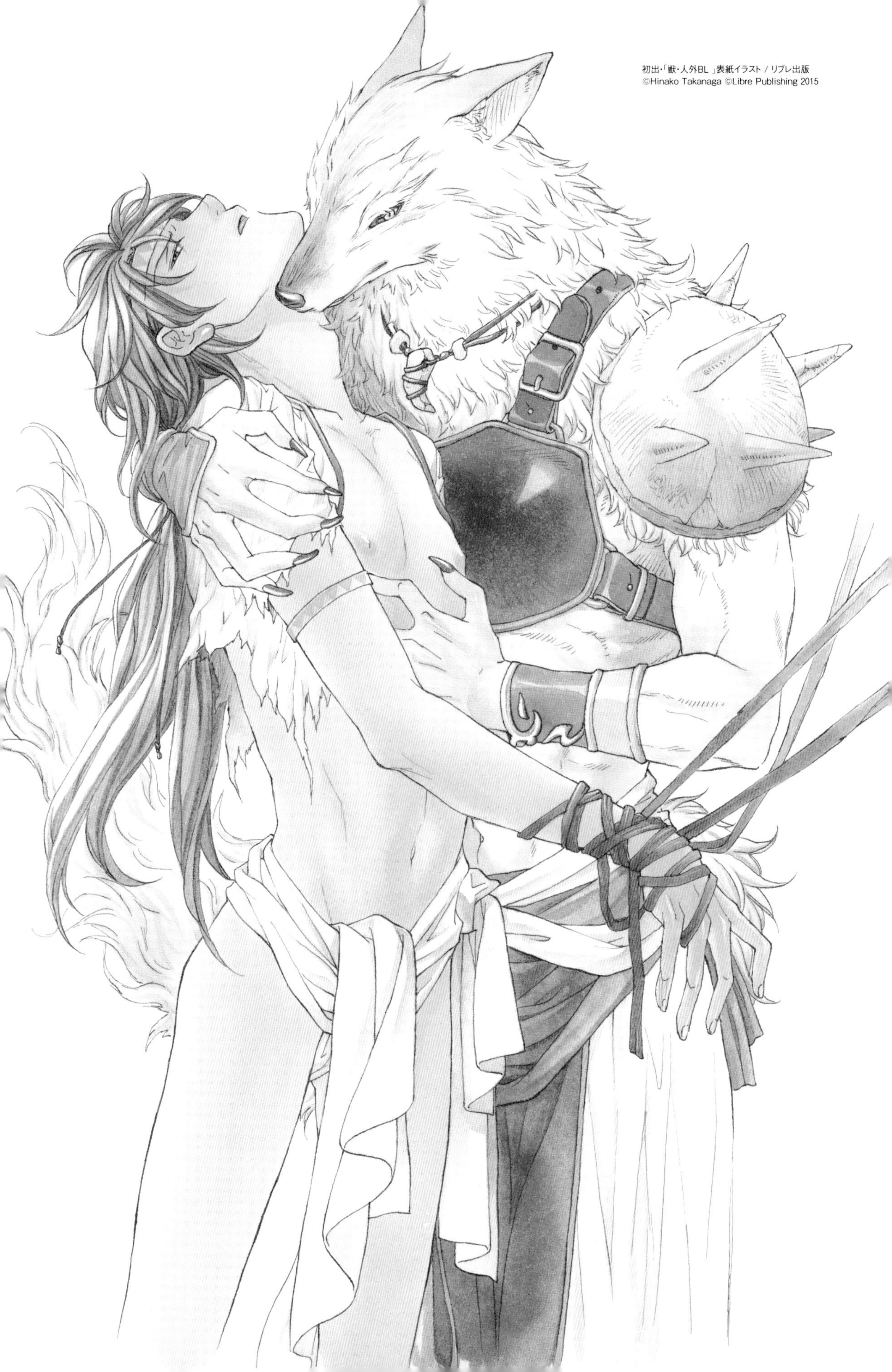

初出・「獣・人外BL」表紙イラスト / リブレ出版

ためこう
tamekou

M ttmkuu@gmail.com   T tmku1
U http://www.tmku8.com   D Photoshop CS6 ● CLIP STUDIO PAINT EX

Profile	漫画家。オリジナル同人誌の発行がきっかけで出版社にスカウトされ、2014年あたりから本格的に描き始める。作品はボーイズラブが中心。広島県出身。	I'm a manga artist. A publisher found my work in a new self-published magazine, and after being scouted, I began illustrating "for real" around 2014. My works are primarily in the Boys Love genre. I'm originally from Hiroshima Prefecture.
Comments	きれいだったり可愛かったり色っぽいなどの方向のフェチを詰めこみます。作品を見る方に自分のフェチを共感してもらうにはどうすればいいのかを考えながら描きます。すべての基本として、清潔感が漂うように気をつけています。	I fill my illustrations with pretty, cute, and sexy passions. As I draw, I imagine viewers identifying with my illustrations in terms of their own fetish. I am careful to keep a clean feel as the foundation for everything I do.

Personal Work「桃」

Personal Work「未」

「下衆」/ 下衆BL (シトロンアンソロジー)ピンナップイラスト / リブレ出版

「蓮」/ 号外onBLUE vol.4 表紙イラスト / 祥伝社　©ためこう / 祥伝社

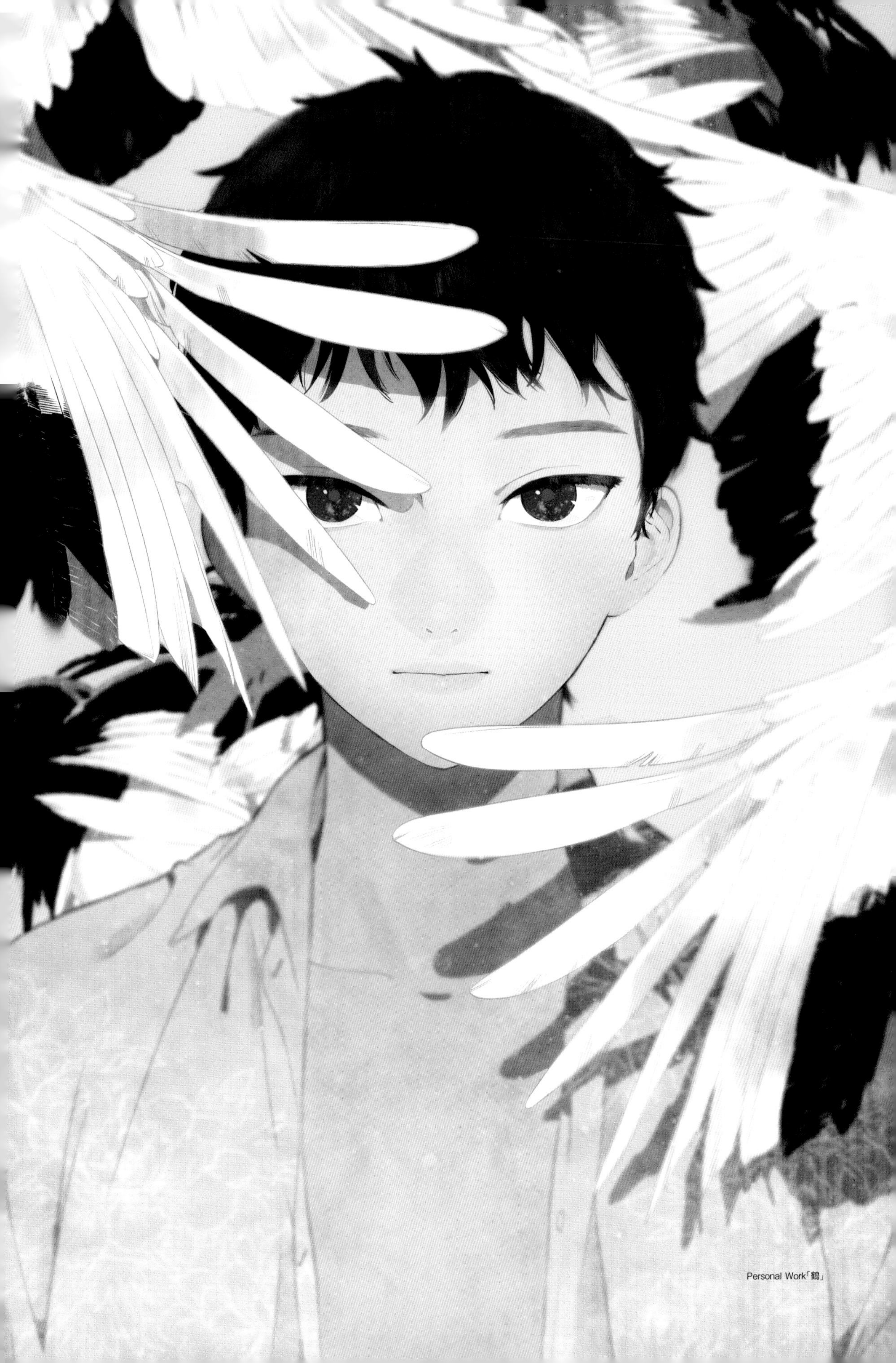

Personal Work「鶴」

問七

toinana

M simile meta@gmail.com
T toinana7
U http://toinana.tumblr.com
D SAI ● Photoshop CS5 ● Illustrator CS5

Profile

愛知県出身。ゲームのキャラクターデザイン、書籍、CDジャケット、雑誌への描き下ろしなど、様々な媒体で活動中。夢のあるファッションが好き。

I'm from Aichi Prefecture. I work in a variety of media, designing game characters and drawing for books, CD jackets, and magazines. I like fashion inspired by dreams.

Comments

キャラクターの服や装飾を考えるのが好きです。自分が着てみたい、こんな服があったらいいな、を絵にしています。既にあるものを正確に描くことよりも、自分で一から世界観を考えるのが好きです。男の子は特に少年期が好きで、幼さと色気が共存しているようなキャラクターが描けたらといいなと思って心がけています。

I love thinking of clothes and accessories for the characters. I draw clothes that I myself would love to wear, or that I wish existed. Instead of making careful drawings of things which already exist, I like to create my own understanding of the world from scratch. I particularly like drawing adolescent males, and think it would be great if I could learn to incorporate youthful innocence and sexiness simultaneously into my characters.

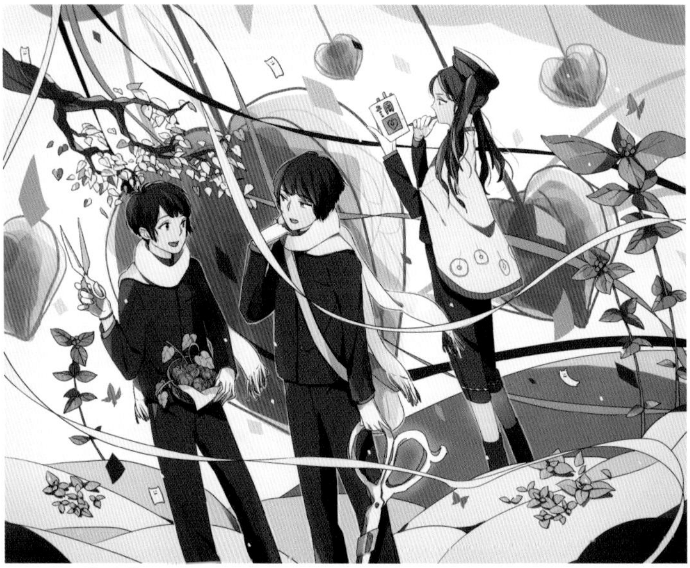

Personal Work「ホオズキ」

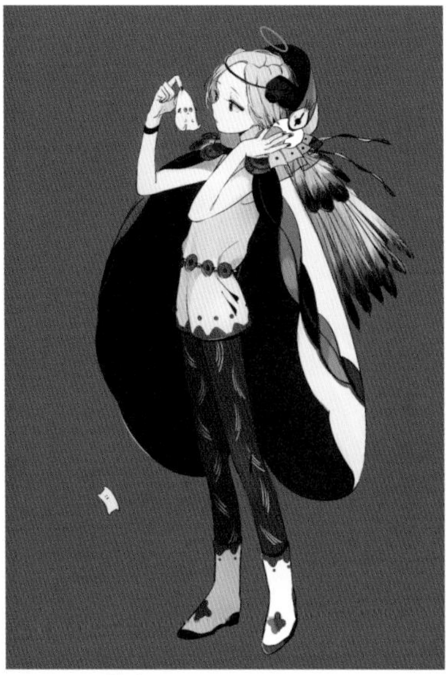

Personal Work「何味?」

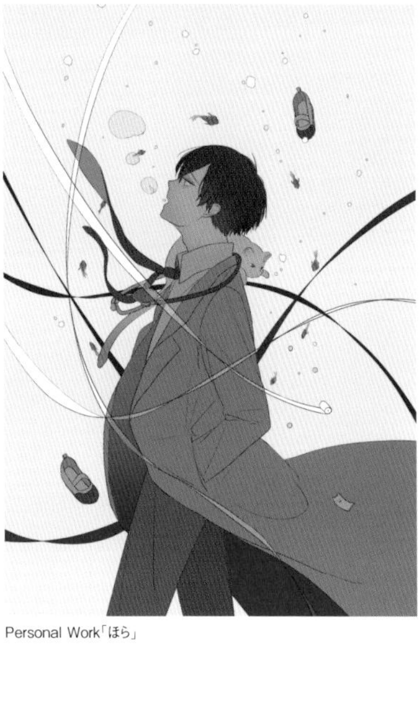

Personal Work「ほら」

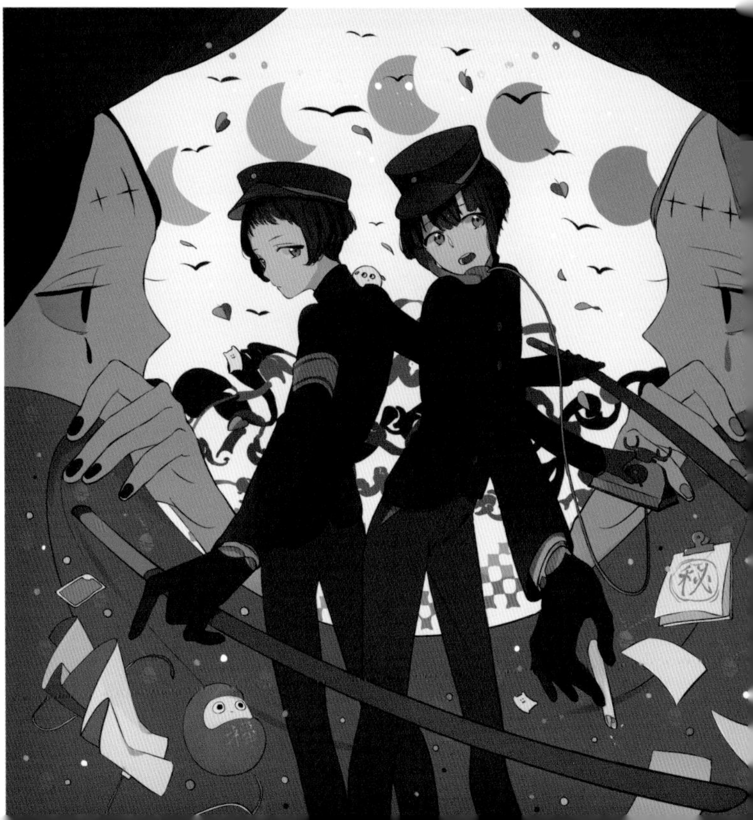

Personal Work「黒の学徒」

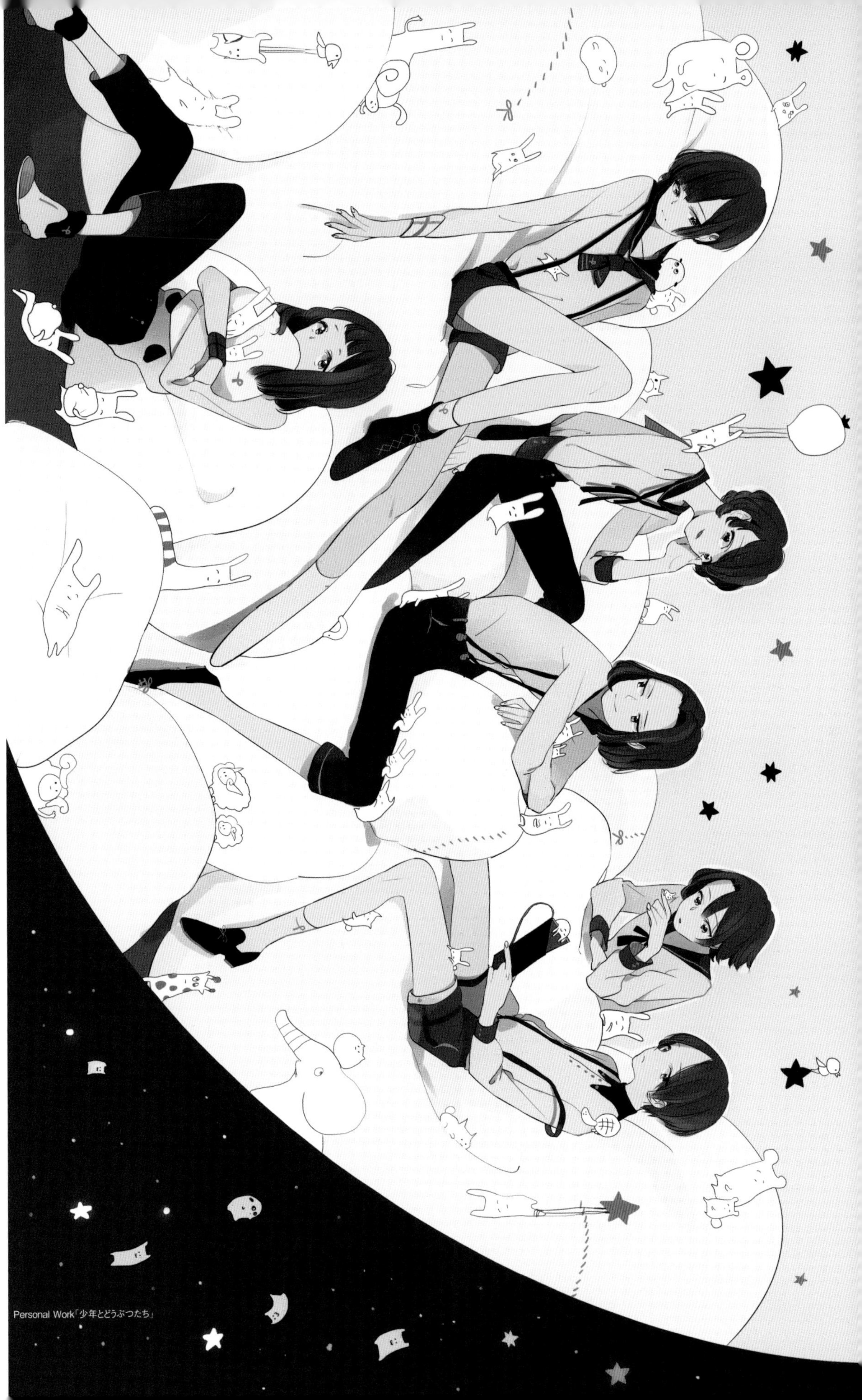

Personal Work「少年とどうぶつたち」

澄
toru

M clown56@jg.chips.jp T ---
U http://pixiv.me/lauralaura D SAI ● Photoshop

Profile	商業及び同人で活動中。ゲームやシチュエーションCDのキャラクターデザイン、女性向けの書籍の表紙等を手がける。	I work for both commercial and dojin publishers. I create character designs for games and situation CDs, and book covers aimed at the female market in addition to other endeavors.
Comments	和服や軍服姿の青年や、少年を描くのが好き。イラストのテーマによってアニメ塗りや重ね塗りを使い分ける。	I enjoy portraying young men in traditional Japanese clothes and military uniforms, as well as drawing boys. I choose anime painting or layered painting software, depending on the theme of the illustration.

「妖カシノ恋 第二巻 鬼編」CDジャケットイラスト / ASGARD ©noctiluca

「妖カシノ恋 第三巻 ぬらりひょん編」CDジャケットイラスト / ASGARD ©noctiluca

「私好みの貴方でございます。」藤谷 郁 / カバーイラスト / エタニティ文庫
アルファポリス ©藤谷郁 / アルファポリス

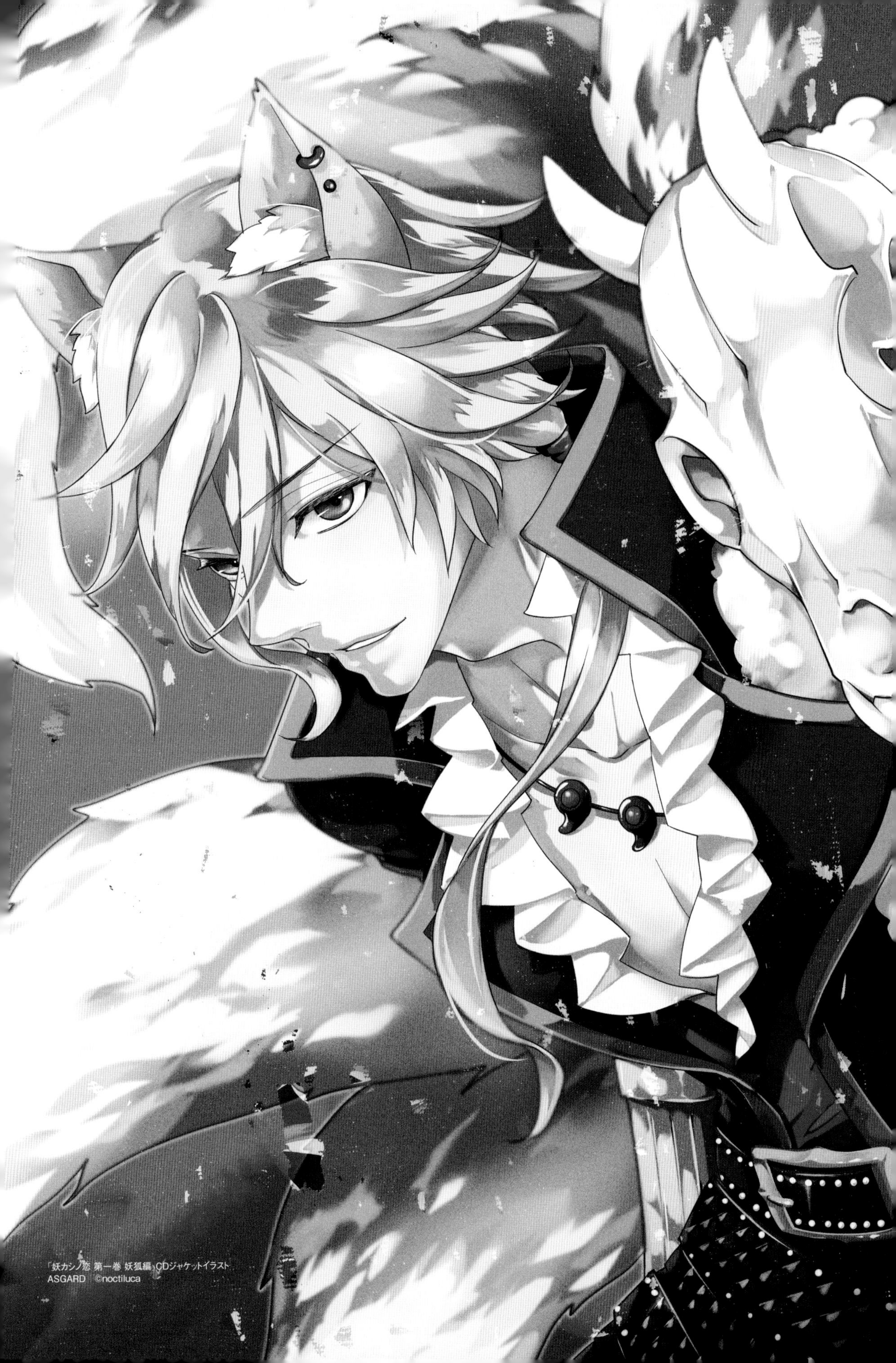
「妖カシノ恋 第一巻 妖狐編」CDジャケットイラスト
ASGARD ©noctiluca

トミダトモミ

TOMIDA Tomomi

M tomato_mts@yahoo.co.jp
U http://migitehidarite.web.fc2.com
T tomitomo_
D SAI ● Illustrator ● Photoshop

Profile

岐阜県在住。カードイラスト・乙女ゲーム・シチュエーションCDなど描いています。歴史ものや和風イラストが得意で、オリジナルイラストは国内・海外展示にも出展しています。

I live in Gifu Prefecture. I illustrate trading cards, otome games, and situation CDs. I'm good with historical and traditional Japanese illustrations, and exhibit my original work both in Japan and abroad.

Comments

作家おまかせの部分では自分の好きなものがイラストの+αになるよう作画しています。BL表現も対応可です。

When given free rein on a job, I like to add my own preferences, providing that extra plus to my illustrations. I also take on BL work.

「籠女ノ唄～吉原夜話～第一話 山吹」/ CDジャケットイラスト / 花鏡　©2015花鏡

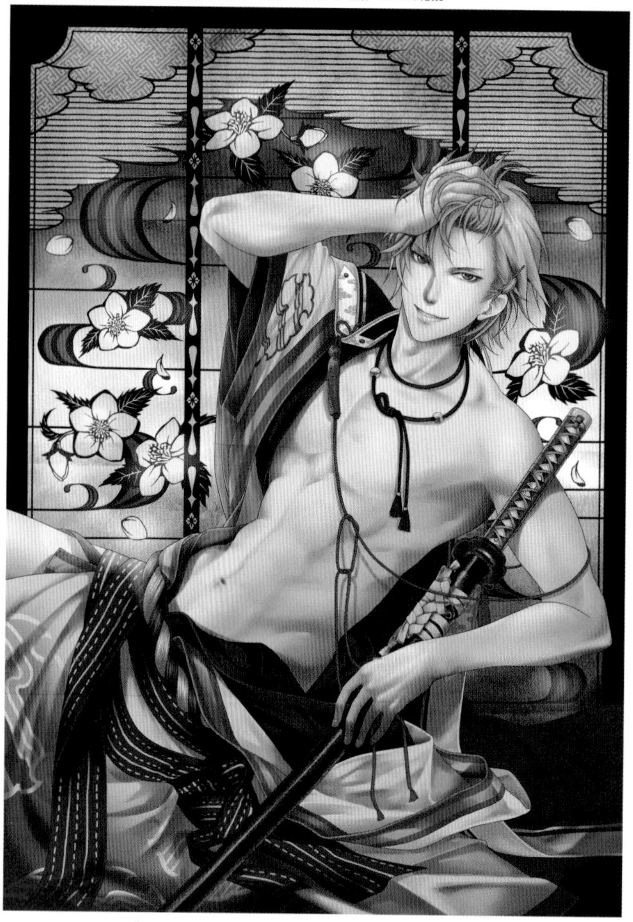

COSPLAY MODE 2015年5月号増刊「剣装」/ カバーイラスト
ファミマ・ドット・コム　©famima.com 2015

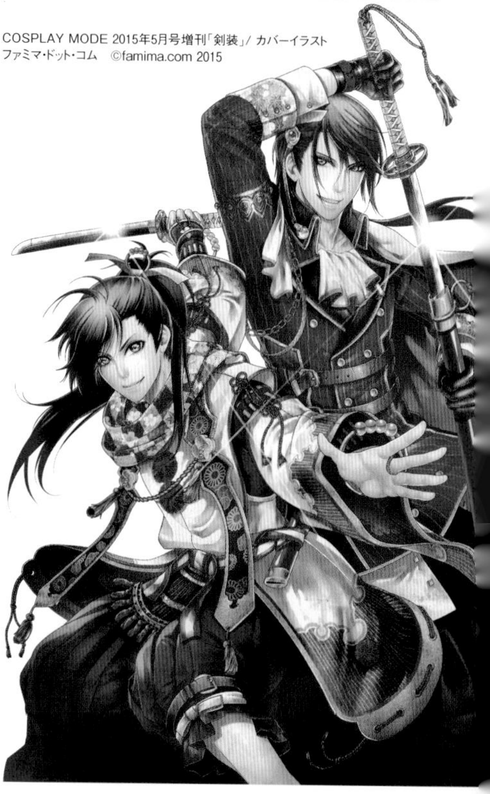

相馬野馬追応援企画「第四回武者絵展」/ 出展イラスト
相馬野馬追「武者絵展」実行委員会 / 2015

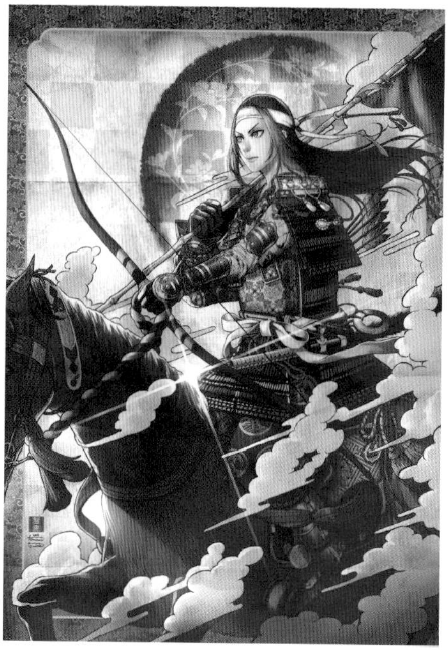

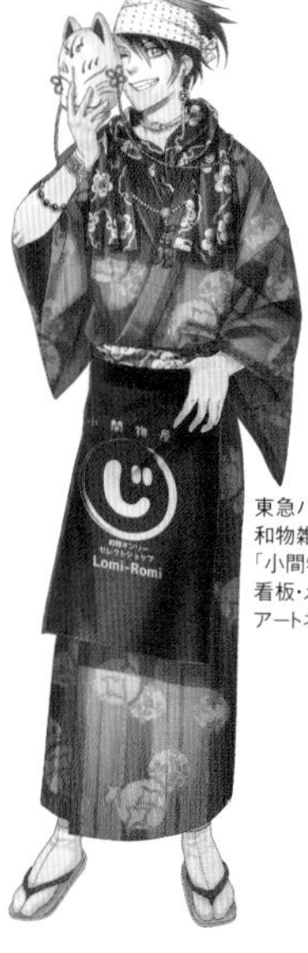
Lomi-Romi

東急ハンズ池袋店
和物雑貨オンリーイベント
「小間物屋じゃぱねすく!!」
看板・メインビジュアル
アートネクストLomiRomi / 2015

「刀剣乱舞-ONLINE-」
キャラクターイラスト
©2015 DMMゲームズ/Nitroplus

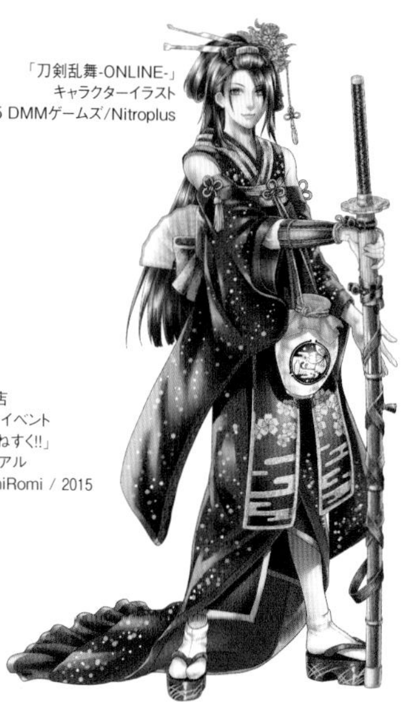

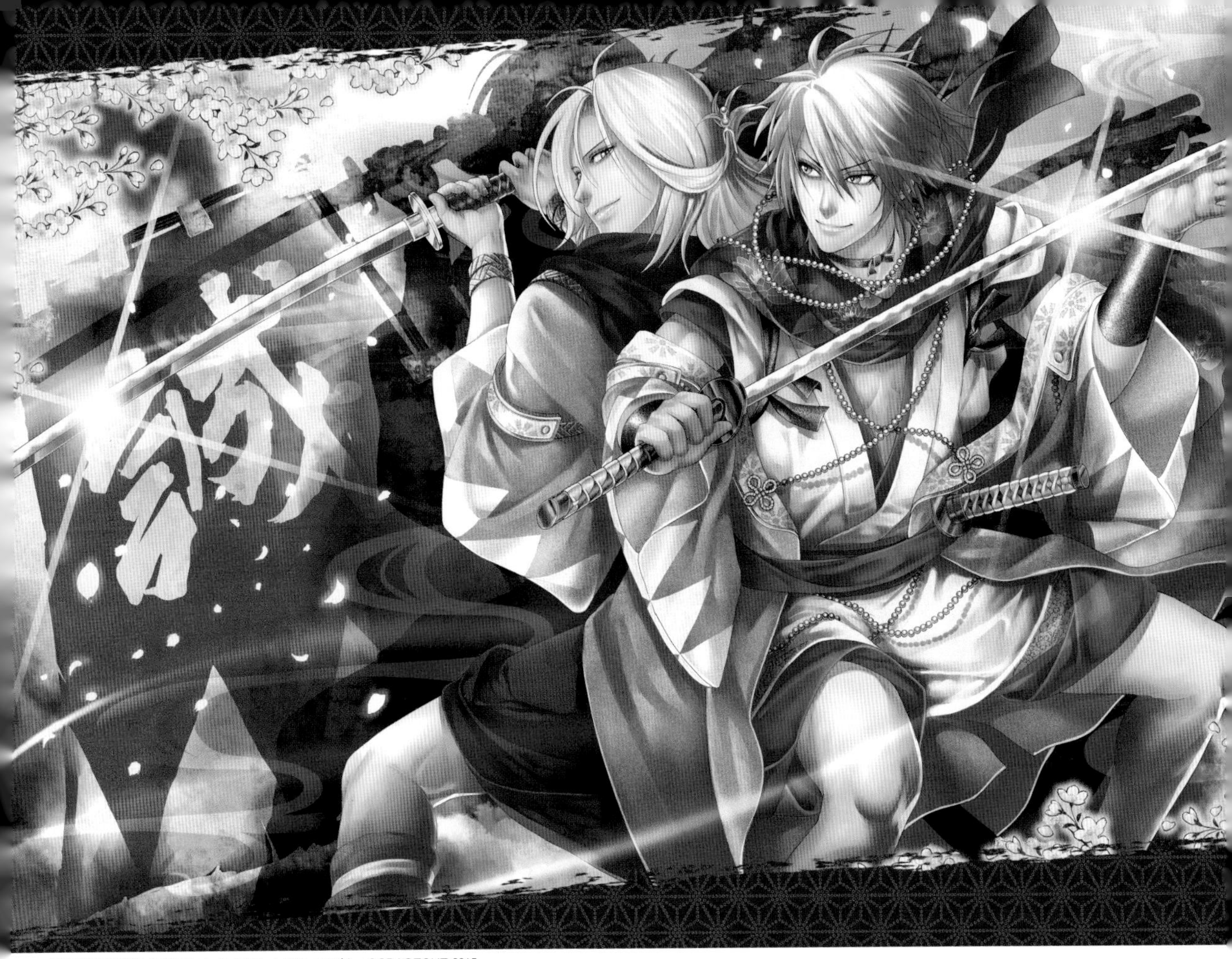

「真◆幕末新撰組」/ プロモーションイラスト / スペースアウト ©SPACEOUT 2015

「真◆幕末新撰組」/ プロモーションイラスト / スペースアウト ©SPACEOUT 2015

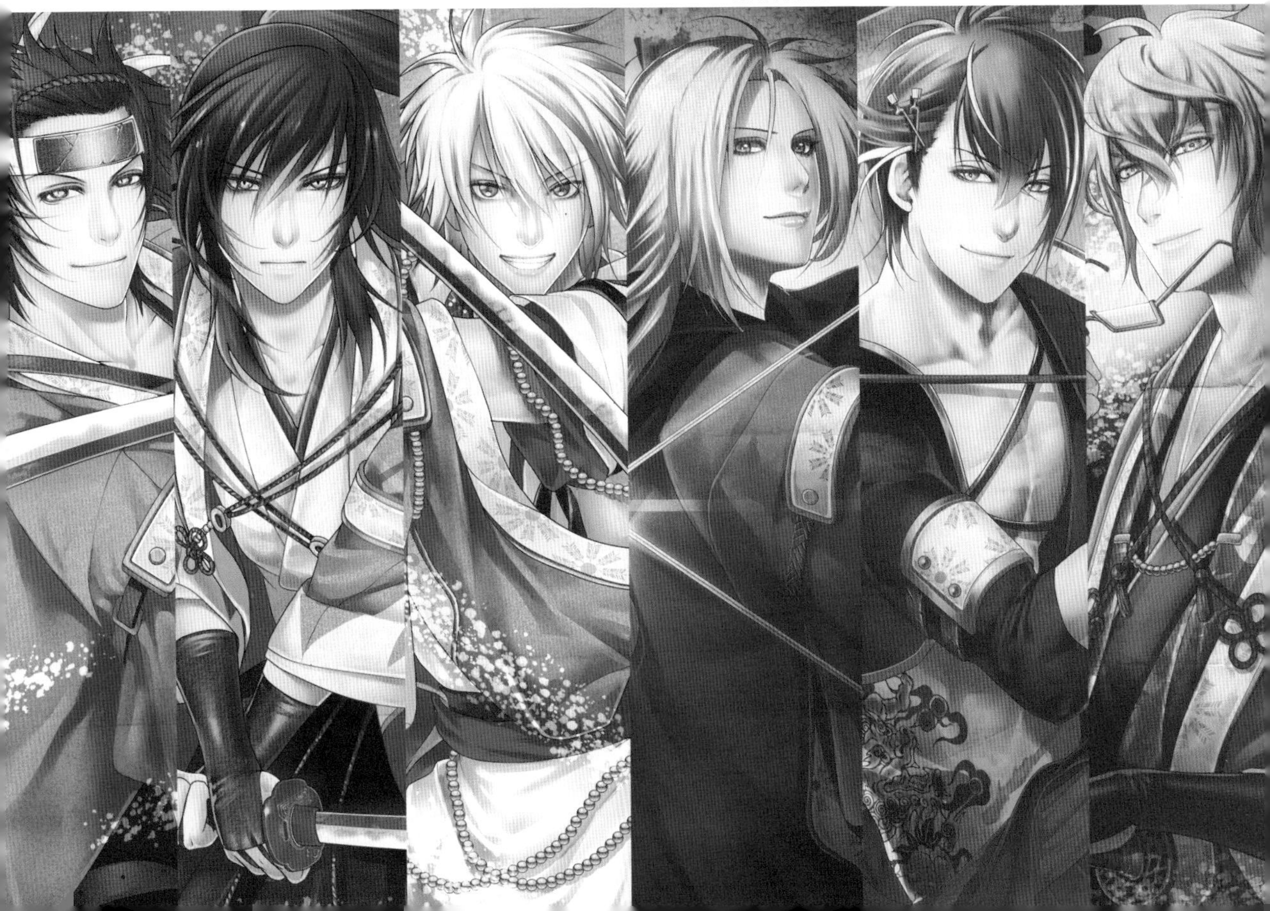

THORES柴本

THORES SIBAMOTO

M thores@mail.goo.ne.jp   T thoresiva   U http://brog.goo.ne.jp/thores

D Liquitex • ACRYL GOUACHE • MODELING PASTE • COPIC MULTILINER

Profile

雑誌投稿から小説『トリニティ・ブラッド』装画デビュー。豪奢な衣装や緻密な画を得意とし、装画とデザインを中心にSF 、伝奇、ファンタジー、ホラー、ミステリー、ライトノベルから文芸、ノベライズまで小説等の装画を幅広く担当。オリジナルは『シザーズクラウン』。受注限定で画集を2冊出版。

I began with magazine submissions and then debuted the cover for the novel *Trinity Blood*. I'm pretty good at creating elaborate outfits and precise lines, and work mainly on book covers for a wide variety of genre including SF, romance, fantasy, horror, mystery, "light novels" (unique category of shorter novels for teenage to under thirties), literature, and novelization. *Scissors Crown* is my original work. Two volumes of my artwork have been published and are available on an order basis only.

Comments

どの角度からでもイメージを大切にしています。作品のイメージ、キャラクターのイメージ、自身の作風のイメージなど。そのイメージを踏まえた上で、視覚的に良いと思う方向で制作をしています。頽廃感のある世界観や衣装のデザイン、機械的なガジェットが好きなのでその方向を得意としています。男性キャラの依頼が多いのですが、実は個人的には女性の衣装が好きなので、本来は余り男性を描くのは得意では有りません。

I value artistic images from every angle: those of the completed work, of the character, and of my own artistic style, among others. I approach my work based on those images, targeting a visually good angle. I like creating decadent atmospheres and costumes along with mechanical gadgets, so I tend to be good at that sort of thing. Although I include a lot of male costumes, I actually prefer female outfits, and am inherently not all that skilled at drawing males.

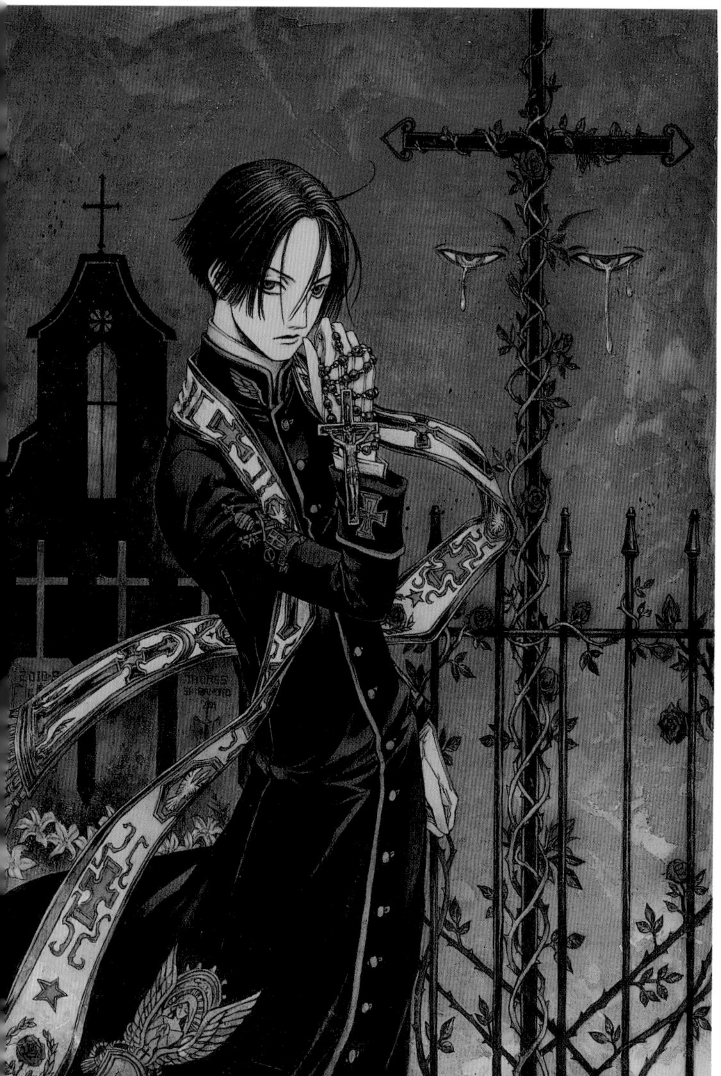

「バチカン奇跡調査官 黒の学院」藤木 稟 / 装画
角川ホラー文庫 / KADOKAWA

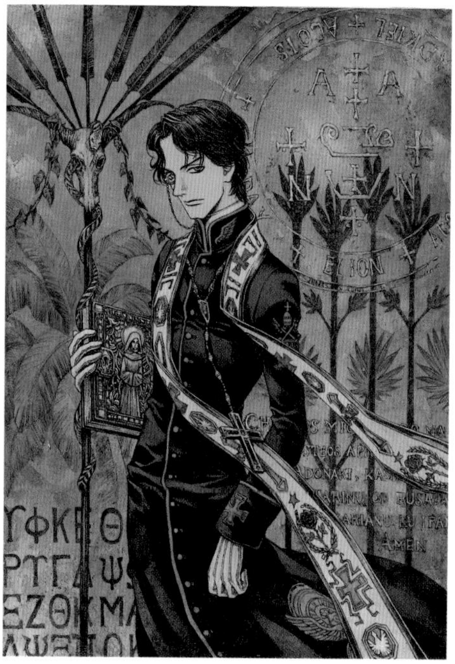

「バチカン奇跡調査官 サタンの裁き」藤木 稟 / 装画
角川ホラー文庫 / KADOKAWA

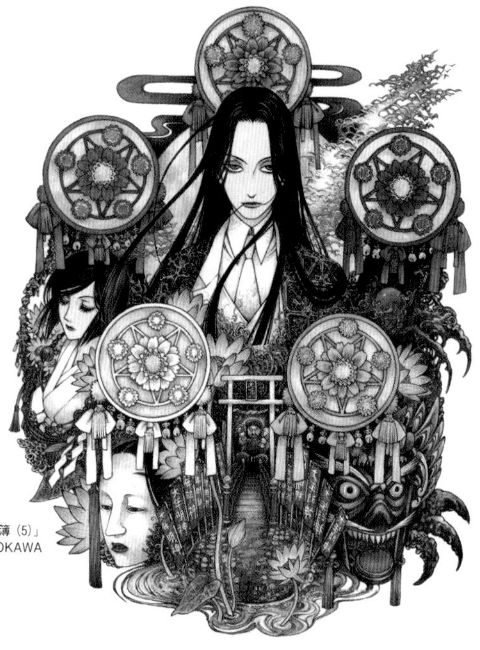

「大年神が彷徨う島 探偵・朱雀十五の事件簿 (5)」
藤木 稟 / 装画 / 角川ホラー文庫 / KADOKAWA

「からくり同心 景」谷津矢車 / 装画 / 角川文庫 / KADOKAWA

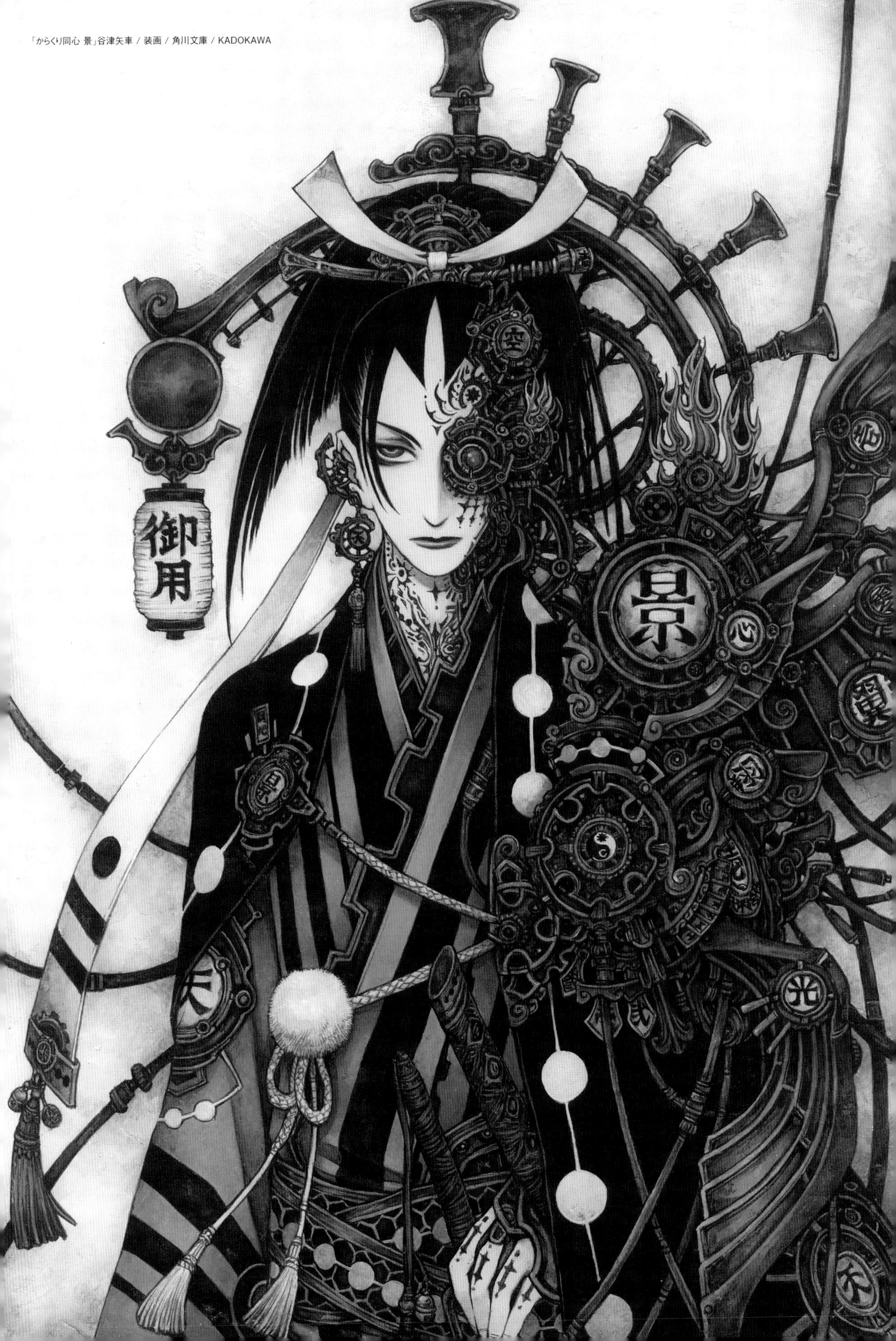
御用
景

直江まりも
Naoe Marimo

Ⓜ marimo@kpland.com
Ⓤ http://www.kpland.com
Ⓣ ---
Ⓓ SAI ● Photoshop

Profile
イラストやマンガのお仕事の他にビジネス書の挿絵なども描かせていただいております。
I create illustrations and manga, and also illustrate business books.

Comments
性別を問わず可愛くて少し色気のあるキャラクターを描くべく心がけております。
I feel I should do my best to draw cute and somewhat sexy characters, regardless of gender.

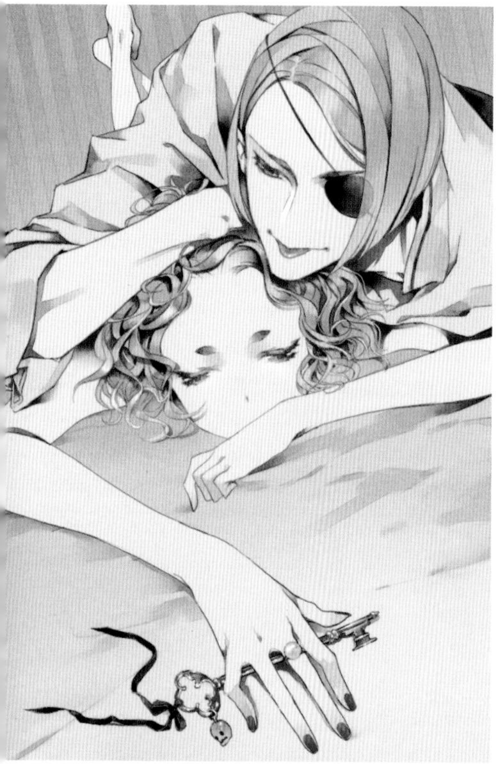

「淫夢に囚われて〜緊縛のベッド」渡辺やよい(電子書籍)
カバーイラスト / KADOKAWA

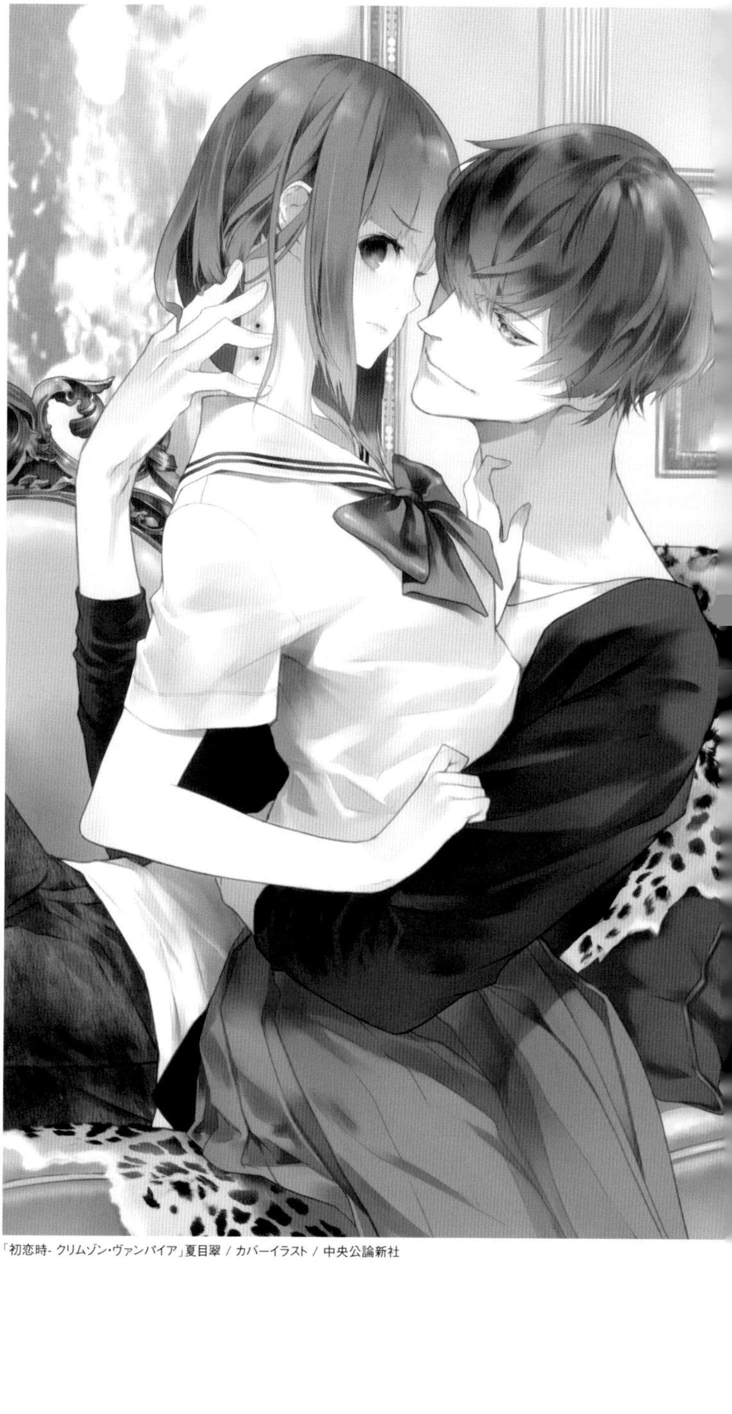

「初恋時- クリムゾン・ヴァンパイア」夏目翠 / カバーイラスト / 中央公論新社

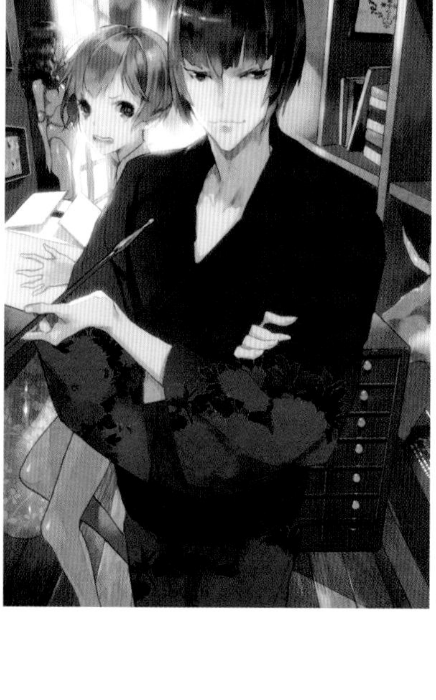

「ナイナイの箱——祓屋黒上スグル」神楽坂あお(電子書籍) / カバーイラスト / KADOKAWA

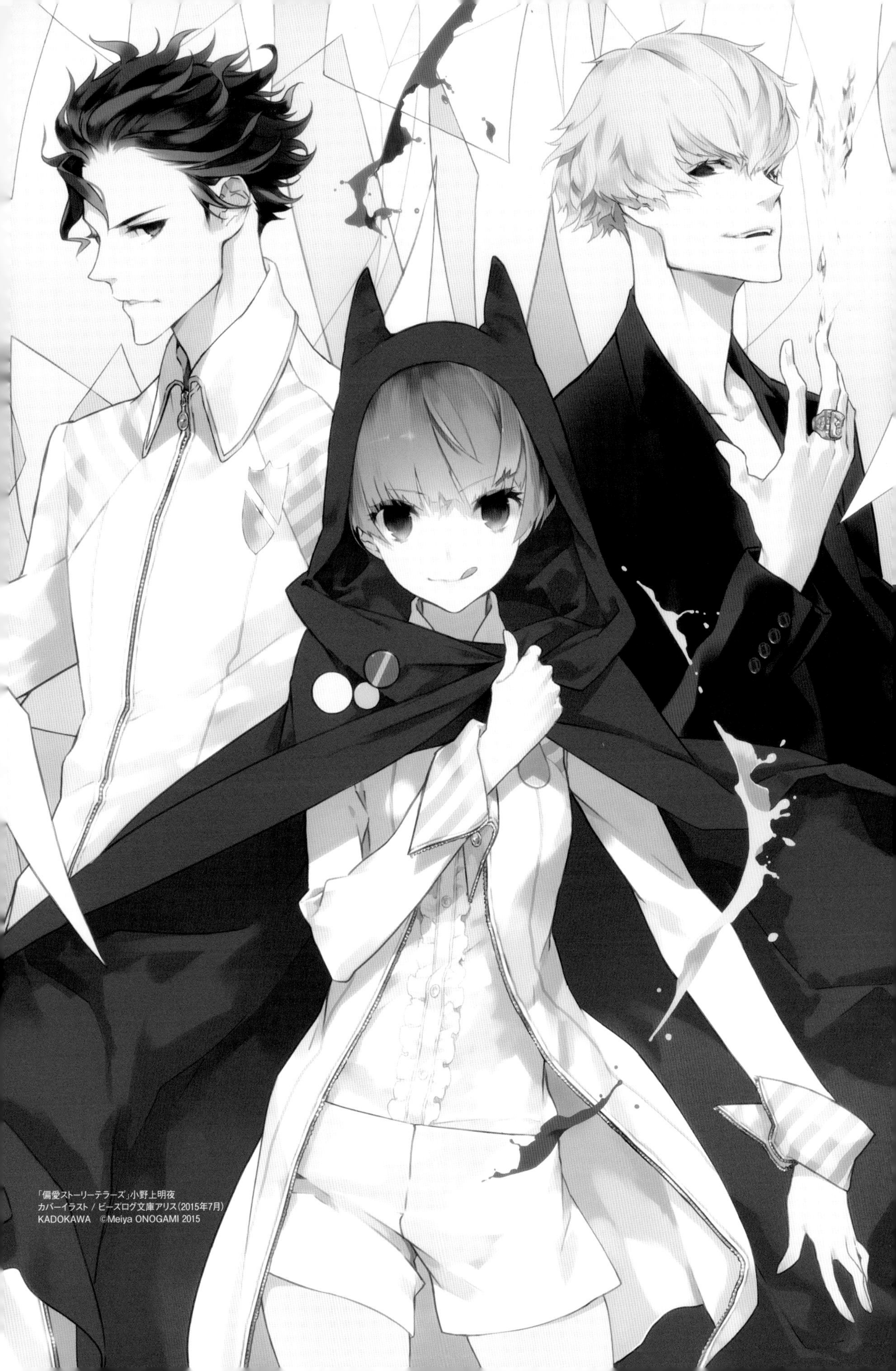

尚月地

nao tsukiji

Ⓜ ---
Ⓤ http://naotukiji.main.jp
Ⓣ adekanofficial
Ⓓ Photoshop / Painter

Profile

第40回ウィングス新人大賞努力賞受賞作『雑貨に埋もれた乙女』が '07年ウィングス3月号に掲載されデビュー。同年、小説ウィングス夏号より『好漢仕事記艶吹雪』を連載。'08年タイトルを『艶漢』に改題し、第1巻を刊行。'09年には連載誌をウィングスに移し、現在に至る。2016年3月に『艶漢』が舞台化。主な作品に『艶漢』『金色騎士』画集『ノスタルヂア』『極彩少年』(すべて新書館)、『廃墟少女』(講談社) などがある。

I debuted in the March 2007 edition *Wings* with *Zakka ni Umoreta Otome*, which was awarded the 40th Wings First Prize for Effort by a Novice. That same year, my work *Koukan Shigoto-ki Ade-fubuki* was published in the summer edition of *Shosetsu Wings*. In 2008, the first volume of the work was published under the series title *Ade-kan*. The serialization continues to this day after moving to Wings in 2009. *Ade-kan* will be performed on stage in March 2016. Some of my primary works include *Ade-kan, Kiniro Kishi, Nostalgia* (a compilation of art work), *Gokusai Shonen* (all published by SHINSHOKAN), and *Haikyo Shoujo* (published by KODANSHA).

Comments

行ってみたい所や見たい場面の絵を描くようにして います。

I usually draw places I would like to visit or scenes I would like to see.

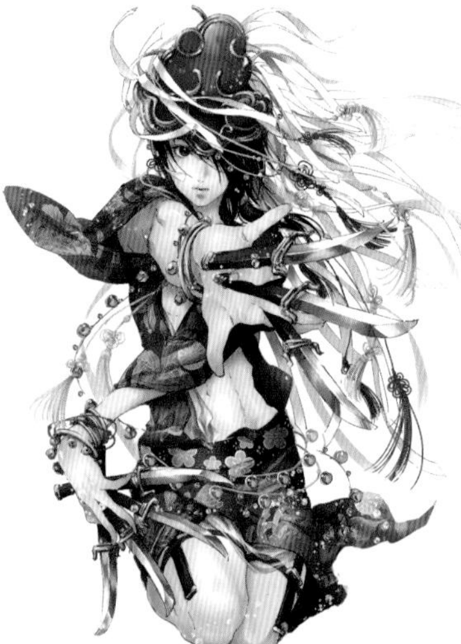

「艶漢」尚月地 / 3巻カバーイラスト / 新書館
©尚月地 / ウィングス・コミックス / 新書館

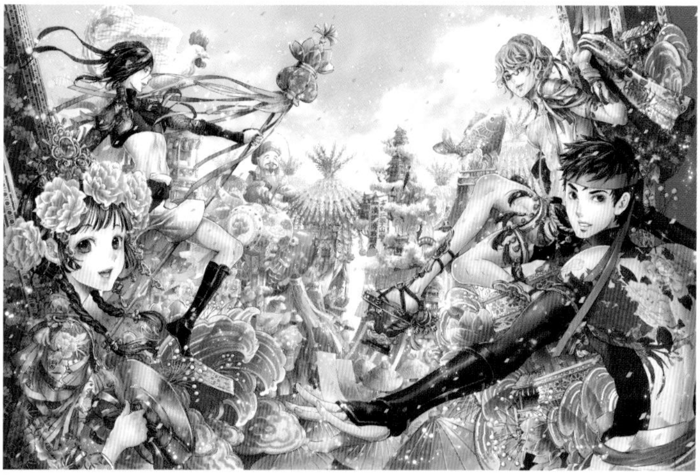

「艶漢」尚月地 / 5巻カバーイラスト / 新書館　©尚月地 / ウィングス・コミックス / 新書館

「艶漢」尚月地 / 1巻カバーイラスト / 新書館　©尚月地 / ウィングス・コミックス / 新書館

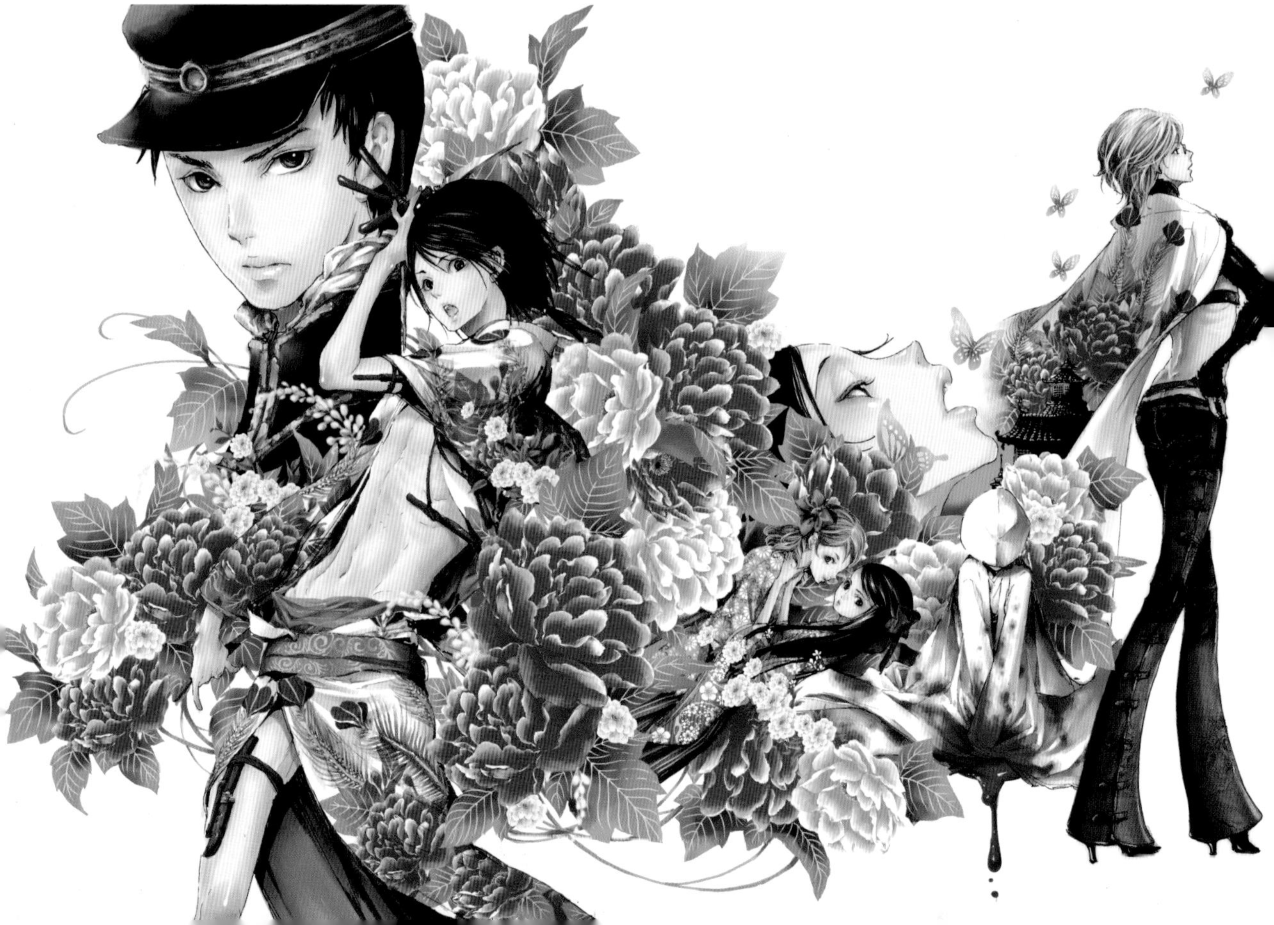

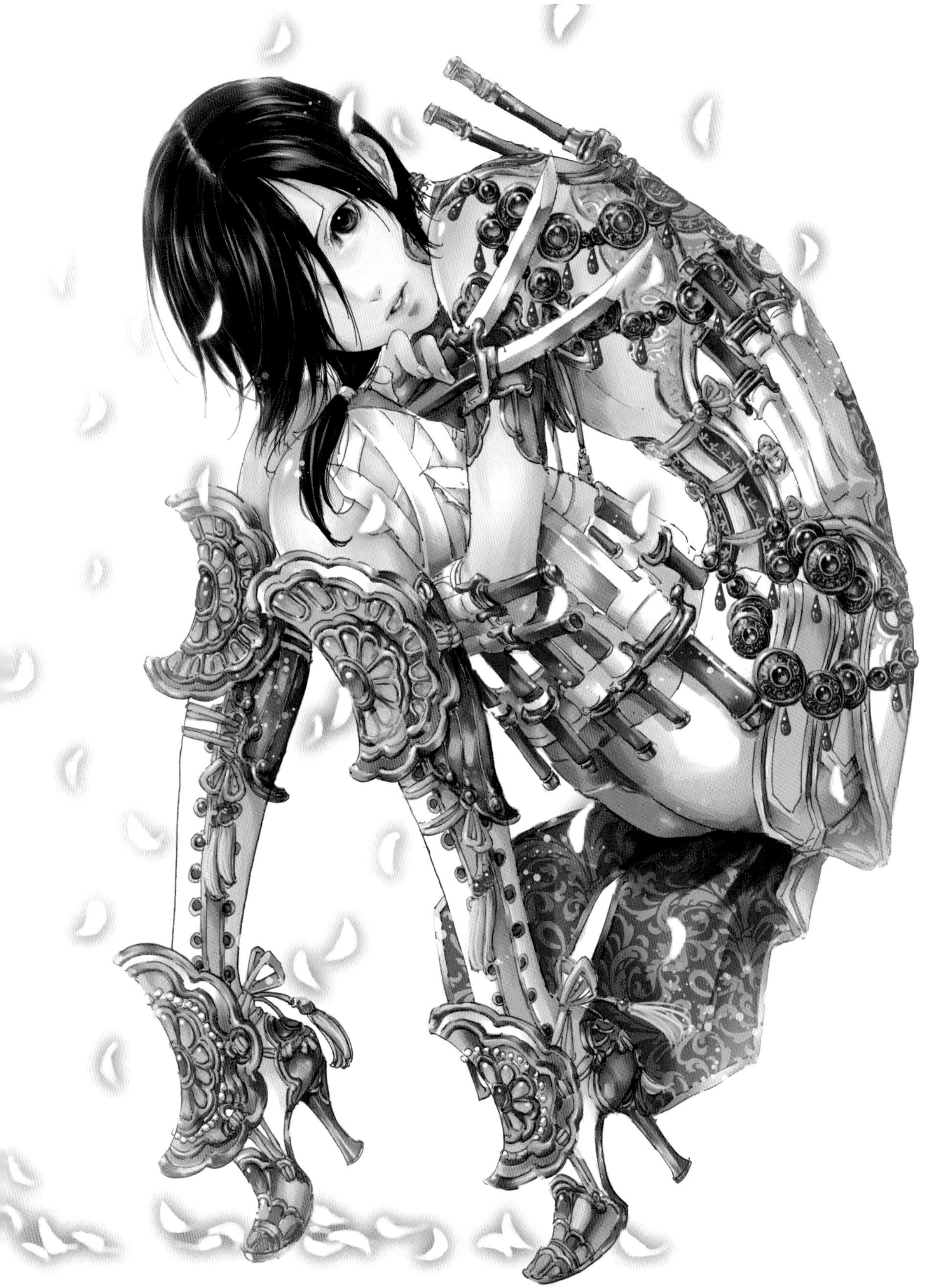

「艶漢」尚月地 / 4巻カバーイラスト / 新書館

流れないテッシュ

nagarenaitessyu

M nycyf820@yahoo.co.jp

T NGgtessyu

U http://ngtessyu.blog.fc2.com

D SAI ● ComicStudio EX 4.0

Profile

関西在住の漫画家・イラストレーター。2013年にBL漫画とイラストでデビューし漫画を中心に活動中。

I'm a Kansai-based manga artist and illustrator. I debuted in 2013 with BL manga and illustrations, and now work mainly with manga.

Comments

主に学生の男の子をメインテーマにしています。キラキラだけどドロドロしているような見た人の心のどこかに刺さるようなイラストになるよう心がけています。また、彩度の高いイラストと彩度の低いイラストのどちらも得意です。

My work highlights male school kids. I'm aiming to melt the hearts of viewers with illustrations that sparkle but have another, rather messy, layer underneath. I'm good at handling both high- and low-intensity color in my illustrations.

Personal Work「おやすみなさい」

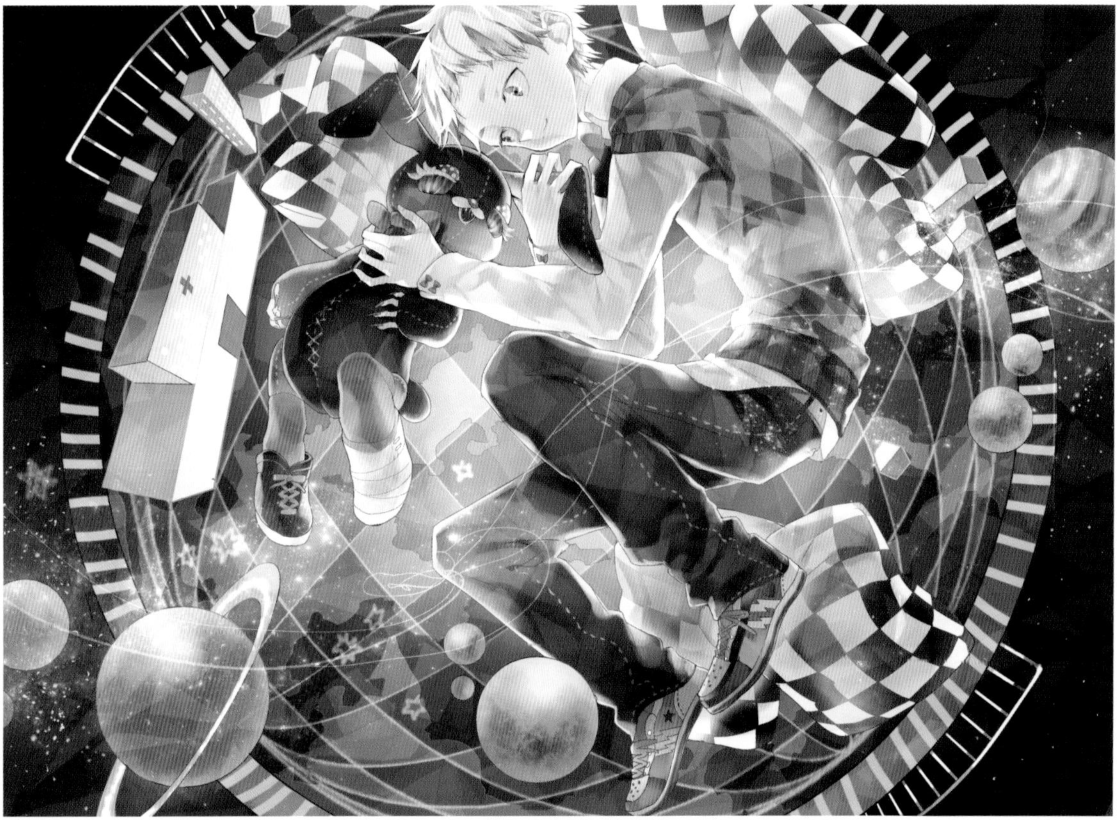

Personal Work

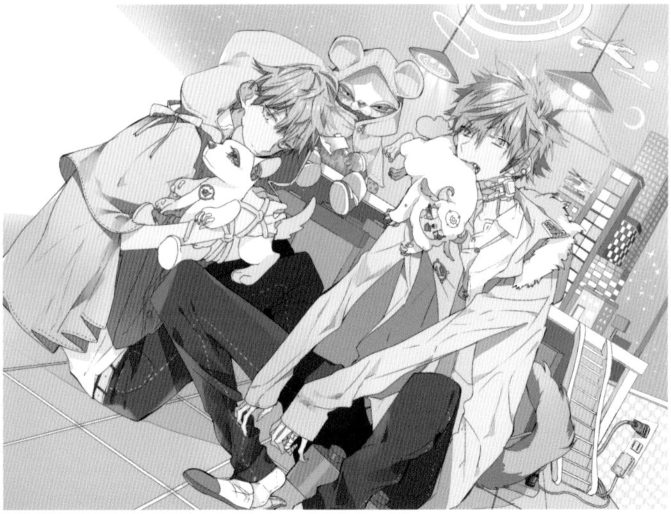

Personal Work「この広い世界のどこにも」

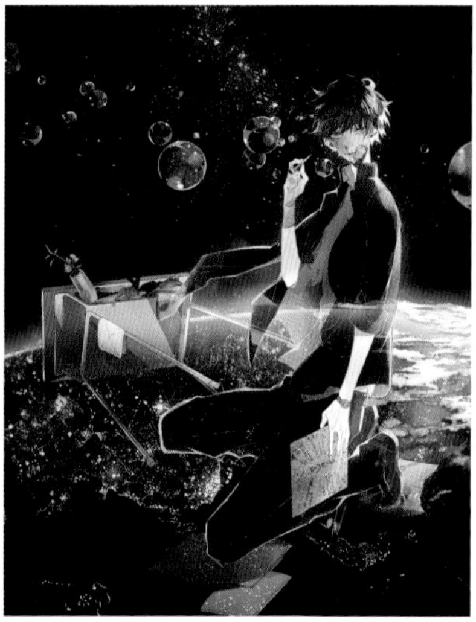

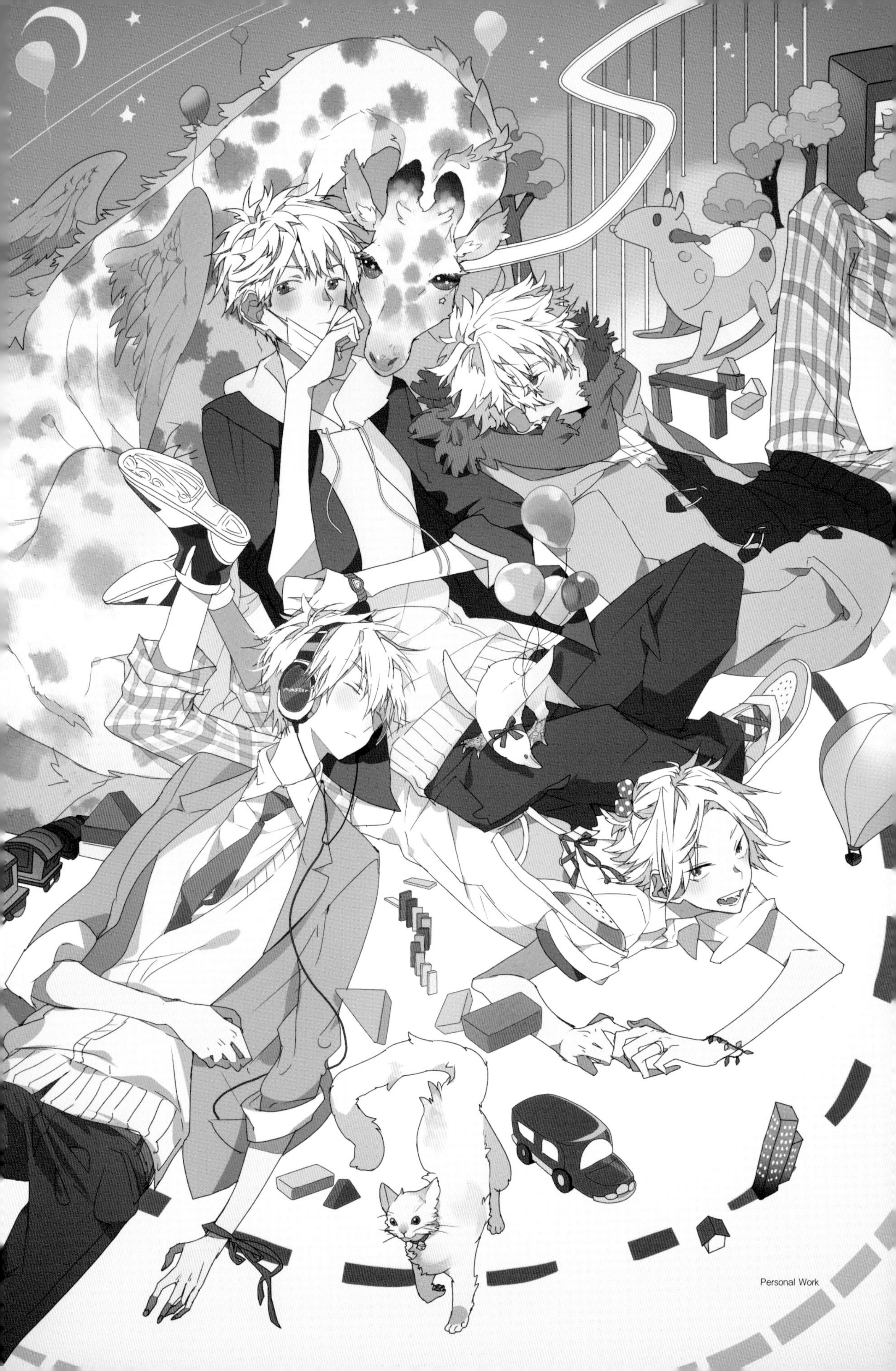

Personal Work

梨 とりこ
Nashi Torico

M gomao@torico.biz
T torico_n
U ---
D Photoshop CS6 • ComicStudio EX 4.0 • CLIP STUDIO PAINT

Profile	主に小説の挿画を描いています。	I primarily illustrate novels.
Comments	キャラクターの関係性と、読者さんに興味を持ってもらうためにどう表現したら良いかを常に意識しています。	As I draw, I always think about which expressions will best portray character relationships and also capture the reader's interest.

「凍える吐息」和泉桂 / 口絵 / 幻冬舎コミックス
©IZUMI KATSURA, NASHI TORICO, GENTOSHA COMICS 2011

「渇命」宮緒葵 / 口絵 / プラチナ文庫 / ブランタン出版　©梨とりこ / プラチナ文庫

ガッシュ文庫「追憶の庭」栗城偲 / カバーイラスト / 海王社　©栗城偲 / 海王社

「彼は死者の声を聞く」佐田三季 / カバーイラスト / 心交社　©心交社

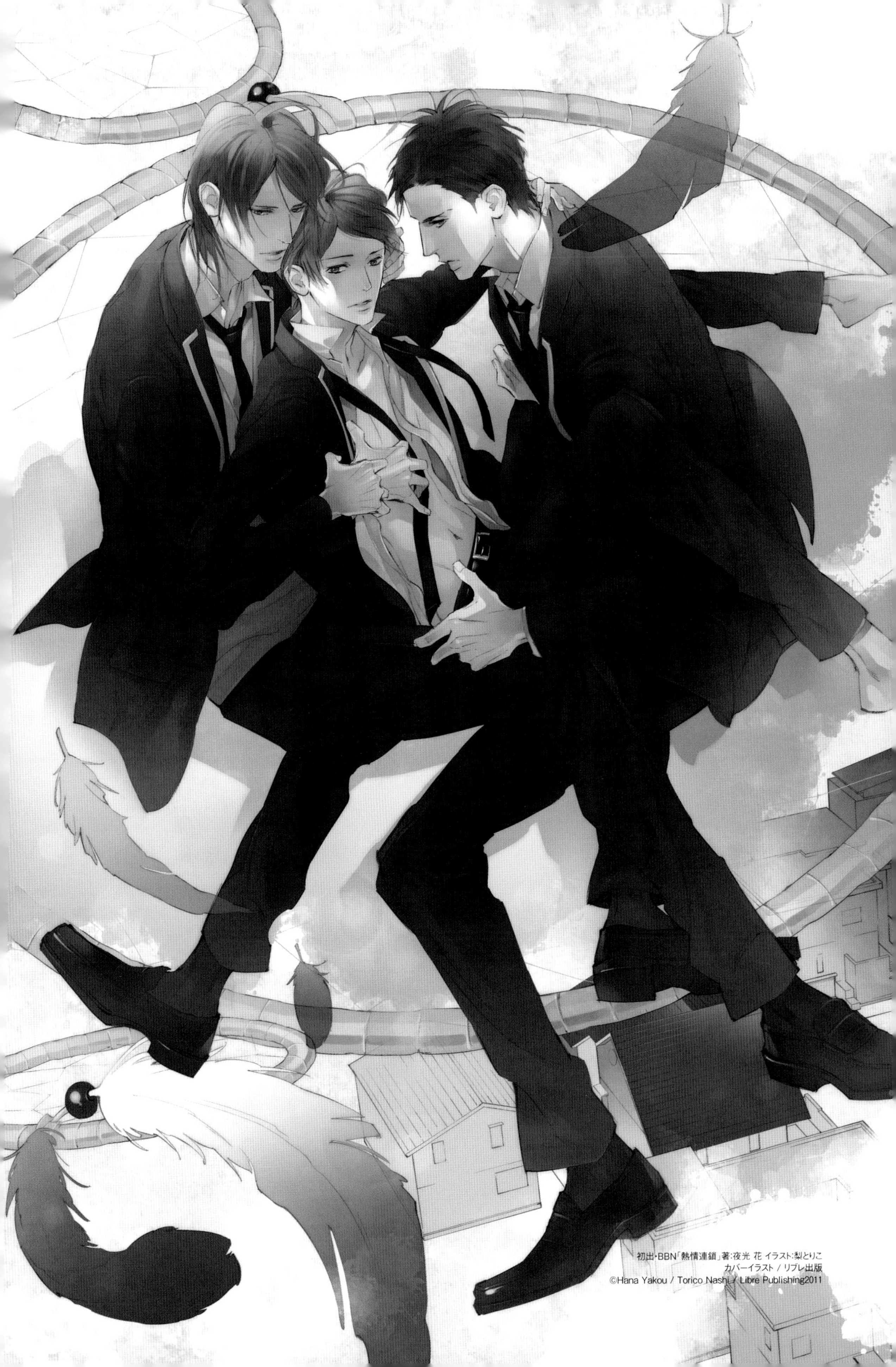

初出・BBN「熱情連鎖」著:夜光 花 イラスト:梨とりこ
カバーイラスト / リブレ出版

西のり子

Nishi Noriko

M info@nishi.moo.jp
U http://nishi.moo.jp
T nishi_noriko
D CLIP STUDIO PAINT • Photoshop

Profile

2014年10月からBL漫画家やってます。色々試しながら、自分に合った描き方を模索中。日々男子ばかり描いています。

I've been a BL manga artist since October of 2014. I'm trying a variety of things in search of my own style as an illustrator. I specifically draw young men.

Comments

見た人が物語を想像できるような絵を描きたいなあ、と思って描いています。ルールは一旦置いといて、自分が描いてて気持ちいい線を引いたり、塗っていて楽しい色を塗ったりと、自分の欲望に正直に描いたほうが、相手に訴えかける力があるものが出来上がる気がします。

While I'm drawing, I always feel that I'd love to create pictures allowing the viewer to imagine the story. I believe that if I draw lines which feel good and use colors which please me, that frankness will communicate itself powerfully to others.

Personal Work

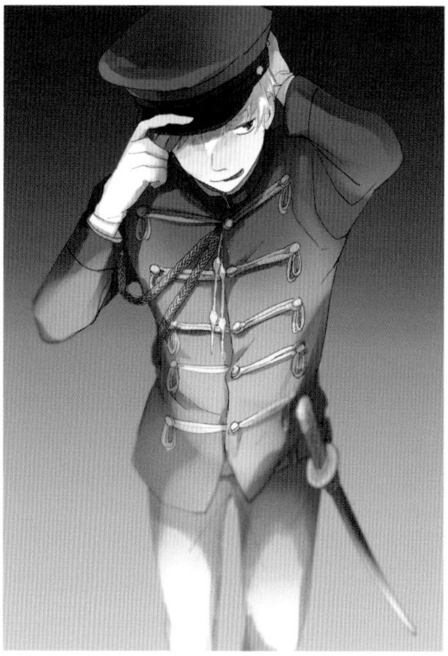

Personal Work

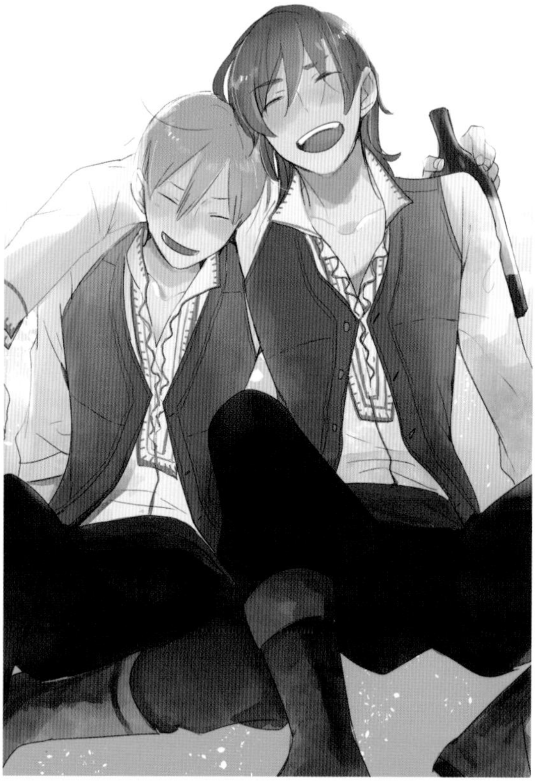

Personal Work

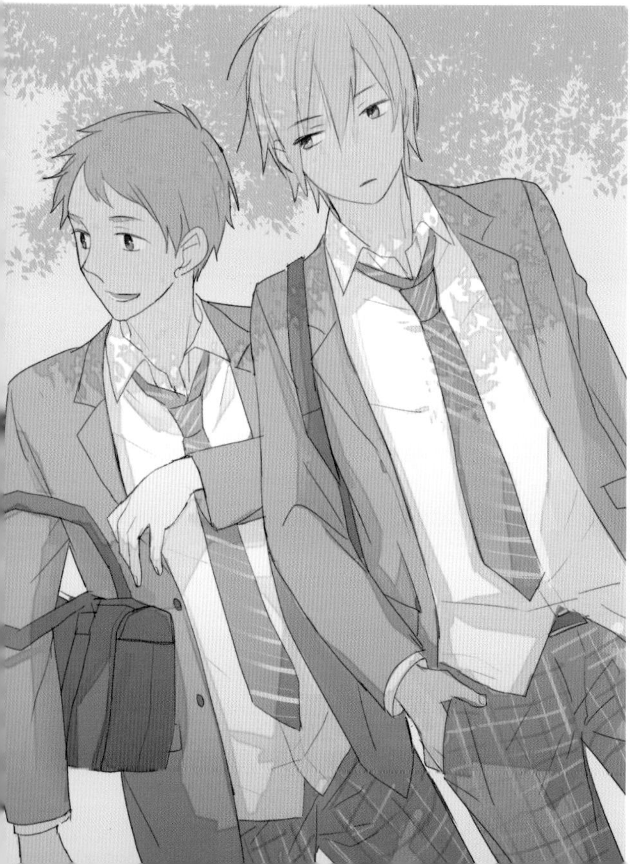

Personal Work

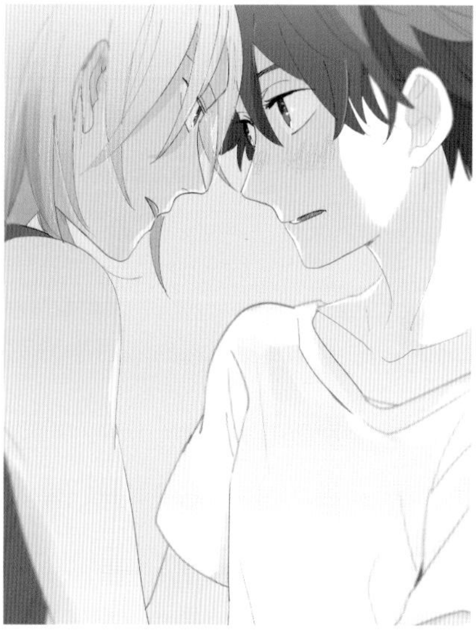

「フォーカス2」西のり子 / カバーイラスト / KADOKAWA / ©Noriko Nishi

「フォーカス」西のり子 / カバーイラスト / KADOKAWA / ©Noriko Nishi

「フォーカス」西のり子 / カバーイラスト / KADOKAWA / ©Noriko Nishi

乃一ミクロ
noici micro

M mc_kago@yahoo.co.jp
U ---
T noici_micro
D SAI ● Photoshop CS5 ● ComicStudio

Profile

2007年頃から趣味として絵を描き始め、2010年にイラストレーターとしてデビュー。女性向け、一般向け、ゲーム系など幅広いジャンルで活動中。漫画等も執筆しています。

I began drawing as a hobby around 2007, and in 2010, became an illustrator. I work in a wide range of areas, including both the female and the general-interest markets, along with game-centered endeavors. I also create manga and other products.

Comments

キャラクターの表情や視線、空間を表現するための色などに、気を使って描いています。あえて"嘘"の色を使うことも多く、その違和感が自分の個性として引き立つ様に現在も試行錯誤中です。天才肌ではないので職人としての絵を目指しています。

I draw using colors and other tools to boost character expression and gaze as well as atmosphere. I often employ colors that are defy reality, and am now trying, through trial and error, to capitalize on that feel of uneasiness and put my own unique stamp on my work. I'm not a gifted prodigy, so I'm simply aiming to produce pictures through craftsmanship.

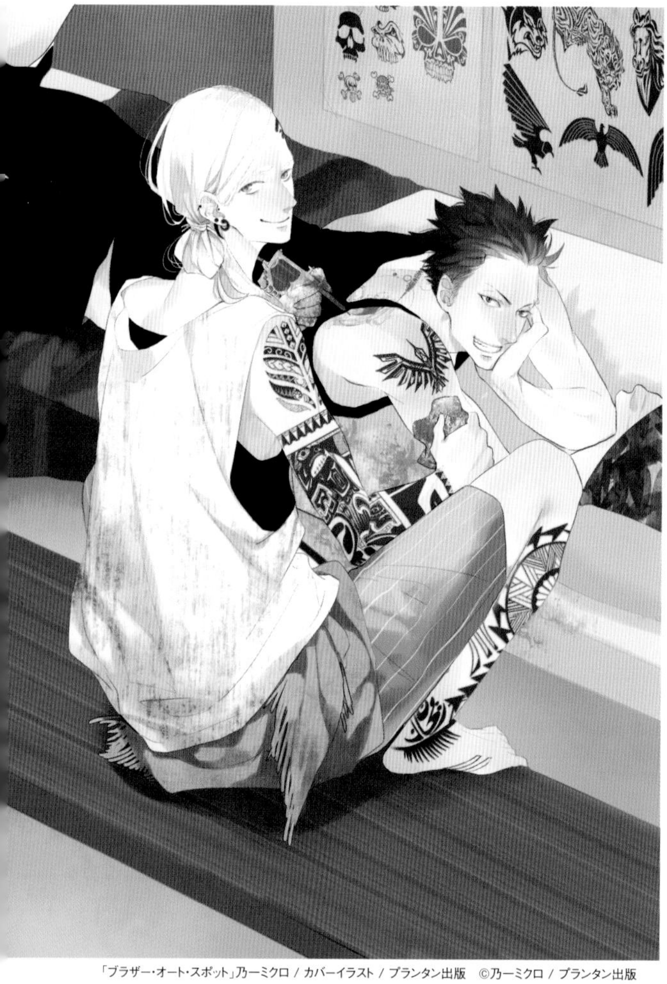

「ブラザー・オート・スポット」乃一ミクロ / カバーイラスト / プランタン出版　©乃一ミクロ / プランタン出版

「H·K(ホンコン)ドラグネット1」原作:松岡なつき　作画:乃一ミクロ / カバーイラスト
Charaコミックス / 徳間書店　©松岡なつき・乃一ミクロ / 徳間書店

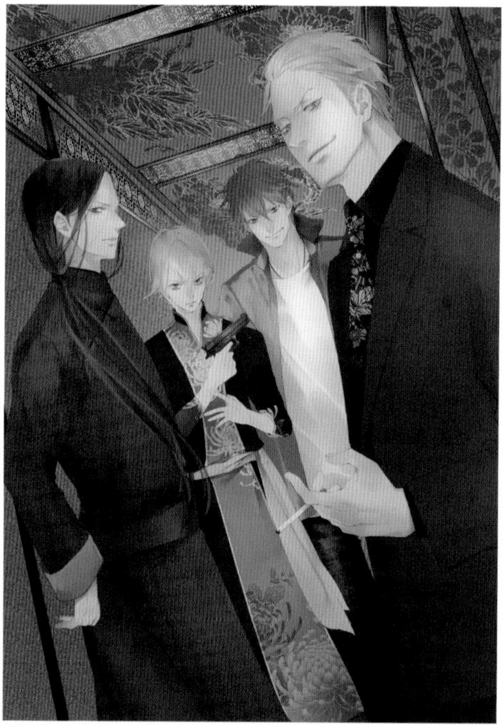

Personal Work

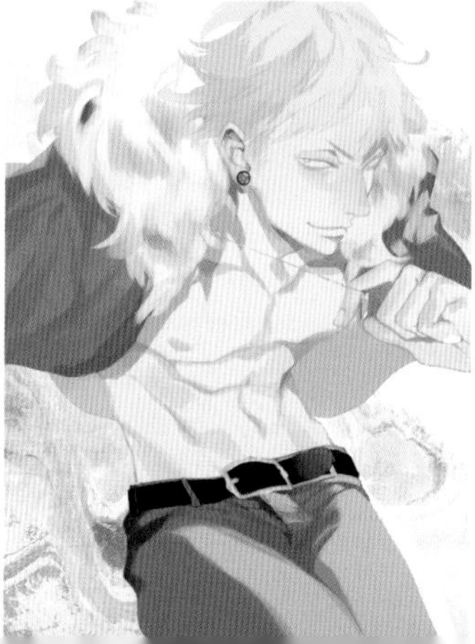

「H·K(ホンコン)ドラグネット4」松岡なつき / カバーイラスト / キャラ文庫
徳間書店　©松岡なつき・乃一ミクロ / 徳間書店

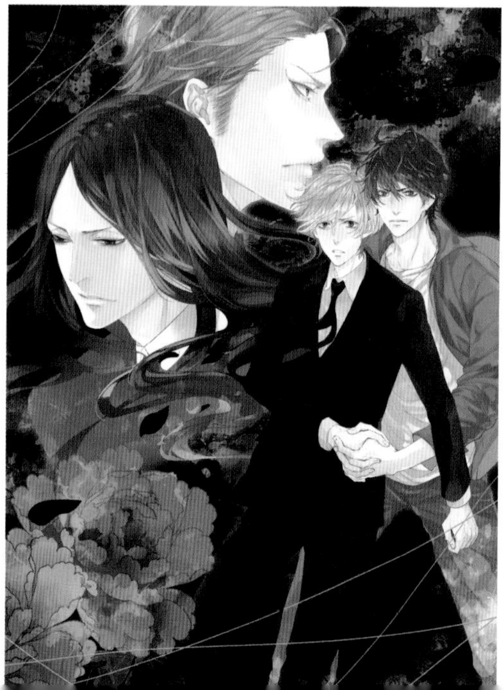

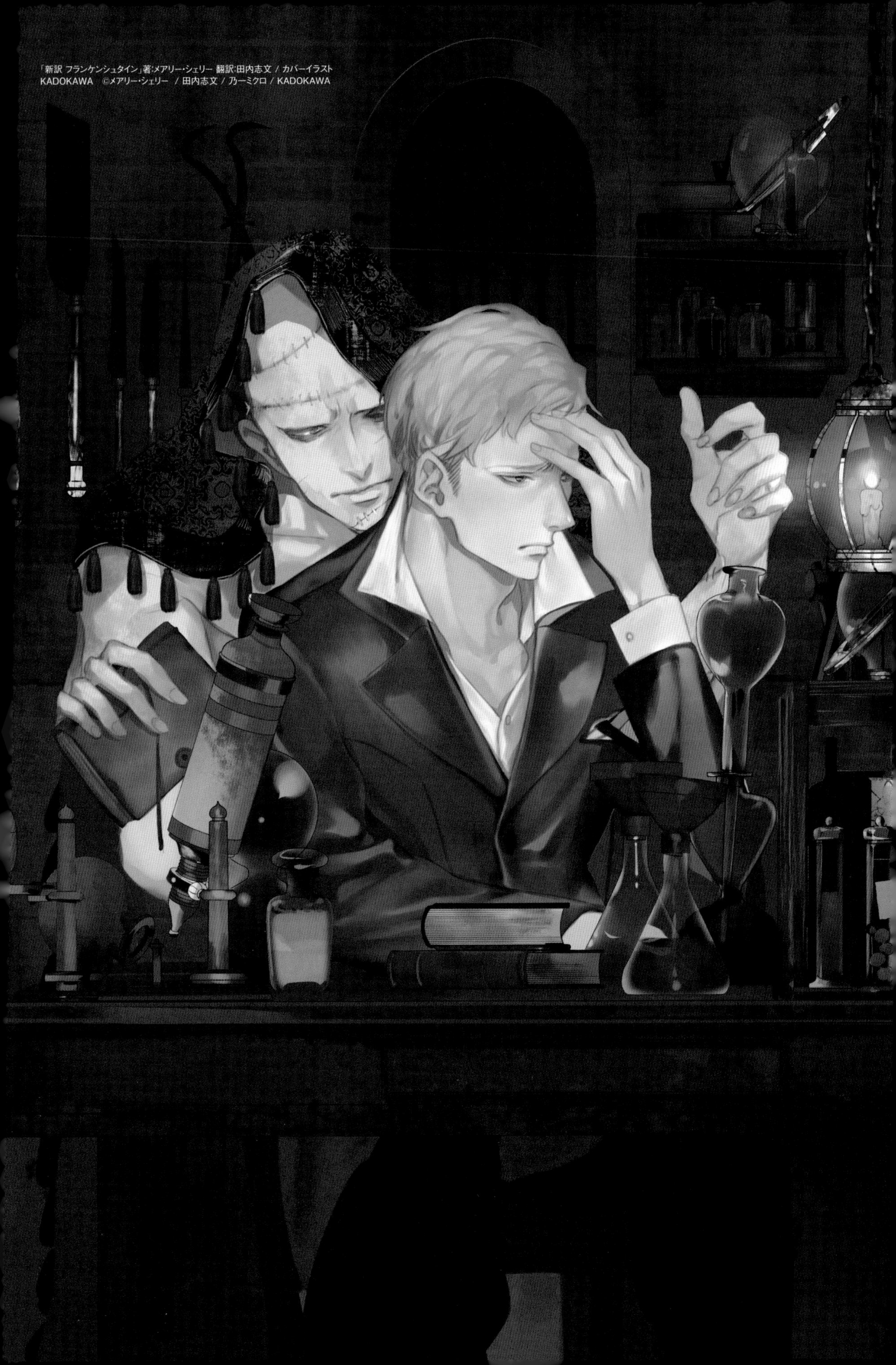
「新訳 フランケンシュタイン」著:メアリー・シェリー 翻訳:田内志文 / カバーイラスト
KADOKAWA ©メアリー・シェリー / 田内志文 / 乃ーミクロ / KADOKAWA

白皙
hakuseki

Ⓜ hakuseki_0730@yahoo.co.jp   Ⓣ _hakuseki_

Ⓤ http://about.me/hakuseki   Ⓓ SAI • Photoshop CS5

Profile	主に、デジタルロックシンガー「VALSHE」のイメージ・パッケージイラスト等を制作しています。そのほか、女性向け恋愛アプリのキャラクター原画、イラストメイキング制作など。
Comments	男性を描く際には、見る人に男性ならではの色気を感じてもらえるように…！と念じながら手を動かしています。また、作品内の空気感や世界観も大切にして制作しています。色っぽい少年が好きです。スタイリッシュだったりダークな世界観が特に得意です。軍服、スーツ、ゴシック、パンクロック…あと厨二病っぽい感じも大好きです。

My prime focus is on creating images and producing illustrations used in packaging for the digital rock singer VALSHE. I also design manga characters and produce illustrations for apps focusing on romantic themes for female consumers.

While I'm drawing, I always think, "I hope I'm conveying the sex appeal of the male characters to the viewer!" The ambience and interpretation of the setting are important to me as I work. I like sexy young boys. My forte is turning out stylish yet dark moods. I also love military uniforms, suits, goth, punk rock ..... and the pubescent look.

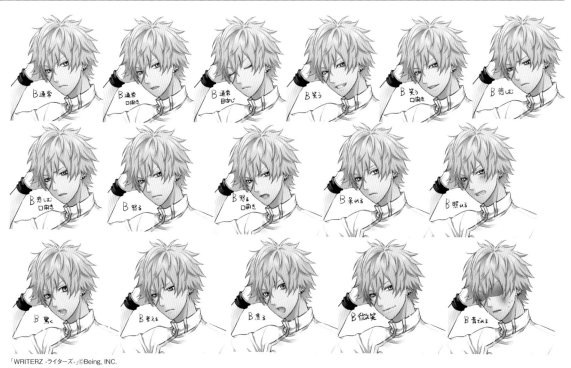

「WRITERZ -ライターズ-」©Being, INC.

Personal Work

Personal Work

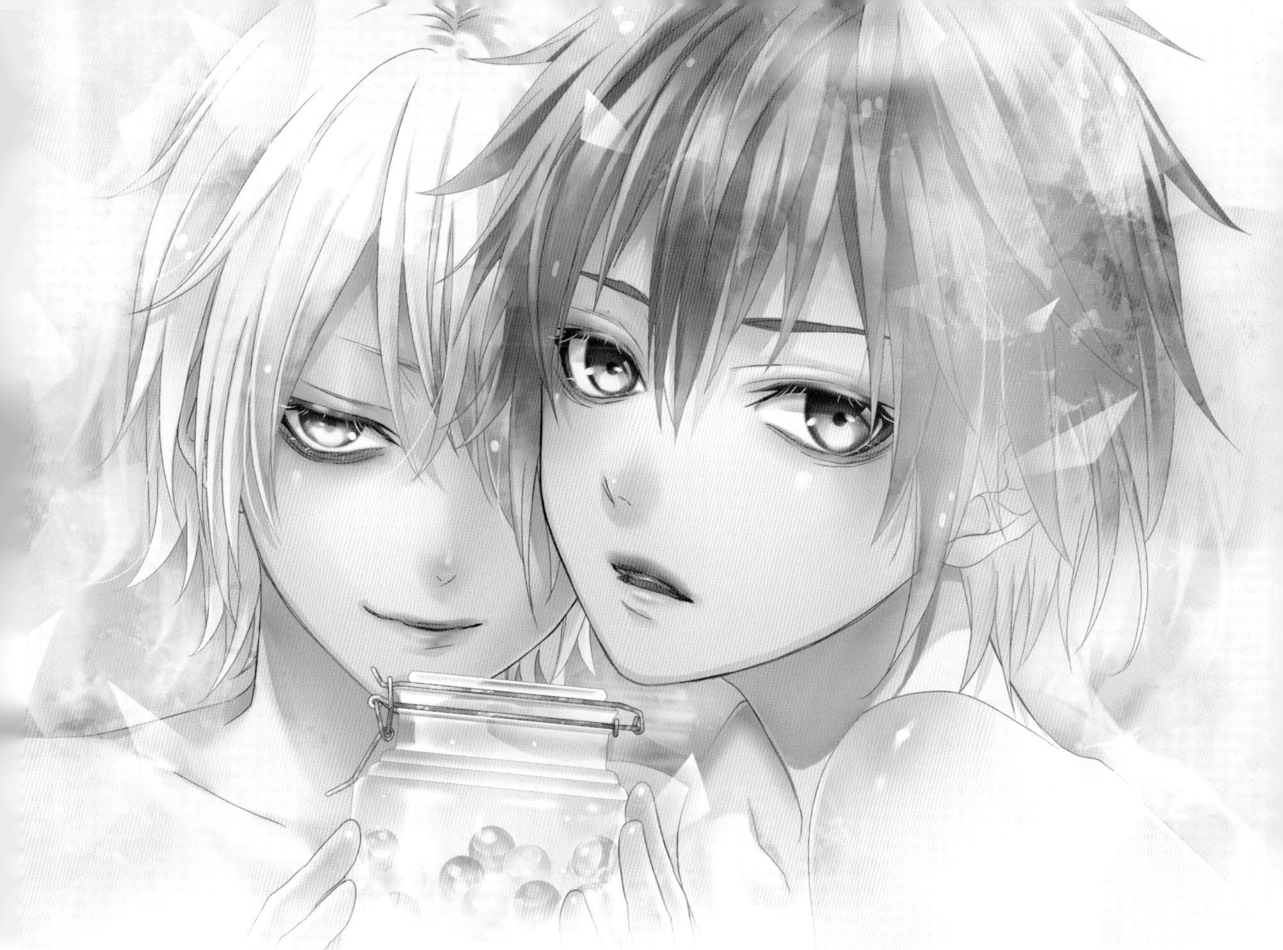

Personal Work

「WRITERZ -ライターズ-」©Being, INC.

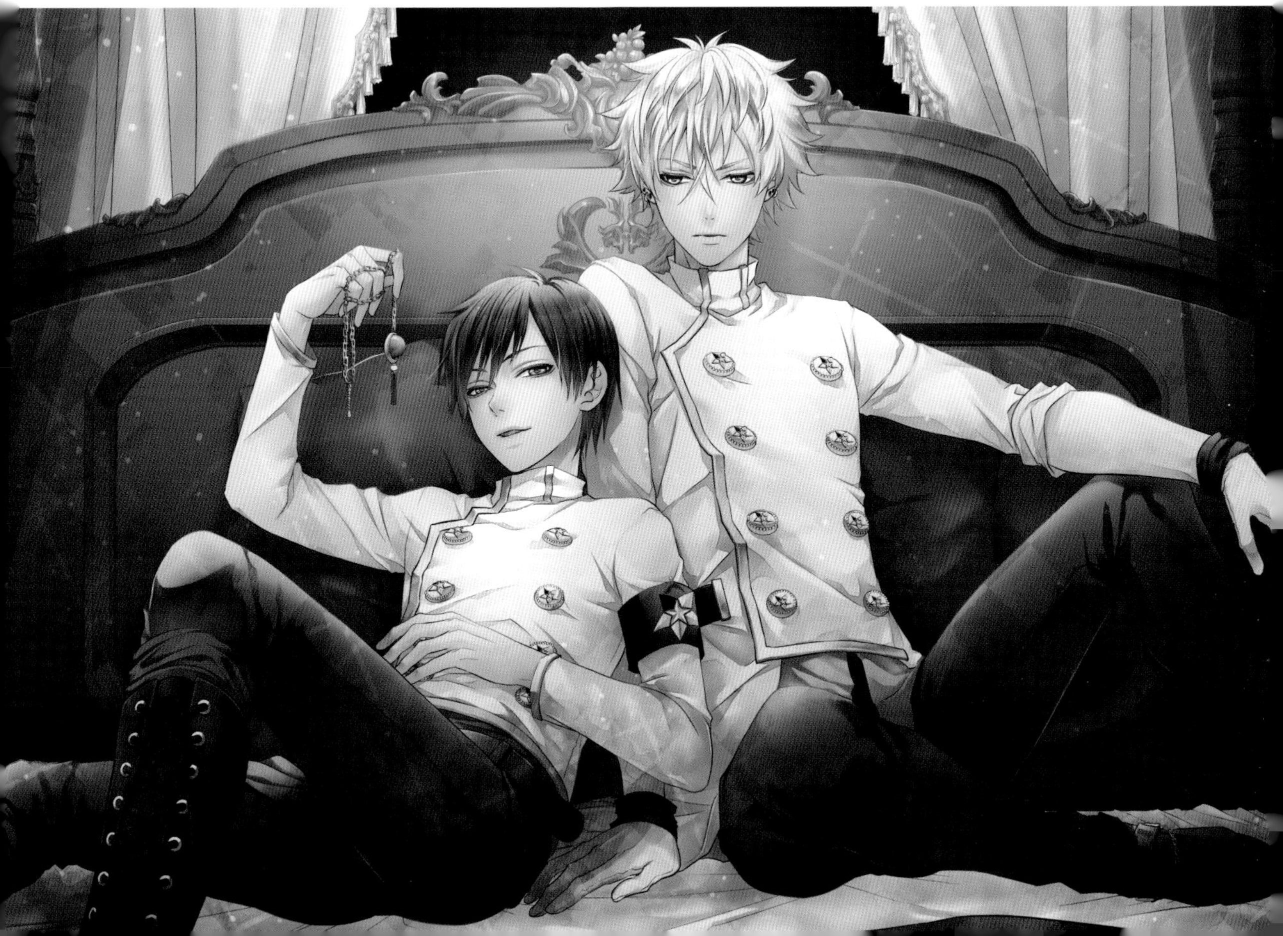

ぱこ
pako

Ⓜ pako@e-mail.jp   Ⓣ ---

Ⓤ ---   Ⓓ Painter 2015

Profile	キャラクター中心に絵を書いております　まる	I illustrate with a focus on the characters themselves.
Comments	世の中にあると楽しい物をつくるためならなんなりと	I basically want to create anything that brings fun and joy into the world.

「スカーレッドライダーゼクスゼノン」著:永川成基　監修:レッド・エンタテインメント
イラスト:pako / 星海社　©星海社 / 永川成基 / レッド・エンタテインメント

キャラクターCD「SRX THE BEST 青盤」/ ジャケットイラスト / レッド・エンタテインメント
©2014 RED / Rejet / STORY RIDERS

アニメ専門フリマアプリ・オタマートの
店員 キャラクター　© 2014 otamart

ドラマCD「PIECE OF XENON」/ ジャケットイラスト / レッド・エンタテインメント　©2014 RED / Rejet / STORY RIDERS

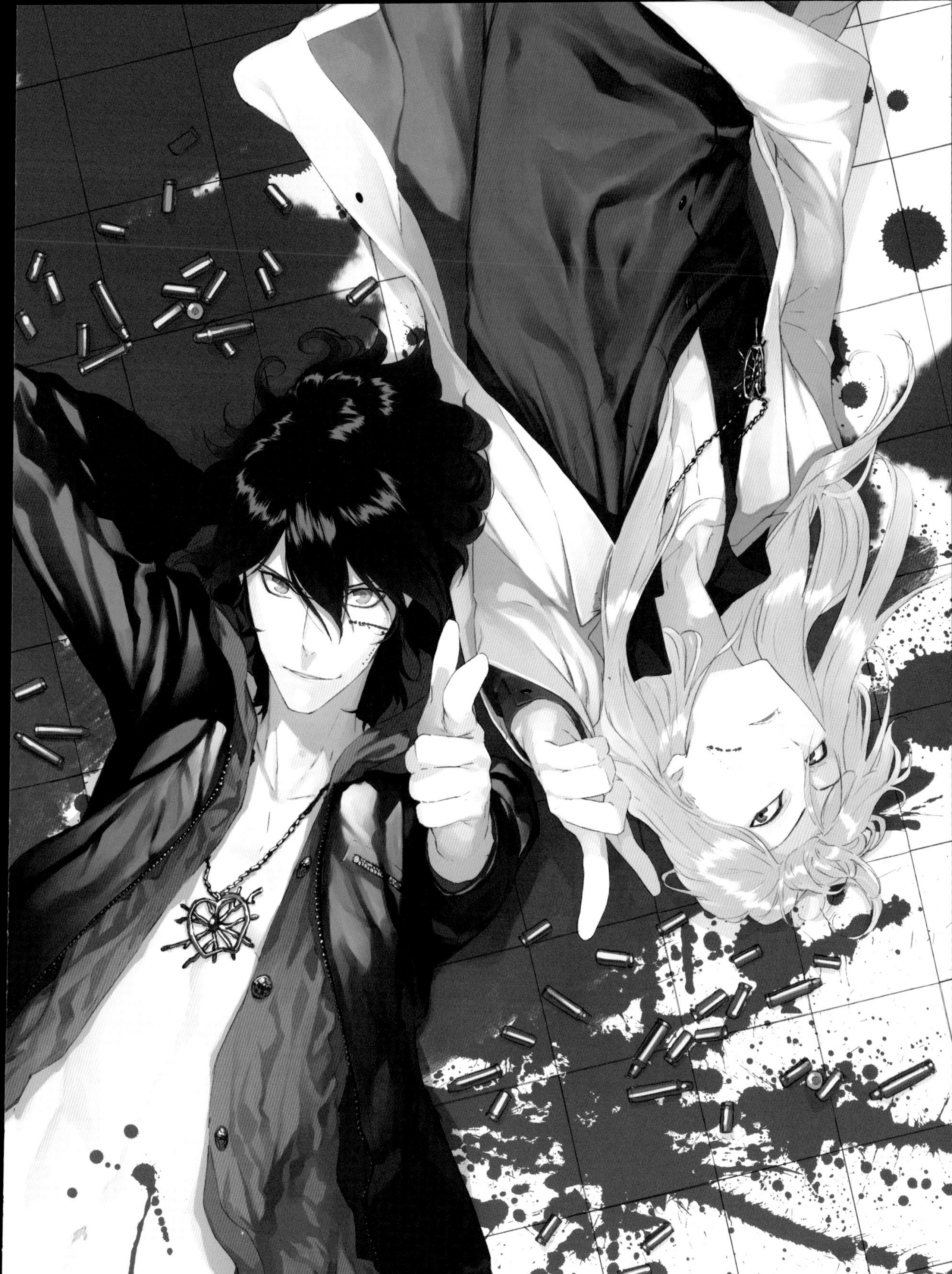

キャラクターCD「愛のZERO距離射撃 -loveshoooooot!!!!!-」発売元:5pb. / ジャケットイラスト / レッド・エンタテインメント ©2010 RED / Rejet / STORY RIDERS

ハッカワークス

HaccaWorks*

M infor@haccaworks.net
U http://haccaworks.net
T haccaworks
D Photoshop ● SAI

Profile

同人ゲームの制作サークルとして活動中。メンバーは現在4名。主な作品は「花帰葬」「あかやあかしやあやかしの」。原作のPCゲームからPS2・PSPへのコンシューマ移植をはじめ、ドラマCD、コミカライズなどにメディア展開されている。

I'm involved in a group creating *dojin* games. There are currently four of us. Our main titles thus far are: *Hana Kiso* and *Akaya Akashiya Ayakashino*. These original computer games have expanded into other formats, being transplanted to consumer products such as PS2 and PSP, drama CDs, manga, etc.

Comments

世界観を大事にした創作を心がけています。掲載作品は和が多いですが、洋も好きです。おおむね退廃的で時々シュールです。仄暗い雰囲気のシチュエーションと、目付きが悪いか薄幸そうな男子が得意分野。

I concentrate on producing work which meaningfully reflects a world view. Most of my published efforts have a Japanese flavor, but I also like Western motifs. I most often portray decadent themes, but occasionally do the surreal. My fortes are situations with gloomy atmospheres and male characters with unpleasant or sad eyes.

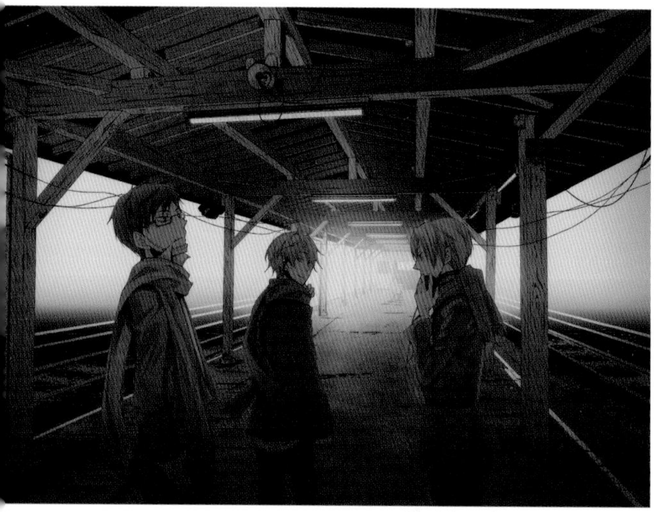

「あかやあかしやあやかしの」© HaccaWorks*

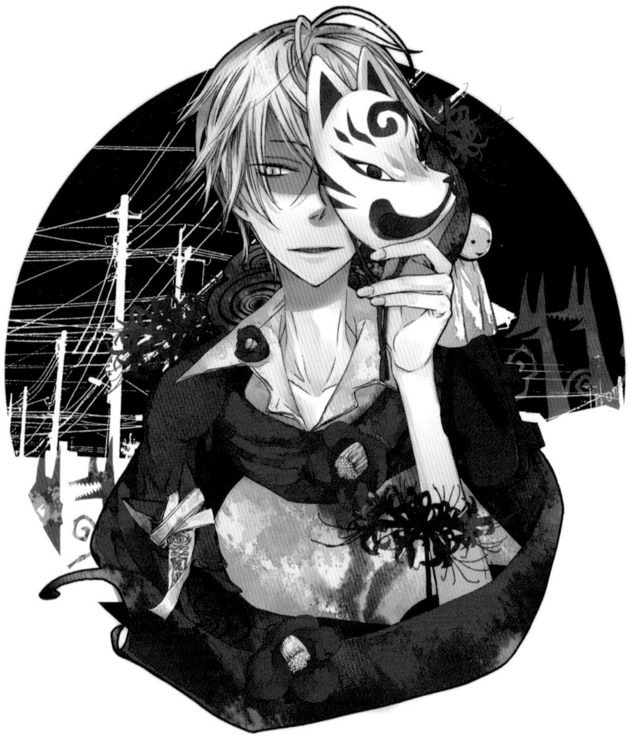

「あかやあかしやあやかしの」© HaccaWorks*

Personal Work

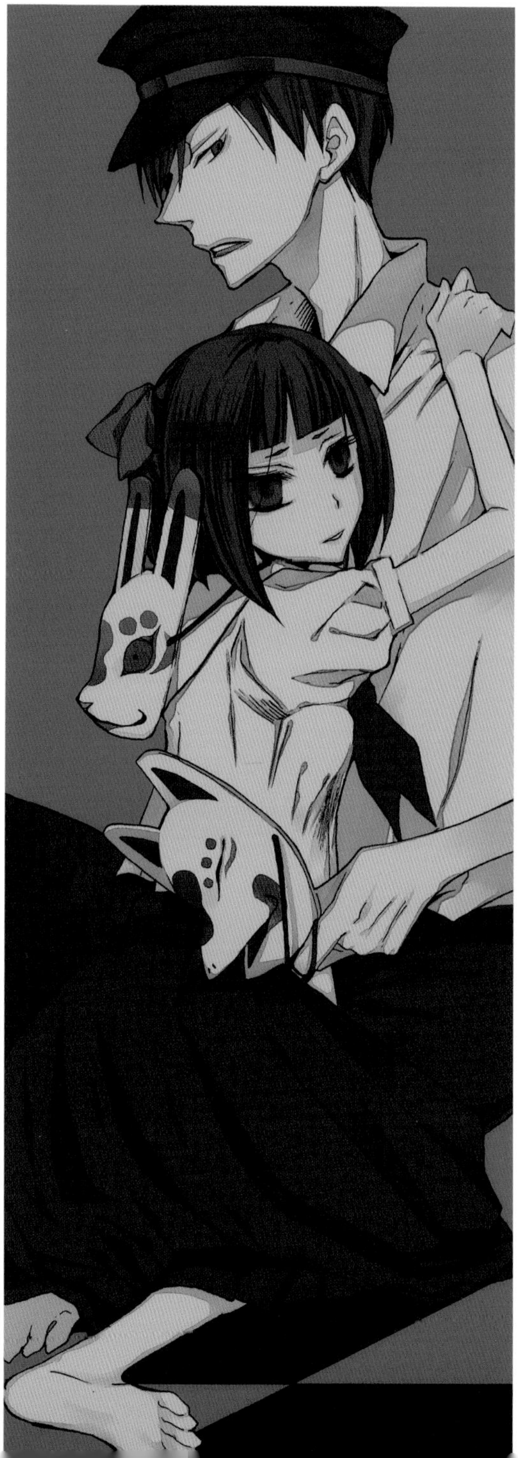

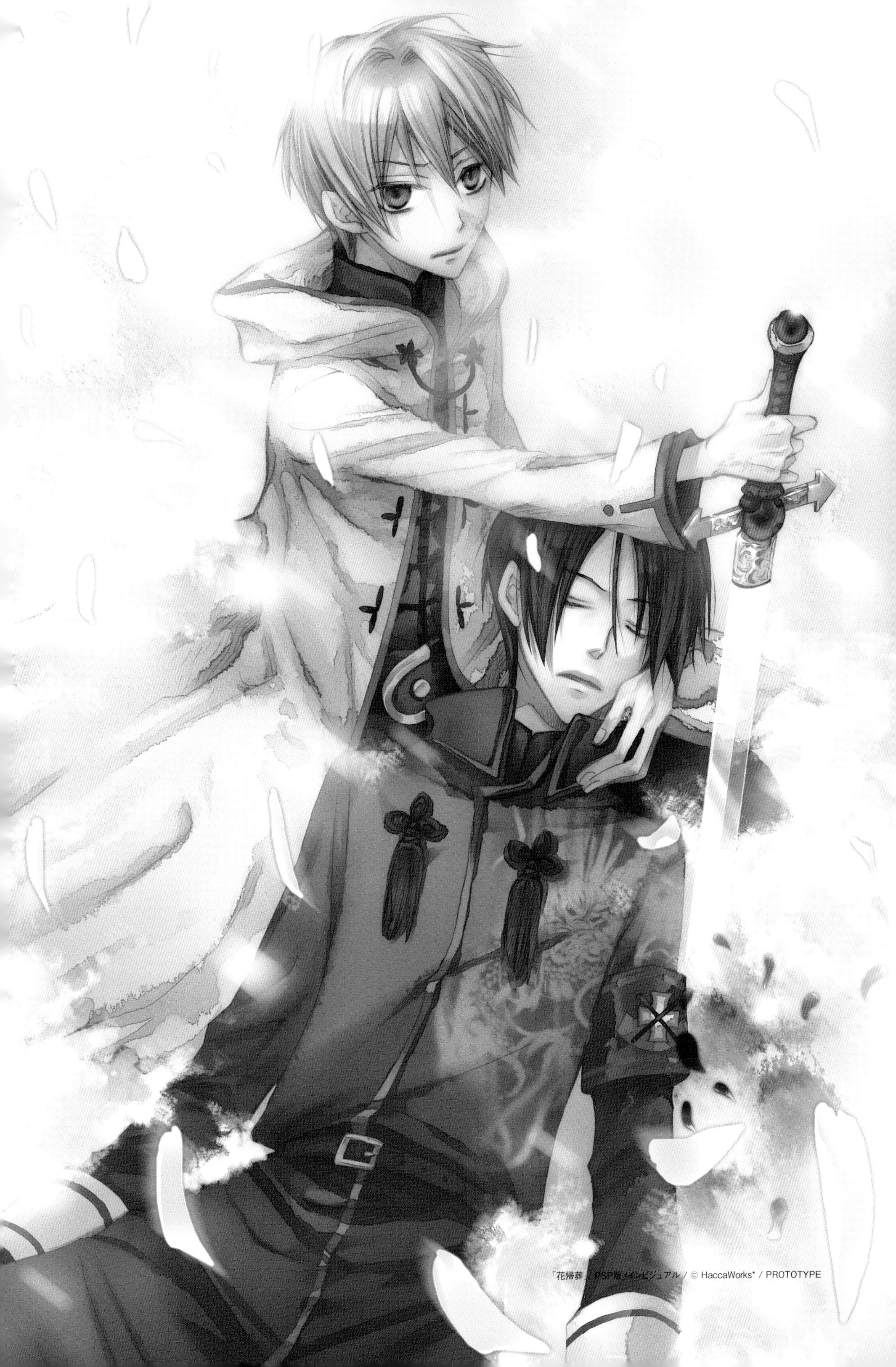

「花帰葬」/ PSP版メインビジュアル / © HaccaWorks* / PROTOTYPE

羽鳥まりえ
Hadori Marie

M johnnysiden@nifty.com　T ---　U http://eggnut.fc2web.com

D Photoshop CS6 ● CLIP STUDIO PAINT ● Mechanical pencil

Profile

千葉県在住。漫画やイラストを描いております。

I live in Chiba Prefecture. I draw manga and illustrations.

Comments

人物の内面やその場の温度、風の匂いなど、さまざまなことが伝わるといいな〜と思いながら描いてます。ノスタルジックなものやファンタジー、あと自然科学（白衣メガネ含む）を題材にした作品を描くのが好きです。

When I draw, I yearn to capture the essence of the characters and the mood and flavor of the moment. I draw on nostalgia, fantasy, and natural science (such as in Hakui Megane) in my work.

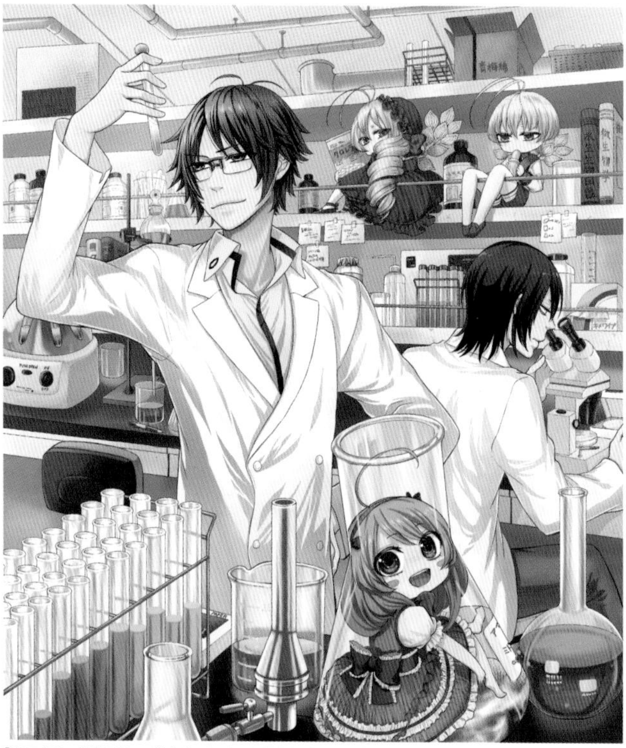

「ミクロネスト」羽鳥まりえ / 1巻カバーイラスト / ©羽鳥まりえ 2014 / 新潮社

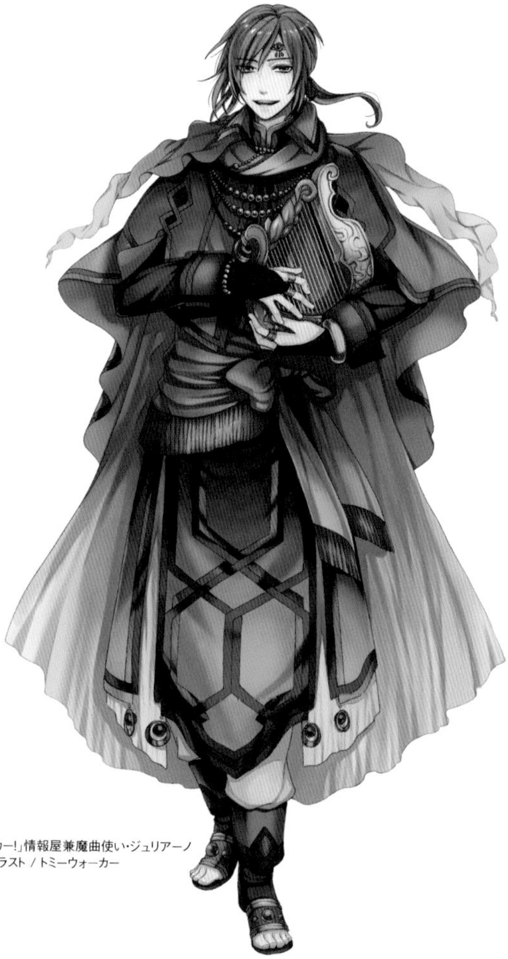

「エンドブレイカー!」情報屋兼魔曲使い・ジュリアーノ
キャラクターイラスト / トミーウォーカー

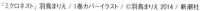

「ミドリムシは植物ですか?虫ですか? I・II」羽鳥まりえ / カバーカット / B's -LOG COMICS / KADOKAWA

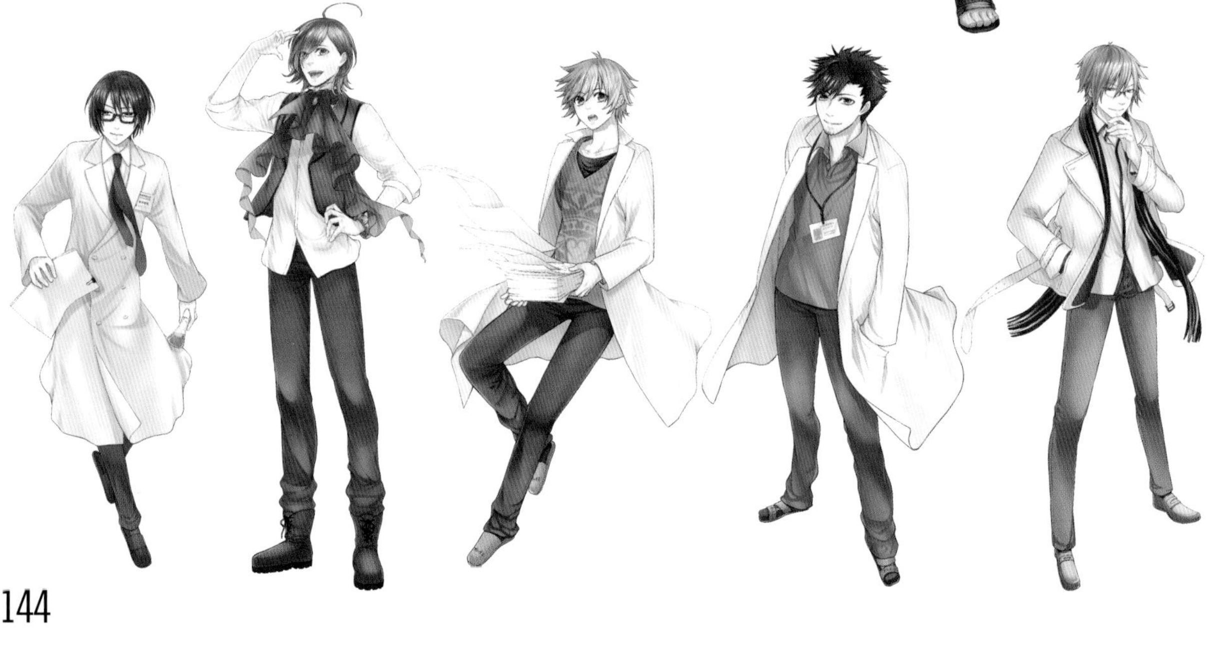

Personal Work「蒼の源」

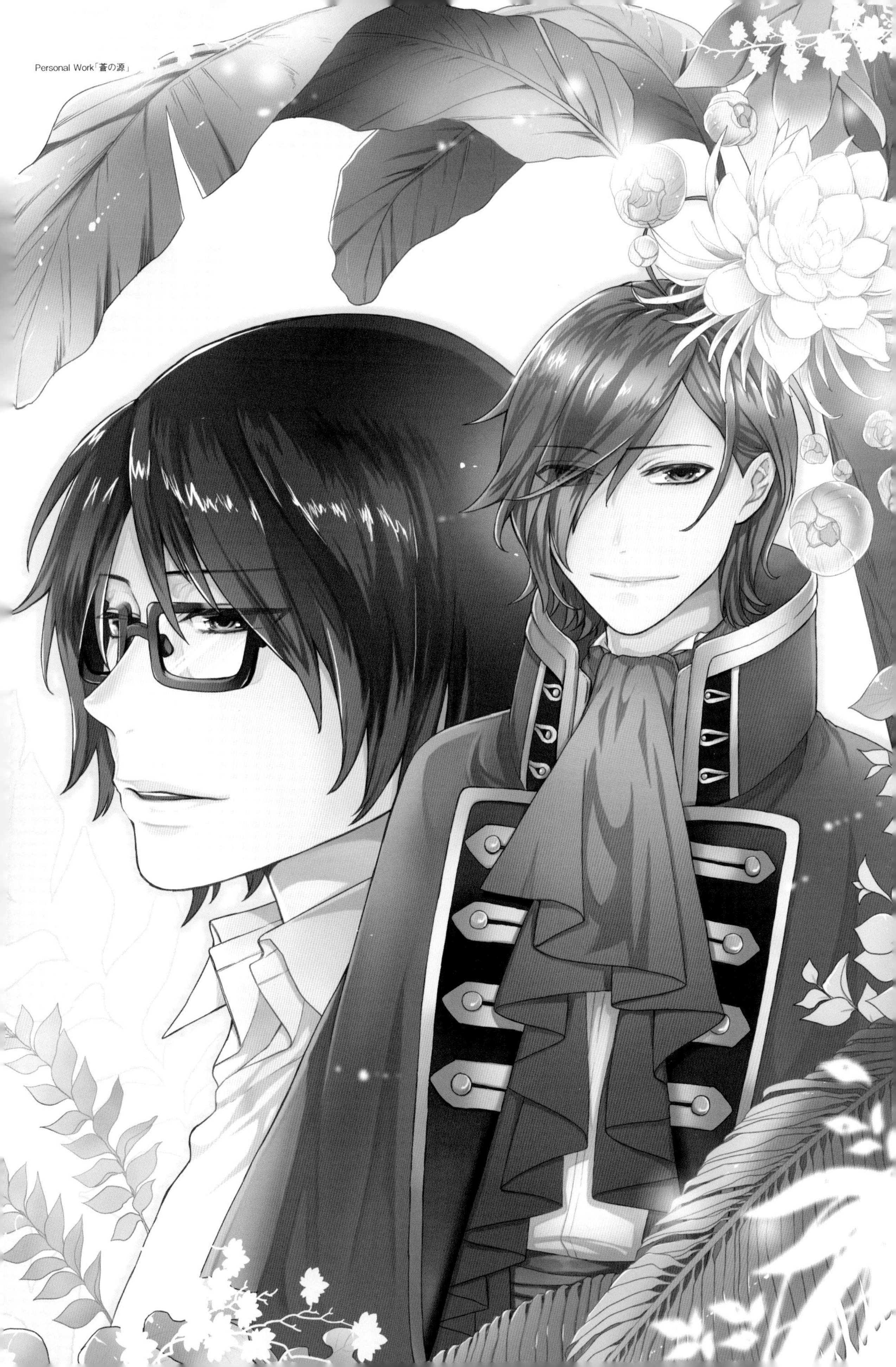

BISAI

M junmurasakikiseki@yahoo.co.jp T ---
U http://pb-b.com D ---

Profile

TCGやキャラクターデザイン、カバーイラスト、CDジャケットなど描いております。

I draw TCGs (trading cards), character designs, book covers, CD jackets, and the like.

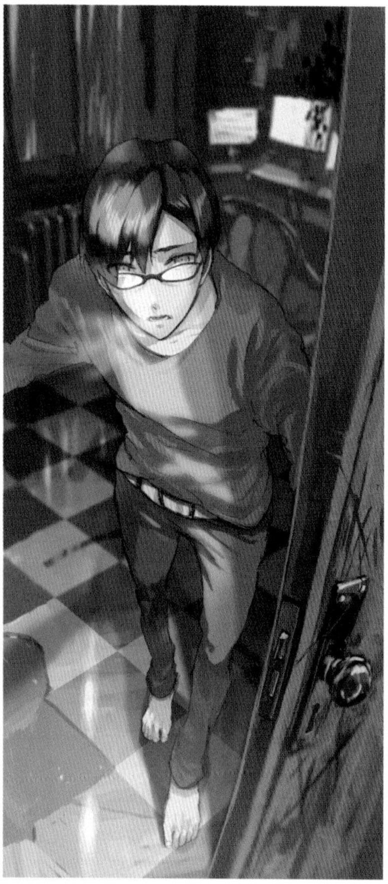

Personal Work

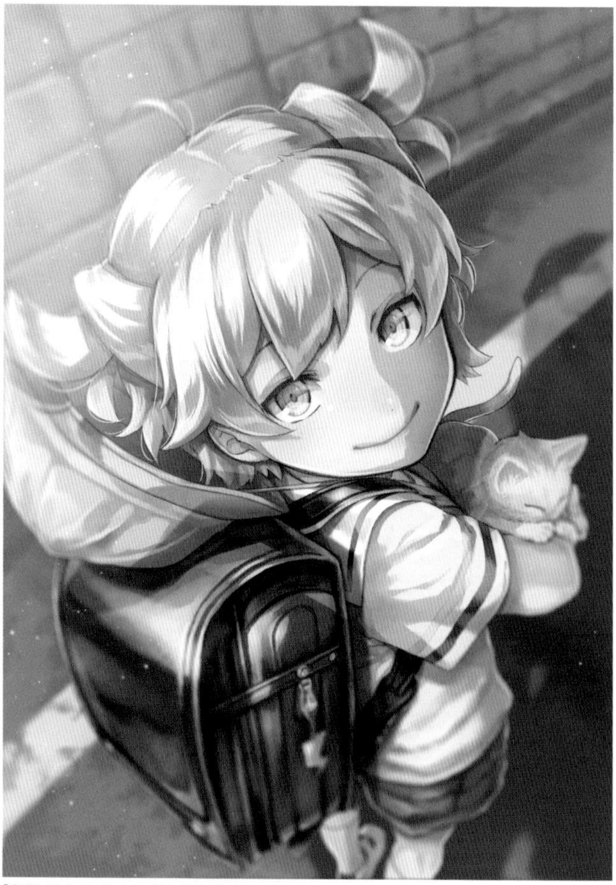

「安眠+カレシ」/ コミック Be 2014年9月号 表紙イラスト
ふゅーじょんぷろだくと ©BISAI / FUSION PRODUCT

Personal Work

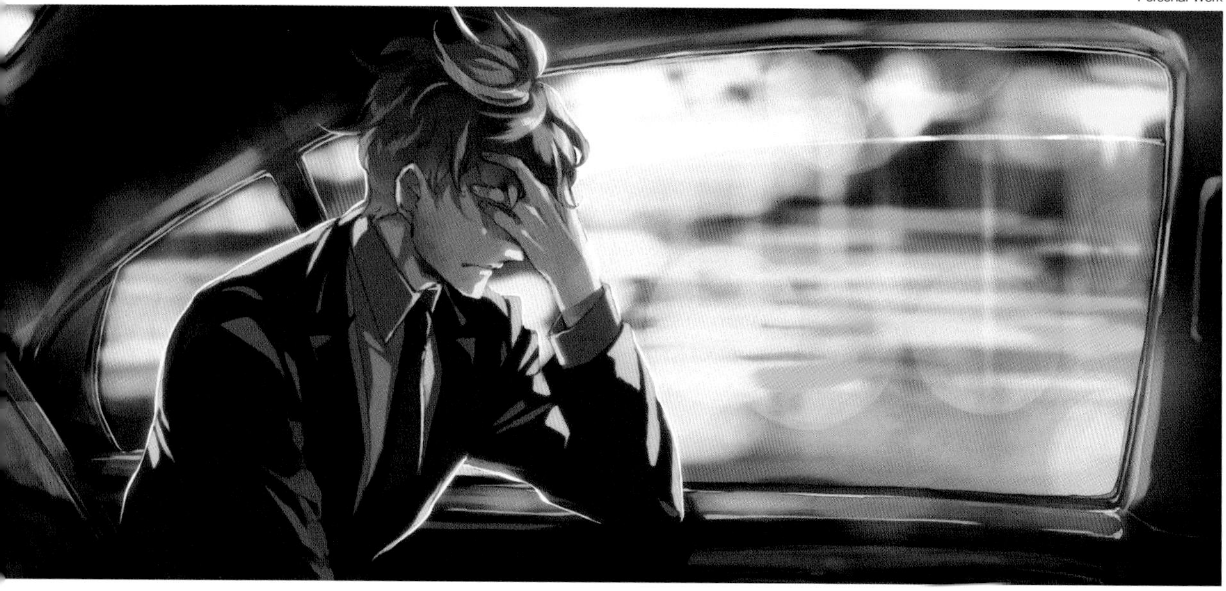

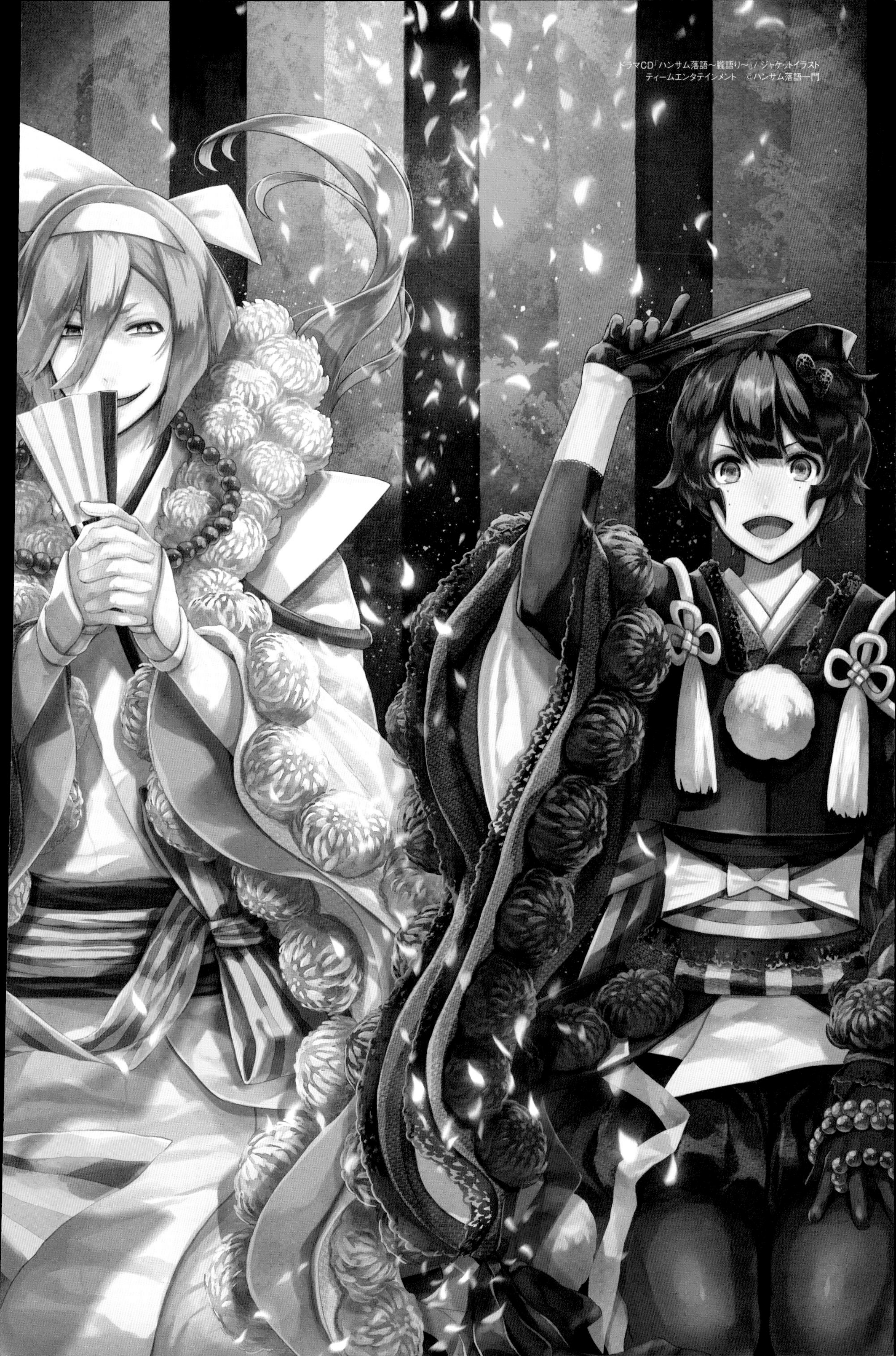

ドラマCD「ハンサム落語〜朧語り〜」/ジャケットイラスト
ティームエンタテインメント　©ハンサム落語一門

ひだかなみ

Hidaka Nami

M origin@hi-na.sakura.ne.jp
U http://hi-na.sakura.ne.jp
T hidakanami
D CLIP STUDIO PAINT EX ● SAI ● Photoshop

Profile	小説挿画、ゲーム用イラスト等を中心に絵を描かせて頂いております。	I mainly create illustrations for books and games.
Comments	見て下さる方に楽しんで頂けたり、絵から色んなことを想像して頂けるようなものが描けたらと思っております。	My hope is to turn out illustrations which will please people, and which will allow their imaginations to run wild.

「百鬼夜行の少年 鏡ヶ原遺聞 壱ノ巻」天堂里砂 / カバーイラスト / 中央公論新社

「姫神の裔と鏡の伝説 鏡ヶ原遺聞 参ノ巻」
天堂里砂 / カバーイラスト / 中央公論新社

「妖虎の主人と金髪の神父 萬屋あやかし事件帖 其の参」
天堂里砂 / カバーイラスト / 中央公論新社

「魔界カンパニー そのお願い、悪魔が承ります!」
夜野しずく / カバーイラスト / 角川ビーンズ文庫 / KADOKAWA

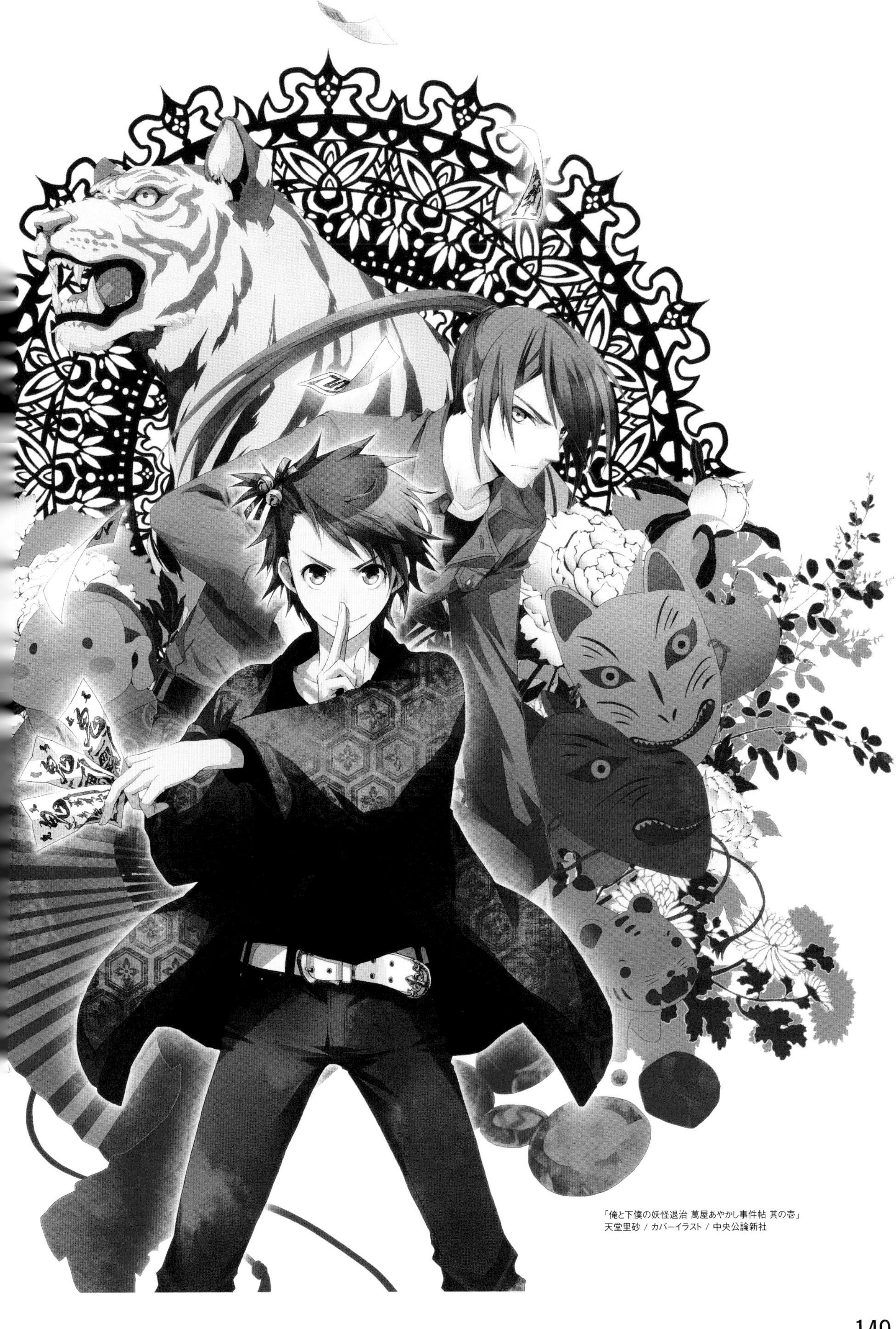

「俺と下僕の妖怪退治 萬屋あやかし事件帖 其の壱」
天堂里砂 / カバーイラスト / 中央公論新社

日向ろこ
Himuka Roko

M hituji_color@yahoo.co.jp **T** 55roko

U --- **D** SAI ● photoshop CS5 ● Illustrator CS5

Profile	ゲーム会社でデザイン・イラスト作成の経験を経て現在はフリーで装画やキャラクターデザインを担当させて頂いております。	After gaining experience working for a company in design and illustrating, I'm now freelancing, creating book-cover and character designs.
Comments	イラスト全体の雰囲気や設定されたキャラクターであればその色を画面に出すようにしています。和装・洋装・ファンタジーなイラストが得意でその中でも特にオリジナルの制服や軍服のデザイン、細かい装飾を描くのが大好きです。	I work on making sure the overall mood of the illustrations and the unique personalities of the set characters are fully expressed on screen. I'm good with kimono, Western clothing, and fantasy outfits, and really love the detail work on my original military and other uniforms.

「千夜一夜の恋物語～ランプに導かれし運命～」©OKKO

Personal Work

Personal Work「Rewind Seven Ⅳ」

Personal Work「Rewind Seven Ⅲ」

Personal Work「Rewind Seven Ⅰ」

Personal Work「Rewind Seven Ⅱ」

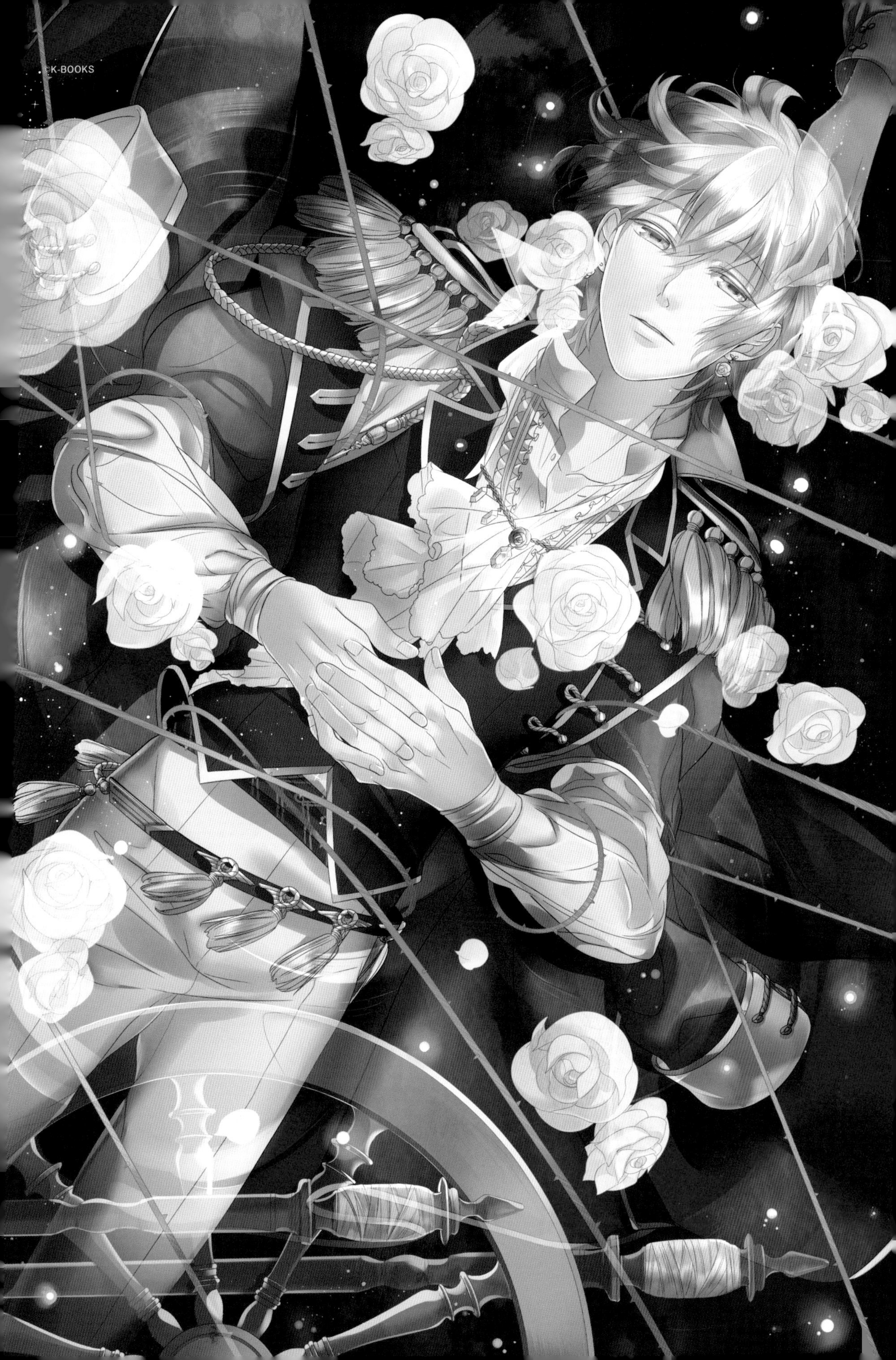

ビリー・バリバリー

Billy Balibally

M billybalibally@gmail.com T onikushock
U http://shokona2.blog.fc2.com

D Dip pen ● Pencil ● CLIP STUDIO PAINT ● SAI

Profile

漫画家です。2013年にBLコミック雑誌でデビュー後、漫画・挿絵を中心に活動しています。

I'm a manga artist. Since debuting in a BL comic magazine in 2013, I have fundamentally created manga and illustrations.

Comments

受け取り手に余韻を残せるような作品づくりを目指しています。髪の先から瞳の中まで楽しんで頂けますように…と気持ちを込めて線を引いています。

My goal is to create works which will reverberate in the minds of those who experience them. I pour myself into creating lines which readers will enjoy, from the tips of hair strands to pupils in characters' eyes.

「ばら色の研究と花喰らふきみ」ビリー・バリバリー / カバーイラスト「love sofa」/ ダリアコミックス / フロンティアワークス ©ビリー・バリバリー / フロンティアワークス

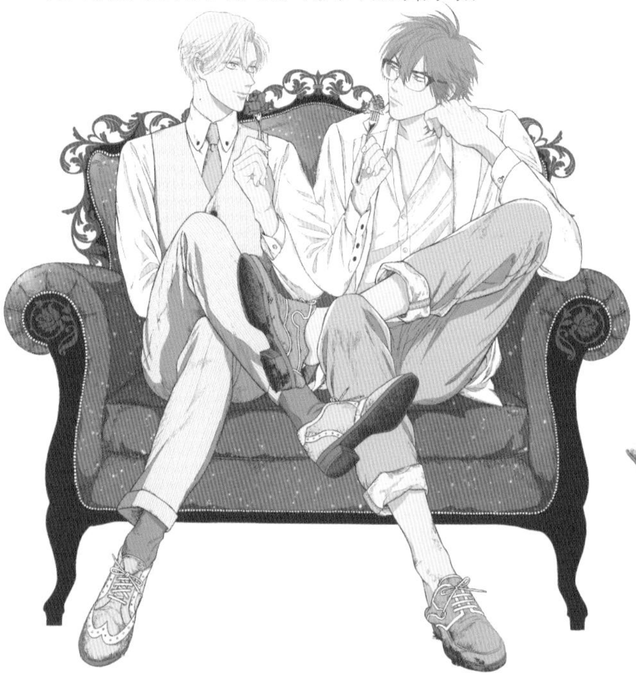

「ばら色の研究と花喰らふきみ」ビリー・バリバリー / 口絵「温室」/ ダリアコミックス / フロンティアワークス ©ビリー・バリバリー / フロンティアワークス

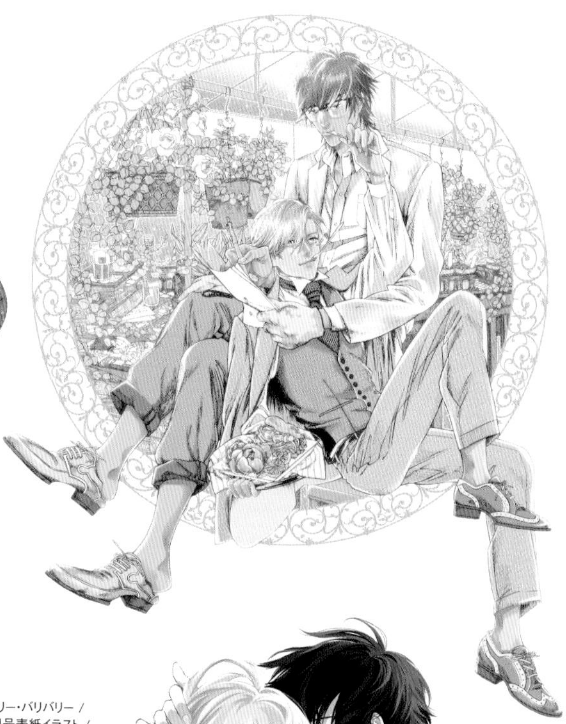

「朝とミーチャ」ビリー・バリバリー / Daria 2015年4月号表紙イラスト / フロンティアワークス ©ビリー・バリバリー / フロンティアワークス

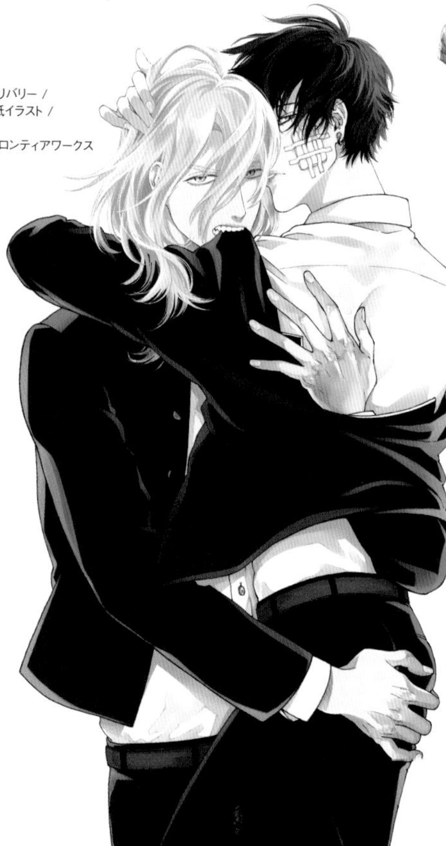

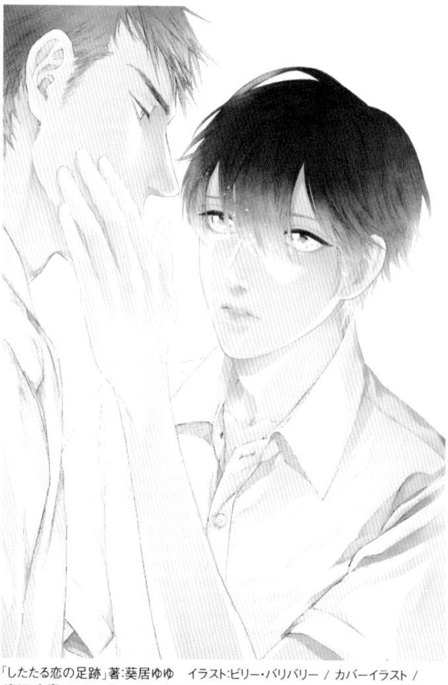

「したたる恋の足跡」著:葵居ゆゆ イラスト:ビリー・バリバリー / カバーイラスト / ダリア文庫 / フロンティアワークス ©葵居ゆゆ・ビリー・バリバリー / フロンティアワークス

「真夜中のオルフェ #1」ビリー・バリバリー / 初出・MAGAZINE BE×BOY 2015年9月号 作品扉イラスト / リブレ出版

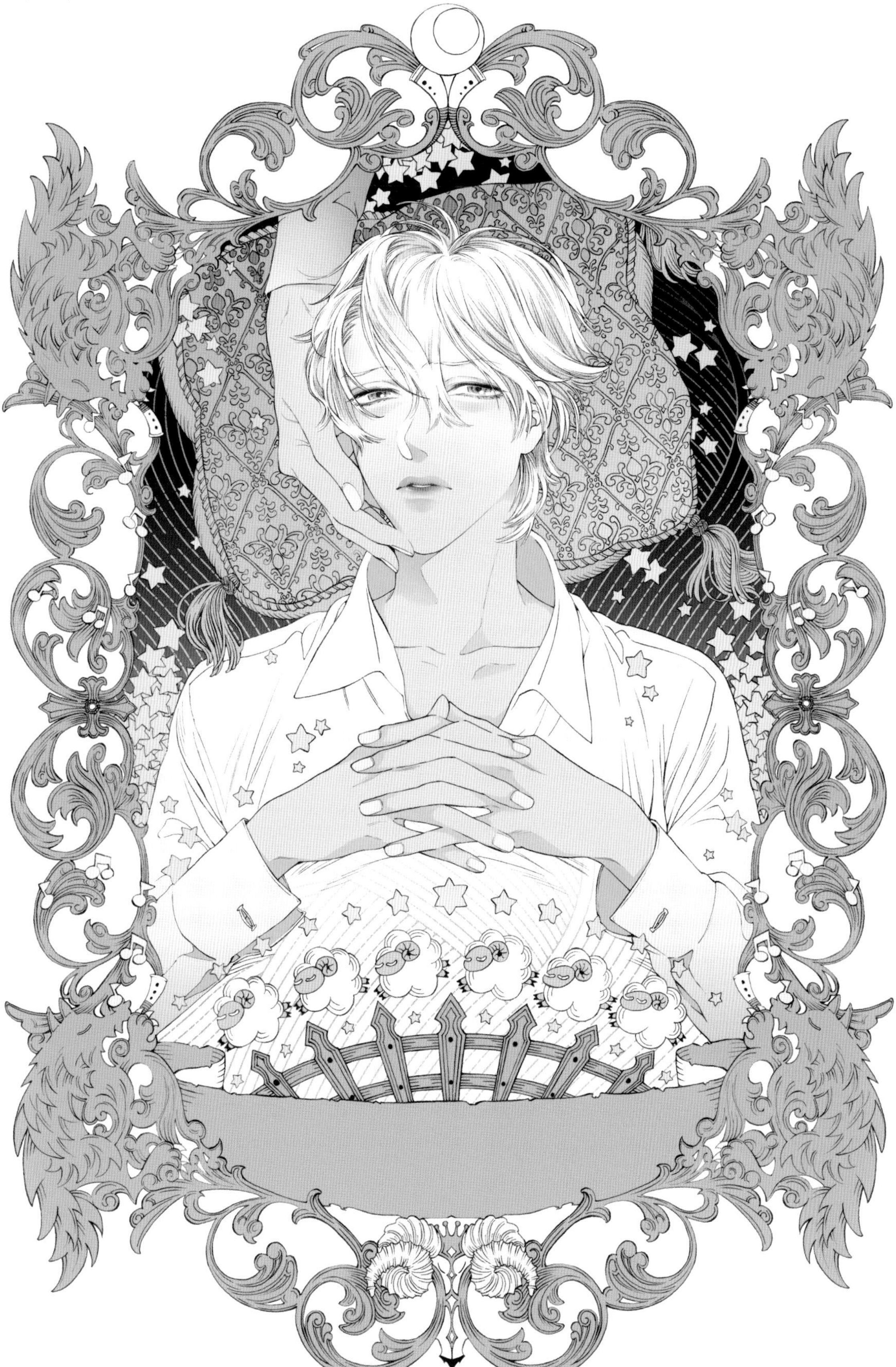

藤末都也
fuji mitsuya

M mitsuya@ali-chino.com
U http://ali-chino.com
T fuji_mitsuya
D SAI ● Photoshop CS3, CS6 ● Painter 8

Profile

こんにちは、藤末都也(ふじ みつや)です。2012年ゲーム会社を退職後フリーランスとして活動。ゲームイラスト、書籍、ドラマCD等で男性キャラクターをメインに制作しています。和と動物とかっこいい男性キャラを描くのが楽しいです。

Hi – I'm Mitsuya Fuji. I've been working as a freelancer since I left the game company where I was working in 2012. My primary work is creating male characters in game illustrations and for books and drama CDs, among other outlets. I find it fun to draw Japanese themes, animals, and trendy male characters.

Comments

和が大好きなので趣味で描く絵は和風なのが多いです。和物が描ける機会は大歓迎です。逆に仕事では作品ごとにテイストを変えたりします。個性をアピールするのも大切ですが、乙女向けで描いていると、印象が被らないよう作品にあった塗りも求められるので。そうすると着地点が見つからないときもありますが、投げ出さないことを気をつけています。

I love Japanese themes, so they tend to predominate in pictures I draw as a hobby. I always welcome opportunities to draw Japanese things. On the other hand, when it comes to work, I change the flavor around with each piece. It's important to have a unique selling point, but when drawing for the otome (young female) market, one is expected to employ coloring which does not overwhelm the impression of the work. Sometimes that hampers my initial efforts, but I soon get the hang of each piece and am able to create freely.

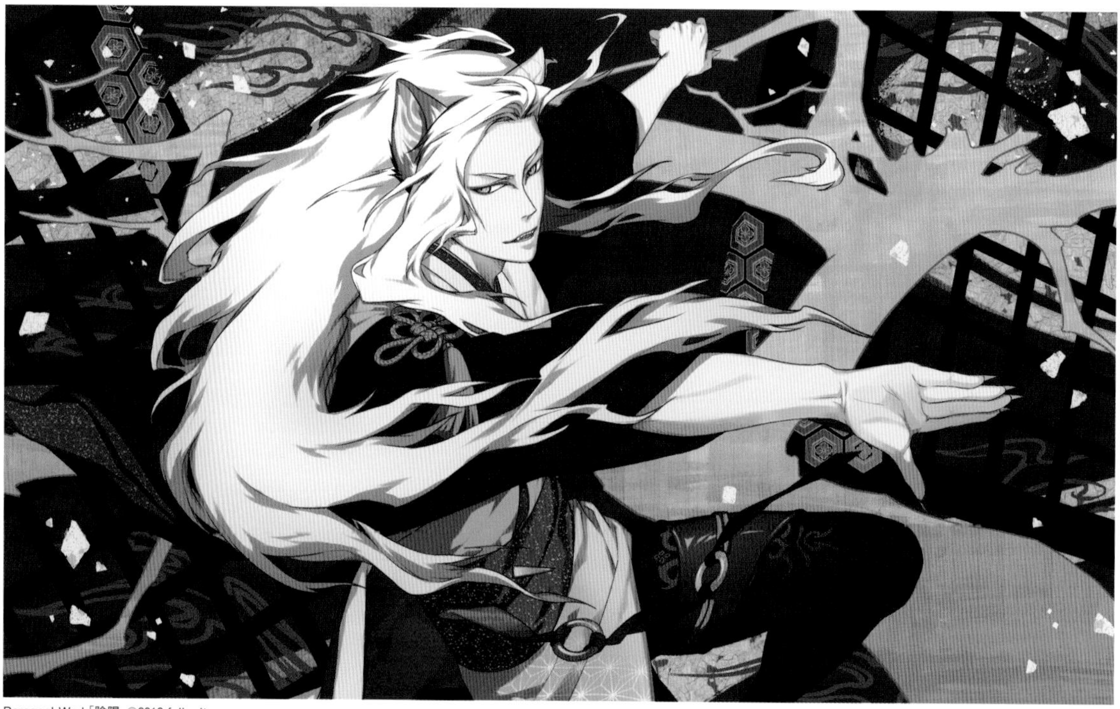

Personal Work「陰陽」©2012 fuji mitsuya

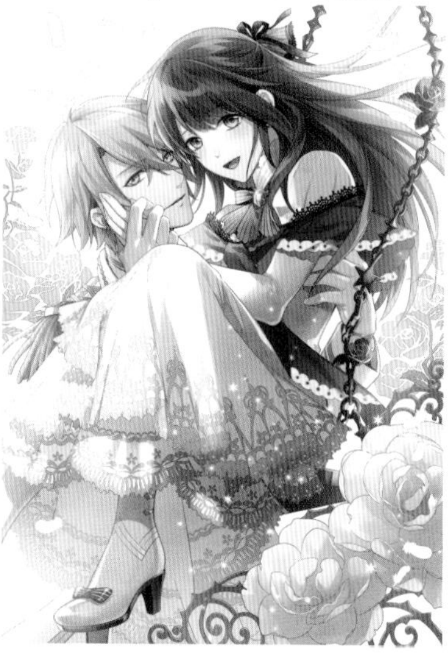

「ヒメコイ! 天に架かる七色の恋」香月沙耶 / カバーイラスト
ビーズログ文庫 ©Saya KOHZUKI 2015 / KADOKAWA

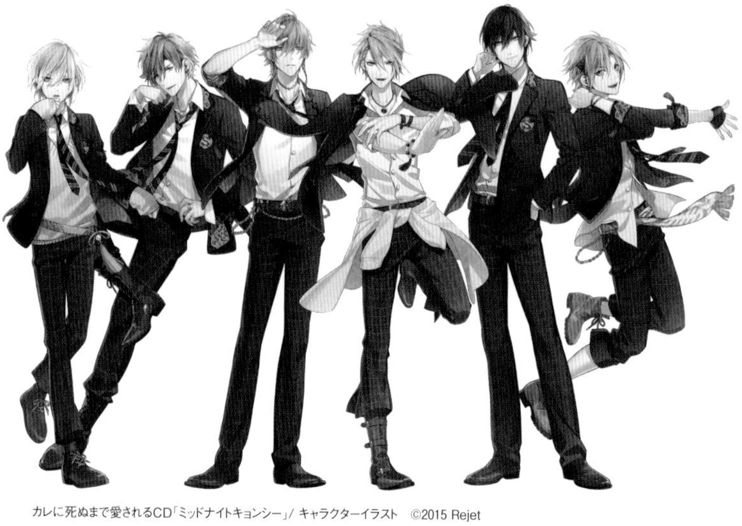

カレに死ぬまで愛されるCD「ミッドナイトキョンシー」/ キャラクターイラスト ©2015 Rejet

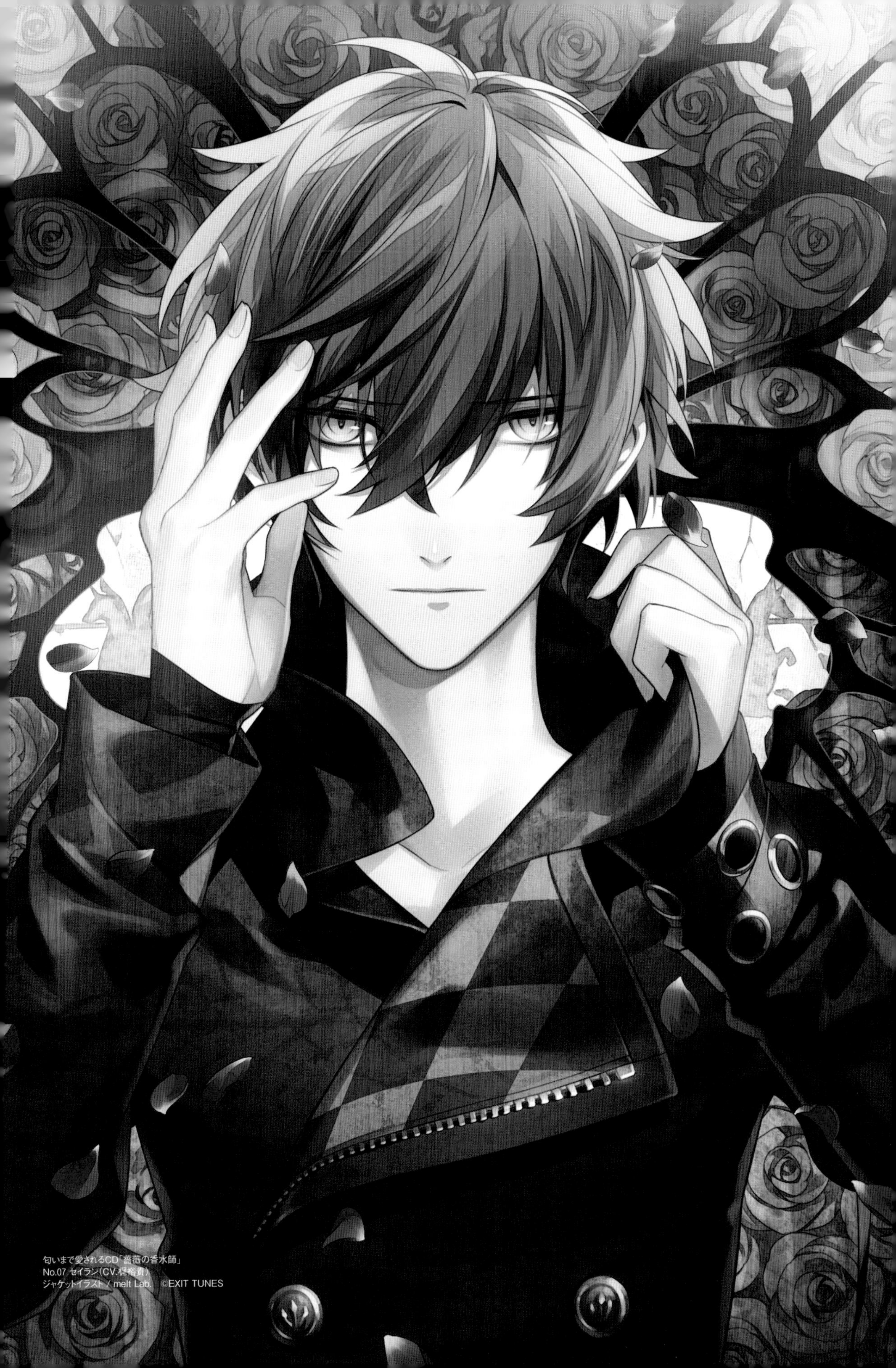
匂いまで愛されるCD「薔薇の香水師」
No.07 セイラン（CV.梶裕貴）
ジャケットイラスト / melt Lab.　©EXIT TUNES

冨士原良
Fujiwara Ryo

wsise47@hotmail.co.jp
---
http://wsise.blog40.fc2.com
SAI • Photoshop CS4

Profile

イラストレーター、漫画家。PCゲーム「DYNAMIC CHORD」キャラクターデザイン・原画、角川つばさ文庫「名探偵シャーロック・ホームズ 緋色の研究」挿絵、KADOKAWA「死神姫の再婚」コミカライズ全3巻 等。

I'm an illustrator and manga artist. Some of my efforts have included character design and original illustrations for the PC game *Dynamic Chord*, illustrations for the Kadokawa Tsubusa Bunko *Mei Tantei Sherlock Holmes: A study in scarlet,* and the manga version of KADOKAWA's *Shinigami Hime no Saikon* three-volume set.

「DYNAMIC CHORD」/ パッケージイラスト / ©honeybee black

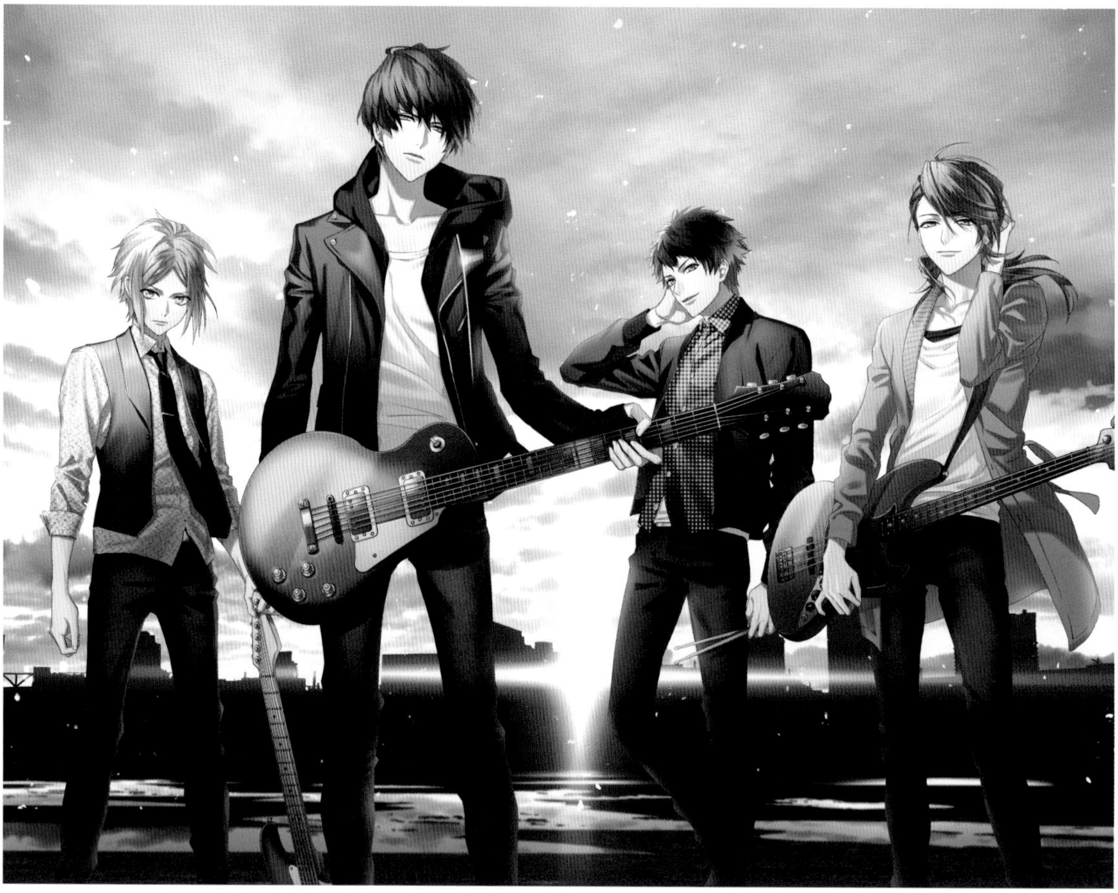

「ネクロ×マジック～陰陽男子ともう一人の末裔～」
著:狩田眞夜　イラスト:冨士原 良 / カバーイラスト / フィリア文庫 / フロンティアワークス　©狩田眞夜·冨士原良 / フロンティアワークス

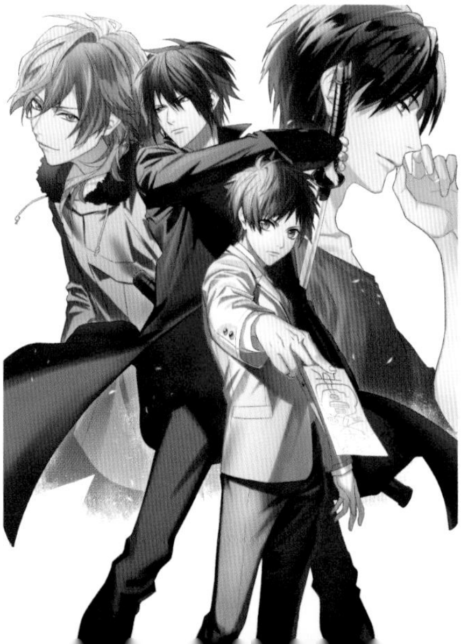

「DYNAMIC CHORD」/ パッケージイラスト / ©honeybee black

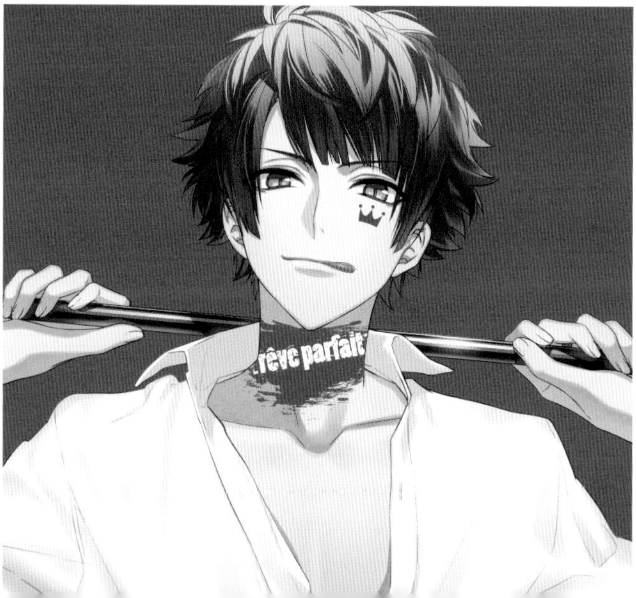
rêve parfait

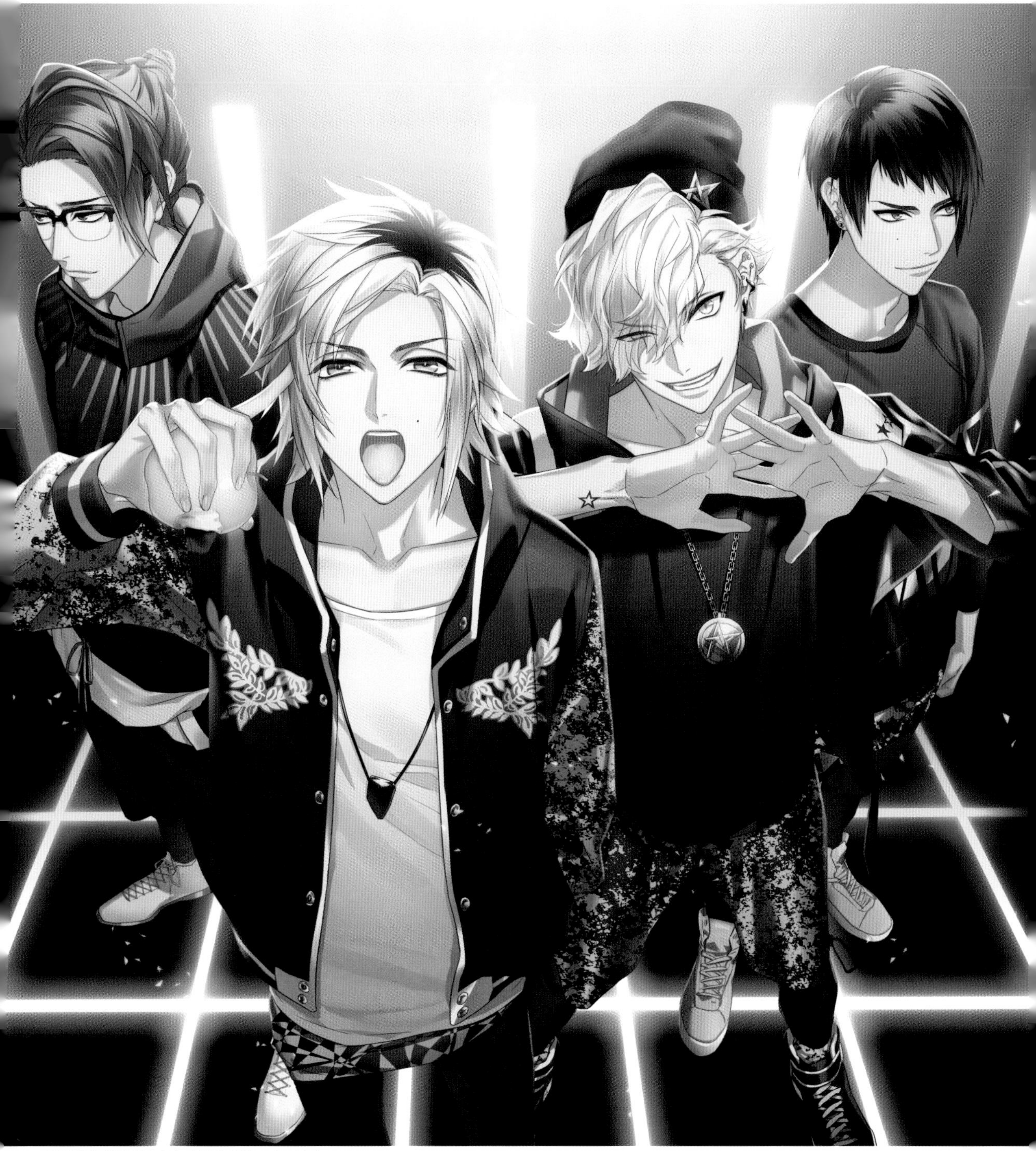

「DYNAMIC CHORD」/ ジャケットイラスト / ©honeybee black

古屋モコ
Furuya Moco

M - - -　　　**T** - - -
U - - -　　　**D** SAI ● Photoshop ● Pencil

Profile	「MANSHIN荘シークレットサービス」- キャラクターデザイン、ジャケットイラスト他。その他 - 挿絵、イラスト、キャラクターデザイン等。

I create character designs, jacket illustrations, etc. for *MANSHIN-So Secret Service*. My other work includes book and other illustrations along with character designs.

Comments	全体的なバランス、キャラクターの個性が伝わりやすいポージングや表情、視線を意識して描いています。

I keep in mind overall balance as well as poses, expressions, and gazes which can easily communicate each character's individuality.

Personal Work「男子高生と刀」

「MANSHIN荘シークレットサービス Karte.1」/ ジャケットイラスト / 創作工房　©長万部総合病院

「MANSHIN荘シークレットサービス 恐怖! 廃病院に突入せよ!」
ジャケットイラスト / 創作工房　©長万部総合病院

「MANSHIN荘シークレットサービス
～スクール×スクランブル! 星ノ森学園に潜入せよ!～」
ジャケットイラスト / 創作工房　©長万部総合病院

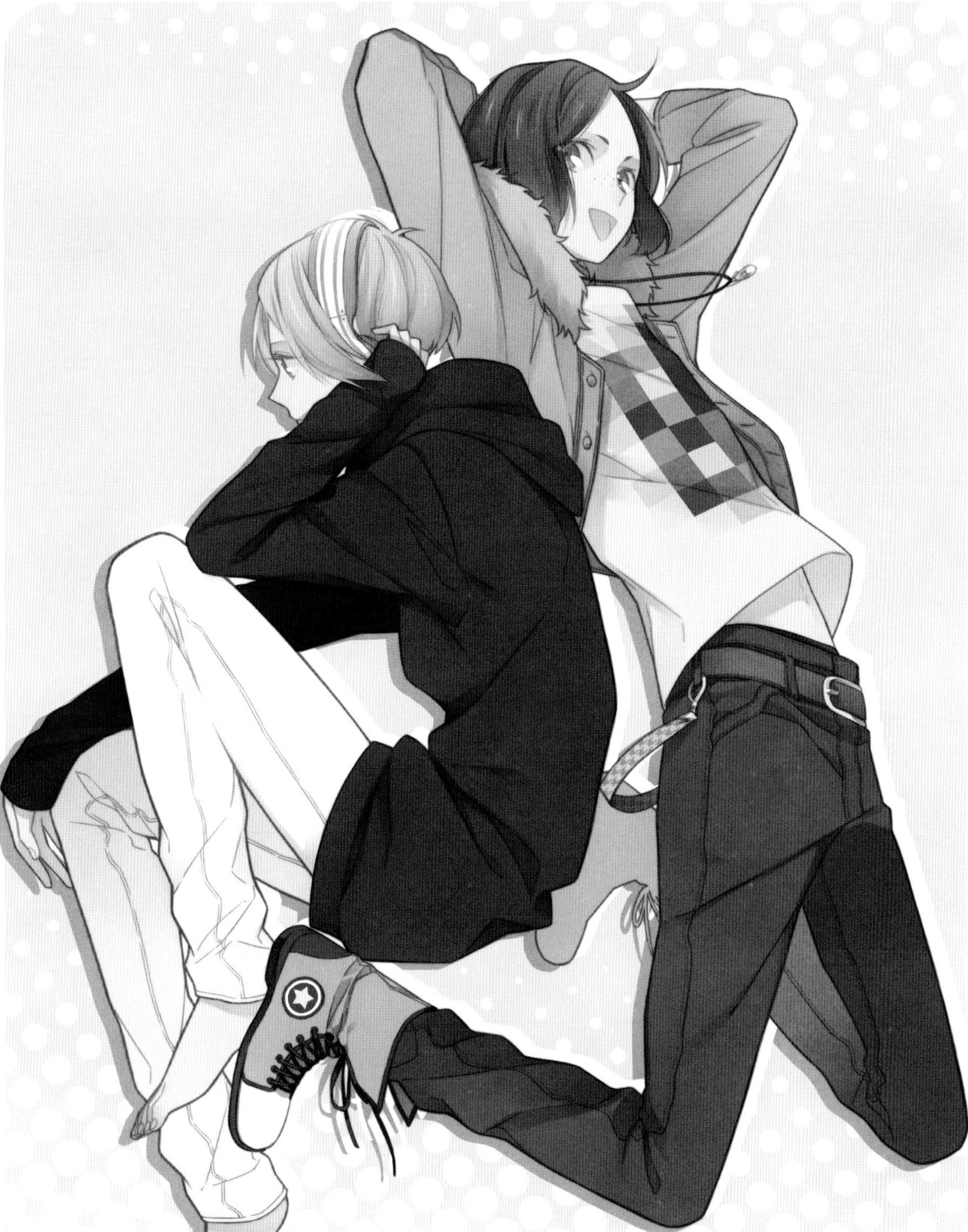

Personal Work「凸凹」

ma2

M sss.chon30@gmail.com
T ---
U http://pixiv.me/chon30
D SAI ● Photoshop CS5

Profile

2013年、小説表紙・挿絵のお仕事で声を掛けて頂きました。まだまだ駆け出しです。

In 2013, I was asked to do cover and other illustrations for a novel. I'm still a complete beginner.

Comments

スーツが好き・リーマンが好きな気持ちを絵に込めて、色っぽい男性を描くべく、仕草や目つき・表情も意識しています。

I feel like I should reflect my affinity for suits and businessmen in my drawings, and that I should create sexy male characters; I also remain conscious of gestures, looks, and facial expressions.

Personal Work「懇願」

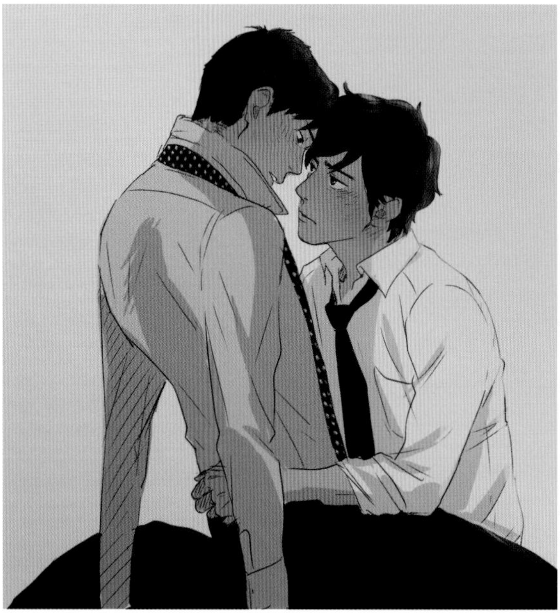

Personal Work「Mr. NAVY」

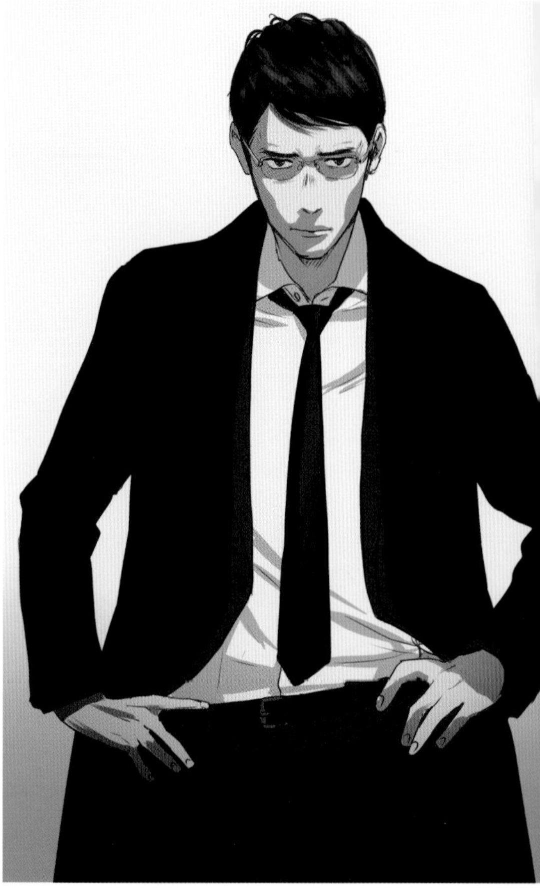

Personal Work

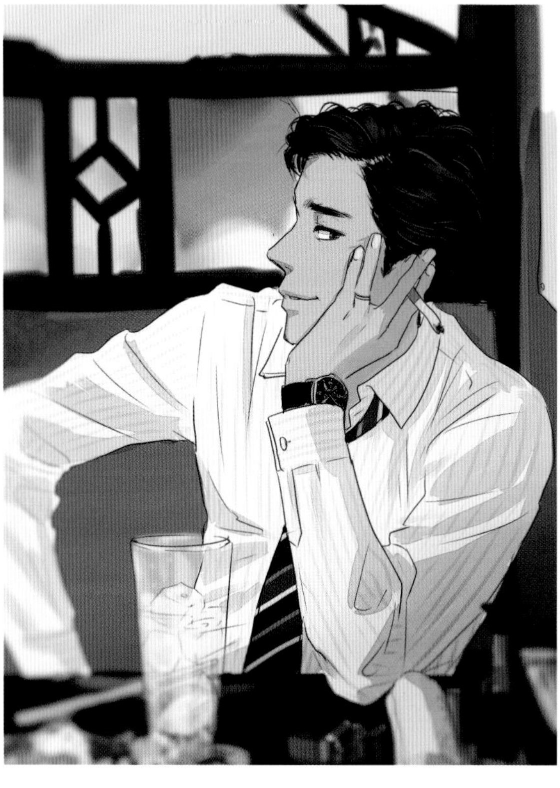

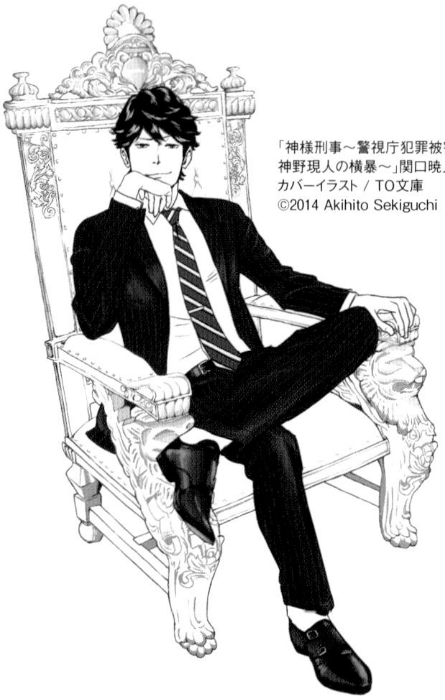

「神様刑事～警視庁犯罪被害者ケア係・神野現人の横暴～」関口暁人
カバーイラスト / TO文庫
©2014 Akihito Sekiguchi

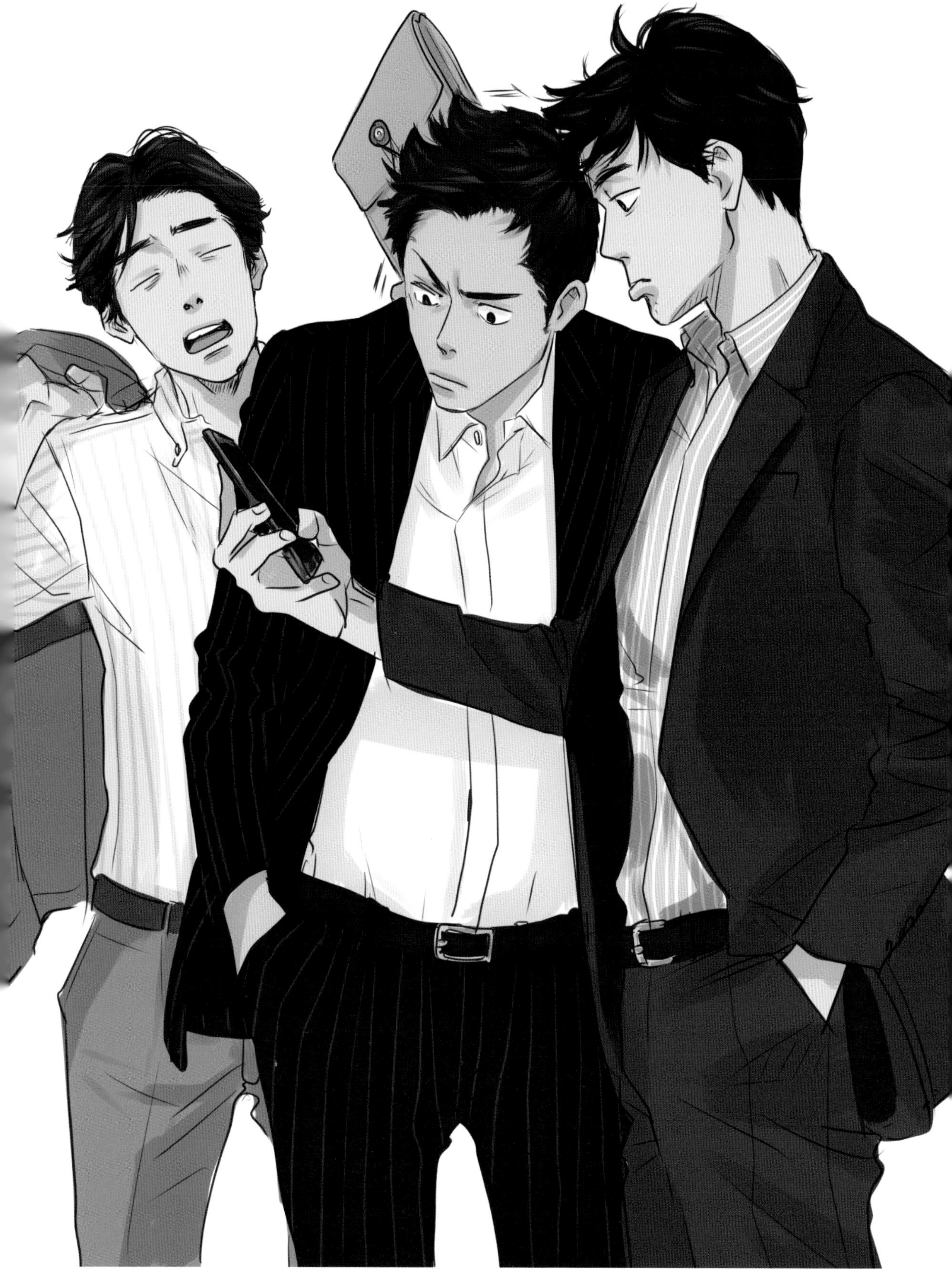

みずかねりょう
MIZUKANE RYOU

M --- T --- U http://mercurius.vc

D Photoshop CC 2015 ● CLIP STUDIO PAINT

Profile	宮城県出身、埼玉県在住。イラストレーター。女性向ライトノベル、一般書籍にて挿画を担当。愛犬家。	I'm from Miyagi Prefecture, but now live in Saitama Prefecture. I'm an illustrator. I illustrate *light novels* targeting young women along with general-interest books. I love dogs.
Comments	作品の雰囲気をこわさないよう願い、気を付けながら。	My hope is that I will not destroy the atmosphere of the works to which I contribute, and I take care not to do so.

「恋してる、生きていく」夕映月子 / 口絵 / ディアプラス文庫 / 新書館
©夕映月子 ©みずかねりょう ©2015新書館

「恋してる、生きていく」夕映月子 / カバーイラスト / ディアプラス文庫 / 新書館
©夕映月子 ©みずかねりょう ©2015新書館

「守護者がさまよう記憶の迷路」神奈木智 / カバーイラスト / Chara文庫 / 徳間書店
©神奈木智 ©みずかねりょう ©2015徳間書店

「守護者がさまよう記憶の迷路」神奈木智 / 口絵 / Chara文庫 / 徳間書店
©神奈木智 ©みずかねりょう ©2015徳間書店

Personal Work ©みずかねりょう

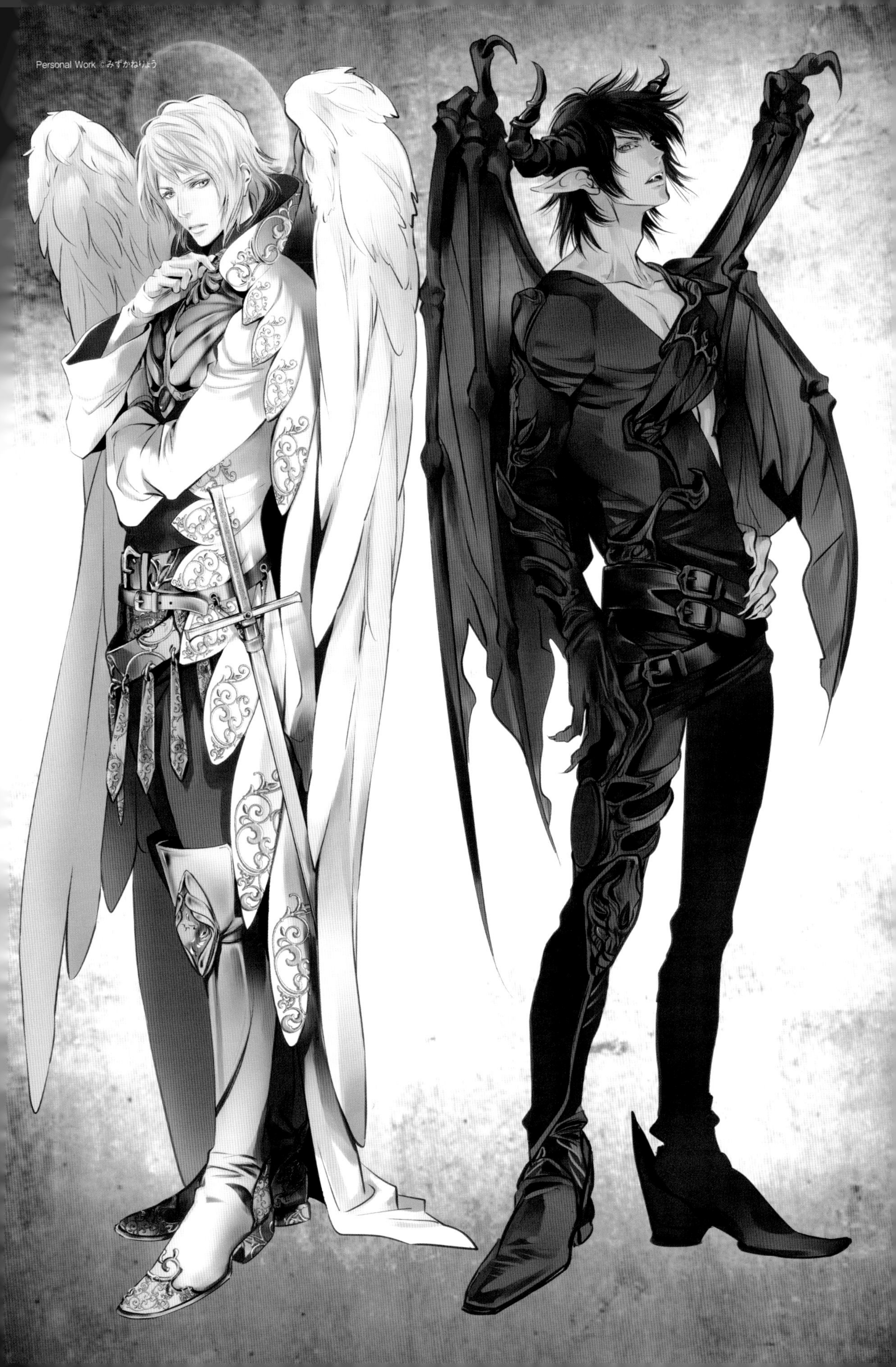

水輿ゆい

Minakoshi Yui

M http://highkick.jp/contact

T y_minakoshi

U http://minakoshi.highkick.jp

D Photoshop CS6 ● SAI

Profile

女性らしい繊細なタッチで、原色を使ったPOPなイラストから、水彩風のものまで幅広く描き分ける。「月蝕のエゴイスト ー愛しすぎて、壊したいー」〜緋色の空〜で、デビュー。その後、「花咲くまにまに」シリーズ、「渇望メソッド」シリーズ等を手掛ける。

I draw a variety of styles, from those with a subtle feminine touch to pop illustrations using primary colors to works featuring a watercolor look. I debuted with illustrations for the song “Hiiro no Sora” from *Gesshoku no Egoist: Aishisugite, Kowashitai*. Since then, my work has included illustrating two series: *Hanasaku Mani Mani* and *Katsubo Method*.

Comments

はじめまして、水輿ゆいと申します。イラストのお仕事を頂くようになってから一年半が経ちました。花や小物、中世ヨーロッパの世界観が好きなので、これからたくさん描ければと思っています。楽しみながら描くということを忘れないようにしています。制作しているイラストの雰囲気に合った音楽を聴きながら作業をするのが好きです。

Hi _ I'm Yui Minakoshi. About a year and a half has passed since I began work as an illustrator. I like flowers, bric _ brac, and the Medieval European atmosphere, and hope I can plentifully incorporate each into my work. I will try not to forget to enjoy myself as I draw. I like to listen to music evoking the atmosphere of what I'm illustrating as I work.

Personal Work

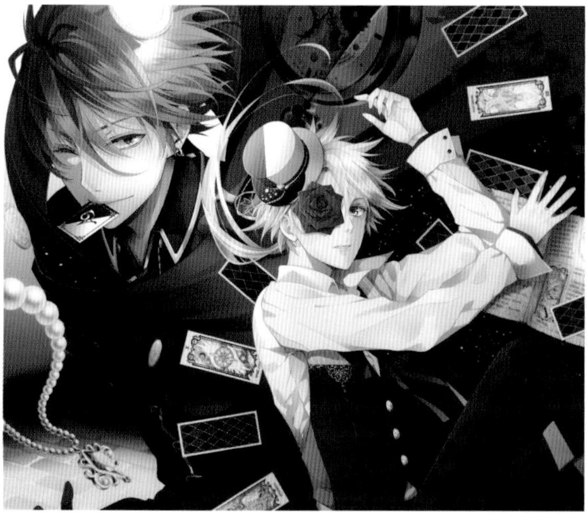

エゴイスティックサスペンスシミュレーションドラマCD
「月蝕のエゴイスト ー愛しすぎて、壊したいー」〜緋色の空〜 / ジャケットイラスト
発売元:5pb. 販売元:KADOKAWA メディアファクトリー ©2014 5pb.

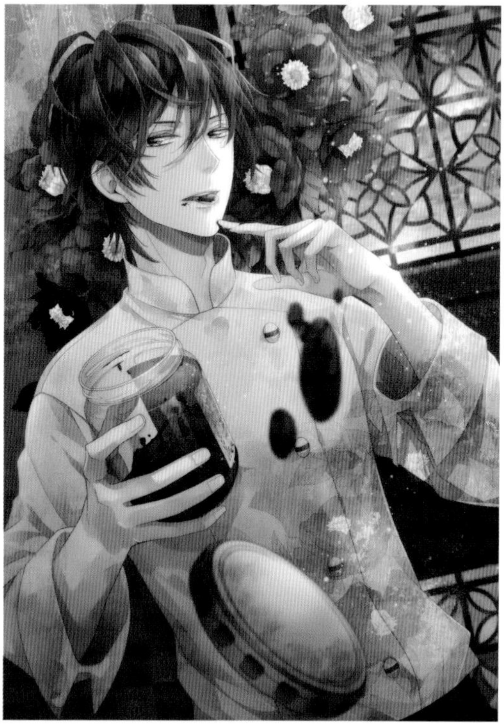

「渇望メソッド」/ ちびキャラクター
発売元:ティームエンタテインメント
©IDEA FACTORY/axcell

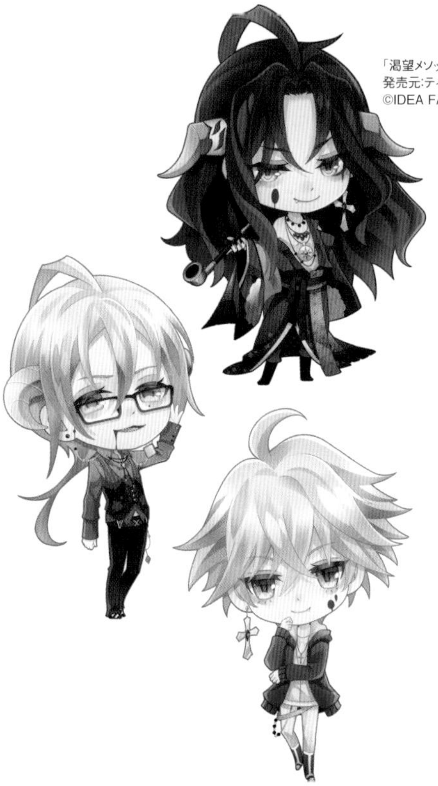

明治吸血奇譚「月夜叉」テーマソング「Accepted Blood」MIKOTO / ジャケットイラスト
発売元:5pb. 販売元:KADOKAWA メディアファクトリー ©2014 5pb.

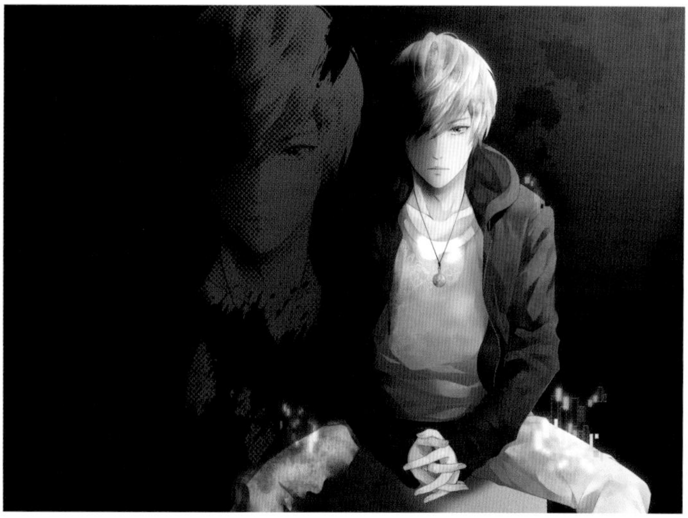

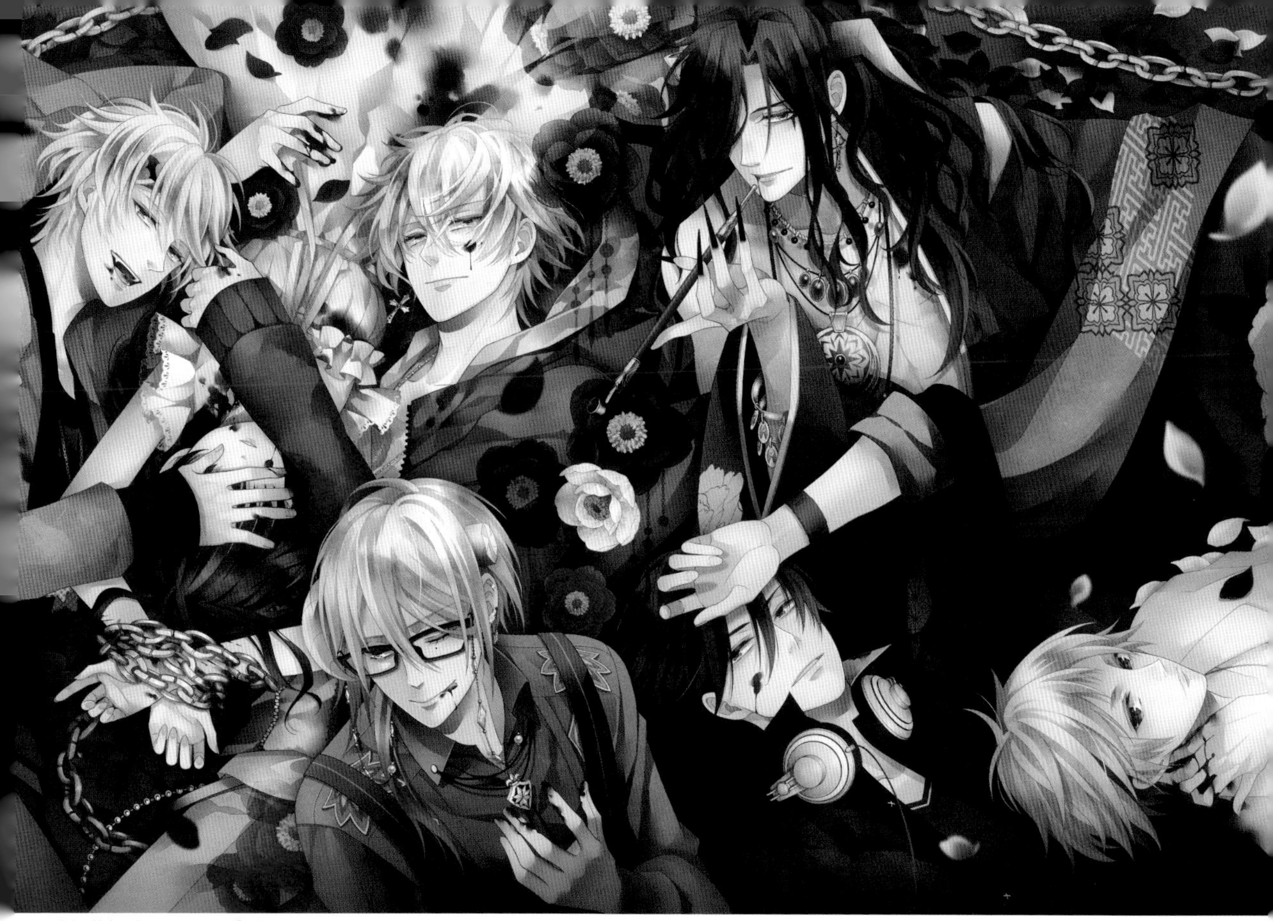

吸血の快楽に囚われるCDシリーズ「渇望メソッド」/ キービジュアル
発売元:ティームエンタテインメント ©IDEA FACTORY/axcell

女性向け恋愛アドベンチャー『花咲くまにまに』キャラクターソングCDシリーズ「鏡歌水月」「百歌爛漫」/ ジャケットイラスト
キャラクター原案:redjuice / 発売・販売元:マリン・エンタテインメント ©MAGES./5pb./redjuice

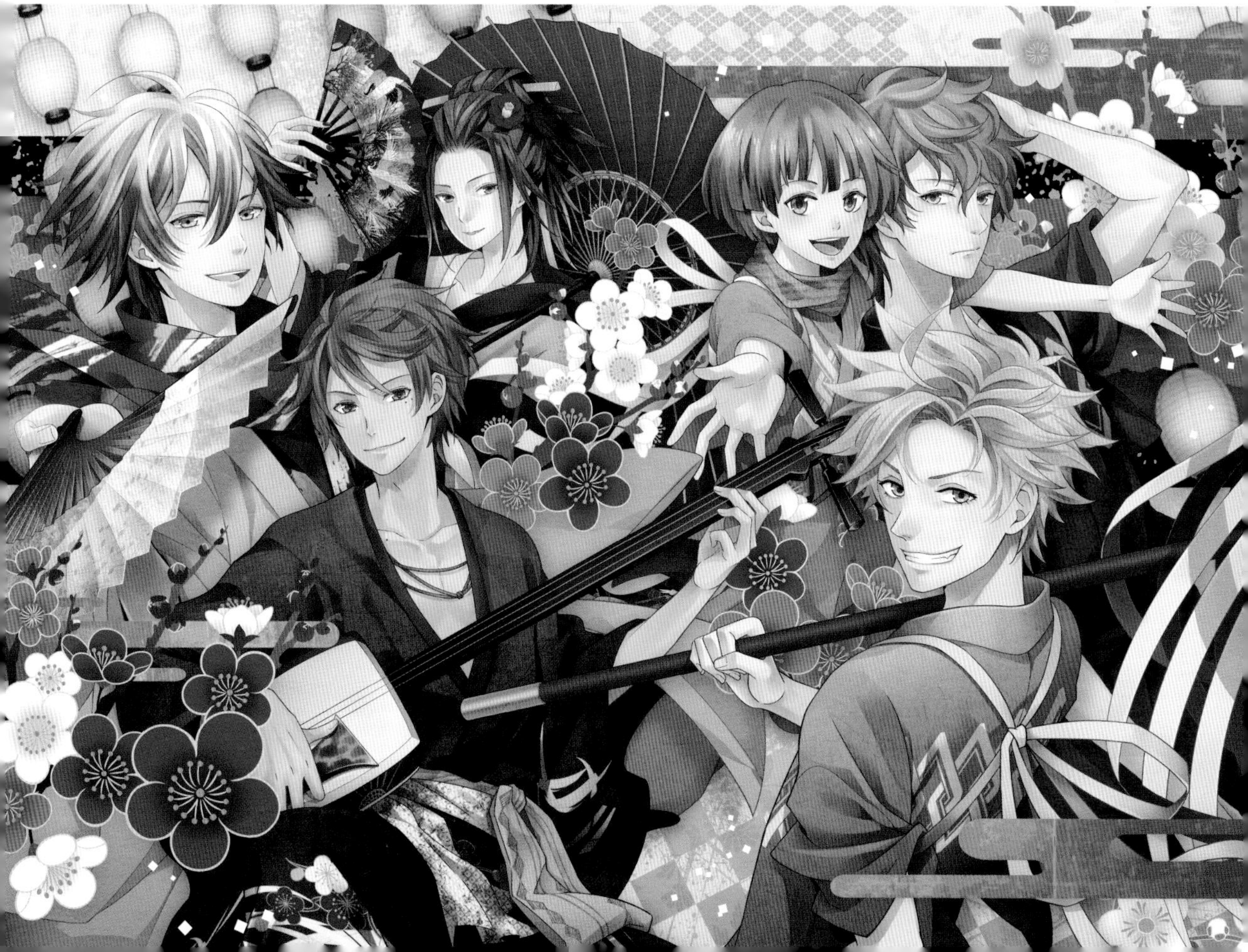

睦月ムンク

Mutsuki Munku

M munku@xt.sunnyday.jp
U http://munku.sunnyday.jp
T m_munku
D Photoshop CS4, CC ● SAI

Profile

フリーランスイラストレーター。京都嵯峨芸術大学短期大学部客員准教授。近年の代表作に「陰陽師-瀧夜叉姫-」(夢枕獏原作/徳間書店COMICリュウ) コミカライズ連載。書籍装画・挿絵、漫画、キャラクターデザイン等、各商業媒体で活動中。

I'm a freelance illustrator and a visiting associate professor at the the Kyoto Saga University of Arts Junior College. My recent artwork includes the comic book serialization of *Onmyoji – Taki Yashahime* (original work by Yumemakura Baku/Tokuma Shoten Comic Ryu). I draw cover and other illustrations for books, I create manga, and I work on character designs and other projects for a variety of media.

Comments

イラスト内のバックグラウンドを色々と想像・予想でき、尚且つキャラクターの魅力も楽しんで頂ける作品を心がけています。

I'm dedicated to creating illustrations with backgrounds allowing viewers to imagine and predict a variety of things, and with characters whose appeal viewers can enjoy.

「遺跡発掘師は笑わない 出雲王のみささぎ」桑原水菜 / カバーイラスト
KADOKAWA 角川文庫 / 2015

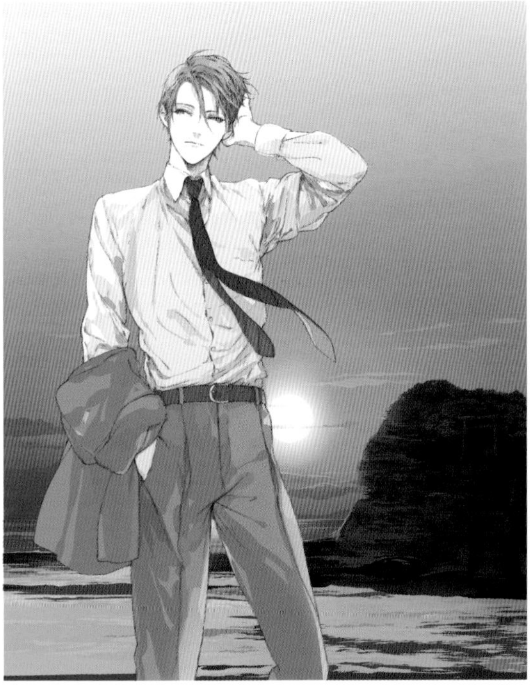

Personal Work「悪源太義平」/ 2015

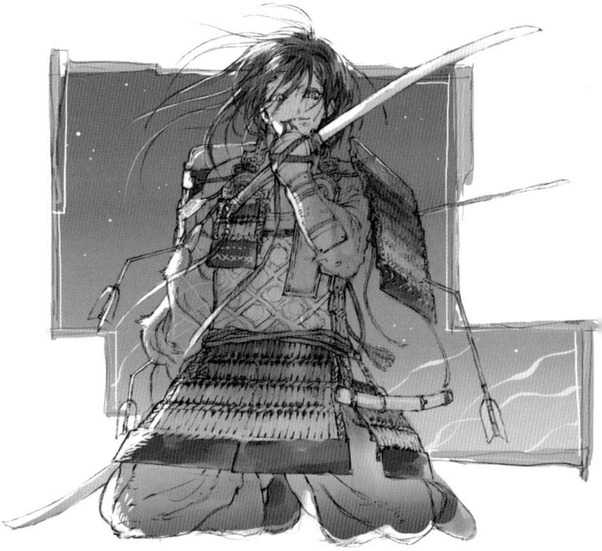

Personal Work「男子高生2」/ 2015

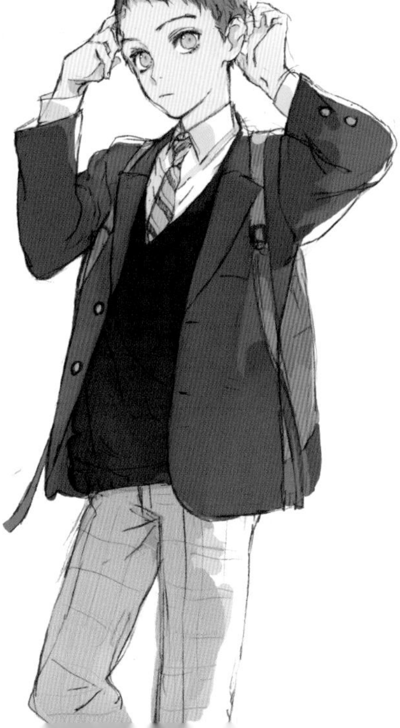

「遺跡発掘師は笑わない まだれいなの十字架」桑原水菜 / カバーイラスト
KADOKAWA 角川文庫 / 2015

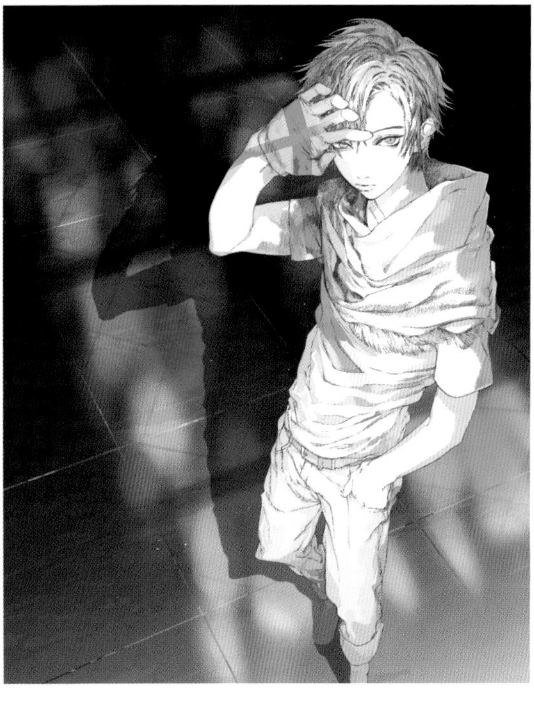

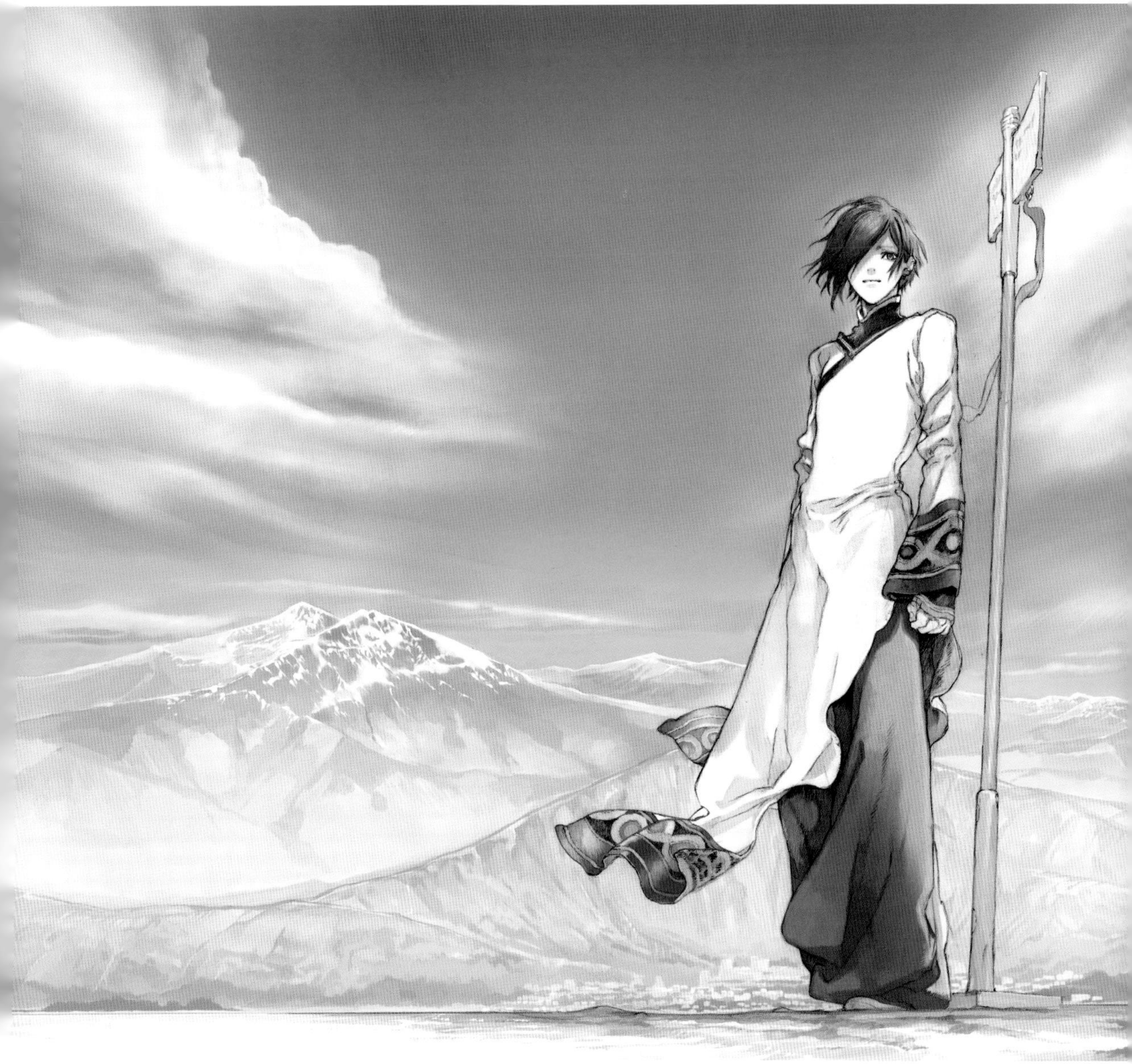

Personal Work / 2014

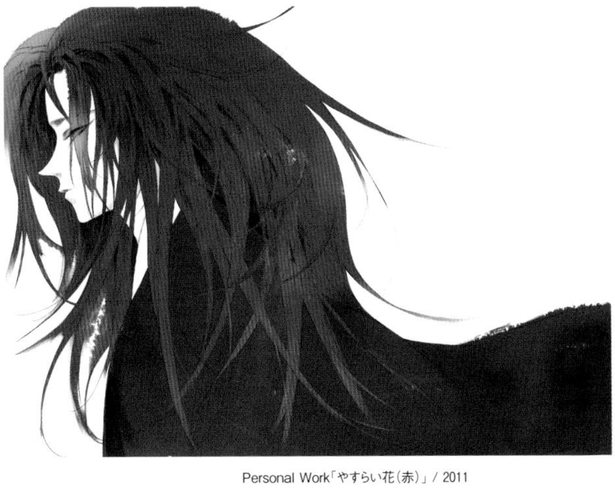

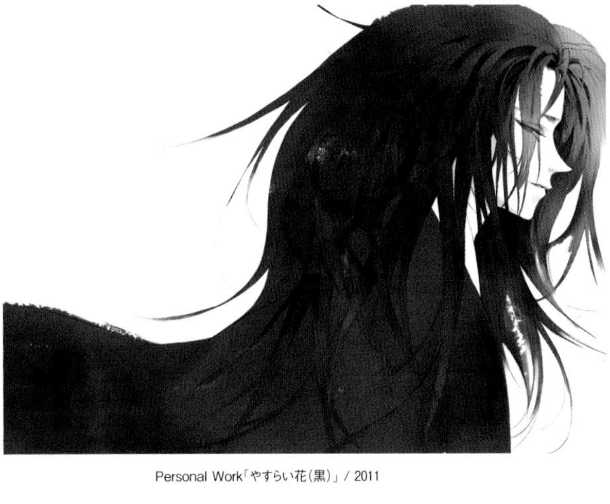

Personal Work「やすらい花(赤)」/ 2011

Personal Work「やすらい花(黒)」/ 2011

六七質
munashichi

M syk_3276771@yahoo.co.jp **T** munashichi **U** http://www.geocities.jp/syk_3276771/index.html

D Photoshop CS5 ● SAI ● CRIP STUDIO PAINT PRO ● Shade3D ver15 ● Pencil

Profile	青森県出身。2008年よりフリーランスのイラストレーターとして活動中。小説の装画、コンセプトデザイン、TCGなどの仕事をしている。風景、建物を描くことが特に好き。絵を描くこと以外では旅行が趣味。	I'm from Aomori Prefecture. Since 2008, I have been working as a freelance illustrator. I do book cover designs for novels, concept design, TCG, and other work. I particularly enjoy drawing landscapes and buildings. I enjoy travel as a hobby.
Comments	キャラは全体の雰囲気で個性をだせるといいなあと思っています。いろんな衣装を着せるのが楽しいです。作品は背景世界感と一緒に考えて描いています。	I would love to be able to extract a character's individuality from the overall atmosphere. It is so much fun to let characters wear all kinds of outfits. I keep the contextual outlook in mind as I draw.

「幽落町おばけ駄菓子屋 夏の夜空の夢花火」蒼月海里 / 装画 / 角川ホラー文庫 / KADOKAWA

「幽落町おばけ駄菓子屋 思い出めぐりの幻灯機」蒼月海里 / 装画 角川ホラー文庫 / KADOKAWA

Personal Work「秘密基地」

「パーティー」初出・pixiv 5th Anniversary Book/ KADOKAWA

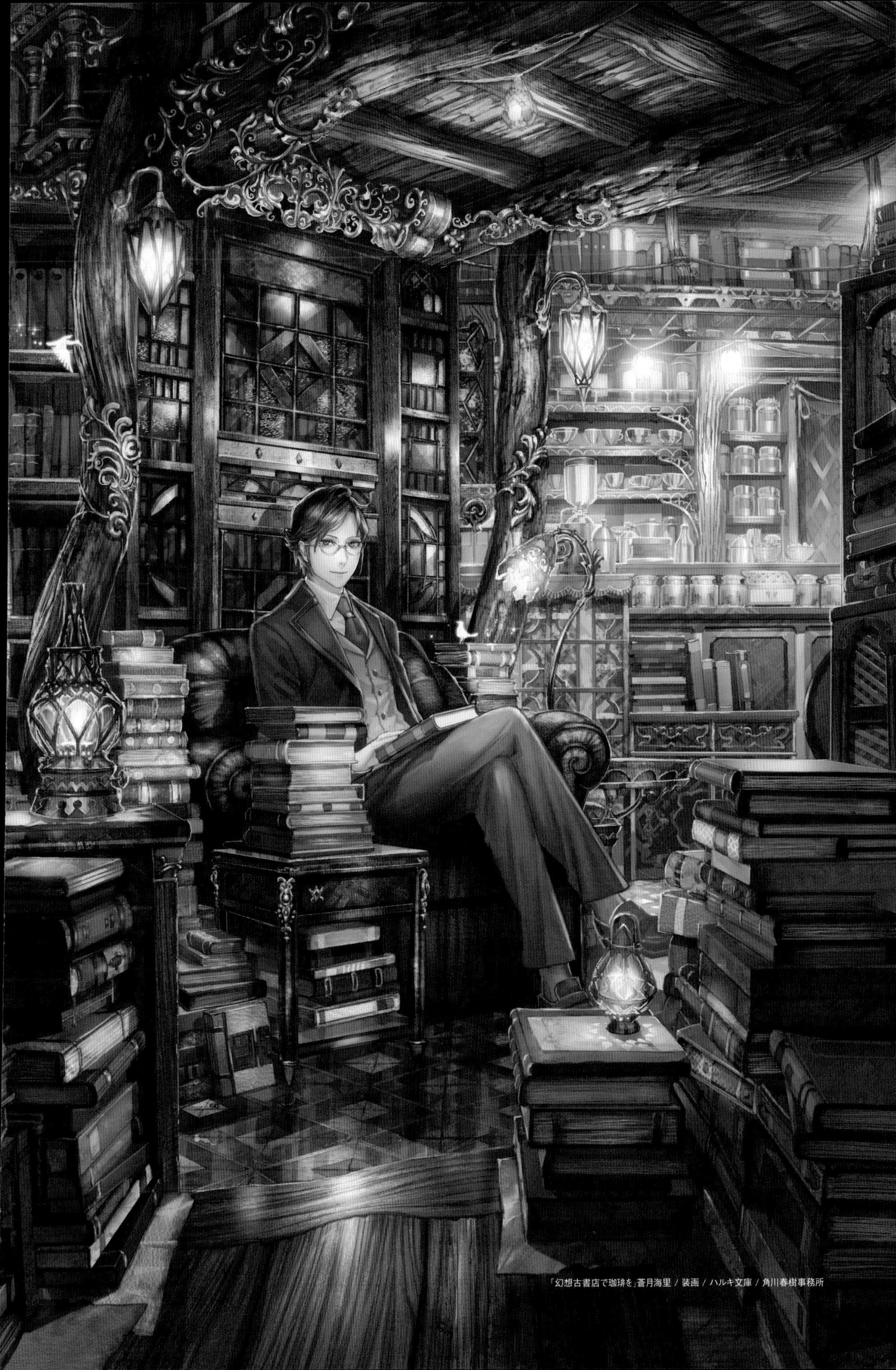

「幻想古書店で珈琲を」蒼月海里 / 装画 / ハルキ文庫 / 角川春樹事務所

めろ
melo

M melowxxxxx@gmail.com
T melo0228
U http://mlwkblog.blog.fc2.com
D SAI ● Photoshop

Profile	主に女性向け作品のゲーム・CDのイラストを描かせて頂いております。他、書籍の表紙や挿絵なども担当しています。	I mainly illustrate games and CDs for the female market. I am also responsible for designing covers and illustrations for non-entertainment books.
Comments	描いている時はそのイラストの雰囲気が伝わるようにと心がけています。他はできるだけ沢山の色を使うようにしています。	I try to convey atmosphere in my illustrations. I also try to use a wide range of colors.

「√HAPPY+SUGAR=DARLIN」/ キービジュアル / ©2014 Rejet

「仲吉商店街、恋の湯 営業中!」/ キービジュアル / ©bisCROWN

「大正×対称アリス episodeⅡ」/ 限定版ジャケットイラスト / ©Primula

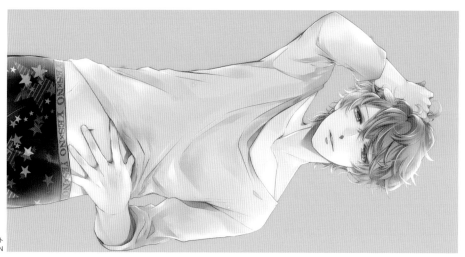

「YES×NO」/ ジャケットイラスト
©bisCROWN

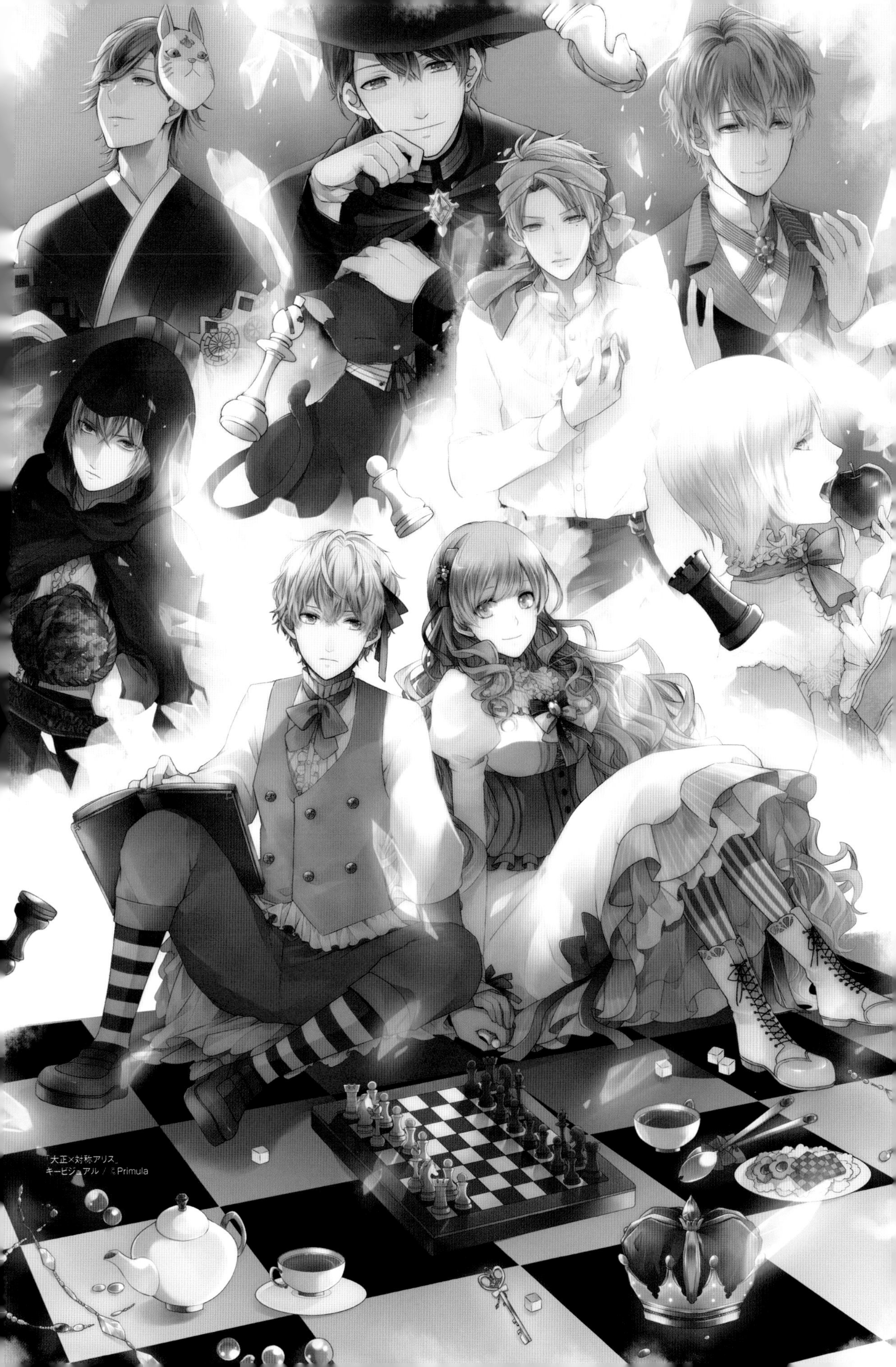
「大正×対称アリス」
キービジュアル / ©Primula

ヤマコ

yamako

M night_stars_berry@hotmail.com   **T** yamako2626

U http://soc.ikidane.com   **D** SAI ● Photoshop CS6

Profile	主にHoneyWorksでイラスト・動画制作しています。ライトノベルの挿絵や、時々漫画も描きます。学生イラストが好きで、少女漫画風の絵を中心に描いていますが、アクションものやファンタジー系も大好きです！	I mainly create animated anime and illustrations for HoneyWorks. I also occasionally do manga and illustrations for *light novels*. I enjoy drawing students, and most of my works are manga-like drawings of young girls, but I also love action and fantasy!
Comments	特に男性キャラクターを描くのが好きなので、自分の好きな要素、フェチなどを盛り込んで楽しく描いています。ストーリー性のあるPVイラストを作成することが多いので、前後の流れを想像し、一瞬を切り取ったような表情、場面を描くよう心がけています。	I particularly enjoy drawing male characters, incorporating my own elements and passions. I'm often asked to do promotion video (PV) illustrations with a storyline, so imagine what happens before and after, and attempt to draw the scene as though frozen in time, facial expressions and all.

「東京サマーセッション」/ PVイラスト / HoneyWorks（sana×CHiCO）©HoneyWorks ©2015 MusicRay'n

「アイのシナリオ」/ PVイラスト / CHiCO with HoneyWorks
©HoneyWorks ©2015 MusicRay'n

「春日坂高校漫画研究部 第3号 井の中のオタク、恋を知らず!」あずまの章
カバーイラスト / 角川ビーンズ文庫 / KADOKAWA
©あずまの章・ヤマコ / KADOKAWA

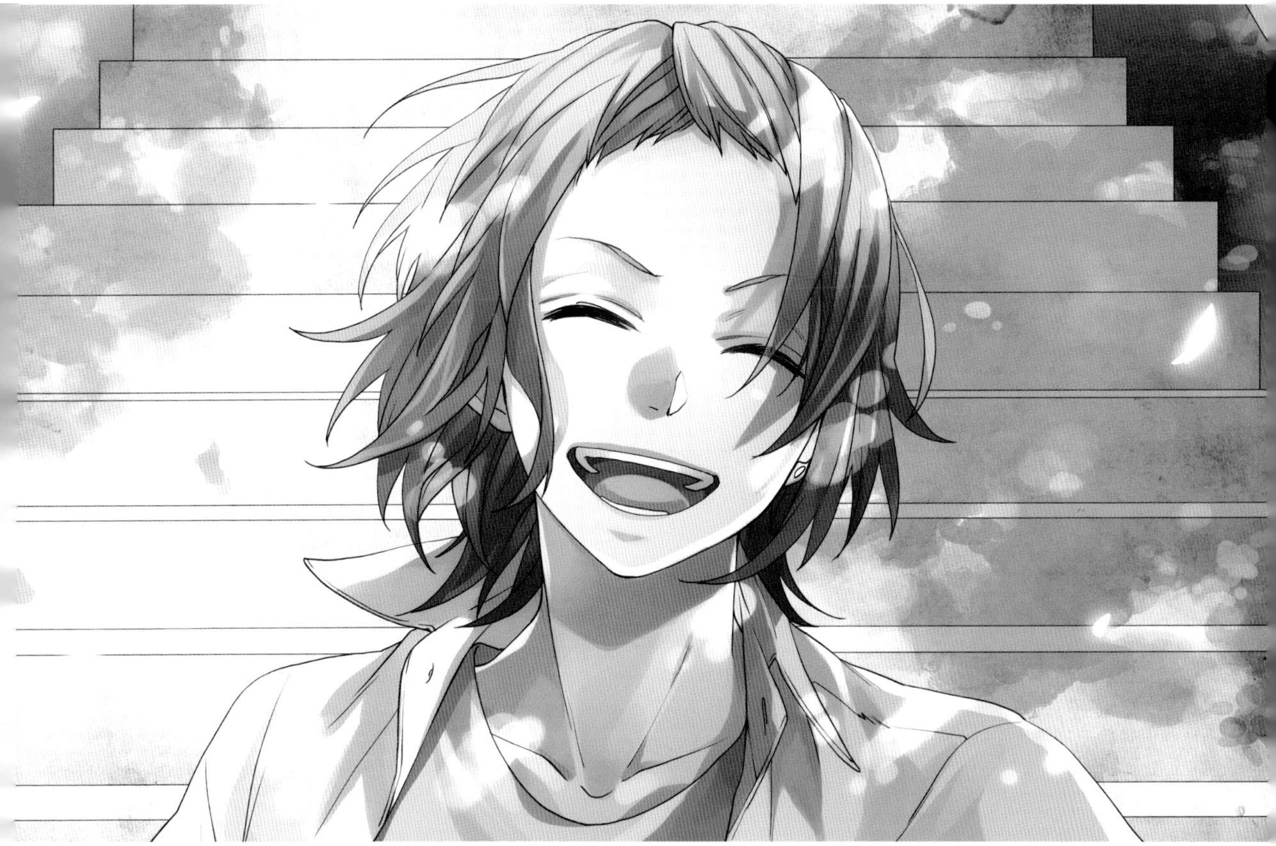

「イジワルな出会い」/ PVイラスト / HoneyWorks feat.初音ミク　©HoneyWorks ©2015 MusicRay'n

「言葉のいらない約束」/ PVイラスト / sana　©HoneyWorks ©2015 MusicRay'n

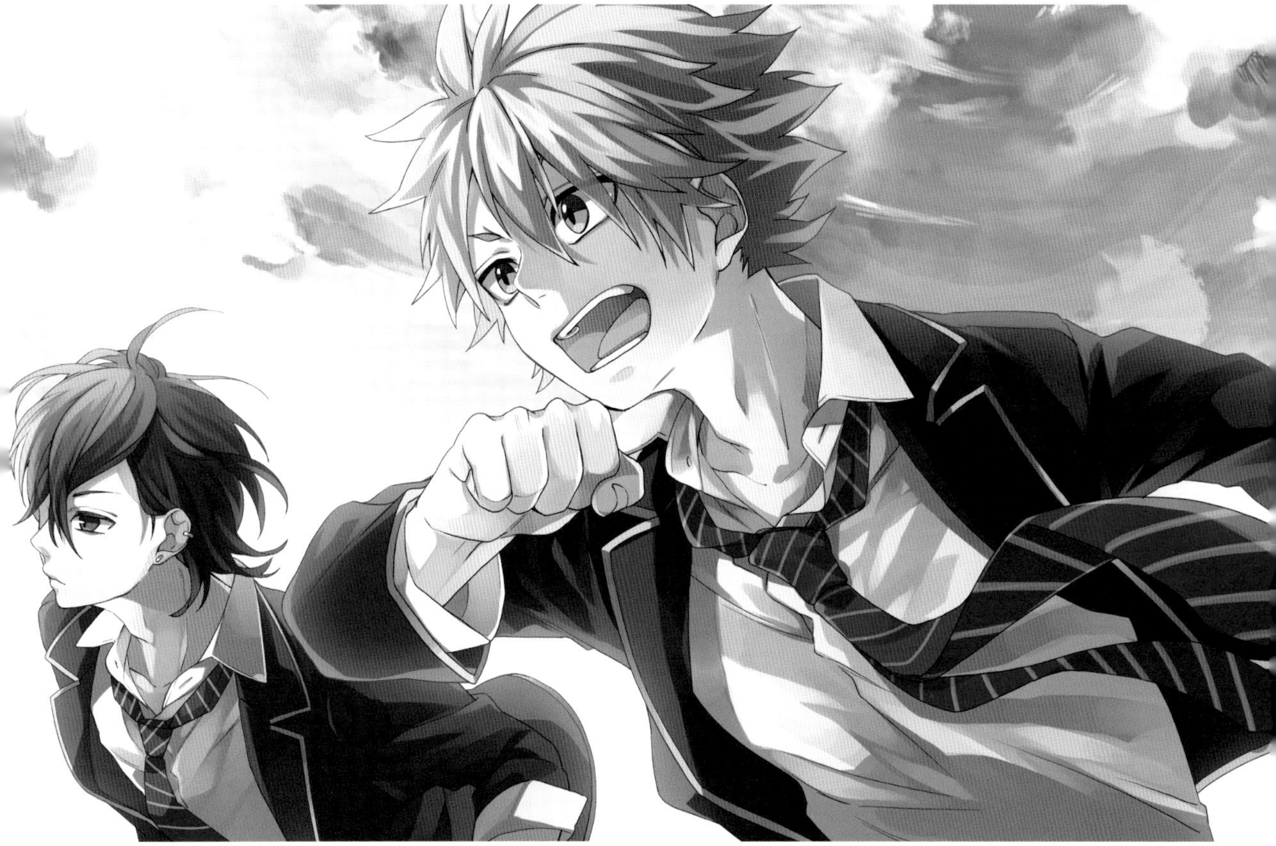

山田シロ
yamada shiro

M soul@do.sub.jp
T yamashiro_k
U http://work.soul.sub.jp
D Photoshop ● SAI ● Painter

Profile	女性向けの小説挿絵、キャラデザ、ゲーム原画、漫画など幅広くお仕事させて頂いております。	I work on a broad spectrum of female-oriented projects, including book illustrations for novels, character design, game illustrations, and manga.
Comments	ファンタジー系や、和もの系のデザイン、音楽系のキャラを描くのが好きですが、現代ものや大人向けのイラストのお仕事も沢山しています。どこか、ビビっと心をくすぐる気になるイラストを描ければと思っております。	I enjoy drawing fantasy- and Japan-related designs, and music-related characters, but I do a lot of work involving modern themes and adult-oriented illustrations. I hope to draw vivid illustrations which entertain the heart.

「ファンタジー彼氏」/ キャラクターデザイン 立ち絵 / マリン・エンタテインメント ©MARINE ENTERTAINMENT

「Tap Trap Love」/ CDジャケットイラスト /5pb. ©2012 5pb.

「スクランブル☆スター」山田シロ / 扉絵
角川書店ASUKA ©KADOKAWA

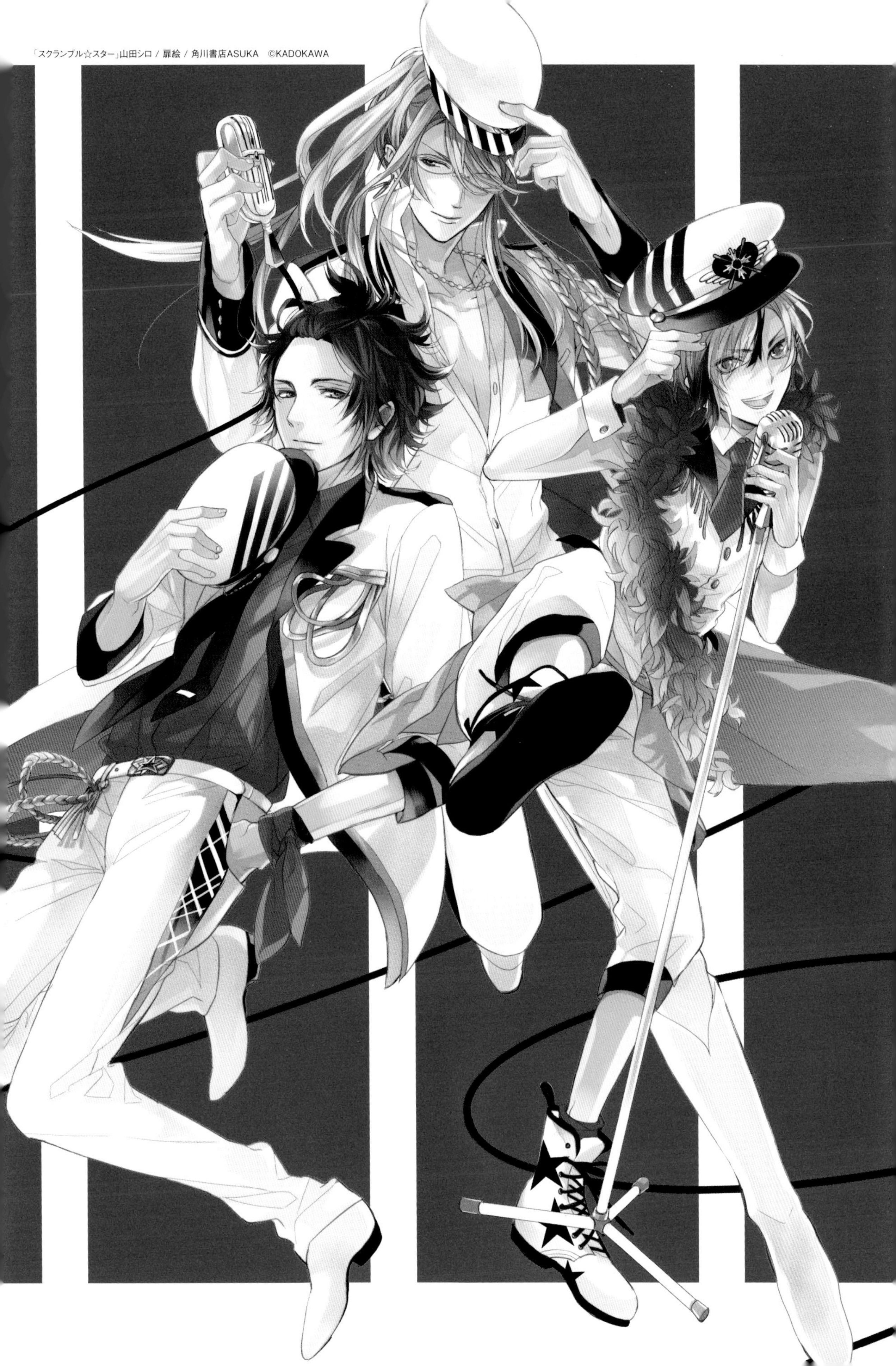

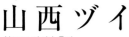
山西ヅイ
Yamanishi Zui

M cell70000@gmail.com　T yamazui70　U http://yamanishi968.tumblr.com

D SAI ● Photoshop CS6 ● CLIP STUDIO PAINT EX

Profile	フリーランスのイラストレーター。沖縄出身、東京在住。現在ソーシャルゲームのカードイラストやキャラクターデザインを主に制作しています。	I'm a freelance illustrator. I was born in Okinawa, but now live in Tokyo. I mainly design characters and do card illustrations for social network games.
Comments	特に和風のモチーフが好きです。制作中は主観をあまり信用しないように心がけています。	I particularly like traditional Japanese themes. I try not to be too subjective while I am in the midst of creating something.

Personal Work

Personal Work

「OZ Chrono Chronicle」ミカエル / キャラクターイラスト / DMMゲームズ

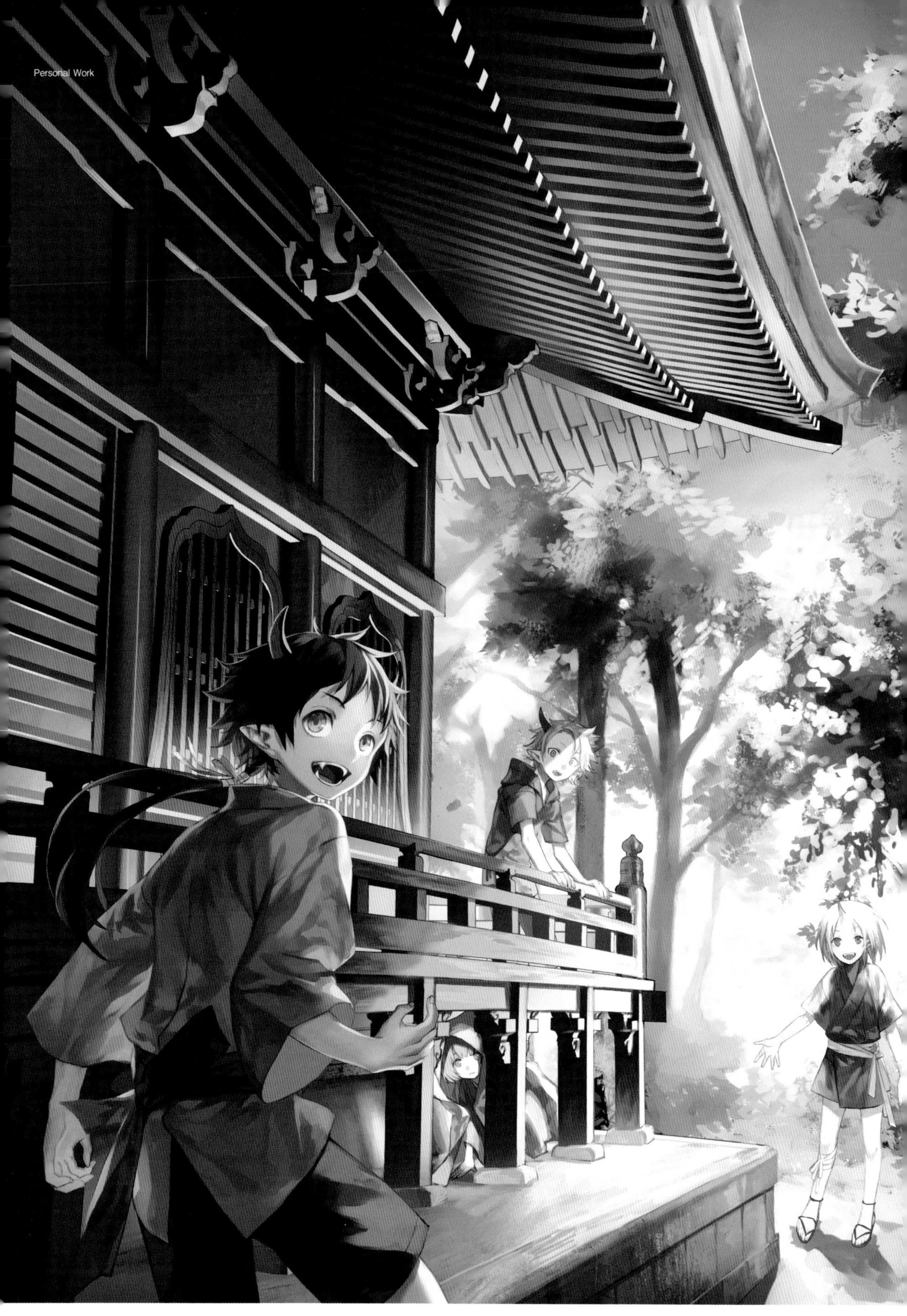

山本アタル
Yamamoto Ataru

M viviarocca@yahoo.co.jp
T ub107
U ---
D ComicStudio • Photoshop

Profile	2013年から商業活動をしています。女装男子と可愛い男の子を描くのが好きです。	I've been illustrating for commercial magazines since 2013. I like drawing cute males and male cross-dressers.
Comments	ポップで可愛いイラストを目指しています	I'm trying to produce cute and trendy illustrations.

「変身しちゃう?」山本アタル / 同人誌表紙

「いくじなしのスペクテイター」山本アタル / カバーイラスト / リブレ出版

「弱虫カレシとろくでなし」山本アタル / カードイラスト / リブレ出版

「いくじなしのスペクテイター」山本アタル / 扉イラスト / リブレ出版

「偽×恋ボーイフレンド」山本アタル / カバーイラスト / リブレ出版

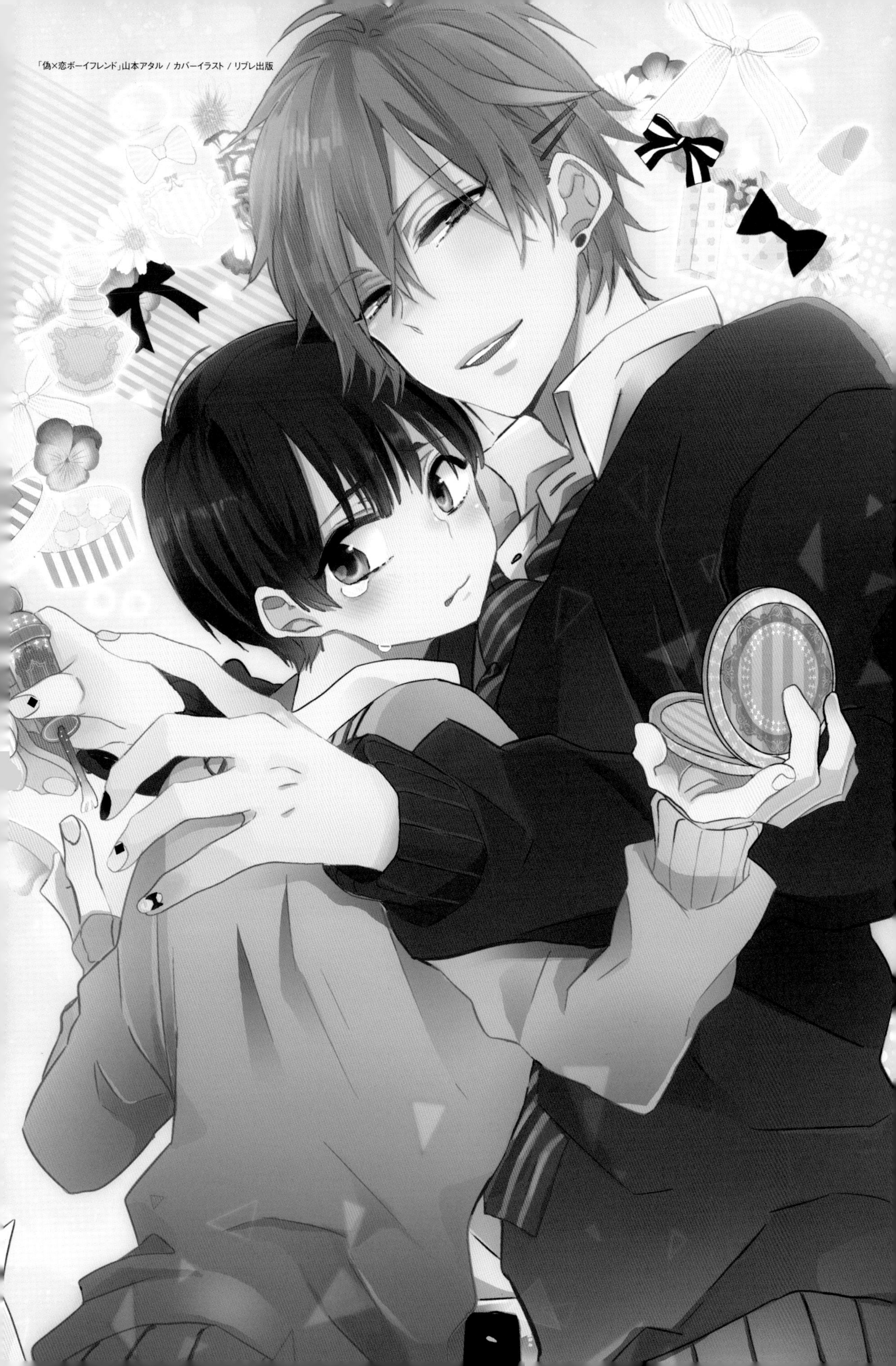

雪広うたこ
Yukihiro Utako

M mail@77x16.com
U http://77x16.com
T mielelatte
D CLIP STUDIO PAINT EX

Profile	漫画媒体中心に、その他小説の挿画やキャラクターデザインなどイラストの場でも活動しています。おもな作品に漫画「魔界王子devils and realist／原作：高殿 円」、アニメ「うたの☆プリンスさまっ♪」シリーズコミカライズ、キャラクターデザイン「B-project」など。	Most of my work focuses on the manga medium, but I am also active in the field of illustration, creating artwork for novels and producing character designs, for example. My major efforts include the manga versions of *Makai Oji devils and realist* (original work by Takadono Madoka) and *Uta no Prince-sama♪* (manga version), and comic illustrations and character design for *B-project*.
Comments	色彩の楽しさが伝わるようなカラーリングと、コンセプトに合わせた彩色で企画の意図を明確に伝えられるよう努力することを心がけています。	I try to ensure that the fun of coloring comes across in my drawings, and that coloring complements and clearly communicates the intent of the project.

「φの方石 −白幽堂魔石奇譚−」(著：新田周右)／カバーイラスト／
メディアワークス文庫／KADOKAWA アスキー・メディアワークス

COMIC it vol.1 表紙イラスト／KADOKAWA アスキー・メディアワークス

「うたの☆プリンスさまっ♪マジLOVE2000%」／3巻カバーイラスト
作画:雪広うたこ 原作:紅ノ月 歌音・ブロッコリー キャラクターデザイン原案:倉花千夏
キャラクターデザイン・総作画監督:森 光恵 監修:うた☆プリ2製作委員会
KADOKAWA アスキー・メディアワークス ©UTA☆PRI-2 PROJECT

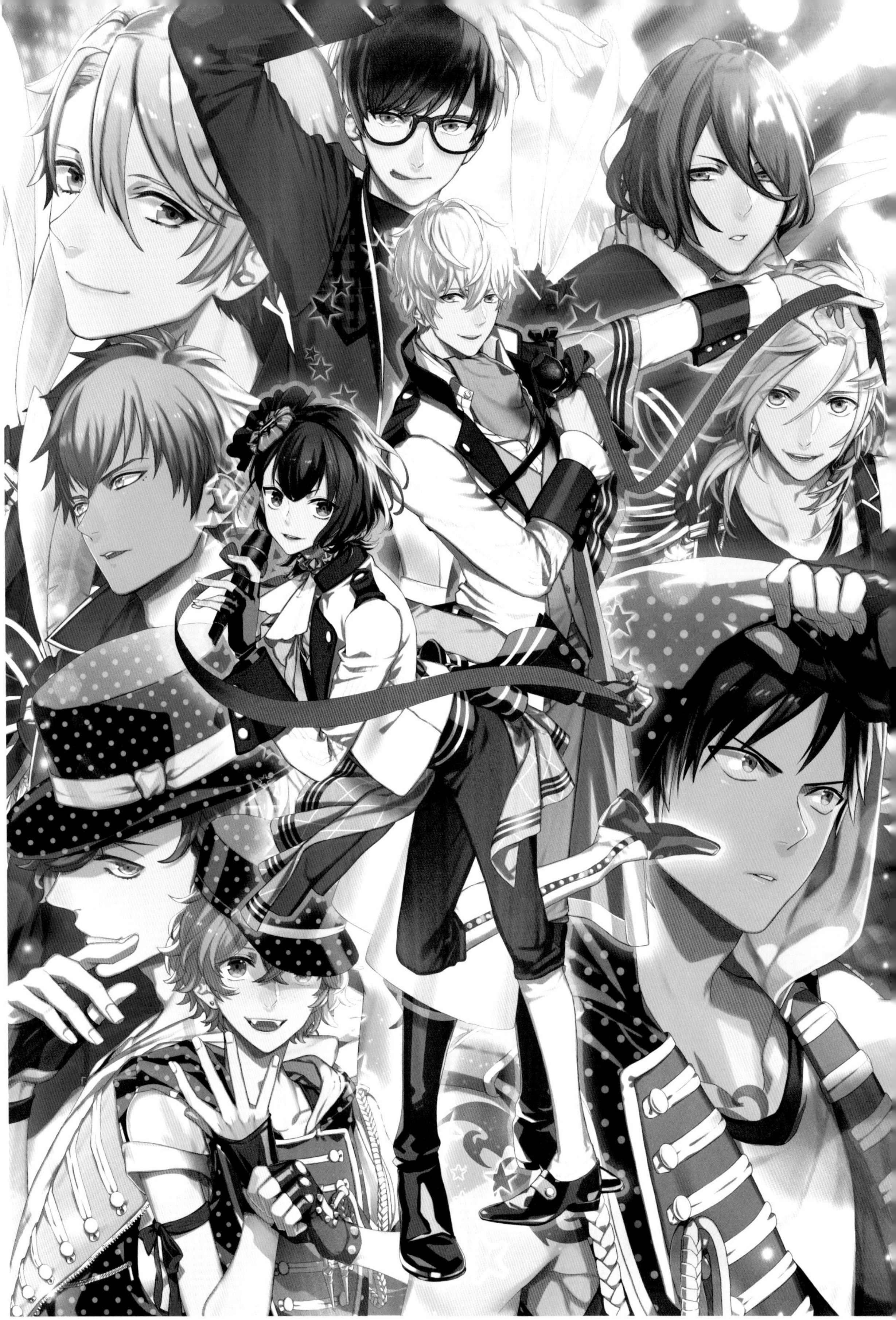
「B-project」/ キービジュアル / MAGES.　©B-project

由良

yura

M ---

T ---

U http://www.tennenouji.net

D Photoshop CC

Profile

初めまして、由良です。主に女性向けゲームのプロデュースと原画を担当しております。過去作品：「絶対服従命令」「みらくるのーとん」「ラッキードッグ１」。

Greetings! I'm Yura. I primarily design games for female users along with original manga. Some of my past works include *Zettai Fukuju Meirei, Mirakuru No-ton, and Lucky Dog 1.*

Comments

なるべく新しい要素を入れ込み、楽しいゲーム作りを目指しております。システムなどはBLゲームには珍しい、ボードゲーム、アクションゲーム、クイズゲームなどを制作し、リリースさせて頂いております。今後は演出面を強化していきたいと思っております。

I try to include new elements whenever possible to create fun games. Some of the systems I have created for BL games have been released and are rather rare, such as systems for board, action, and quiz games. From here on out, I'd like to strengthen my directing credentials.

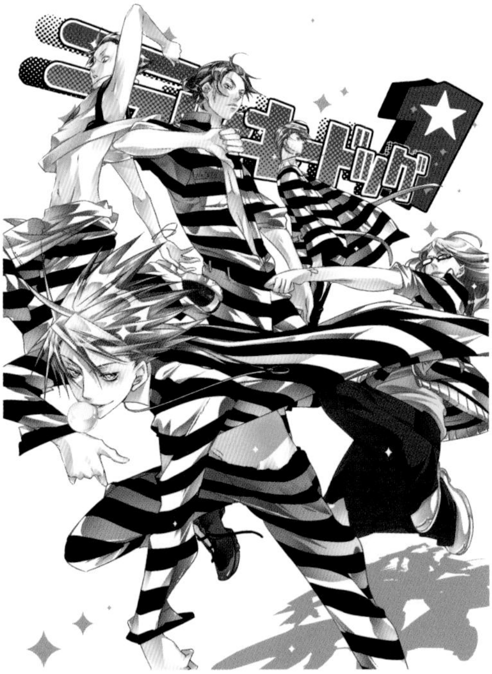

「ラッキードッグ1」メインビジュアル / ©Tennenouji

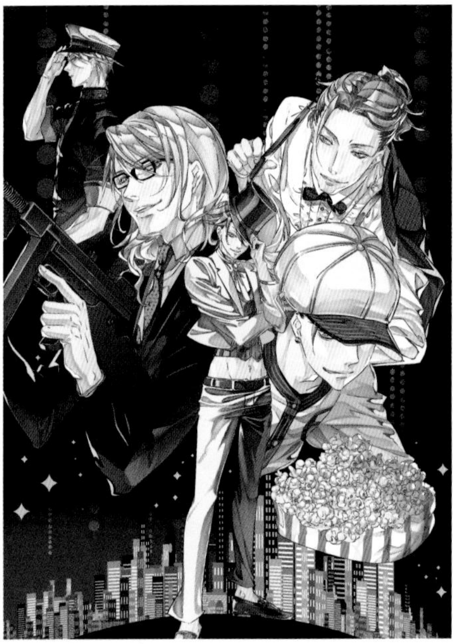

「Gian・carlo'S Lucky Happy Life」メインビジュアル / ©Tennenouji

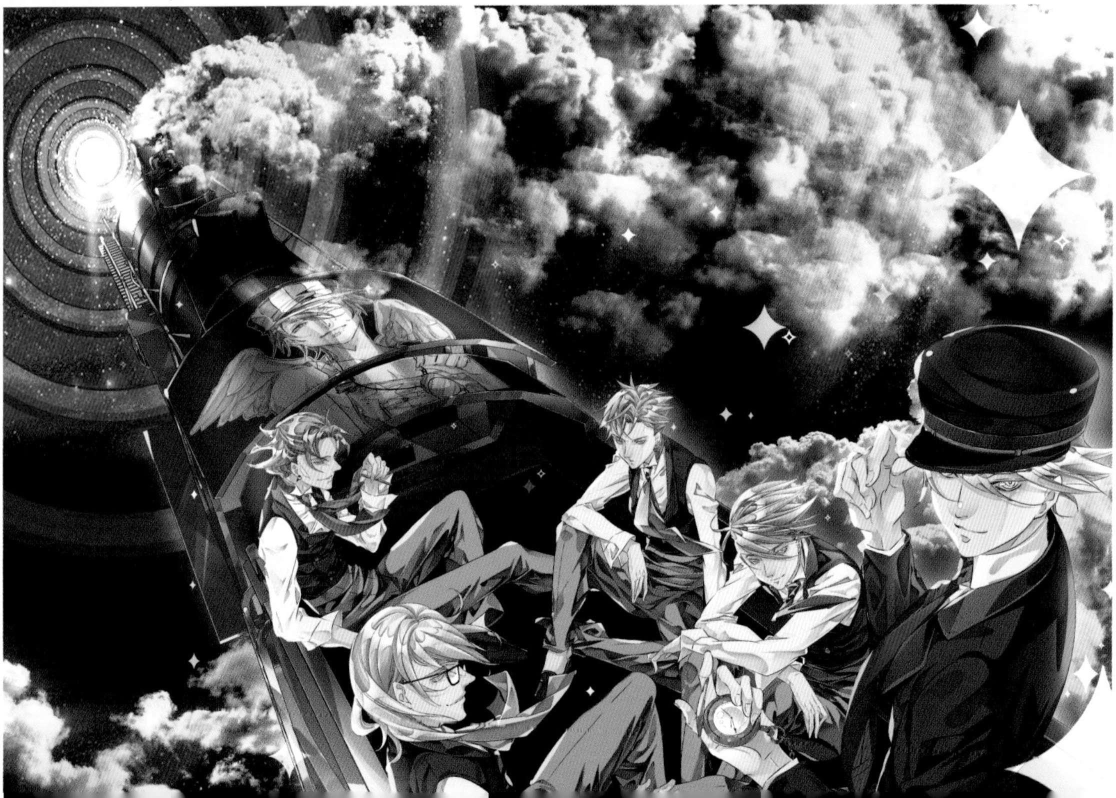

「ラッキードッグ1 3rd anniversary」メインビジュアル / ©Tennenouji

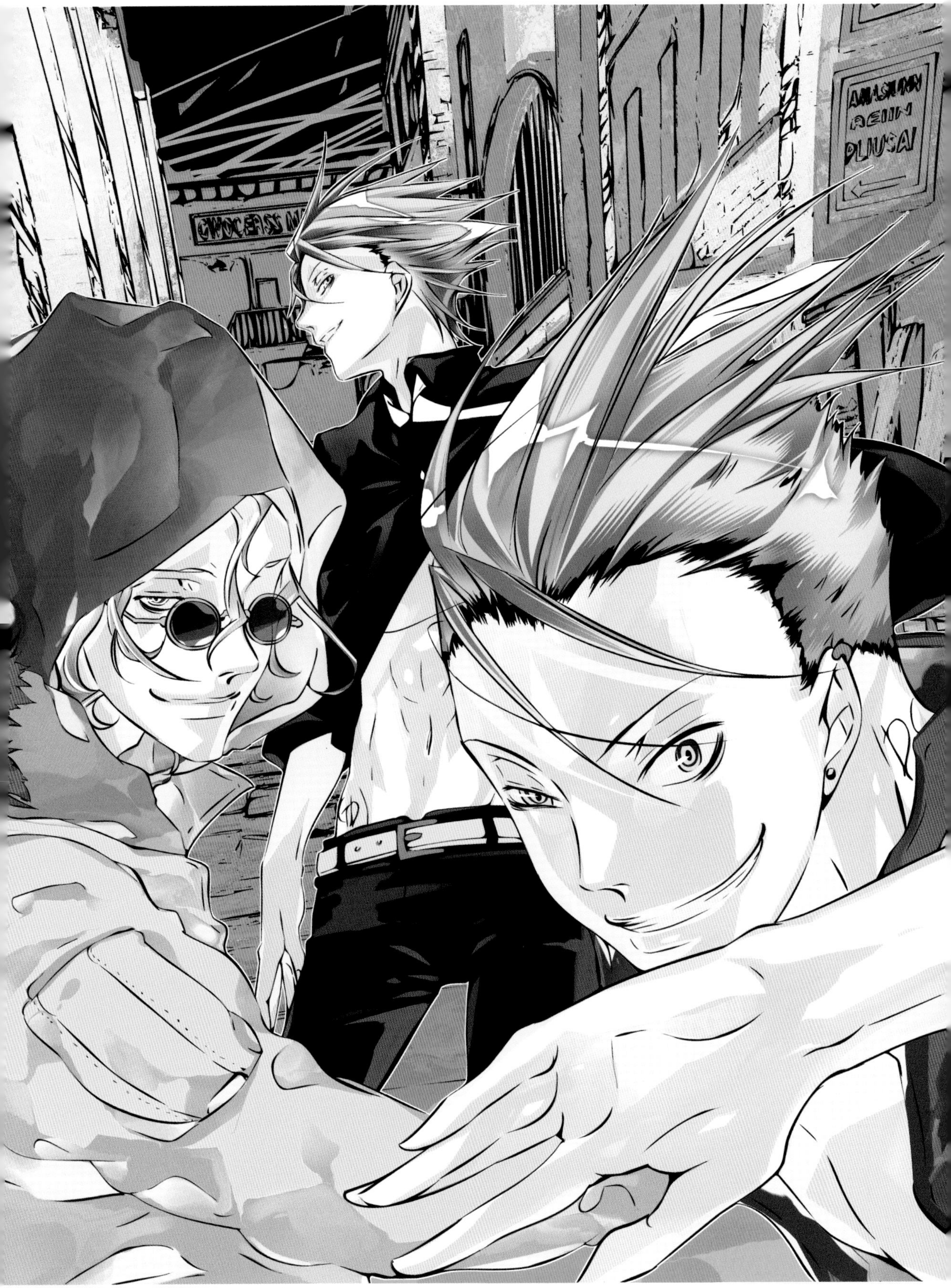

「ラッキードッグ1」雑誌 Cool-B 表紙イラスト / ©Tennenouji

yoco

M babyrain322@yahoo.co.jp　　T ---
U http://ocoy.tumblr.com　　D Photoshop 5 ● ComicStudio Pro 4

Profile	イラストレーター。BL小説や関連書籍の装画などを手がけています。	I'm an illustrator. I am working on book cover designs for BL novels and similar works.
Comments	自分の感じた空気感や物語を読んでいて見えてきた風景を絵に起こせるように心がけています。その世界の色んな場所からカメラを向けるような一瞬を切り取った絵を描きたいです。	I try to reawaken the feeling and atmosphere I imagined while reading the story. I would like to draw as though lifting a momentary scene from that world captured by many cameras trained on many angles.

「Heaven's Rain 天国の雨」著:朝丘戻　イラスト:yoco / カバーイラスト / ダリアシリーズ / フロンティアワークス　©朝丘戻・yoco / フロンティアワークス

「BLカルチャー論 ボーイズラブがわかる本」西村マリ / カバーイラスト / 青弓社

「メメント・モリ」英田サキ / カバーイラスト / 白泉社

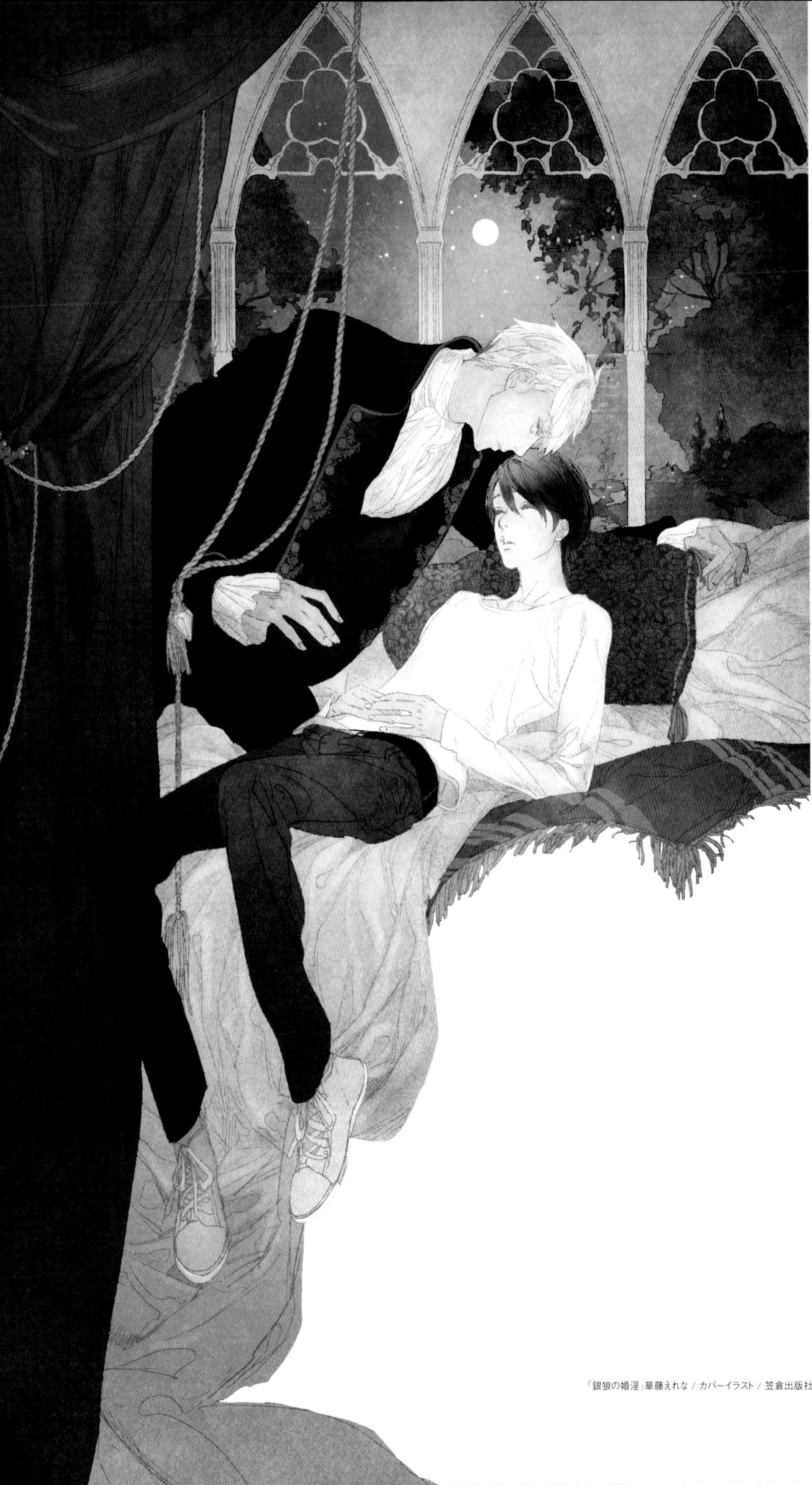

「銀狼の婚淫」華藤えれな / カバーイラスト / 笠倉出版社

横井ヨシサト

Yokoi Yoshisato

M yokoi.tentaikansoku@gmail.com T misato09292000

U http://amefurashi.michikusa.jp D Acrylic paint • Dip pen • COPIC • Photpshop

Profile

神奈川県川崎市出身。阿佐ヶ谷美術専門学校視覚デザイン科卒業。2015年5月実業之日本社リュエルコミックスより単行本『彼の作る弁当は何かと問題が多い。』発売。漫画、イラストの仕事の他、同人イベントや展示などにも参加している。

I'm from Kawasaki City in Kanagawa Prefecture. I graduated from the visual design department of Asagaya College of Design and Art. In May of 2015, my book *Kare no Tsukuru Bento wa Nanika to Mondai ga Oi* was published by Jitsugyo no Nihon Sha, Ltd. as part of the Comic Ruelle division. In addition to manga and illustrations, I participate in dojin events and exhibitions.

Comments

アナログにこだわりイラストや漫画を描いております。少年と猫とちょっと懐かしい感じの風景を好んでよく描く事が多いです。BL関連のものは「ヨシサト」名義で制作しております。主にアクリルでの着彩がメインですが、イラストの用途によってはコピックなどを使用したりもします。

I draw illustrations and manga with an analog approach. I like to draw youths, cats, and nostalgic landscapes. I draw BL-related illustrations under the name Yoshisato. I usually employ acrylics for color, but depending on the requirements of my illustrations, I sometimes also rely on Copic markers.

「彼の作る弁当は何かと問題が多い。」/ 口絵 / 実業之日本社 /©ヨシサト

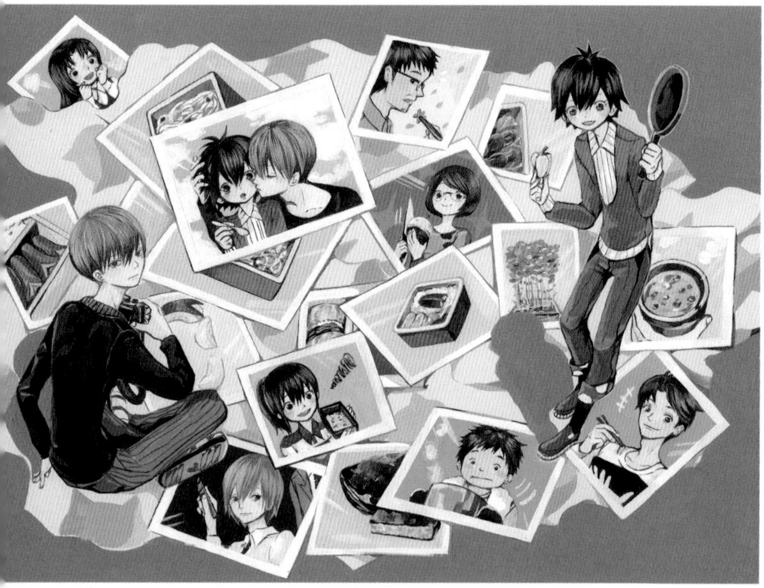

Personal Work「僕の誓い」

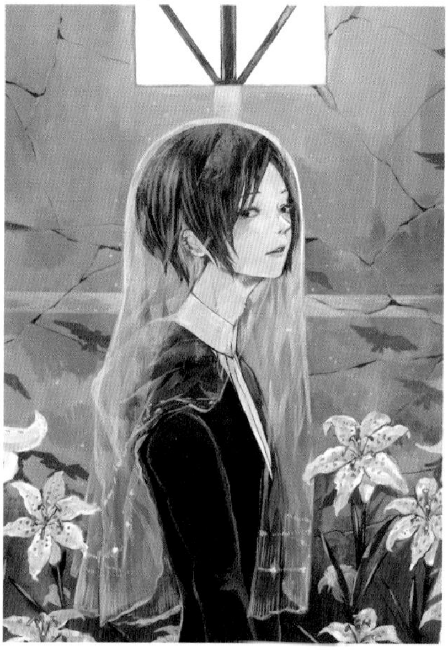

「未来点灯夫」/ 創作音声劇 CDジャケットイラスト / 碧空プラネタリウム

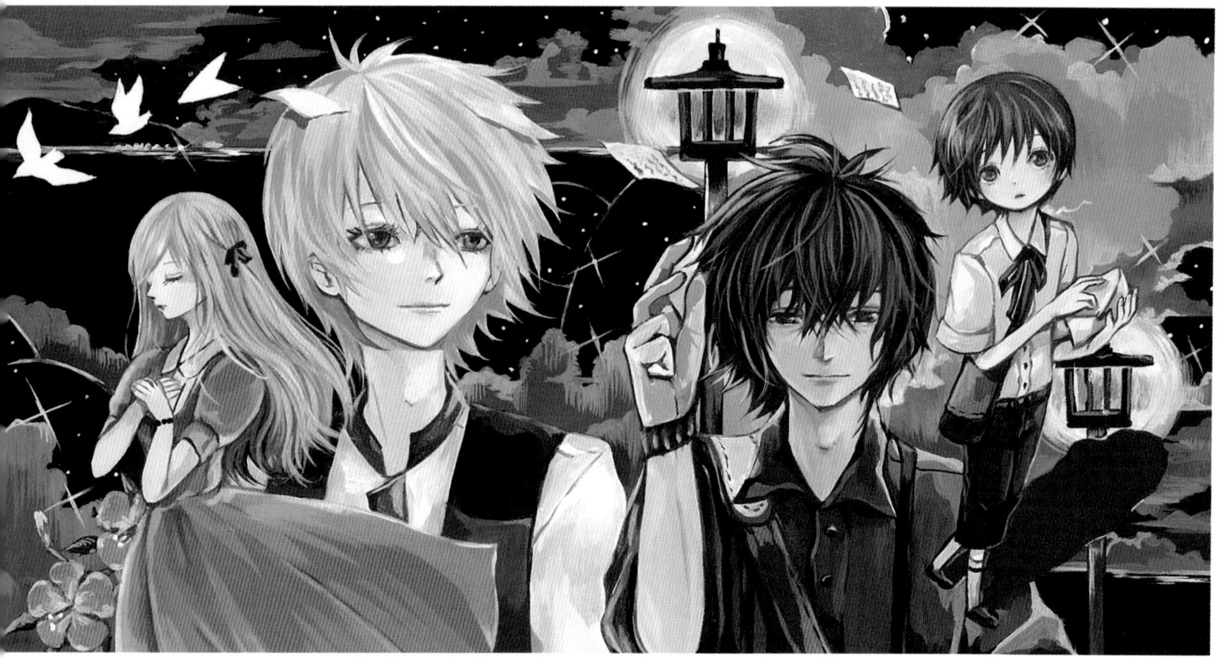

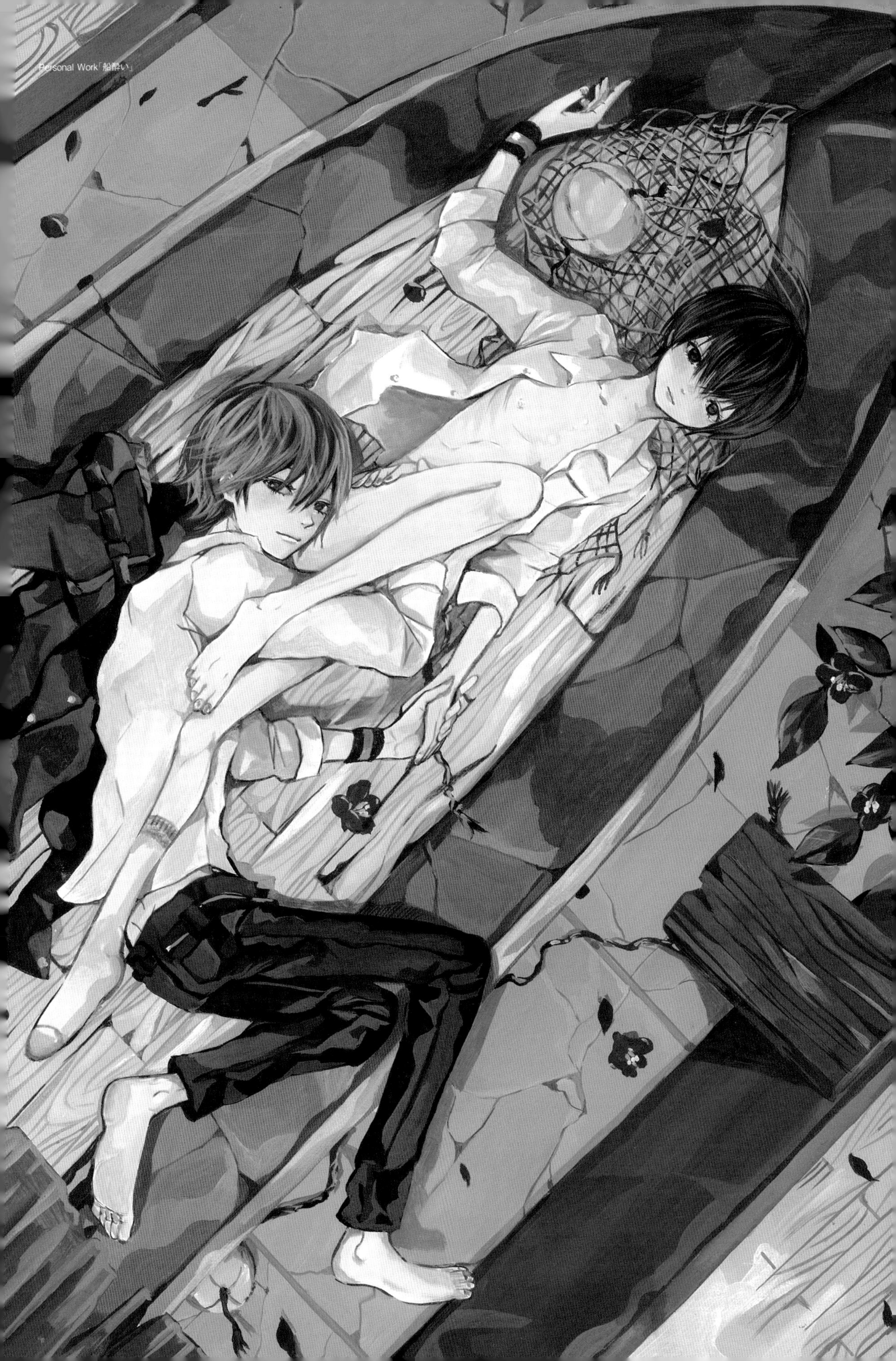
Personal Work「船酔い」

淀川ゆお
yodogawa yuo

M kuroa1112@hotmail.com
T yuo_zero
U http://chaosswitch.x.fc2.com
D ComicStudio ● Photoshop CS5 ● SAI

Profile

2008年から㈱KADOKAWA エンターブレインさんのBL電子書籍レーベル「BL☆美少年ブック」でBLコミック作品を描かせて頂いており、基本漫画を描いておりますが、挿絵等のイラストも描いたりしております。

I have been drawing for KADOKAWA Enterbrain's BL (*Boys Love*) electronic books label since 2008, contributing BL comics for "BL☆Bishonen Books." I basically illustrate standard manga, but I also create book illustrations and other artwork.

Comments

創作イラストを描くときはキャラクターの瞳の強さに力を入れて描く事が多く、また一番楽しいと思える部分です。そして表情やしぐさにも気を遣って描いてます。

When creating original illustrations, I place emphasis on producing powerful eyes for each character, as I find the eyes the most enjoyable part of manga. I also focus on facial expressions and gestures.

Personal Work

Personal Work

Personal Work

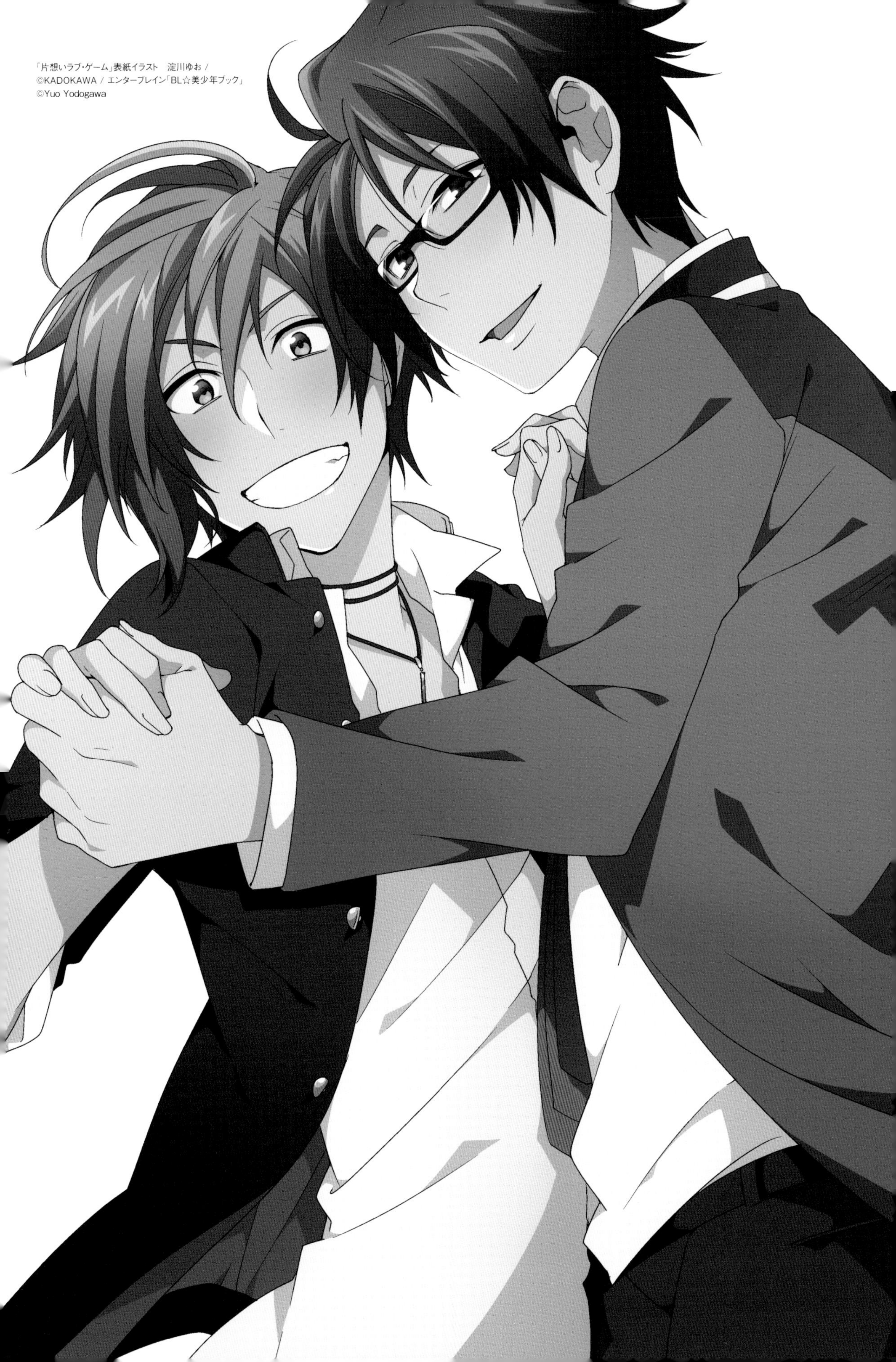